COMPLETE BABY AND CHILD CARE

Dr. Miriam Stoppard

A DORLING KINDERSLEY BOOK

For Will and Ed

DORLING DK **KINDERSLEY**

LONDON, NEW YORK, SYDNEY, DELHI, PARIS,
MUNICH AND JOHANNESBURG

ORIGINAL EDITION
Created and produced by
CARROLL & BROWN LIMITED

REVISED EDITION
Senior Managing Editor Corinne Roberts
Senior Managing Art Editor Lynne Brown
Senior Editor Julia North
Senior Art Editor Karen Ward
Editor Jinny Johnson
US Editors Constance Robinson, Jill Hamilton
Production Maryann Rogers

First published by Dorling Kindersley in 1995; reprinted 1996, 1997
Revised American Edition, 2001

2 4 6 8 10 9 7 5 3 1

Published in the United States by
Dorling Kindersley Publishing, Inc., 95 Madison Avenue
New York, New York 10016

Library of Congress Cataloging-in-Publication Data
Stoppard, Miriam.
   [Complete baby and child care]
   Dr. Miriam Stoppard's complete baby and child care/Miriam Stoppard. – 1st
American ed.
     p. cm.
  Includes index.
  ISBN 1-56458-850-5
  1. Child care. 2. Infants–Care. 3. Child development.
    I. Title. II. Title: Dr. Miriam Stoppard's complete book of baby and child care
RJ61.S8947 1995   94-26720
649'.1–dc20   CIP

Reproduced by Colourscan, Singapore
Printed and bound in Singapore by Star Standard Industries (Pte.) Ltd

See our complete
catalog at
www.dk.com

COMPLETE
BABY AND
CHILD CARE

PREFACE

There would hardly seem to be room for another baby book. Having worked on this subject for over 20 years, however, I've always felt that even the best baby books have gaps. Very few, for instance, deal with three- to five-year-olds. So what happens after three? Traditionally it's an age that's been ignored. I also feel sure that parents who have children with special needs or children with chronic ailments and disabilities feel shortchanged by most baby books, including mine, because their babies aren't given enough space or emphasis. Fathers continue to be a neglected group, and there's a tendency to overlook the impact of a new addition on the family as a whole. With more mothers in the 1990s working outside the home, choosing child care is a more universal problem than it once was.

In my previous books, there was never enough space to deal with important subjects like caring for twins, to illustrate the treatment of illnesses, from earaches to diabetes, and to go fully into complicated subjects like baby first aid. Most of all, I never felt that I had the freedom to explain how a baby's physical, mental, and social development relates to the acquisition of skills. This is a subject that's crucially important to parents. For instance, without the knowledge that a baby cannot hold a bladder full of urine until her nerves and muscles have matured, parents will continue to enforce "toilet training" – a completely outdated and cruel idea.

The scope of this book has given me the chance to plug some of those gaps and to enlarge on those two very important preschool years. Three-year-olds make huge strides in all areas of development when they're introduced to nursery and preschool classes and need a great deal of patience, understanding, and support from parents if they're going to realize their full potential – which is every child's birthright, after all.

In twenty years of writing about child care, my aim has always been to help parents feel independent, confident, and free to follow their instincts – which are nearly always right. For the first time I feel I have the space to do that. In this book, I've been able to fill out, augment, and introduce the latest research in many areas where previously I felt curbed. While this book is not definitive, it's as nearly complete as I've ever hoped for.

CONTENTS

INTRODUCTION

Whether you are a mother expecting your first baby, have just given birth, or are an expectant or new father, you may be feeling apprehensive about your new role. Don't worry: while parenting may be one of the most responsible and challenging jobs around, it's also one of the most rewarding.

THE NEWBORN BABY

You have just experienced the creation of newborn life. Your baby is probably smaller than you imagined, and she may seem very vulnerable. You may be overwhelmed by feelings of joy, but you will also be anxious to know whether your baby is all right, and whether the sounds and movements she makes are normal. Your child's doctor will be able to reassure you, and you will probably be surprised at just how much your baby can do.

EVERYDAY CARE

In the first months of life, your child depends on you for everything: you will have to feed, dress, and change him, and carry him around. If it is your first child, you are bound to be nervous. You may wonder whether he is getting enough milk and putting on weight fast enough, whether he is waking too often in the night, or why he seems to cry so much. You will be surprised at how quickly caring for your baby becomes second nature; in fact, you will hardly believe there was once a time when you didn't know how to change a diaper! You will be surprised, too, at how quickly the time comes when your child is able to do things for himself: to spoonfeed himself, to walk, to dress himself, to use a potty…. Your job is to help him reach the stage where he can look after his own basic needs and is ready to go to school.

PLAY AND DEVELOPMENT

Sharing your child's pleasure in new skills and knowledge is one of the great joys of parenthood; it's also the most important thing you can do to promote your child's healthy development: physically, by allowing her to explore her own capabilities in a challenging and safe environment; mentally, by taking time to talk to and play with her; and socially, by providing her with the love and security that will make her a happy and well-adjusted child. In these early years, play is the main tool for learning. By understanding how she learns and develops, you can help her get the most from play and from her toys.

FAMILY LIFE

However much getting married or deciding to live with your partner may have changed your life, the birth of your child will change it far more. You need to balance your partner's needs and the needs of your baby with your own. If you've had twins, you will be very much in need of practical help and support. Your extended family may suddenly start to figure more largely in your life. Whether you see this as a good thing will depend on all sorts of personal factors, but your child will undoubtedly benefit from the loving interest of his relatives, and this continues to be true even – or rather especially – if the relationship between you and your partner is under strain.

CHILDREN WITH SPECIAL NEEDS

Every mother wants her baby to grow up a happy, well-adjusted adult, and to live a rich and fulfilling life. If your child has special needs – and this applies to a wide variety of children, from those who are very gifted to those born with a chronic physical condition such as cerebral palsy – achieving this is going to require a lot of extra effort from you. If your child is ill, you will also have to cope with your own feelings of confusion, anxiety, and perhaps guilt. Over the months that follow the diagnosis of your child's condition, however, you will learn a lot about what you can do to help your child, and you will almost certainly cope better than you had thought possible. There are many support networks available that offer help to parents of children with special needs; be sure to make use of them.

MEDICINE AND HEALTHCARE

You are responsible for promoting your child's good health, recognizing when he is ill, and acting accordingly. Your child cannot always tell you what is wrong with him, but you will become sensitive to the signs that tell you something is amiss, and you will learn when you can look after him yourself and when he needs a doctor. It is your duty as a parent to learn basic first-aid procedures, and you should attend a training course to do this rather than try to learn from a book. (The American Red Cross and various local organizations such as Ys and hospitals offer courses for parents.) Learn emergency first-aid procedures by heart, and refresh your memory often.

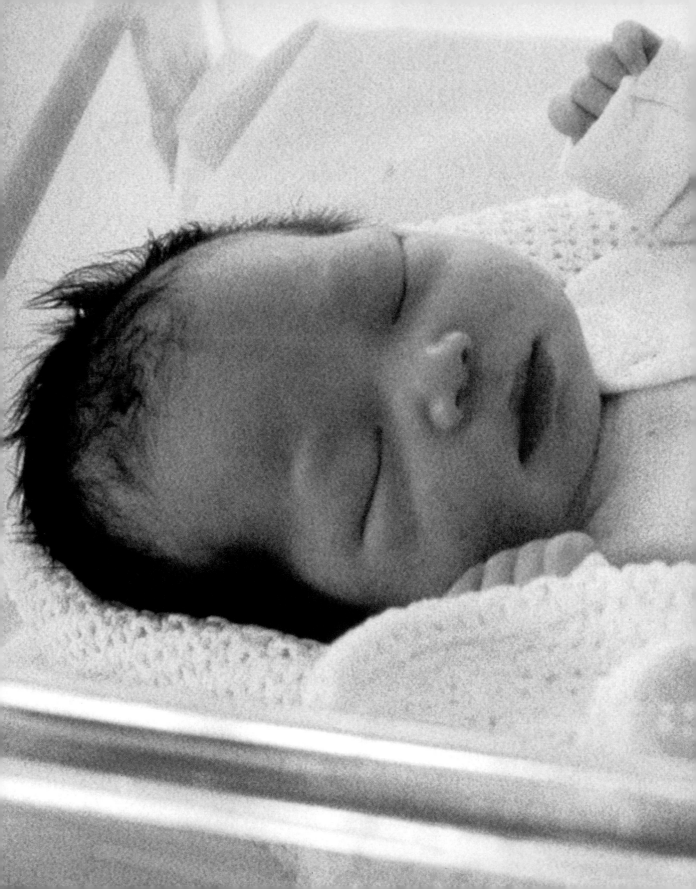

CHAPTER 1

The NEWBORN BABY

Your feelings on the birth of your new baby are likely to be pride, wonder, and exhilaration mixed with exhaustion. You may feel fiercely attached to your baby right away, or bonding may take a little longer. You will almost certainly be surprised at his appearance: his oddly shaped head, wrinkled face, and tiny hands and feet.

From the moment of birth your baby will exhibit reflexes and behavior that help him survive. In such things as his sleeping patterns and crying bouts you will be able to discern the beginnings of a personality.

The first question in every new mother's mind is "Is he all right?" and medical staff will carry out tests immediately after the birth and in the first few days to reassure you on this score. Your baby will be given all the special attention that they consider necessary. If he is premature or small for dates he may need to be kept in a special care unit, but you'll still be able to bond with him and take part in his care.

Your New Baby

Loving your Baby

Most mothers find they establish a tangible bond with their new-born babies within the first 72 hours, but a "bond" doesn't necessarily mean instantaneous and ecstatic love at first sight.

Attending to the physical needs of your newborn baby is so exhausting that it's easy to forget your baby also has an active emotional life. In the long term, the most serious damage to a baby's health may stem from inadequate love and attention – so in the next few weeks and months heap as much upon your baby as you can.

Mother love is partially hormonal. One of the hormones that stimulates lactation is also, in part, responsible for mother love.

Some mothers are shocked to find that they lack maternal feelings when they first hold their babies. This may be due to a variety of factors, such as complications with the delivery, unrealistic expectations of childbirth, sheer exhaustion, fluctuating hormone levels, and even the mother's own experience in early childhood. Maternal "indifference" can last from an hour to a week, but rarely much longer.

Bonding
Your baby will be happiest next to your skin, where she can feel your warmth and hear your heartbeat.

Whatever you had expected – bigger, smaller, quieter, less slippery – your baby will surprise and delight you. Experienced parents discern a personality at birth, but first-time parents may think their newborns are insensitive to the world about them. Babies, however, rapidly build up a storehouse of sensory experiences from birth; when awake, she will be alert and listening. She responds when spoken to, recognizes you by smell, and has an intent gaze. At birth she can see a human face and she will move her head in response to noise. She is born wanting to communicate and will "converse" with you if you talk animatedly about 8–10 inches (20–25 centimeters) from her face where she can see you clearly. She will react to your smile by moving her mouth, nodding, protruding her tongue, or jerking her whole body.

Handling your baby

The need for physical contact throughout childhood is well documented, and this is especially true of the first weeks of life. The majority of newborns spend much of their time asleep, so it is important that you are there to to hold your baby and play with her when she's awake. If your baby is in an incubator, ask to stroke her and change her diaper. One young mother I met recently, whose ten-day-old baby had been in an incubator for the first 48 hours, was too terrified to pick him up because she thought he might "break." Babies are stronger than you think.

BREATHING

After an initial outburst of crying, you may not be able to hear anything more from your baby because it can be difficult to hear a newborn's light breathing. In some cases a baby may even stop breathing entirely for a few seconds, but this isn't abnormal. All babies make strange noises when they breathe – usually a noisy snuffling sound – and their breathing is often irregular.

Your baby's lungs are still immature, which means her breathing is naturally much shallower than yours or mine. This is nothing to worry about, as her lungs will gradually mature.

SUCKLING

For the first three days after your baby's birth, your breasts produce not milk, but colostrum, a thin, yellow fluid that contains water, protein, sugar, vitamins, minerals, and antibodies for protection against infectious diseases. During her first few weeks of life, colostrum helps protect your baby against infections. To stimulate your breasts to produce milk, you need to feed her frequently; the sucking action of the baby stimulates hormones that, in turn, stimulate milk production. Even if you do not intend to breastfeed, it is a good idea to suckle your baby as soon as she is born, because the colostrum will be beneficial to her and the act of suckling will help you bond with your baby.

As soon as your baby is born, you can put her to your breast. She will have a natural sucking reflex and the sucking action will encourage the production of the hormone oxytocin. Oxytocin makes the uterus contract and expel the placenta. Touch your baby's cheek on the side nearest your nipple to stimulate her rooting reflex. Rather than just sucking on the nipple, her lips should be on the breast tissue with the whole of the nipple in her mouth.

INVOLVING YOUR PARTNER

Because the experience of childbirth is so focused on the mother, it is common for the father to feel neglected or excluded. It is important for father and baby to bond, too: touch, smell, and sound are good ways to do this. If at all possible, her father should hold her against his skin soon after his baby is born; this way his baby will come into contact with his specific smell and over a period of weeks she will learn to associate this with comfort and reassurance. The father should also speak to his child so she will become familiar with his voice.

It is common for the mother to take prime responsibility for a newborn's care, but the father should be encouraged to take an equal role. He should learn how to hold his baby and should build up a tactile relationship with her. Make sure he becomes involved with day-to-day routines such as bathing and diaper changing. Even if the baby is breastfed, he can bottlefeed her using expressed breast milk. Although having two parents is the ideal, many babies are born to single mothers and into a variety of nontraditional family settings. Significant others, whether family members or other adults, can also establish a bond with a newborn.

Don't be alarmed if your newborn cries vigorously – this is exactly what you want to hear.

In the uterus your baby gets oxygen from the placenta; her lungs are inactive, and are collapsed.

With the baby's first breath, her lungs expand and increased pressure in them shuts a valve just beyond the heart; blood that once passed to the placenta for oxygenation now goes directly to the lungs. These two steps make her independent, able to survive without you; they occur in an instant.

Nothing should interfere with your baby's first breath. That's why doctors and midwives clear her air passages immediately; this also often encourages breathing.

Newborn babies cannot make vitamin K, so it is injected into your baby soon after birth.

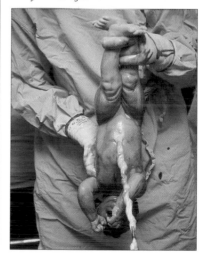

Crying
The intake of air that accompanies crying helps your baby clear her airways at birth.

YOUR BABY'S APPEARANCE

SPOTS AND RASHES

Most newborns have harmless skin irritations such as spots and rashes in the first few days. They generally clear up as the skin begins to stabilize at about three weeks of age.

Milia *These small white spots, found mainly on the bridge of the nose but also elsewhere on the face, are the result of a temporary blockage of the sebaceous glands, which secrete sebum to lubricate the skin. Never squeeze them – they will disappear on their own within a few days.*

Heat rash *If your baby is too warm he may get small red spots, especially on his face. Make sure that he isn't wrapped in too much clothing or blankets, and that the room is not too warm (see p.123).*

Urticaria *This is a harmless rash whose spots have a white center and a red halo (see p.292). It is quite common in the first week, and may recur for a month or so. There is no need to treat it; it will disappear on its own.*

When you are given your baby to hold for the first time you will probably be surprised by his appearance. Although your baby is undoubtedly a bundle of joy, many mothers mistakenly expect a clean and placid bundle, similar to the ones that appear in baby-food commercials. As you now suddenly discover, however, real life is a little bit different.

Skin Your baby's skin may be covered in a whitish, greasy substance called vernix, which is a natural barrier cream to keep the skin from becoming waterlogged. In some hospitals, the vernix is removed immediately, but in others it may be left on to give your baby some natural protection against minor skin irritations, flaking, and peeling.

Your baby's skin may be rather blotchy in color; this is because the tiny blood vessels are prominent. African-American children are often light-skinned at birth, but the skin darkens as it begins to produce the natural pigment melanin; it will reach its permanent color by about six months.

Head Your baby's skull is made up of many large bony plates that have not yet fused. These sliding skull bones enabled him to withstand the pressure from your vaginal walls during labor and to pass through the birth canal without hazard, although his head may have become slightly elongated or misshapen in the process. This is entirely normal and does not affect the brain. There may also be some bruising or swelling, but it will disappear during the first few days or weeks.

The soft spots on the top of your baby's skull where the bones are still not joined are called the fontanels. In a sense, they are the windows into a baby's body. The skull bones will not fuse completely until your baby is about two.

Eyes Your baby may not be able to open his eyes right away due to puffiness caused by normal pressure on his head during birth. This pressure may also have broken some tiny blood vessels in your baby's eyes, causing small, red semicircular marks in the whites of the eyes. Entirely harmless, they require no treatment and will disappear within a couple of weeks. A yellow discharge around the eyelids is quite common. Although this is not usually a serious condition, it should always be treated by a doctor.

Your baby can see clearly up to a distance of 8–10 inches (20–25 centimeters), but beyond that cannot focus both eyes at the same time; this may cause him to squint or look cross-eyed. Both of these conditions will clear up as his eye muscles develop (usually within a few months). If your baby is still cross-eyed (see p.287) at three months you should consult his doctor. You may find it difficult to get your baby to open his eyes at first, but never try to force them open. One of the easiest ways I have found to get a baby to open his eyes is to hold him above my head.

Most newborn babies' eyes are blue regardless of race. Your baby's eye color is likely to change after birth because it is only then that babies acquire melanin, the body's natural pigment.

Hair Some babies are born with a full head of hair, while others are completely bald. The color of your baby's hair at birth is not necessarily the permanent color he will acquire later in life. The fine downy hair that many babies have on their heads and bodies at birth is called lanugo, and it falls off soon after birth.

Genitals Many babies, both male and female, appear to have enlarged genitals shortly after birth, and babies of both genders may have "breasts." This is due to the massive increase in hormone levels that you've experienced just before giving birth, some of which have passed into your baby's bloodstream.

With a baby boy this can lead to an enlarged scrotum and enlarged breasts; he may even produce a little milk. This is not abnormal, and the swelling will gradually subside. A baby girl may have a swollen vulva or clitoris and a small "period" shortly after birth.

Umbilicus The umbilical cord, which is moist and bluish white at birth, is clamped with forceps and then cut with scissors. Only a short length of cord remains, and this dries and becomes almost black within two to four hours. The stump will dry up and fall off about 1–3 weeks after birth, but your baby will not feel any pain as a result of this.

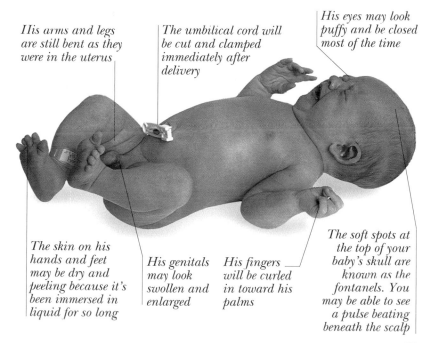

His arms and legs are still bent as they were in the uterus

The umbilical cord will be cut and clamped immediately after delivery

His eyes may look puffy and be closed most of the time

The skin on his hands and feet may be dry and peeling because it's been immersed in liquid for so long

His genitals may look swollen and enlarged

His fingers will be curled in toward his palms

The soft spots at the top of your baby's skull are known as the fontanels. You may be able to see a pulse beating beneath the scalp

UMBILICAL HERNIA

Some babies develop a small swelling near the navel – an umbilical hernia – caused by incompletely developed abdominal muscles, which allow the intestines to push through a little.

Umbilical hernias are most obvious when the abdominal muscles are used for crying. They are very common, and virtually always clear up within a year. If your baby has one and it enlarges or persists, consult your pediatrician.

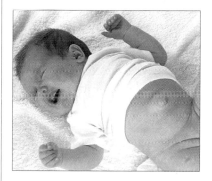

Site of swelling
The hernia forms where the umbilical cord entered the baby's abdomen, because there is a gap in the abdominal muscles at that point.

ABOUT BIRTHMARKS

If you haven't found a blemish anywhere on your baby's body, it's probably because you haven't looked long enough.

Virtually every child is born with some type of birthmark, no matter how tiny. Most marks will fade and disappear on their own by the time your child is three years old, although some of them remain and increase in size.

Both my sons had stork bite birthmarks at the back of the neck just under the hairline (which is a very common place to find them). They disappeared, however, by the time they were six months old.

Other likely places are the eyelids, the forehead, and the neck, although one might be found on any part of your baby's skin.

Superficial birthmarks are nothing to worry about. They do no harm and need no treatment.

MEASUREMENTS

Your baby's weight, head circumference, and length will be measured to give an indication of her maturity and development. These measurements can be used as a baseline for her future development if necessary. Although routine measurements are inevitably compared to "the average," don't worry about this too much. An average is just an arithmetical calculation, so the "average child" is only theoretical and doesn't exist.

Weight Newborns differ greatly in weight. Nutritional, placental, and racial factors all have a bearing. The weight range for babies born around their expected time is 5 pounds 8 ounces to 9 pounds 14 ounces (2.5–4.5 kilograms). If you are tall or heavy or if you are diabetic, your baby is likely to weigh more.

Women who suffer from chronic hypertension, vascular or renal disease, or preeclampsia, and women who smoke during pregnancy are likely to have lighter babies. A woman whose pregnancy is shorter than 40 weeks is also likely to have a lighter baby. Girls generally weigh slightly less than boys, and babies born as twins or other multiple births are each likely to weigh less than singletons.

It is normal for your baby to lose weight in the first few days after birth as her body adjusts to new feeding requirements. She must now process her own food, and it will take a while for her to feed consistently. The usual weight loss at this time is about 4–6 ounces (115–170 grams). After five to seven days, you can expect your baby's weight to begin increasing.

The significance of a baby's weight gain is what it tells us of her overall physical health. Steady weight gain indicates that her food intake is sufficient and is being absorbed, whereas poor or erratic weight gain or weight loss signals that food intake is insufficient or that it isn't being absorbed normally. Your baby will be weighed frequently by the pediatrician. There's no need to monitor her weight at home unless the doctor advises it.

Head circumference Your baby's head is disproportionately large in comparison to her body size, and takes up one quarter of her entire length. The younger a baby is, the larger her head will be in

Head circumference is an important indicator of healthy development

Measurements
Your baby's length and head circumference will be measured, and then he will be weighed.

proportion to the rest of her body. The average circumference of a newborn baby's head is about 14 inches (35 centimeters) but the range can be anything from 12½–15 inches (31.5–38 centimeters).

Measuring head circumference is regarded as an essential part of the examination of a baby because the growth of the head reflects the growth of the brain. An unusually large or small head circumference may be an indication of an abnormality of the brain.

Chest and abdomen The circumference of your baby's chest will be smaller than that of her head. Her stomach might appear to be very large and even distended, but given the immaturity of her abdominal muscles, this is to be expected.

THE FIRST DIAPERS

Your baby's stools and urine may not look as you expect them to, and if you have a baby girl there may be some vaginal discharge. None of these mean that something is wrong.

Stools Your baby's first bowel movement will consist of meconium, which is mainly digested mucus and looks blackish green. Some of this is accumulated from swallowing amniotic fluid while inside your uterus. The first meconium stool should be passed within the first 24 hours and her next bowel movement may not occur until two days later; this is especially true if you are breastfeeding (check, however, that your baby is wetting her diaper regularly). After the fourth day she may pass four or five stools daily.

You will notice that the color and composition of her stools change from dark, greenish black sticky meconium to greenish brown, and then to a yellow semisolid type. If you are bottle feeding your baby, the stools might resemble scrambled eggs.

Most babies fill their diapers as soon as they have eaten, due to a perfectly healthy gastrocolic reflex, which makes the bowel empty itself as soon as food enters the stomach. Some babies pass stools much less frequently, but as long as your baby does not have to strain too much and her stools are a normal color and soft, there is no need for concern. If her stools are very hard or infrequent after the fourth day of life, you should consult her doctor.

Urine A newborn baby passes urine almost continuously because her bladder muscles are immature. She's unable to hold urine for any length of time – usually no longer than a few minutes – so it's quite normal to find that she wets her diaper up to 20 times in 24 hours. When she does, her urine will contain substances called urates, which may occasionally stain the diaper dark pink or red. This, too, is normal for a newborn.

Vaginal discharge Newborn girls sometimes produce a clear or white vaginal discharge. In some cases you may notice a small amount of vaginal bleeding due to hormone changes, but this is perfectly normal and will clear up naturally after a couple of days. If you are concerned about this, talk with your baby's doctor.

TYPES OF BIRTHMARK

Most birthmarks are just collections of small blood vessels under the skin. They are harmless and do not cause your baby any pain. Here are some of the most common types:

Strawberry marks These usually first appear as small red dots that are not always obvious. They may grow rather alarmingly during the first months of life into red raised lumps, but during the second year most shrivel and disappear without leaving a scar.

Salmon patches Also called stork's marks or stork bites, these pink discolorations of the skin usually fade with time, often within a few months.

Spider birthmarks (nevi) These small marks appear shortly after birth as a network or a cobweb of dilated vessels. They generally disappear after the first year.

Pigmented nevi These brownish patches can occur anywhere on the body. They are usually pale and nearly always enlarge as the child grows, but they seldom become darker.

Port-wine stains Found anywhere on the body, these bright red or even purple marks are caused by dilated capillaries in the skin. Although permanent, they can be removed with lasers or camouflaged with special makeup.

Mongolian spots It is common for dark-skinned babies to have harmless, dark bluish black discolorations of the skin, usually on the back or buttocks; these will fade naturally.

NAME *Katharine Winterton*

AGE *31 years*

PAST MEDICAL HISTORY *High blood pressure (140/190)*

FAMILY HISTORY *Several cases of high blood pressure on paternal side*

OBSTETRIC HISTORY *First pregnancy. Mild pre-eclampsia (a condition that causes swelling of the legs, fingers, and face) diagnosed in sixth month. Occasional bleeding gums*

During pregnancy Katharine's whole view of giving birth changed drastically. She had originally decided to do everything naturally, she didn't want any drugs, and the thought of a cesarean horrified her. When she was told she had high blood pressure, she began to panic. Symptoms that virtually all pregnant women experience at some point, like faintness, headaches, and indigestion, seemed terrifying to her.

NEW PARENTS

Katharine was very concerned that she might develop eclampsia during labor, which can lead to convulsions or seizures. In fact, as I explained to her, this is a rare condition that is unlikely to occur even when preeclampsia has been diagnosed. Due to her high blood pressure and the weight of the baby (estimated at about 9 pounds/4 kilograms), Katharine agreed to be induced when she was two weeks overdue.

THE LABOR

Although it was long (17 hours), labor went relatively smoothly for Katharine. She was induced at 9:00 a.m. on Monday, and at 1:00 p.m. felt relaxed enough to send her husband Adam to her mother's for lunch… on the condition that he bring her back some of her favorite cake.

Katharine used a TENS machine, which is supposed to stimulate natural painkillers through the transmission of electrical impulses. She was put on it late, however, so she's not sure whether it helped or not. At midnight, 15 hours later, she asked for an epidural – something she had sworn not to do – and after that everything was all right. At 1:45 A.M. on Tuesday she was given an episiotomy (which she didn't feel at all), and about ten minutes later the doctor used forceps to pull Natasha out.

FIRST REACTIONS

"I got a bit of a shock when I saw her," recalls Katharine, "because her face was very red and scrunched up, her head looked slightly lopsided and indented because of the forceps, and she seemed to be gasping for air but not making any sound. I kept on asking, 'Is she all right?! Is she all right?!' The nurse turned away for a second and I was absolutely convinced that Natasha was dead. That was actually the worst moment during the whole labor, and I started to cry uncontrollably.

"In fact, the nurse was only doing the Apgar scores and, as it turned out, Natasha scored high. About 30 seconds later we were handed a perfect little baby girl breathing normally.

"I was quite surprised that she had her eyes wide open and seemed to be looking at me and Adam in a very alert, quizzical manner. She just sat staring for about five minutes without crying at all. Natasha is my first child, and so I wasn't prepared for the combination of sheer joy, love, and relief that flooded over me when she was placed in my arms for the first time.

"The placenta came out after only ten minutes, which I'm told is a bit unusual without the use of oxytocin, and then the nurse clamped the umbilical cord in two places and Adam cut it."

LOOKING BACK AT THE BIRTH

The one thing Katharine regrets about the whole pregnancy is having had an episiotomy. She is sure she would have dilated enough had she been given another half hour. Although she felt no pain at the time, due to the epidural, she says the episiotomy was the only physical problem associated with the birth that didn't clear up in the first two weeks.

Three months later the episiotomy scar is still sensitive, and she says that the worry of tearing during intercourse has made her avoid sex completely. I explained to her that although this fear is genuine, it is almost certain she would have lost her sexual appetite for a time after giving birth, with or without an episiotomy. In any event, a forceps delivery almost always necessitates an episiotomy.

THE FIRST DAYS

Katharine found that despite her elation after the birth of Natasha, she soon got what are commonly known as the "baby blues," a feeling of deep depression that stayed with her for three days. She found it very difficult to relate to all the people around her, including Adam. She also felt guilty because she had not expected these feelings to accompany the birth of a normal, healthy baby.

"Baby blues" are caused by the huge increase in hormones which occurs in a woman's body during childbirth. It takes quite a while, sometimes weeks or even months, for the body to readjust completely, and in the meantime a new mother may have to deal with difficult bouts of depression.

In Katharine's case, things improved when she arrived home from the hospital. Although she was physically exhausted, psychologically she felt much more in control.

"It was only when we walked through our own door with Natasha for the first time that I felt the three of us were a real family. Having said that, Natasha seemed to take up every last second of our time, although I was lucky to have Adam there to help – he did about 40 percent of all the work."

KATHARINE'S TIPS

- Try to be flexible and positive. The only thing to be sure of is that it probably won't turn out as you planned – but that isn't necessarily a bad thing.

- Although I only had my husband with me during labor, a lot of women I spoke to on the ward also had a friend or a relative. I will definitely consider this next time if the hospital allows it.

- If you reach the stage where the pain becomes overwhelming, don't be afraid to ask for a pain-killer – it really did make a difference for me, and after that I enjoyed the birth much more.

- Ask your midwife or doctor to let you stretch naturally rather than attempt an episiotomy too early.

NAME *Adam Winterton*

AGE *30 years*

Because he had gone through three years of medical school, Adam was sure he would be able to take the birth in his stride. Having his wife as the patient, he admitted, contributed to the loss of a lot of his usual composure.

"To begin with, it seemed to be going very slowly, and Kath sent me away to get some lunch. When I got back she was obviously in a lot of pain, and I couldn't believe I had been selfish enough to leave her for two hours. I felt incredibly guilty, and also a bit useless.

"Just before midnight, Kath really started to scream, and that was the worst point for me. All I could do was squeeze her hand tightly, which made me feel terrible.

"I was virtually jumping for joy when they gave her the epidural, something we both decided beforehand we didn't want. After that we knew it was just a matter of waiting, and because Kath was no longer in excessive pain, it was something we could really enjoy together. That was when I felt the most useful, because she needed someone to take her mind off what was going on. We even started planning what we were going to do once we got Natasha home."

NEWBORN BEHAVIOR

Your baby will close his eyes, blink, or move them from one side to the other, depending on what is happening around him.

• *If light shines in his face, he will blink – usually whether he has his eyes open or not (you should never shine bright light directly in your baby's eyes)*

• *He will also blink if you tap the bridge of his nose or blow gently across his eyes, or if he is startled by a sudden noise*

• *If you lift your newborn up and turn him to the left or right, his eyes will normally not move with his head, but will stay fixed in the same position momentarily. This is known as the "doll's-eye response," and will usually disappear after about ten days*

It may take you a while to get used to your baby's behavior. It is worth studying his reactions to various stimuli and becoming familiar with some of the traits that will mark his personality as he grows. Young babies have far more individuality than they are usually credited with, and this is a useful fact to bear in mind as you get to know your child.

REFLEXES

One thing common to all healthy babies is a number of reflexes that can be stimulated from the very first moments after birth. These reflexes are involuntary movements that eventually, at about three months, start to be replaced by voluntary movements.

Grasp reflex
If you put something in the palm of your baby's hand, he will clench it surprisingly tightly. The grasp of a baby is often tight enough to support his entire body weight (although you should never try this).

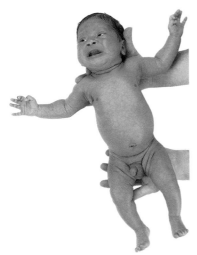

Moro reflex
When your baby's head is allowed to drop back, he will quickly extend his arms and hands with fingers outstretched, then let them fall back slowly.

He will turn to a finger stroking his cheek

The rooting reflex
This is the most basic instinct: the one that helps your newborn baby find your breast and suck it. If you gently stroke your baby's cheek he will turn his head in the direction of your finger and open his mouth. If you touch the center of his upper lip, you will also see that his mouth opens.

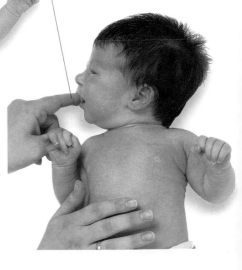

He instinctively opens his mouth to suck

You might notice that your newborn baby responds in a positive way to your presence by momentarily contracting his whole face and body. As he learns to control his movements, you will see that his reactions become more directed and less random. For instance, at six weeks, instead of scrunching up his whole face, he may show you a distinct smile.

TESTING REFLEXES

Until your baby's physical and mental capabilities develop, it will be his instinctive reflexes that provide an indication of his maturity. Doctors can test these reflexes to check your baby's general health and see that his central nervous system is functioning well. Premature babies will not react in the same way as full-term babies.

Although there are more than 70 primitive reflexes that have been identified in newborn babies, your doctor is likely to test only a selected few. The two most commonly recognized reflexes that you can easily test yourself are the rooting and the grasp reflex. Don't try to test the Moro reflex at home, as this could distress your baby and make him cry.

Walking reflex
If you hold your baby under the shoulders so that he is in an upright position and his feet are allowed to touch a firm surface, he'll move his legs in a walking action. This reflex disappears in three to six weeks, and is not what helps your child learn to walk.

Your baby takes up a crawling position when placed on his stomach

Placing reflex
This is quite similar to the walking reflex. If you hold your baby in an upright position and bring the front of his leg into contact with the edge of a table, he will lift his foot as if to step onto the table. The same reflex is present in the arm; if the back of your baby's forearm touches the table edge, he will raise his arm.

"Crawling"
When you place your baby on his stomach, he will automatically assume what appears to be a crawling position, with his pelvis high and his knees pulled up under his abdomen. When he kicks his legs he may be able to shuffle in a vague crawling manner. It is not real crawling, however, and this behavior will disappear as soon as his legs uncurl and he lies flat.

CRYING

Assume that your baby will cry a lot and you might be pleasantly surprised if she doesn't. If you think she won't cry and then she does, you may find yourself overwhelmed and disorientated.

Remember that there are really only three states your newborn baby can be in: asleep, awake and quiet, and awake and crying. If she is crying there are a variety of reasons for it. The most likely causes are tiredness, hunger, loneliness, and discomfort – she is too hot or too cold, is in an uncomfortable position, or needs changing. You must accept sometimes, though, that a baby will cry for no discernible reason. This type of crying can be the most stressful for a parent.

Responding to crying Leaving a child to cry on her own is never a good idea, even though you will hear this advice often. If a baby is denied attention and friendship in her early weeks and months, she may grow up to be introverted, shy, and withdrawn. Research on newborns shows that if parents are slow to respond to their baby's crying, the result may be a baby who cries more rather than less. A recent study found that babies whose crying was ignored in their first few weeks tended to cry more frequently and persistently as they grew older.

Often people confuse spoiling a child with loving a child. In my opinion a baby cannot be "spoiled" enough. A six-month-old baby who is picked up, nursed, cuddled, and talked to soothingly and lovingly is not learning about seeking attention; she is learning about love and forming human relationships – and that is one of the most important lessons a child will ever learn in terms of her future emotional and psychological development. What we tend to call spoiling is both a natural response of a mother to a distressed child and the natural need of the baby.

SLEEP PATTERNS

Once you bring your newborn home, you'll have some sleepless nights unless you are very lucky. Although most newborns usually sleep when they are not feeding – typically spending at least 60 percent of their time asleep – some will remain active and alert for surprisingly long periods during the day and night.

One young mother was shocked to find that her new baby never dozed for longer than one or two hours at a time until she was four months old. This is a very long time for any parent to survive without a full night's sleep, especially when your body may be in need of rest after an exhausting pregnancy and birth. If you have a very wakeful baby, be consoled by the fact that as long as she isn't left bored on her own, every minute that she's awake she's learning something new – and in the long run you will be rewarded with an eager, bright child.

All babies are different, and their sleep requirements depend on individual physiology. For this reason it's nonsensical to lay down rigid sleeping times that correspond to the average baby. As I've said before, the average baby doesn't exist.

COPING WITH COLIC

When a baby cries inconsolably for several hours on end, often pulling her legs up to her chest as though in response to abdominal pain, the chances are she is suffering from colic (see p. 298).

The first thing to do is make sure the problem really is colic. Once a pediatrician has ruled out other, potentially serious problems, the most important thing is for the mother to marshal support to endure a trying period.

Enlist the help of your husband and other family members, friends, neighbors, and hired caregivers. There is nothing more difficult for a mother than to have to face a ceaselessly crying baby alone and without respite.

Because caring for a colicky baby can leave a mother at her wit's end, it is essential to get support before frustration causes negative changes in a mother's feelings for her baby.

The good news is that babies with colic are generally healthy children. Except for their crying bouts, they eat and sleep well, gain weight normally, and show no ill effects from the colic. The other piece of good news is that colic doesn't last forever; most colicky babies "grow out" of it by about three to four months.

Most newborns fall asleep soon after feeding. At first, a baby's wakefulness is likely to depend on how much feeding she needs, which in turn depends on her weight (see below).

SOUNDS YOUR BABY MAKES

Babies make a variety of strange noises, whether asleep or awake, and this is quite normal. Most of these are due to the immaturity of her respiratory system and will soon disappear.

Snoring Your baby may make some grunting noises when she's asleep. This is not a true snore, and is probably caused by vibrations on the soft palate at the back of her mouth as she breathes.

Snuffling Your baby may snuffle so loudly with each breath that you think she has a cold or that she has mucus at the back of her throat. In most babies, these snuffling noises are harmless and are caused because the bridge of the nose is low and air is trying to get through very short, narrow nasal passages. As your baby grows older, the bridge of her nose will get higher and the snuffling sound will gradually disappear.

Sneezing You may also think your baby has a cold because she sneezes a lot. In fact, sneezing is common in newborn babies, particularly if they open their eyes and are exposed to bright light. This sneezing can actually be beneficial – it helps clear out your baby's nasal passages.

Hiccups Newborn babies hiccup a lot, particularly after a feeding. This leads some mothers to fear that their baby has indigestion, but this is rarely the case. Hiccups are due to imperfect control of the diaphragm – the sheet of muscle that separates the chest from the abdomen – and they will disappear as your baby's nervous system control of the diaphragm matures.

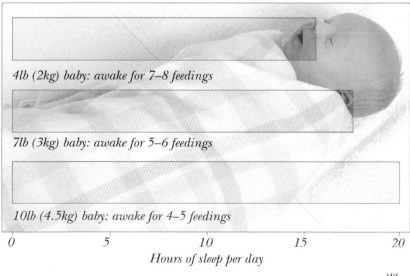

4lb (2kg) baby: awake for 7–8 feedings

7lb (3kg) baby: awake for 5–6 feedings

10lb (4.5kg) baby: awake for 4–5 feedings

| 0 | 5 | 10 | 15 | 20 |

Hours of sleep per day

WHY BABIES SLEEP WHEN THEY SLEEP

How much a baby sleeps is influenced by how long she can go between feedings, as well as individual factors in her temperament. Although new parents dream of the day their baby will "sleep through the night," this is not likely to occur before about 9 weeks, if it happens at all.

Before that age, a baby really needs a middle of the night feeding (around 2 A.M.) to grow at a healthy rate. A baby who regularly skips that feeding may make it up by taking more at other times of the day, but she should be watched carefully for weight gain because she may not be getting enough nourishment.

Some babies sleep and wake around the clock; others do most of their sleeping at night with briefer naps during the day. In general, babies adapt to the pattern of life around them: They will tend to be most awake and alert at times of the day (or night) when the most interesting things and people are around.

Newborn sleep requirements
A newborn's sleep pattern is determined by her weight and feeding requirements. This means that in the first weeks of life, the less your baby weighs, the more often she will need to be fed and the less time she will spend sleeping, and vice versa. The chart is a very rough guide to sleep requirements according to varying birth weights.

NEWBORN HEALTH

Immediately after birth your baby will undergo five short tests to assess his health

Your baby is given a score of 0, 1, or 2 for each category. If he scores over 7, he is in good condition. If he scores under 4, he needs help and will receive resuscitation. Most low-scoring babies score high when tested again a few minutes later. The five checks are:

Color *A pink skin color shows his lungs are working well.*

Heart rate *Indicates the strength and regularity of the heartbeat.*

Reflex *Facial expressions and responses show how alert your child is to stimuli.*

Muscle tone *Shows the health and tone of his muscles.*

Respiration *Breathing shows the health of his lungs.*

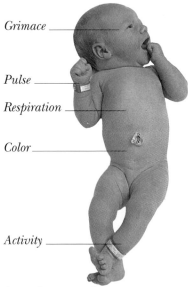

Grimace

Pulse

Respiration

Color

Activity

Assessing a newborn
The baby is checked to ensure his lungs and heart are working and his responses are healthy.

Whether your baby is born in a hospital, birthing center, or at home, the doctor or midwife will see to it that he is given uninterrupted expert attention until breathing is well established. Any major problems should be identified within a matter of minutes, so that if special care is required it will begin at the earliest possible moment.

Immediately after delivery, and then again five minutes later, the doctor or midwife will test your baby against the Apgar scale (see left), a series of short tests to determine his general physical well-being. Devised by the late Dr. Virginia Apgar, a renowned anesthesiologist, they are designed to detect whether your baby is in need of immediate special attention. The doctor will then examine your baby to assess his general condition.

THE INITIAL EXAMINATION

A doctor will give your baby a thorough examination shortly after birth and again 24 hours later, to ensure that nothing was missed and that no new problems have developed. Once the initial tests and examination have been carried out and you've held and suckled him for as long as you and your partner want, your baby will be wrapped up snugly and put in his bassinet to keep warm. The sort of checks done involve:

- Making sure that your baby's facial features and body proportions are normal.

- Turning your baby over to see that his back is normal and there is no spina bifida (see p. 28).

- Examining his anus, legs, fingers, and toes.

- Recording the number of blood vessels in the umbilical cord – normally there are two arteries and one vein.

- Weighing your baby.

- Measuring your baby's head and body length.

- Checking your baby's temperature and warming him if he needs it.

If you are in the hospital, you should ask to be informed when the second examination is to take place, so that you can be there. You will have the opportunity to ask the doctor questions and to discuss any worries you may have.

For both examinations, your baby is placed on a flat surface in a good light and at a convenient height for the doctor, who may be seated. You can have the examination at your bedside if you are immobile, but should you be absent, never fail to get the results of the examination. Generally the doctor will start examining at the top of the head and work down to the toes.

Head and neck The doctor will look at the skull bones and the fontanels, and check for any misshaping that occurred when the head passed through the birth canal during delivery. He will look at the eyes, ears, and nose, and check the mouth for any abnormality, such as cleft palate, and for any teeth. Although it is rare, some newborn babies do have teeth. If they are loose or growing at an unusual angle they will be removed so that there is no risk of their falling out and being swallowed. The doctor will also check your baby's neck for cysts or swellings.

Chest and heart The heart and lungs are checked with a stethoscope. The lungs should be expanded and working normally. The work load of a baby's heart increases substantially when he becomes responsible for his own circulation, sometimes causing what sounds like a heart murmur, but the vast majority of murmurs disappear spontaneously and quickly. Your child will be examined during the postnatal checkup to see if a heart murmur persists.

Arms and hands The doctor will check each arm for a pulse, and for normal movement and strength. He will also check your baby's fingers and palm creases. Nearly all babies have two major creases across each palm; if there is only a single crease, the doctor will look for other physical abnormalities.

Abdomen and genitals The doctor will press his hands gently into your baby's abdomen to check the size and shape of the liver and spleen. Both may be slightly enlarged in a newborn baby. The testes will be checked to ensure that they are properly descended if your baby is a boy; if you have a girl, a check will be made to see that the labia are not joined and the clitoris is a normal size. The doctor will also check the lower spine and anus for congenital abnormalities (see pp. 28–29).

Hips, legs, and feet The doctor will hold both thighs firmly and move each leg to see whether the head of the thigh bone is unstable or lies outside the hip joint, suggesting congenital dislocation of the hip. Testing the hips is not painful, but your baby may cry at the movement. The doctor will examine the legs and feet to make sure they are of equal size and length and that no skeletal abnormalities are present.

Nerves and muscles The doctor will put your baby's arms and legs through a range of movements to make sure that they are not too stiff or floppy. This will tell about the health of your baby's nerves and muscles. The doctor will make sure that the normal newborn reflexes, such as the grasp, stepping, and Moro reflexes (see p.20) are present, and check your baby's head control.

JAUNDICE

Jaundice is not a disease and, in the majority of newborn babies, is not dangerous.

Jaundice is likely to occur when a baby is about three days old. It is caused by the breakdown of red blood cells shortly after birth. This breakdown creates an excess in the blood of a pigment called bilirubin, giving a yellowish tinge to the baby's skin. A blood test is used to measure bilirubin levels.

A newborn is unable to excrete the bilirubin sufficiently rapidly to prevent jaundice until his liver is more mature, at about one week. Treatment for jaundice is usually just a short time under an ultraviolet light, but even without this, the condition should clear up by itself within a week.

If there is an incompatibility between the blood types of mother and baby (usually a Rh-negative mother with a Rh-positive baby) a more serious type of jaundice can appear; this requires treatment within the first two days. All your medical staff will have taken preventive steps before you give birth. Other, less common, causes of jaundice are hepatitis and biliary atresia, a rare condition in which the bile duct fails to develop properly.

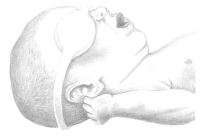

Phototherapy
Jaundice in a newborn may be treated by exposure to ultraviolet light for about 12 hours.

SPECIAL-CARE BABIES

About 7 percent of all babies born in the U.S. weigh less than 5½ pounds (2.5 kilograms), either because they are premature or for other reasons. All low birth-weight babies need special care.

When we say a baby is premature we mean that he has not yet matured to the point where he can cope easily outside the security of his mother's uterus. Although the chances today that a premature or low birth-weight baby will survive and thrive are vastly improved in comparison to our mothers' generation, it's still a difficult experience to see your baby being taken away to a special-care or intensive-care unit immediately after the delivery. Understanding why a baby needs special treatment for a few days or weeks will help lessen your anxiety. Premature babies have very weak muscle tone and don't move much. They often have calcium and iron deficiencies, as well as low blood-sugar levels. If they are very premature their eyes may still be sealed. They have very red and wrinkled skin. Their heads are disproportionately large in comparison to the rest of the body, and the bones in their skull are soft. They are more than usually prone to jaundice (see p.25).

SPECIAL NEEDS

A premature or low birth-weight baby needs to be fed more frequently than a full-term baby because he burns calories more quickly. You can understand why he needs to be fed so often if you think of a tiny hummingbird; it never stops feeding since its weight is so low compared to its volume that it needs constant food to stoke up the metabolic burners and keep the temperature normal. The smaller the baby, therefore, the more often he needs to feed and the less time he spends asleep (see p.23). For premature babies the challenge of living outside the uterus is clearly an exhausting

BONDING

You should make every effort to establish bonds with your baby as soon as possible through your smell, your voice, and your touch, especially if he will have to remain in a special-care unit.

Much research has been done to illustrate the positive effects of physical contact on young babies, and this applies equally to those who are premature and of low birth-weight.

If you are a new mother expecting to have your baby in your arms right after birth, it is obviously distressing to find that he will be kept behind a glass screen, surrounded by many machines.

Mothers who do not have early contact with their babies may start to feel cheated of motherhood. They are likely to blame themselves for having "failed" their babies, and these feelings of guilt are intensified because they are unable to comfort their babies, who are obviously in need of help.

It is important to realize, though, that effective bonding can take place with your baby in an incubator – indeed, it is essential that it does. No baby is so ill that you can't place your hand inside the incubator and stroke him gently. Try not to be intimidated by all the machinery; ask the hospital staff to show you what to do.

Incubators
A premature baby will be placed in a closed, thermostatically controlled cabinet to maintain his body temperature, and given oxygen if necessary. His temperature and breathing will be constantly monitored.

one. The lack of stimulation from being in an incubator and the inability to move very much means that, apart from frequent feeding, these premature babies spend most of their time sleeping.

BREATHING PROBLEMS

A baby with respiratory distress syndrome (RDS) may stop breathing for a short time. This is called apnea. Although it sounds very frightening, apnea is not uncommon, and most babies start breathing again after gentle stimulation such as a tap or a stroke. Other respiratory problems can arise from fluid inhaled into the lungs or a lack of surfactant – a substance produced in the lungs that keeps them from collapsing. If a baby's lungs do not have enough surfactant coating, they don't expand as well as they should. This can cause the smaller air sacs to collapse, leading to hyaline membrane disease, a condition common in babies born before 28 weeks.

Babies suffering from any of these complications can be given oxygen either by way of a face mask or by a small tube inserted directly into the windpipe and attached to a ventilator.

TUBE FEEDING

Most premature and low birth-weight babies do not have the strength to suck milk from a nipple or bottle, and their intestines may be too weak to absorb food. There are three alternative ways of feeding:

• Intravenous feeding is used for babies who are very ill or so premature that they cannot swallow or digest food for themselves. It may continue for weeks and subsequent feeding will be through a nasogastric tube.

• With nasogastric feeding, a tube is passed through the baby's nose and into the stomach or intestine. Because the tube is very fine and soft, the baby hardly knows it's there, so it's a very comfortable way to feed.

• When your baby is older, a combination of breast or bottle and tube feeding will suffice; the baby feeds as much as he can from breast or bottle, and the feeding tube supplies the rest. Combination feeding can be used once the rooting and sucking reflexes (see p.20) are established and will continue until the baby is strong enough to feed from breast or bottle only.

PROGRESS

The development of a premature baby can be slow and erratic. It is often a great shock to see just how tiny a premature baby is but he will have a great will to live.

For a premature baby every day can be an uphill battle. Periods of improvement may be followed by setbacks, and this constant uncertainty can make you and your partner feel anxious, moody, and restless. It is encouraging to know, however, that most babies born after 32 weeks will develop normally. Of those babies born at 28 weeks (three months early), six out of seven will survive.

HEALTH RISKS

Premature and low birth-weight babies are ill-prepared for life outside the uterus, and can have the problems listed below.

Breathing Due to the immaturity of their lungs, premature and low birth-weight babies are at risk for developing difficulty in breathing, known as respiratory distress syndrome (RDS). Treatment with a surfactant helps diminsh RDS.

Immune system An underdeveloped immune system and a body that is too weak to defend itself properly means there is a greater risk of infection.

Temperature regulation A premature baby's temperature control is inefficient and he is likely to be too cold or too hot. He has less heat insulation because he lacks sufficient body fat underneath the skin.

Reflexes Inadequate development of his reflexes, particularly his sucking reflex, creates difficulties in feeding. Premature and low birth weight babies often need tube feeding.

Digestion A premature or low birth-weight baby's stomach is small and sensitive, which means he is less able to hold food down and is more likely to vomit. The immaturity of his digestive system can make it difficult for him to digest essential proteins, so they may have to be given in a predigested form.

SPINA BIFDA

If the neural tube (the developing spine) doesn't fuse properly at around four to six weeks in the developing fetus, the meninges (the coverings of the brain and spinal cord) may be left exposed.

The affected part of the spine may be covered by skin and marked only by a dimple or a tuft of hair (spina bifida occulta); the meninges may protrude and the bulge may be covered with skin (meningocele); or in the most serious form, the spinal cord itself may protrude as a raw swelling over the spine (myelocele). Eighty percent of all spina bifida babies have some degree of hydrocephalus (see opposite).

Spinal openings should be corrected by surgery soon after birth. In babies with severe defects, problems may include complete paralysis of the legs, double incontinence, and mental retardation. Urinary incontinence can be helped by the use of a catheter (a sterile tube inserted into the bladder), and physiotherapy is important to encourage mobility.

Spina bifida can be detected in pregnancy by ultrasound. In the U.S., spina bifida will occur in 1 in 1,000 live births; women who have had one spina bifida pregnancy are at greater risk of having another. Seventy-five percent of spina bifida births could be prevented by taking 0.4 milligrams (400 micrograms) of folic acid daily. Because the defect occurs before week 8 of pregnancy and often so early that a woman does not yet know she is pregnant, folic acid supplements should be started before conception and continued throughout the pregnancy.

CONGENITAL CONDITIONS

Congenital handicaps are rare. Some are genetic, whereas others are due to the effects on the fetus of drugs, radiation, infections, or metabolic disturbances. The fetal tissues that are most actively growing at the time when the adverse factor operates are the ones most likely to be affected. An increasing number of defects can be detected before birth and successfully treated just after birth.

Talipes (Club foot) Some infants – twice as many boys as girls – are born with the sole of one or both feet facing down and inward, or up and outward. The cause of club foot is not fully understood, but it may be inherited. It may be associated with spina bifida. The foot will be manipulated over several months, and braced or splinted in position between manipulations. If surgery is necessary, it can be carried out between the ages of 12 weeks and nine months.

Dislocated hip In about 0.4 percent of infants, the ball at the head of the thigh bone does not fit snugly into its socket in the hip bone. In a newborn, this is a potential rather than an actual problem. It is much more common in girls than in boys, and following breech births and pregnancies where there is an abnormally small amount of amniotic fluid in the uterus. A doctor will check your baby's hips for excessive mobility as part of routine tests after birth (see p.24). Treatment such as manipulation and splinting can prevent trouble in later infancy. In severe cases, an operation may be needed.

Epispadias and hypospadias In a very small number of male babies – about 0.3 percent – the urethral opening is not situated at the end of the penis. In epispadias, the opening is on the upper surface of the penis; in hypospadias, the opening is on the underside of the glans (head). In severe cases, the penis may curve upward or downward. Rarely, the urethral opening lies between the genitals and the anus; the genitals may appear to be female. Corrective surgery is usually done before the age of two years, allowing normal passage of urine and, in later life, normal sexual intercourse. Neither condition, even in the severe form, causes infertility.

Congenital heart disease The most common form of heart disease in newborns is a hole in the ventricular septum – the thin dividing wall between the right and left ventricles (pumping chambers). About four weeks after birth, blood will "shunt" from left to right through the hole and the oxygenated blood will flow to the lungs instead of to the body. Symptoms include breathlessness, particularly during feedings; crying; and poor weight gain. There may be no symptoms, and a murmur will lead the doctor to pick up the condition during a routine examination. In some cases, the hole seals by itself, but if it doesn't, an operation will be necessary.

Cleft lip and cleft palate A cleft is a split or separation of parts. During the early part of pregnancy, separate areas of the baby's face and head develop individually, then join together. When joining does not take place or is incomplete, the baby can be born with a cleft lip on one or both sides, with or without a cleft palate. Breastfeeding is sometimes possible, perhaps using a nipple shield; if not, special bottles and nipples are readily available. Some milk may return down the nose but this doesn't matter.

A cleft lip can be surgically closed soon or some weeks after birth. The palate can be closed from about six to nine months. Further operations may be necessary for some children.

Affected children are looked after by a cleft-palate team which will monitor speech, hearing, and teeth and will intervene should this become necessary. Support for parents is available (see **Useful addresses**, pp.344–45).

Down syndrome This is by far the most common of a range of conditions called trisomies, in which one pair of chromosomes has an extra chromosome, making three. In Down syndrome, there are three number 21 chromosomes. Affected infants characteristically have a round face, small features, a tongue that protrudes, and slanting eyes with folds of skin at their inner corners. They tend to be rather floppy infants and have short, wide hands. They may also suffer from congenital heart disease.

Down syndrome babies are usually mentally handicapped, though the degree of handicap varies widely; many are near normal. They are usually affectionate and happy children. With careful attention and early education, they often do very well, and some manage to live independently as adults.

Pyloric stenosis In this condition, the pylorus, the passage that leads from the stomach into the small intestine, is narrow because of a thickening of the muscle. The cause is unknown, and it is more common in boys than in girls. Symptoms usually first appear at two to four weeks, though they can appear earlier or later. The stomach contracts powerfully in an attempt to force a buildup of food through the narrow pylorus. This is impossible, however, and the contents of the stomach are vomited up so violently that they may be propelled up to 3 feet (1 meter) – projectile vomiting. The baby may also suffer constipation and dehydration. Ultrasound and a barium swallow may be used to confirm the diagnosis. A simple operation to widen the pylorus can be performed, curing the condition completely.

Imperforate anus In rare cases, a baby's anus is sealed at birth, either because there is a thin membrane of skin over the opening or because the anal canal, which links the rectum with the anus, has not developed. The rectal pouch may be connected to the vagina, urethra, or bladder, and surgery must be performed at once. This condition is routinely checked for at every birth (see p.24), and is treated immediately if present.

HYDROCEPHALUS

Commonly called water on the brain, hydrocephalus often occurs with spina bifida or other neurological defects.

Hydrocephalus is rare, most commonly occuring after a brain hemorrhage in a preterm baby. Normally, cerebrospinal fluid bathes the brain and spinal cord and protects them from injury. Restrictions in the circulation of this fluid or its excessive formation can lead to too much fluid within the skull. The head swells because the skull bones are still soft, and the soft tissues between the skull bones (the fontanels) become wide and bulging.

If hydrocephalus is suspected, frequent CT scans will be done and the baby's head circumference measured every one to two weeks. If a child is born with hydrocephalus, a shunt may be inserted to drain off the fluid. Mental development may be adversely affected, but some children with advanced hydrocephalus are of normal intelligence.

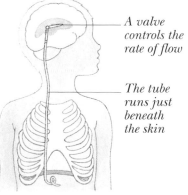

A valve controls the rate of flow

The tube runs just beneath the skin

Shunt
A system of tubes with a valve drains off excess cerebrospinal fluid to where it can pass into the bloodstream, usually the abdominal cavity. The entire device is enclosed in the body.

CHAPTER 2

Everyday CARE

Confronted with a newborn baby, many parents worry that they will not know what to do. Will she start to breastfeed automatically? How much sleep should she have? How much food does she need? What if she refuses food?

Fortunately, looking after a baby does not require specialized skills – just some basic knowledge, common sense, and a willingness to ask for advice. In the space of a few weeks your confidence and experience will increase dramatically, and you will know the best way to change, hold, comfort, and feed your baby. You will learn that if she needs something she will usually find a way of communicating with you.

As your child gets older, she will become more independent. By the age of four she will be able to feed, wash, and dress herself and she may be quite opinionated about the clothes and foods she does and doesn't like. Her physical needs will no longer take up so much of your time. Your role in her everyday care is to keep her strong and healthy by meeting her dietary needs and looking after her health and hygiene.

YOUNG BABY

EQUIPPING THE NURSERY

SAFETY

When planning a nursery, bear in mind that your child will be mobile before long.

• *Make sure there are no sharp edges or corners on the furniture.*

• *Choose a nonskid floor covering and consider putting bars and locks on the windows*

• *The furniture should be stable so your child can't pull it over*

• *Toys should be stored at floor level so your child doesn't have to stretch to reach them*

• *Choose wall-mounted lamps to avoid trailing cords*

• *Don't overheat the nursery; overheating is a risk factor in crib death (SIDS) (see p.122)*

• *Secure drapes and blinds well up from the floor*

Your baby may have a room of his own or share yours; once he is sleeping through the night, however, he should have his own space. You'll need little special equipment, and you can improvise with household items – a sink will do as well as a baby bath, for example, and a folded towel serves as a changing pad – but many parents delight in equipping a nursery.

If this is your first child, ask friends with children which items they found most useful (or which items they bought and never used), and weigh their advice against your own lifestyle. If there's anything you're unsure about, shop around and study catalogs from children's stores before making a final decision. There will often be many things that you can manage without. The only essentials are somewhere for the baby to sleep, clothes and diapers (see pp.82–83 and 106–107), and feeding equipment.

You don't have to buy everything brand new; watch for secondhand items advertised in local papers or on bulletin boards in local grocery stores. A bassinet will last only a couple of months, because babies grow so quickly, so it makes sense to borrow one from friends if you can. If you buy secondhand items, check for general wear and tear, and make sure that all surfaces are smooth and rust-free for your baby's safety. Check, too, that they comply with the latest safety regulations. Beware of painted items; older paints may contain lead, which is poisonous. Never buy secondhand car seats.

BASIC EQUIPMENT

Sleeping

Bassinet or crib

Mattress with waterproof cover

Fitted crib sheets

Thermal blanket (for newborn)

Receiving blankets

Baby monitor

Transportation

Carriage that lets baby lie flat
(suitable from birth)

Sling

Infant car seat

Bathing

Baby bath

Cotton balls

Large soft towel

Washcloth or sponge

Baby brush

Baby bath lotion

Blunt-ended scissors

Other

Bouncing chair or baby seat

Clean, soft cloths for diaper changes

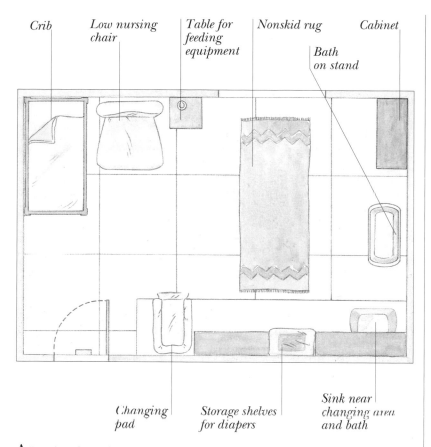

Crib
Low nursing chair
Table for feeding equipment
Nonskid rug
Cabinet
Bath on stand

Changing pad
Storage shelves for diapers
Sink near changing area and bath

ARRANGING A NURSERY

Planning your nursery, like buying equipment, is best done before your baby is born: once you bring him home you'll be far too busy feeding and changing, and you're likely to be tired, too.

Try to ensure that the room is as easy as possible to keep clean, with wipe-clean surfaces. Choose furniture without sharp edges or corners and make sure that any painted surfaces are nontoxic and lead-free. You will need plenty of storage space, especially near the changing area. This could be a wide-topped chest of drawers with some shelf space above, or you may want to build your own. Be sure the top is wide enough for the changing pad and smooth as well as washable. Wall-to-wall carpeting is an ideal floor covering for the nursery, as it is warm; choose a stain-resistant type.

The baby's room does not have to be especially warm, but should be kept at a constant temperature. Around 65°F (18°C) is suitable if your baby wears a heavyweight fleece sleeper and is covered with a blanket; if the room is warmer, he should wear lighter sleeping clothes (see p.122). If your baby is tucked snugly in his crib, then all-night heating may not be necessary except during very cold weather; a thermostatically controlled room heater is the most suitable. It is a good idea to install a dimmer switch so that you can gently bring up the lights without frightening the baby. If you like, the light can be left on low as an alternative to a nightlight.

DECORATING THE NURSERY

Although a newborn's vision is limited, cheerful colors and decorations will provide a stimulating environment.

• *Light, cheerful colors are the most suitable for your baby's room. Yellow, blue, and grassy green – the colors of nature – will be soothing to your baby, and vivid splashes of primary colors will enliven the room*

• *A newborn baby has a very limited range of vision – only 8–10 inches (20–25 centimeters) so hang mobiles above the crib and the changing area. Their colors and movement will make your baby alert to his surroundings*

• *Put an unbreakable mirror on the side of the crib so your baby can see his face; the human face is rivetingly interesting to very young babies*

• *Choose fabrics and wallcoverings that are washable*

• *A folding screen may be useful to shelter the crib from bright sunshine or from cold drafts*

• *Carpet is warm and will absorb noise; a good alternative is a vinyl floor covering with a couple of nonskid rugs*

Mirror made from unbreakable plastic

Visual stimulation
A sturdy mirror placed in the crib will allow your baby to see his own face.

SLEEPING

The best choice for your newborn is a Moses basket, cradle, bassinet, or a carriage with a bassinet; some carriages like this convert to strollers for use when the baby is able to support herself sitting up. Your baby will outgrow baskets or cradles quite quickly, so don't waste money on an expensive one unless you're sure you can afford it. When your baby outgrows her bassinet or cradle, you'll need a full-sized crib. Choose one with side rails that are set closely together – a distance of no more than $2\,^3/_8$ inches (6 centimeters) is suitable – and drop sides so you can lift your baby out easily. The

SLEEPING EQUIPMENT

Your newborn will spend much of her time asleep, and she'll be able to sleep almost anywhere. A bassinet or Moses basket is best at first, and easily portable, but once she outgrows these she'll need a crib.

The shade protects your baby from drafts and direct sunlight

Air holes in mattress allow your baby to breathe if she rolls over onto her front

Make sure the cover is washable

A waterproof cover will keep the rain out

Handles should be near the hood end to take the weight evenly

The spaces between the bars should be no more than $2\,^3/_8$ inches (6 centimeters)

The drop side should have safety locks so your child can't let the side down

Casters for maneuvering and for "rocking"

Caster locks

mattress should fit snugly, so your baby can't get her arm or her leg, or even her head, trapped down the side. The crib will last you until your baby is big enough to climb out, when you'll need to buy a bed – at about two or two and a half years, or 36 inches tall. The crib mattress should be a firm foam type, with air holes that allow your child to breathe if she turns over onto her front while asleep. Portable cribs are very useful for going on vacation or taking your baby out for the evening. They have fabric sides and are collapsible so they can be carried easily.

Because a young baby can't regulate her body temperature effectively, you should use a cotton sheet and thermal blankets for the crib so you can easily add one or take one away. Once she is a year old, a comforter will be suitable. Check the label on any mattress, cribs, and bedding you buy to make sure that it is flameproof and conforms to current safety standards.

Sleeping temperatures and suffocation risks Research has shown that babies who get too hot are at a greater risk of crib death. While nursery temperature is important, how the baby is covered is even more so. If the nursery is at 65°F (18°C), a sheet and three blankets will keep your baby at an ideal temperature. These days, fleece sleepers are not advised because the baby may become overheated. If it is warmer, use fewer blankets (see p.123). Avoid lambswool fleeces and mattress pads and natural sheepskins; they have been implicated in a few cases of suffocation and SIDS in infants. Be sure bumpers are securely tied, and don't give your baby a pillow.

BABY MONITORS

A baby monitor will allow you to keep in touch with your baby, even when she's in another room.

• *Baby monitors are available in different versions: battery, electrical, or rechargeable*

• *Lights indicating whether the batteries are low, or the baby unit is out of range, are useful*

Keeping in touch Monitors come in two parts – the baby's transmitter and the parent's receiver

SLEEPING ACCESSORIES

Comforter (babies over one year)

Cotton sheets

Cotton thermal blanket

Warm blanket

Tie-on waterproof sheet to protect mattress

Safety foam mattress with airholes

WALKING AND CARRYING

Your baby will spend most of her time being carried, wheeled, or secured in some way, and there is a wide variety of strollers and carriers available. When choosing equipment of this kind, safety and portability will be your main considerations.

Slings are the most popular way of transporting a newborn; they're light and comfortable, and allow you to carry your baby close while keeping both hands free. Try one on with your baby in before you buy it. Backpacks, which can be used once the baby can sit up on his or her own, have supportive frames that will make it easier to bear a larger baby's weight. Make sure backpacks have a safety strap for your baby and a stand so you can put it on without any help.

For longer journeys you will need a carriage or stroller in which your baby can sit or lie down. Choose one that will let your baby lie flat for the first three months, until she has head control. Consider where you will keep it and whether you will need to take it on buses and trains or up stairs. Whatever stroller you choose, it should have a safety harness or rings to install one.

CHOOSING A STROLLER

For the first three months, your baby must be able to lie flat. Reclining strollers are most common, but a carriage with removable bassinet is more versatile. Some models have an extra "sitting" unit.

Add a canopy for sun protection

A hood shield will protect your baby from rain

The top lifts off and can be used as a bassinet

A safety harness will keep your baby securely strapped in

A basket is useful for carrying changing equipment or shopping

Safety locks prevent the frame from collapsing when the stroller is in use

Make sure the brakes are easy to use

CARRYING YOUR BABY

A sturdy frame takes the strain off your back

The sling should have a support for your baby's head

Using a backpack
You can carry your baby in a backpack once he can sit up by himself. Make sure he is comfortable and is not restricted by the leg openings.

Using a sling
Your baby will feel safe and secure inside a sling, and it leaves your arms free.

BOUNCING CHAIR

Your baby can be propped up in a specially made chair so that she can look around her. When she's on solids, you can sit her in the chair and feed her, but ensure that she is safely strapped in to keep her from slipping.

Put the chair on the floor, never on a table or desk

SAFETY HARNESSES

Your young baby has no fear of falling, so wherever she sits she will have to be strapped in for her own safety.

- *A five-point harness, which has straps for the shoulders as well as the waist and crotch, is safest*

- *Your baby's stroller should have a built-in harness or rings so that you can attach one*

- *High chairs should have a built-in crotch strap and seat belt*

- *Some harnesses come with reins that can be attached when your baby is old enough to walk*

FEEDING AND NUTRITION

MILK: THE IDEAL FOOD

In the first few months of life, your baby will get all the nutrients she requires from breast or formula milk.

Calories *The energy content of food is measured in calories. Infants require about two-and-a-half to three times more calories than adults for their body weight.*

Protein *Vital for building body cells and tissues, a baby's protein needs are three times as great as an adult's on a body-weight basis.*

Fats *Minute traces of fatty acids are needed for growth and repair.*

Carbohydrates *These are the major source of calories.*

Your baby depends on you for the provision of adequate nutrition, and for a newborn, breast or bottled milk will provide all she needs. Breast milk is the ideal food for a baby (see below), but if you choose to bottlefeed, rest assured that your baby will still thrive. Feeding takes a great deal of a parent's time, so it's important to choose a method that is suitable for both parent and baby. Well before delivery you should decide whether you are going to breast-feed or bottlefeed and prepare for whichever you choose.

It's quite normal for all babies, breastfed or bottlefed, not to take much colostrum (see p.40), at first, for they take a while to get the hang of feeding. Your baby will cry when she is hungry, and you should take your lead from her in setting the pattern of feeds.

Babies grow most rapidly during the first six months of life – most babies double their birth weight in around four to five months. Your baby's nutritional needs reflect this tremendous growth. A healthy baby's food has to contain adequate amounts of calories, protein, fats, carbohydrates, vitamins, and minerals (see left and opposite), and until she's at least four months old, your baby will receive all these nutrients from breast or formula milk.

WHY BREAST IS BEST

Human breast milk is the perfect food for babies. Because it doesn't look as rich and creamy as cows' milk, you may think that it is not good enough, but don't be put off. It contains all the nutrients your baby needs, and in just the right amounts.

Breast milk has many benefits for your baby. Breastfed babies tend to suffer less than bottlefed babies from such illnesses as gastroenteritis and chest infections. This is because antibodies from the colostrum and the mother's milk are absorbed into the bloodstream, where they act to protect the baby against infections. In the first few days of life, they also protect the intestine, reducing the chances of intestinal upsets.

Breast milk has other advantages for a baby's digestion. Breastfed babies don't get constipated, since breast milk is more easily digestible than cows' milk, although they pass few stools because the milk is so completely digested that there is little waste. They are less prone to ammoniacal nappy rash (see p.110), too. From a mother's point of view, breastfeeding is far more convenient than bottlefeeding: there is no need for the milk to be warmed up, there are no bottles to sterilize, no formula to be

Breastfeeding
Suckling helps to form a very strong bond between you and your new baby.

made up, and no equipment to buy. Breastfed babies usually sleep longer, suffer less from wind, and posset – that is, regurgitate food – less, and the posset smells less unpleasant. It is difficult to overfeed a breastfed baby, so don't worry if your baby seems fatter than other babies of her age. Each baby has its own appetite and metabolic rate, and yours will be the right weight for her own body.

Some women worry that breastfeeding will make their breasts sag. This is not the case: breasts may change in size or sag after a baby is born, but these changes are due to being pregnant, not to breastfeeding itself. In fact, breastfeeding is good for your figure, as it promotes the loss of any weight gained during pregnancy. While you are breastfeeding, the hormone oxytocin (see p.40), which stimulates milk flow, also encourages the uterus to return to its pre-pregnant state. Your pelvis and waistline will also get back to normal more quickly.

Studies have shown that breast cancer is rarer in those parts of the world where breastfeeding is the norm, and it is possible that breastfeeding may provide some protection against the disease.

BOTTLEFEEDING

Every woman is capable of breastfeeding her baby, and you should try to do so. Many women feel that they must breastfeed to be a good mother, and feel guilty if they decide not to. On the other hand, some women find it emotionally or psychologically difficult to breastfeed; others find that, however much they try, they cannot master breastfeeding. If this is the case, then you should forget about it and concentrate on giving your baby a good bottlefed diet: she will still thrive. If you decide not to breastfeed at all, you will probably be prescribed hormones to suppress your milk supply.

You may consider bottlefeeding because you feel that breastfeeding will tie you down, particularly if you intend to return to work very soon after the birth. This may be the best solution for you, but remember that it is also possible to express enough milk so that your partner or a childminder can feed your baby in your absence. That way your baby can have the benefits of your milk, and you can still have the flexibility of bottlefeeding and the freedom that this gives you.

One of the benefits of bottlefeeding is that your partner can be involved with feeding the new baby. He should try to do this as soon as possible after the birth, so that he can learn to handle the baby confidently, and if possible he should share the feeding equally with you. Encourage him to hold the baby close and talk to her while feeding, so that the baby gets used to the feel of his skin, his smell, and the sound of his voice.

Bottlefeeding
Make feeding a time of closeness and intimacy for you and your baby.

VITAMIN AND MINERAL NEEDS

As well as the basic nutrients (see opposite page), milk will supply your baby with necessary vitamins and minerals.

Vitamins Vitamins are essential to health. Formula milks contain all your baby's vitamin requirements, but breast milk does not contain as much vitamin D, which is manufactured by the skin when stimulated by light, as formula milk. You should ask your health visitor whether your baby needs vitamin supplements.

Minerals Calcium, phosphorus, and magnesium, which are necessary for the growth of bone and muscle, are contained in breast and formula milk. Babies are born with a reserve of iron that will last about four months; after this they have to be given iron, either in solids or as supplements.

Trace elements Minerals like zinc, copper, and fluoride are essential to your baby's health. The first two are present in breast and formula milk, but fluoride, which protects against dental decay, is not. Never give fluoride supplements without checking with your midwife or doctor, as excessive amounts can cause fluorosis (discoloration of the tooth enamel).

Taking good care of yourself is the key to a good milk supply. If you stay relaxed, eat well, and drink enough fluids, you will have plenty of milk for your baby.

• *Rest as much as you can, particularly during the first weeks, and try to get plenty of sleep*

• *You produce the most milk in the morning when you are rested. If you become tense during the day, your supply could be poor by evening. Go through your prenatal relaxation routines and make sure you rest every day*

• *Let the housework go; do only what is absolutely necessary*

• *Try to give yourself a few treats; relax with a glass of wine at the end of the day*

• *Eat a well-balanced diet that is fairly rich in protein. Avoid highly refined carbohydrates (cakes, cookies, candy, and so on)*

• *Ask your doctor about iron and possibly vitamin supplements*

• *Drink about three quarts of fluid a day; some women find that it is helpful to keep a drink by them while they are feeding*

• *Express any milk your baby doesn't take in the early feedings of the day to encourage your breasts to keep on producing milk*

• *The combined contraceptive pill decreases your supply, so avoid it for five months after delivery. Discuss alternative methods of contraception with your doctor*

• *Avoid spicy foods, which could affect your milk and upset your baby's stomach*

ALL ABOUT BREASTFEEDING

Breastfeeding has to be learned, and you should seek support and advice from your family, from friends with babies, and from your pediatrician or a lactation consultant. Above all you will learn from your baby, by understanding his signals and discovering how to respond to them. No special action is required to prepare the breasts for feeding unless you have an inverted nipple. If you do, use a breast shell to make your nipple protrude so the baby will be able to latch on. If you are having your baby in a hospital, make sure the nursing staff knows you intend to breastfeed, and don't be afraid to ask for help. Suckle your baby as soon as he is born – in the delivery room, if you are in the hospital – to form a bond with him as early as possible and let him get used to suckling.

COLOSTRUM AND BREAST MILK

During the 72 hours after delivery, the breasts produce a thin, yellow fluid called colostrum, made up of water, protein, and minerals. It contains antibodies that protect the baby against a range of intestinal and respiratory infections. In the first few days, your baby should be put to the breast regularly, both to feed on the colostrum and to get used to latching on to the breast (see p.42).

Once your breasts start to produce milk, you may be surprised by its watery appearance. When your baby sucks, the first milk that he gets – the foremilk – is thin, watery, and thirst-quenching. Then comes the hindmilk, which is richer in fat and protein.

THE LET-DOWN REFLEX

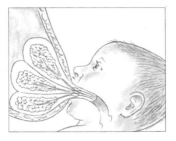

Pituitary gland
Hypothalamus

The sucking action of your baby at the breast sends messages to the hypothalamus, which in turn stimulates the pituitary gland in your brain to release two hormones: prolactin, which is responsible for the manufacture of milk in the milk glands, and oxytocin, which causes the milk to be passed from the glands to the reservoirs behind the areola. This transfer is known as the let-down reflex.

BREASTFEEDING POSITIONS

Lying down is ideal for night feedings; when your baby is very small you may need to put him on a pillow so that he can reach your nipple. You may find a lying position the most suitable if you have had an episiotomy and sitting is uncomfortable. If you have had a cesarean section and your stomach is still tender, try lying with your baby's feet tucked under your arm.

Both you and your baby should be comfortable

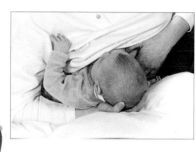

Lying positions
Breastfeeding positions that let the mother lie down offer a restful alternative and can keep wriggly babies off tender cesarean incisions.

Sitting position
Make sure that your arms and back are supported and you are relaxed.

WHAT TO WEAR TO BREASTFEED

You should always wear a supportive nursing bra when you are breastfeeding.

Choose one that has front fasteners and wide straps that won't cut into your shoulders. Drop-front or zipper-front bras are easy to undo with one hand while you hold your baby. A good bra will minimize discomfort if your breasts become sore.

SUPPLY AND DEMAND

Milk is produced in glands that are deeply buried in the breast, not in the fatty tissue, so breast size is no indication of how much milk you can produce; even small breasts are perfectly adequate milk producers.

Milk is produced according to demand – you supply what your baby needs, so don't worry that you'll run out of milk if your baby feeds very often. Your breasts are stimulated to produce milk by your baby's sucking, so the more eagerly he feeds, the more milk they will produce, and vice versa. During the time that you breastfeed, the amount of milk available will fluctuate according to your baby's needs, and once he becomes established on solids, the breasts will produce less milk.

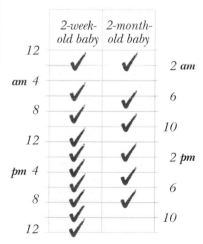

	2-week-old baby	2-month-old baby	
12	✔	✔	2 am
am 4	✔	✔	6
8	✔	✔	10
12	✔	✔	2 pm
pm 4	✔	✔	6
8	✔	✔	10
12	✔		

Frequency of feedings
At first your baby will eat little and often. By about two months, most babies eat roughly every four hours and take more at each feeding than before.

HOW LONG ON EACH BREAST?

You should keep your baby on the breast for as long as he shows interest in sucking.

• *If your baby continues to suck after your breasts have emptied, it may be that he is just enjoying the sensation; this is fine for a few minutes, but more may irritate the nipple*

• *When your baby has finished feeding from one breast, gently take him off your nipple (see below right) and put him onto the other breast. He may not suck as long on the second breast*

• *Alternate the first breast you offer at each feeding. To help remember which breast was used last, put a safety pin on your bra*

Encourage intimacy by talking or singing to your baby

BREASTFEEDING YOUR BABY

Breastfeeding creates a strong bond between mother and baby if feeding time is relaxed and pleasurable for both. Make sure your baby can see you, and smile and talk to him while he is suckling. He will come to associate the pleasure of feeding with the sight of your face, the sound of your voice, and the smell of your skin. Make sure you are both comfortable before you start (see **Breastfeeding positions**, p.41). You should feed your baby from both breasts, and you may want to burp him before changing over (see p.55).

GIVING A BREAST FEEDING

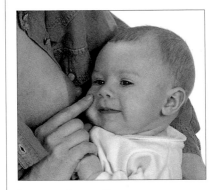

With an open mouth, your baby feels for your nipple

The rooting reflex
Prompt your baby to look for the breast by gently stroking the cheek nearest to it. Your baby will immediately turn toward your breast, open-mouthed.

Latching on
Your baby should take the nipple and a good proportion of the areola into his mouth. The milk is drawn out by a combination of sucking and squeezing the tongue on to the hard palate.

Your baby presses the elongated nipple against the roof of his mouth as he draws out milk

Releasing the nipple
To break the suction, slip your little finger into the corner of the baby's mouth. Your breast will slip out easily instead of being dragged out.

POSSIBLE PROBLEMS

It is perfectly normal for breastfeeding not to go smoothly at first, so don't get worked up about minor setbacks such as your baby refusing a feed. Remember that he too is learning and that it will take time for you to get used to each other, so persevere, and ask your midwife or health visitor for advice and suggestions.

Refusing the breast It is quite usual for a newborn not to suck very vigorously or for very long during his first 24 to 36 hours. If this occurs later, however, there may be a problem that needs to be addressed. Breathing difficulties are the most likely cause of a baby's having problems taking the breast. It may be that your breast is covering his nostrils; if so, gently pull the breast back from the baby's face, just above the areola. If he seems to have a snuffly or blocked nose, consult your doctor; he may prescribe nose drops to clear the nostrils.

If there is no obvious cause for your baby's refusal to feed, he may simply be fretful. A baby who has been crying with hunger, or has been changed or fussed over when he's hungry, can become too distressed to take the breast. You will need to soothe him by holding him firmly and talking or singing; there is no point in trying to feed him until he's calmed down.

If there has been some delay in starting to breastfeed – as with a premature baby who has had to be fed by bottle – your baby may find it more difficult to take the breast, and you will have to be patient and persevering. Your midwife or health visitor will advise you if you need to give expressed milk from a special cup until the baby can take all he needs from the breast. Supplementary bottles are rarely necessary, and they may cause mothers to give up breastfeeding. Giving expressed milk is a better alternative.

Comfort sucking Most babies enjoy sucking on their mothers' breasts for its own sake just as much as feeding. You will learn to tell the difference between actual feeding and comfort sucking. During a feed you may notice that your baby is sucking strongly without actually swallowing. There is no reason why your baby shouldn't suck as long as he wants, provided your nipples are not sore, though he takes most of his feed in the first 3–5 minutes.

Sleeping through feeds If your baby doesn't seem very interested in food during the first few days, make sure that he takes as much as he wants from one breast. If he sleeps at the breast, it means he is contented and doing well, though premature babies should be woken and fed regularly, as they tend to sleep a lot. If your baby does fall asleep at the breast, wake him gently half an hour later and offer a feed; if he is hungry he will perk up.

Fretful feeding If your baby doesn't settle down to feed, or appears not to be satisfied, he is probably sucking on the nipple alone and not getting enough milk. This may also lead to sore nipples. Check that your baby is positioned correctly on the breast.

UNDERFEEDING

You may feel anxious that you can't see how much the baby has taken, but it is rare for a breast-fed baby not to get enough milk.

• *If your baby wants to continue sucking even though he's finished feeding from both breasts, it doesn't always signify hunger; he may just enjoy sucking*

• *Thirst may cause your baby to go on on sucking after he's emptied your breasts. Try giving about 30 millilitres of cooled, boiled water from a special cup*

• *If he seems fretful and hungry, have him weighed at your baby clinic to check if he is gaining weight as quickly as expected. If not, then your milk supply has been reduced – perhaps because you are tired and run down. You may be advised to give supplementary feeds (see p.45) from a special cup until your supply is back to normal. If you are at all worried contact your health visitor or doctor.*

• *Low-milk syndrome, recently described in the US, is a rare condition when a newborn baby fails to get enough nutrition. This is nearly always due to difficulties in learning how to latch on and suckle. In a very few cases it may be due to a mother's failing to produce enough milk. This doesn't preclude breastfeeding, but supplementary bottles will be needed. I cannot stress enough that mothers and babies must be given time to get the hang of breastfeeding.*

• *One warning sign of low-milk syndrome is in the nappies; if your baby wets fewer than six nappies a day, check with your midwife or health visitor.*

EXPRESSING MILK

*Make expressing milk as easy on
yourself as possible, and take
care to store your milk correctly.*

Expressed milk can easily be stored either in the refrigerator or in the freezer. This will free you from feeling tied down by breast-feeding, and allows your baby to be fed with your milk if you are away. It also allows your partner to share in feeding your baby.

Milk can be expressed from your breasts using either your hands or a breast pump, which may be manual or electric. Although small battery pumps are very easy to use, many women find hand expressing to be easier and more convenient. Before you start, you will need a bowl, a funnel, and a container that can be sealed. All equipment must be very clean.

In the first six weeks, hand expressing is nearly always a bit difficult, as the breasts have not reached full production, but don't give up. Because breasts produce milk in response to demand, you may need to express milk in order to keep your supply going – if your baby does not suck well at first, or is premature and can't yet breastfeed, for example. Even if you use a pump, it is worth learning the technique of hand expressing in case you need it. The best time to express milk is in the morning, when you'll have the most milk, although when your baby drops the night feeding you may find the evening the best time.

- *If you have to lean over a low surface, expressing may give you a backache. Make sure the container is at a convenient height*

- *Expressing should be painless. If it hurts, stop immediately. Ask your doctor or lactation consultant if you are expressing correctly*

- *The more relaxed you are, the easier it will be to express. If the milk won't start to flow, place a warm washcloth over your breasts to open the ducts, or try expressing in the bath*

- *If you're concerned that your baby might not go back to breast-feeding after getting used to the bottle, try feeding her milk from a specially designed cup, or spooning the expressed milk from a cup*

- *Milk will go sour unless it is stored correctly, and then it could make your baby ill. Refrigerate or freeze your milk as soon as you've collected it. Refrigerated milk will keep for 24 hours; frozen milk for up to six months*

- *Expressed milk should be put into clean, sealable containers. Don't use glass containers in the freezer – they might crack. Sterile plastic bottle liners are ideal*

EXPRESSING BY PUMP

All manual pumps work with suction and have a funnel or shield, pump mechanism, and container. The assembly and operation of different brands of pump will vary slightly, so follow the manufacturer's instructions.

Pump mechanism

Funnel

Container doubles as feeding bottle

Using a pump
Place the shield over your nipple, then squeeze and release the handle. Your milk should be drawn into the vacuum created in the bottle. If this causes you any pain, stop immediately; expressing should be painless. Try again a little later.

EXPRESSING BY HAND

Massaging the outer breast
Make sure your hands are clean. Cup your breast in both hands with the fingers underneath and the thumbs above. Squeeze the outer part of your breast gently and firmly between your fingers and thumbs. Repeat this ten times, moving around the breast as you do so.

Massaging the inner breast
Move your hands closer to the areola and repeat the squeezing procedure as above.

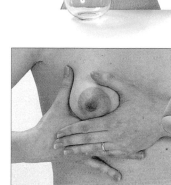

Massaging the breast stimulates milk flow

Press back gently and rhythmically

Make sure the container you use is at a convenient height for you

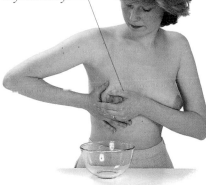

Starting the flow
Place the thumb and fingers of one hand near the areola, press them back into your ribs, then squeeze gently and rhythmically. If the milk doesn't begin to flow immediately, keep trying.

Express from each breast alternately

Emptying the breast
Continue for about five minutes, working around the areola, then move on to the second breast. Repeat the whole procedure for both breasts.

SUPPLEMENTARY BOTTLES

Even though you are breastfeeding, there may be occasions when you have to give supplementary bottles of formula.

If you have a blocked duct or a particularly sore nipple, you may wish to give supplementary bottles, although many mothers prefer to express milk from the affected breast and use this in the bottle.

A baby who has become used to the mother's nipple may dislike rubber nipples. Unfortunately, it can be difficult to tell whether your baby just dislikes the nipple or is not hungry. She'll get used to the bottle if you persist, but you may then find that she doesn't want to go back to the breast. If this happens, try giving the milk from a sterilized spoon or cup.

Bottles containing your own expressed milk can be given to your baby if you are unable to breastfeed or are leaving the baby with someone else.

Although they are not essential, you will find that breast pads and shells will help keep your nipples clean and dry.

Breast shells
When you are feeding from one breast, milk may drip or even flow from the other. A shell can be used to collect this excess milk, which can then be stored in the refrigerator for up to 24 hours or frozen.

Plastic breast shell

Fabric pads are washable and absorbent

Breast pads
Disposable and washable pads are available. They fit inside your bra and protect your clothes from leaks of milk.

MANAGING BREASTFEEDING

Many mothers find that breastfeeding goes smoothly right from the start, but it is also normal to be a bit clumsy at first, for the baby not to suck for very long, or for your breasts to be a bit sore. Remember that it takes time to learn, so if problems arise, persevere until things get easier.

CARE OF THE BREASTS
The daily hygiene of your breasts and nipples is very important. You should cleanse them every day with water or baby lotion (not soap, which defats the skin and can aggravate a sore or cracked nipple), and gently pat them dry. Dry them gently after feeding. Wear your bra all the time, as you will need lots of support, but leave the front flaps down with your nipples open to the air. You may like to use a moisturizing cream on your nipples or, if they become sore, an antiseptic spray.

Once your milk flow is established, the milk may leak out quite a bit. You can use breast pads or clean cloth handkerchiefs inside your bra to soak it up. Change them frequently for cleanliness. A plastic breast shell with a reservoir will help keep your nipples dry and catch leaks of milk, which can be frozen or refrigerated in a clean bottle. Wash and sterilize the shell before reusing.

IF YOU ARE ILL
If you are confined to bed, you can express milk so that your partner can feed the baby when you are not feeling up to it. If you are too ill even to express your milk, then your baby can be given formula by bottle or by spoon and, although she may not like this at first, she will take the milk as she becomes hungrier.

If you have to go into the hospital you can still breastfeed. You should inform the nursing staff that this is what you intend to do so that they can make the necessary arrangements – for example, someone will have to be available to lift and change your baby if you are too tired or ill to do so. If you are having an operation, though, you will not be able to breastfeed afterward because of the anesthetic – you will be too groggy, and, more importantly, the drugs you have been given will have passed into your milk. If you know you will be having an operation, try to express and freeze your milk so your baby can be bottlefed until you have recovered. It will take up to ten days for your milk to return; your baby should suck as often as she wishes in the meantime.

DRUGS AND BREASTFEEDING
If you can, avoid all drugs when breastfeeding. Many medications pass into the breast milk and can affect your baby. Always inform your doctor that you are breastfeeding if you are already taking medications or if you consult her for any new problems; make sure

that she is prescribing appropriate drugs only. If you want to use oral contraceptives, you should take the progestogen-only "mini-pill," as the estrogen in the combined pill may reduce your milk supply. However, as the effects of progestogen on the baby are not yet fully known, it is best to use some other contraceptive method until your baby has been weaned. Your doctor or family planning clinic can help you choose the method that suits you best.

PROBLEMS

Your breasts will be working hard for the next few months, and problems may arise if, for instance, your baby is not latching on properly or if she drags on the nipple as she comes off. The best way to prevent this is to keep your breasts clean and dry and make sure your baby always empties them when she eats. You should also wear a supportive nursing bra. If your nipples do become sore or cracked, take action immediately or they will get worse.

Cracked nipple If sore nipples (see right) are not looked after properly, they may become cracked. If this happens, you will feel a shooting pain as your baby suckles. You should keep the nipples dry with breast pads or clean tissues, and stop feeding from the affected breast until it has healed. Express the milk by hand instead; it can be fed to your baby by bottle or from a cup with a spout.

Engorgement Toward the end of the first week, before breast-feeding has become fully established, your breasts may become overfull and painful and quite hard to the touch. If this happens, your baby won't be able to latch on successfully. Make sure you wear a good bra to minimize discomfort, and gently express some milk before feeding to relieve the fullness. Having warm baths will also help relieve the discomfort by promoting milk flow.

Blocked duct Tight clothing or engorgement can cause a blocked milk duct, resulting in a hard red patch on the outside of the breast. You can prevent this by encouraging your baby to feed often and empty your breasts, and by making sure your bra fits properly. If you do get a blocked duct, offer the affected breast first.

Mastitis If a blocked duct is not treated, it can lead to an acute infection, known as mastitis. The breast will be inflamed and a red patch will appear on the outside, as with a blocked duct. If you can, you should continue to breastfeed because you need to empty the breast. However, you may find nursing too painful. In any case, consult your doctor, who may prescribe antibiotics.

Breast abscess An untreated blocked duct or mastitis can result in a breast abscess. You may feel feverish, and you may have a shiny red patch on your breast that is exquisitely tender. Your doctor should prescribe antibiotics; if this fails, the abscess will have to be drained surgically, but you may be able to continue breastfeeding even if you need this minor operation – ask your doctor's advice.

PREVENTING SORE NIPPLES

Suckling your baby can cause soreness around the nipples, especially if you are fair-skinned. To minimize the possibility of any problems:

- *Always make sure that your baby has the nipple and areola well into her mouth*

- *Always take your baby off the breast gently (see p.42)*

- *Keep your nipples as dry as possible between feedings*

- *Make sure your nipples are dry before putting your bra back on after a feeding*

If one of your nipples does become sore, give that breast a rest from feeding for 24 hours, or until the soreness has gone. Express milk from the affected breast and feed your baby from the other one. To prevent the nipple from becoming cracked, apply a protective cream two or three times a day.

The shield is very soft and allows for a close fit

Nipple shield
This is made of soft silicone and fits over your nipple; the baby sucks through a small rubber nipple on the front. Sterilize before use.

NAME   *Petrina Wehrli*

AGE   *27 years*

OBSTETRIC *Normal*
HISTORY   *pregnancy,*
           Benjamin born
           prematurely at
           28 weeks

PAST   *Appendectomy*
MEDICAL   *at 15 years*
HISTORY

FAMILY   *Twins in previ-*
HISTORY   *ous generations*

Petrina was enjoying a career in real estate when she gave up work to have a baby. A very determined woman, she prepared for her pregnancy by eating well and getting regular exercise. When she became pregnant, she read all the baby books she could, and even practiced expressing milk manually. Mike, her husband, was very involved in these preparations, attending prenatal classes with Petrina and reading baby books with her.

One night while at the movies, only 28 weeks into her pregnancy, Petrina felt sudden uterine pains that quickly escalated to regular, strong contractions. Mike took her directly to the hospital, where Benjamin was born.

FEEDING A PRETERM BABY

It was a shock for both Petrina and Mike to have their baby a full three months before they'd expected him; Petrina, who likes to be in control of everything, was particularly disturbed. It was difficult for her to sit by her new baby so impersonally enclosed in an incubator, unable to hold and, most of all, to breastfeed him, something she longed to do.

MAINTAINING A SUPPLY

I explained to Petrina that although no feeding is straightforward for premature babies, breast milk is especially beneficial for them, as it provides protection against infections in the first few risky weeks of life. Benjamin had to be fed intravenously for several days and then gradually through a stomach tube because he had not had time to develop rooting and sucking reflexes. Petrina expressed her milk from day one and stored it so that it could be used to feed Benjamin when the stomach tube was in place.

She remained adamant that she wanted to breastfeed Benjamin when she could eventually take him home, and as soon as he could be released from the incubator for short periods, the nurses encouraged Petrina to put him on the breast. I reminded her that breast milk is produced in response to demand. If it's not removed by a nursing infant, it must be expressed; otherwise production stops. This meant Petrina had to express milk to keep up production until Benjamin was able to breastfeed regularly.

LEARNING TO EXPRESS

Expressing milk for a premature baby is difficult because all the natural cues for milk let-down are missing: hearing the baby's hungry cry, lifting him up, putting his mouth to the breast. To master the technique of expressing milk (see pp.44-45), Petrina needed great persistence and support from Mike; often she felt like giving up. Her breasts became engorged on day three and she could hardly bear to massage them. She explained her problems to the head pediatric nurse in the hospital nursery, who arranged for nurses to help and encourage her to take off milk every two hours (as a very small baby would) and to store it hygienically (see p.44).

Petrina continued to express milk during the night, every four to six hours. By the second week, she'd become quite expert and was asked to teach other mothers how to express. Now she was feeling useful and competent, her fears about her baby started to wane.

BONDING WITH A PREMATURE BABY

One of Petrina's main concerns was that Benjamin wouldn't bond to her and Mike because he couldn't hear their voices and couldn't smell their skin or enjoy their hugs. The hospital staff, however, showed them how they could put their clean hands into the incubator to stroke and caress Benjamin gently. Within a week Benjamin was showing signs of loving this contact and responded by wriggling when they touched him. Quite naturally they would talk to him as they did this, and during the second week they saw his eyes flicker in recognition at the sound of their voices. They thought of this as their first conversation and continued to babble to him happily during their time together. The hospital staff encouraged both parents to spend as much time as possible with Benjamin, and to help feed and change him as their confidence grew.

COPING WITH THE DEMANDS

Two and a half weeks after Benjamin's birth, Petrina experienced a crisis. The shock of the premature birth, the anxiety of the first few days, and the loss of sleep because of expressing at night were all having their effect, and she felt that she had no emotional resources left. When one of the nurses found her sobbing, she realized immediately that Petrina herself needed some tender loving care. She suggested that Petrina talk to Mike about her feelings. Mike had thought that Petrina was totally absorbed with Benjamin, but was only too willing for them to have some time alone together each day for hugging and sharing. Petrina also started to take some time for herself – to have her hair done, for instance – and to spoil herself now and then with nutritious treats like strawberries out of season or a salad with fresh baby greens. She drank lots of mineral water to keep herself healthy for breastfeeding.

PREPARING TO GO HOME

Before Benjamin was ready to leave the hospital, the staff established him on breast milk from a bottle so that he learned to suck well before he was put on to the breast. In the last week before he was due to go home, he was taking five feedings out of eight from Petrina's breast so she got Benjamin used to the breast in the reassuring environment of the unit. When Benjamin was 38 weeks old, and weighed 5 pounds 8 ounces (2.5 kilograms) – ten weeks after he was born – Petrina and Mike took him home and felt like a real family for the first time. At home, Petrina had to continue expressing so that she always had enough milk if Benjamin ever showed signs of being hungry after a feeding. A week later, Benjamin weighed in at 5 pounds 12 ounces (2.6 kilograms) and was thriving. However, I explained to Petrina that she must think of him as if he were still in her womb: he wasn't two months old, but 39 weeks, and she shouldn't expect him to catch up completely with full-term babies of his age till he was two years old.

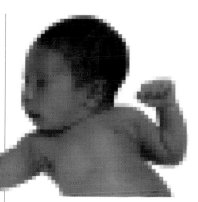

NAME *Benjamin Wehrli*

AGE *39 weeks*

BIRTH WEIGHT *2 pounds 13 ounces (1.3 kilograms)*

MEDICAL HISTORY *Born prematurely at 28 weeks, and nursed in special care unit in an incubator. Sent home at 38 weeks*

BOTTLES AND MILK

The majority of babies end up being bottlefed at some stage – if not continuously right from the start, then often after weaning or with supplementary bottles. New formulas, bottles, and nipples appear on the market regularly, all with the aim of making bottle-feeding as convenient and as similar to breastfeeding as possible.

The one thing you cannot give your baby if you bottlefeed from the start is colostrum (see p.40), so even if you're not intending to breastfeed your baby, you will be giving him a good start if you put him to the breast in the first few days. If you decide not to do this, the hospital staff can take care of your baby's first feedings; he will probably be given sugar water a few hours after delivery.

One of the good things about bottlefeeding is that the new father can be involved at feeding times. Make sure that your partner feeds your baby as soon as possible after the birth. This way he can get used to the technique and won't be afraid to handle the baby. He should open his shirt so that the baby nestles up to his skin when he feeds, and gets to know his smell.

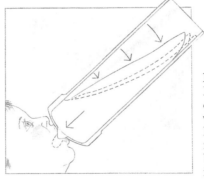

Disposable bottles
Bottles that take disposable liners are convenient, especially when you are traveling. The liner is collapsible, so air does not enter the bottle as your baby draws the milk and there is less likelihood of gas.

FORMULAS

A variety of baby formulas are available, all carefully formulated to make them as close as possible to breast milk: in fact, formula has added vitamin D and iron, levels of which are quite low in breast milk.

Most formulas are based on cows' milk, but you can buy soy-based formulas for a baby who finds cows' milk unsuitable. Some formulas are available both in powder and ready-to-use forms.

Ready-to-use formula comes in cans or ready-to-feed bottles and is ultra-heat treated (UHT), which means it is sterile and will keep in a cool place until the "best before" date. Once the can has been opened, the formula will keep for 24 hours in a refrigerator. Ready-to-use formula is more expensive than powdered formula, but it is convenient, and useful when you are traveling.

If you use powdered formula, it is essential to make it up precisely according to the manufacturer's instructions. Some parents are tempted to add extra powder to make the formula "more nourishing," but this will lead to your baby getting too much protein and fat, and not enough water.

Similarly, if you add too little powder, your baby will not be getting the nutrients he needs for healthy growth.

BOTTLES AND NIPPLES

Bottles (left to right)

Tapered bottle

Waisted bottle

Easy-grip bottle

Disposable bottle with liners

Nipples (left to right)

Universal nipples (2)

Silicone anti-colic nipple

Natural-shaped nipple

Wide-based nipple for disposable bottle

STERILIZING THE BOTTLES

It is wise to practise with your feeding equipment before you go into hospital, so buy it well in advance of your delivery date. Large department stores and drugstores sell bottlefeeding packs that have all the essential equipment.

I always found it most convenient to sterilize and make up a full batch of bottles (see p.52), and refrigerate them until needed. After the feeding, rinse the bottle in warm water and then put it aside. It is a good idea to continue sterilizing all formula-feeding equipment until your baby is a year old.

Most sterilizing units hold only four to six bottles. Your newborn baby, however, will be taking around seven feedings over 24 hours, so you may have to sterilize and prepare the bottles twice a day – morning and evening – to ensure that you have enough formula ready whenever he is hungry. The number of feedings will decline as your baby grows, so you'll only have to prepare one batch a day.

STERILIZING TIPS

- Put all the equipment into a large, covered, plastic container and use sterilizing tablets (or fluid) and water.

- Steam sterilizing units quickly and effectively destroy bacteria on your equipment

- You can sterilize your equipment in the microwave using a specially designed steam unit, as long as the feeding equipment is suitable for microwave use

- Wash the equipment and boil it for at least 25 minutes in a large, covered pot

Cleaning in a dishwasher
After 12 months, if you have a dishwasher, you can put the equipment straight in it. Clean nipples before they go in (see column, right). Run the dishwasher on the normal cycle.

Check that bottles are submerged when boiling

Boiling
You should boil the bottles for five minutes. Then remove and allow to cool down before using.

Wash equipment in hot soapy water

Use a bottle brush to clean the bottle thoroughly

Washing bottles and nipples
All equipment should be washed in hot, soapy water. Scrub the insides of the bottles with a bottle brush and rub the nipples thoroughly to remove any traces of milk. Rinse the bottles and nipples under warm, running water to remove any soap.

Using a ready-made formula is more straightforward than mixing your own, but strict rules of hygiene should still be observed.

- *Before opening the can, scrub the top, paying particular attention to the cutting edge*

- *Use a very clean can opener or can punch to open the formula*

- *If you are not using all of the formula, store the extra in the refrigerator in a clean jar, not in the can. Formula can be stored in the refrigerator for 24 hours*

- *Don't reuse any formula that your baby has left in the bottle; it will have been contaminated with her saliva*

THE FLOW OF MILK

The hole in the nipple should allow the milk to flow in a steady stream of several drops per second when the bottle is inverted.

If the hole is too large, your baby will get too much too fast and splutter; if it is too small, your baby will get tired from sucking before she is satisfied. To make the hole in a nipple bigger, insert a fine, red-hot needle gently through the hole to melt the rubber (stick one end of the needle into a cork and hold it over a flame to heat it).

Sculpted nipples that are shaped to fit the baby's palate and allow her control over the flow are best.

BOTTLEFEEDING YOUR BABY

When you are bottlefeeding, there are a couple of essential points to bear in mind. The formula should be properly mixed so that your baby gets correct amounts of both nutrients and water and is able to draw milk at a comfortable rate. You can make up a bottle at a time, mixing it according to the manufacturer's instructions and then pouring into the bottle, or make a batch of several.

MAKING FORMULA FROM POWDER

Equipment
The equipment should be rinsed with hot water and drained before use.
- Bottles and lids
- Plastic knife
- Measuring scoop from formula package
- Funnel
- Nipples and rings
- Caps
- Measuring cup

Level off powder with back of knife

Measuring
Using the measuring scoop provided with the formula, measure out the required amount. Use a knife to level off each scoopful, and do not pack the formula down into the scoop.

Mixing
Put the required amount of formula into the mixing cup with the boiled and cooled water. Never add extra formula or the mixture will be too concentrated and could be dangerous. Stir the formula and water until you are sure that there are no lumps or residue and the mixture is smooth.

Use a clean funnel to fill the bottles if needed

Storing
Place the clean nipples upside-down in the bottles; secure with the screw-on rings and put on the plastic caps. Refrigerate the bottles immediately, putting them on a tray to keep them upright.

GIVING A BOTTLE

Make yourself comfortable and support your arms well. Hold your baby half-sitting with her head in the crook of your elbow and her back along your forearm; this will allow her to swallow safely and easily. Keep your face close to hers and talk to her frequently.

If you prefer, there are other positions that are suitable for feeding. You could try lying down with your baby tucked under your arm, for example – this position is especially comfortable for night feedings. Try different positions until you decide which one suits you best (see **Breastfeeding positions**, p.41).

Before you begin, test the temperature of the milk; you should already have tested the flow (see opposite). Slightly loosen the cap of the bottle so that air can get in. If your baby has difficulty getting the milk, gently remove the bottle from her mouth so that air can enter the bottle, then continue as before. Hold the bottle at an angle so that your baby doesn't swallow air with the milk.

BOTTLEFEEDING

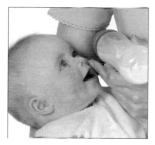

Giving the bottle
Gently stroke your baby's nearest cheek to elicit her sucking reflex. Insert the nipple carefully into her mouth. If you push the nipple too far back she may gag on it.

Feeding
Make feeding times as pleasant as possible by talking to your baby and smiling at her. Let her pause midfeeding if she likes. Burp her and change her onto the other arm at this stage to give her a new view, and your arm a rest.

Removing the bottle
If you want your baby to release the bottle, gently slide your little finger into the corner of her mouth. This will break the suction on the nipple.

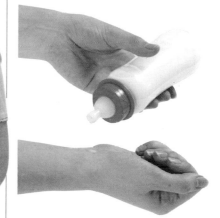

WARMING THE BOTTLE

Some mothers like to warm the bottle, though it will be perfectly all right if it has simply been brought to room temperature. Many babies like their bottles cold. Don't warm the bottle in a microwave; that may create "hot spots" in the milk that could scald your baby's mouth.

Warming the formula
Place the bottle in a bowl of hot water for a few minutes. You could also run it under the hot tap, shaking it all the time.

Testing formula temperature
Try a few drops on your wrist: it should be neither hot nor cold to the touch.

Bottlefeeding is straightforward, but you will need to make sure that your baby can swallow properly, and that he is not taking in air with the milk.

• *Never leave your baby with the bottle propped up on a pillow or cushion; it can be dangerous. He could become very uncomfortable if he swallows a lot of air with the formula, and he could choke. Moreover, he will miss the cuddling and affection that he should enjoy while he eats*

• *Tilt your baby on your arm. It is very difficult for a baby to swallow when he is lying flat, so don't feed him in this position; he may gag or even vomit*

• *If your baby has a stuffed nose he can't swallow and breathe at the same time. Your doctor can give you nose drops to be used before each feeding*

• *Don't change your formula without first consulting your pediatrician, even if you think your baby does not like the one you're using. It is very unusual for a brand of formula to be responsible for a baby's not feeding well; very rarely cows' milk formula causes allergies in babies, and your doctor may advise you to use a soy-based formula*

• *Your baby knows when he's had enough, so don't try to force him to finish the bottle after he has stopped sucking*

BOTTLEFEEDING ROUTINES

Bottlefed babies tend to be fed less frequently than breastfed ones. This is because formula takes longer to digest and contains slightly more protein, and therefore delays hunger longer. A four-hourly regimen of six feedings a day seems to suit most bottlefed babies after the first two or three days, whereas breastfed babies will probably take seven feedings a day. A newborn baby will probably not take much over 2 fluid ounces (60 milliliters) at each feeding, but as he grows he will take fewer and larger feedings.

Never feed your baby according to the clock; let him determine when he is to be fed. He will let you know quite clearly with cries when he is hungry. Your baby's appetite will vary, so if he seems satisfied, allow him to leave what he does not want. Don't feel that your baby has to finish the bottle at each feeding. He will only get overfull and spit it up (see opposite); or worse, become overfed and fat. On the other hand, if your baby is still hungry, give him some extra from another bottle. If this happens regularly, start to make more formula for every bottle.

NIGHT FEEDINGS

Your baby will need feeding at least once during the night, and this break in your sleep on top of all the other things that you have to do to take care of him may make you extremely tired and tense. The problem isn't so much the number of hours of sleep that you lose, but more the way in which your sleep patterns are broken over long periods. For this reason it is important that you get adequate rest, day and night, and since you are doing most of the feeding, try to get your partner to take on some of the other jobs.

REDUCING NIGHT FEEDINGS

At first your baby won't be able to sleep for more than two to four hours at a time without waking with hunger. Once he reaches a weight of about 11 pounds (5 kilograms), try to stretch the time between feedings until you are getting about six hours of undisturbed sleep at night. Although your baby will have his own routine, it's sensible to try to time his last feeding to coincide with your own bedtime, which should be as late as possible. You may find that your baby will still wake up and demand the early morning feeding, no matter how hard you try. If this happens you'll just have to be patient and look forward to when he drops it.

OVERFEEDING

Chubby babies can be cute, but fat cells, once produced, can't be removed, and a fat baby may grow into a fat adult, with all the attendant dangers to health. Unfortunately, it is easy to overfeed a bottlefed baby. The reasons for this are twofold; first, it is tempting to put extra formula into the bottle, but you should always follow the instructions precisely (see p.52); otherwise, you'll be giving the baby unwanted calories. Second, in your anxiety to feed him "properly" you may want to see your baby finish every last drop of his bottle, but you should always let him decide when he's finished. Introducing solids too early and giving sweet, syrupy drinks also cause overfeeding.

UNDERFEEDING

This is rare in bottlefed babies. Your baby should be fed on demand and not at set times; demands may vary from day to day. If your child consistently seems fretful after he drains each bottle, he may well be hungry. Offer him an extra 2 fluid ounces (60 milliliters) of formula. If he takes it, then he needs it.

If your baby demands frequent feedings but doesn't take much, the nipple hole may be too small (see p.52), so that he is having difficulty sucking the formula and is tired before he gets enough.

BURPING

Burping releases any air that has been swallowed during feeding. It's unlikely that gas causes your baby discomfort, and many babies are not noticeably happier or more contented for having been burped. Swallowing air is more common in bottlefed babies, but you can prevent it to some extent by tilting the bottle more as your baby empties it so that the nipple is full of milk and not air. Disposable bottles (see p.50) cut down on the air the baby swallows, because air cannot enter the bottle as the baby sucks the milk.

The good thing about burping, whether you breast- or bottlefed, is that it makes you pause, relax, slow down, hold your baby gently, and stroke or pat him, and this is good for both of you.

SPITTING UP

If your baby tends to bring food right back up – some babies never do – you may wonder if he's keeping enough down. My youngest son was a child who had a tendency to spit up, and I worried that he wasn't getting enough to eat. I simply followed my own instinct, which was to offer him more food. If he didn't take it, I assumed that he had spat up an excess that he didn't require. Babies usually spit up because of a normal gastroesophageal reflex, which is more pronounced in some babies than in others. Overfeeding can also cause spitting up, which is another reason to avoid insisting that your bottlefed baby finish his bottle.

Forcible or projectile vomiting, especially if it occurs after several meals, should be reported immediately to your doctor; vomiting is very serious in a small baby because it can quickly lead to dehydration.

HYGIENE AND PREPARATION

To protect your baby from bacteria, make sure all feeding equipment is scrupulously clean, and be careful with the storage and preparation of formula.

- *Follow all cleaning instructions carefully*

- *Wash your hands before preparing or giving feedings*

- *Never add any extra powder; follow the instructions accurately*

- *Give the formula to your baby as soon as it has been warmed up*

- *When making batches, cool the formula as soon as it is made up. Don't store warm milk in a thermos bottle; germs will easily breed there*

- *Keep all prepared bottles refrigerated until they are needed*

- *Keep any opened ready-to-use formula in a jar (not the can) in the refrigerator*

- *After a feeding, throw away any leftover formula*

Burping your baby
Hold your baby close to you and stroke or pat him gently to help him bring up air bubbles.

GIRLS' WEIGHT

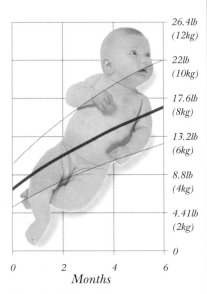

26.4lb
(12kg)

22lb
(10kg)

17.6lb
(8kg)

13.2lb
(6kg)

8.8lb
(4kg)

4.41lb
(2kg)

0

0   2   4   6
Months

Your baby's weight
In the first five months your baby girl will be growing fast and will more than double her birthweight. Any weight within the colored band is normal.

Growth charts
The charts shown here and on pp.62–63, 66–67 and 318–25 show the wide ranges of weight or height within which a "normal" child may fall. The middle line represents the 50th percentile: 50 percent of babies will fall below this line and 50 percent above it. The lines at the top and bottom represent extremes outside which only a tiny proportion of children will fall; if your child does, you should talk to your pediatrician.

INTRODUCING SOLIDS

During your baby's first year there will be a time when you will have to start to wean her onto solid foods, although not before she's four months, and possibly quite a bit later than that. Before this, your baby's digestive tract is incapable of digesting and absorbing complex foods.

Breast milk (or its formula equivalent) is the only food that your baby needs in the early months, and if a baby is introduced to solids too young it can lessen her desire to suck. Breastfed babies will take less milk from your breasts, and you will respond by producing less milk. Either way your baby will end up having an unsatisfactory diet for her needs.

WHEN TO WEAN

As your baby grows, she'll need to drink more and more milk or formula to maintain this growth. But your baby's stomach can only hold a certain amount of milk at each feeding; eventually, she will reach a point when she's drinking to full capacity at each feeding, but still doesn't have enough calories for her needs. Your baby will let you know that she needs more to eat by a change in her feeding habits. She may start to demand more milk and appear very unsatisfied after each feeding, or she may start demanding a sixth feeding, having previously been quite content on five. A classic case is a baby who has been sleeping through the night starting to wake for a night-time feeding. This is the time to introduce solids. Many babies do this at around four months, when their intense desire to suck lessens, though it can be later. You should be aware of the

EXAMPLES OF WEANING STAGES

Feedings	1st week of weaning	3rd week of weaning
1st	Breast or bottle feeding.	Breast or bottle feeding.
2nd	Half breast or bottle feeding. Try one or two teaspoons of puree or cereal, then give remainder of feeding.	Half breast or bottle feeding. Two teaspoons of cereal. Remainder of feeding.
3rd	Breast or bottle feeding.	Half breast or bottle feeding. Two teaspoons of vegetable or fruit puree. Remainder of feeding.
4th	Breast or bottle feeding.	Breast or bottle feeding.
5th	Breast or bottle feeding.	Breast or bottle feeding.

signs that your baby gives you, and be ready to follow her lead for the introduction of solids. The first tooth, if it appears at or after six months, definitely indicates the need for solids.

GIVING THE FIRST SOLIDS

Have a small amount of prepared food on hand and then settle in your normal position to feed the baby. Although your baby is ready for the calories solids provide, she will still prefer what she knows is satisfying – milk or formula. Start by feeding her from one breast or giving half the usual bottle. Then give her one or two teaspoons of food. Begin with the midday meal when your baby is not ravenous but is wide awake and more cooperative. Never force your baby to take more food than she wants. When she's taken the solid food, give her the rest of the milk. Once she becomes used to solids, she may prefer to take them first.

As soon as your baby is having any quantity of solid food she will need water as well as milk or formula to drink. Start her off with ½ ounce (15 milliliters) of water or very dilute fruit juice between and after feedings, and whenever she's thirsty. Give no more than four ounces total of juice and water per day through the first year; she should still be getting most of her nutrition from breast milk or formula. Avoid soda, drinks containing alcohol, and any drinks with added sugar, saccharin, or aspartame as these will damage your baby's teeth and may encourage her to develop a sweet tooth.

SPOONFEEDING

Giving the food
Halfway through her normal breast or bottle feed, scoop up some food on a small spoon and insert it gently between her lips. Don't push the spoon in too far or your baby may gag. She may take a month or so to get used to using a spoon. Your baby may push more food out than she takes in. Gently scrape the excess onto her lips; she will turn away once she's had enough.

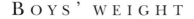

BOYS' WEIGHT

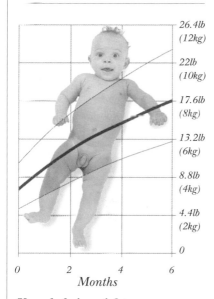

	26.4lb (12kg)
	22lb (10kg)
	17.6lb (8kg)
	13.2lb (6kg)
	8.8lb (4kg)
	4.4lb (2kg)
	0

0   2   4   6
Months

Your baby's weight
Your baby will put on weight faster during this period than at any time in his life, and is likely to more than double his weight in the first five months. Any weight within the colored band is normal.

WEANING TIPS

Your baby may be reluctant to try new foods, so give her time to get used to each food and don't persist if she seems to dislike something.

• *Give one new food at a time. Try it once and wait for several days before giving it again to see if there's a reaction*

• *Use dry infant cereals rather than the ones in jars; dry cereals are more nutritious.*

• *Don't give foods containing gluten, milk, nuts, or egg for at least six months, to avoid developing allergies later*

NAME *Penny King*

AGE *27 years*

OBSTETRIC *First baby, nor-*
HISTORY *mal delivery, no*
complications

Penny and her husband David are vegetarians and have been since they married three years ago. They know that a vegetarian diet that excludes meat, poultry, and fish but contains eggs and milk can provide all the nutrients necessary for health and vitality as long as a proper balance of the different food groups is maintained. They want Oona to be a vegetarian and became particularly concerned when she was six months old and ready to eat a mixed diet.

VEGETARIAN WEANING

Penny was nervous about not giving Oona a really balanced diet with enough protein, vitamins B_{12} and D, calcium, and iron, even though she knows many vegetarian foods are fortified with extra B_{12} and protein. I told her that a growing baby can get all the nourishment she needs from a carefully planned diet, although if she wished to bring up Oona as a vegan (no animal foods whatsoever, not even dairy products or eggs) she would need to see a baby nutritionist for advice.

When Oona was 6 months old Penny started gradually to wean her by replacing breast milk feedings with solid foods so that Oona would end up on three meals a day, using a cup and a spoon at around 11–12 months.

Penny and I planned a schedule in which she would introduce one food at a time, withdrawing it if Oona didn't like it and trying it again ten days later. Oona's diet had to include foods from each of the major food groups (see p.66).

Oona would get protein, essential for growth in a young baby, from beans, cheese, and milk as well as yogurt, soy products, and grains. I pointed out to Penny that egg whites should not be given until Oona was nine to ten months old in order to avoid the possibility of an allergic reaction.

Foods made from cereals and grains provide carbohydrates to give Oona the energy to grow and develop, while fruit and vegetables supply essential vitamins and minerals. I told Penny that vegetarian diets tend to be bulky and lower in calories than a diet including meat. This can be hard for a baby because Oona could get full before she's had all the calories she needs, so Penny should give her a wide variety of foods that are low in fiber such as egg yolks, milk, and cheese. Penny and I drew up a menu plan for Oona together and I gave her a few tips about how to start.

- Penny should choose a time when Oona was hungry but not ravenous, such as the middle of the day, to try the first solids.

- Oona's first foods should be smooth in texture and mild in taste. Baby rice, cooked pureed fruit such as apples and pears, or vegetables such as carrots or potatoes (with no added salt) are ideal.

- Penny should avoid adding lots of seasoning or sugar.

- Adding a spoonful of Oona's usual milk to the food would help her recognize the taste.

I also advised Penny that when preparing fruit and vegetables, she shouldn't overcook or keep foods hot for a long time; this destroys vitamin C content. Fresh fruit should always be peeled and have all stones, seeds, or pits removed. Oona sailed through her weaning. She seemed to really enjoy foods without salt and sugar, foods Penny thought she would find too bland. Penny found that Oona adored pureed lentils, a food she introduced when Oona was seven months old. She also relished the yolk of an egg finely chopped and then mashed with yogurt. The more solid food she ate, the more fluid Oona wanted to drink. In addition to 24-32 ounces of milk, a little orange juice diluted half and half with water became a favorite drink. Since it was summer, Penny found that Oona could easily drink a half-cup of this drink every day.

Oona is now ten months and very much one of the family, eating more and more family food, which only needs mashing to suit her. She loves gravies and sauces, and Penny has found that these help her accept almost any new food. Ice cream has become such a favorite that Penny has to limit this treat to once or twice a week so that Oona isn't getting too much sugar and fat. She's gaining weight steadily, but she's not fat; Penny is very proud of this, and also of Oona's skill at using the spoon to feed herself – something she began to try at seven months.

Since Oona clearly enjoys her food, Penny is eager to introduce her to lots of new flavors. She asked if there were any foods she shouldn't give, and I advised her to introduce strongly flavored vegetables such as broccoli, onions, or peppers only gradually, and not give whole-grain bread, whole nuts, or unpeeled fruit until Oona is a year old.

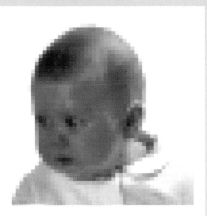

NAME *Oona King*

AGE *10 months*

MEDICAL HISTORY *Born at full term. Umbilical hernia cleared up by six months. Breastfed*

VEGETARIAN MENU FOR NINE-MONTH-OLD BABY

Breakfast.	*Breast or bottle feeding.* *Baby yogurt dessert.*	*Breast or bottle feeding.* *Breakfast cereal with milk.*	*Breast or bottle feeding.* *Baby rice.*
Lunch.	*Diluted unsweetened fruit juice or water.* *Cooked pureed lentils with vegetables.* *Pureed fruit.*	*Diluted unsweetened fruit juice or water.* *Hard-boiled egg and spinach with bread fingers.* *Pureed fruit.*	*Diluted unsweetened fruit juice or water.* *Cheese or mashed tofu with vegetable puree.* *Mashed banana and yogurt.*
Afternoon.	*Breast or bottle feeding.*	*Breast or bottle feeding.*	*Breast or bottle feeding.*
Supper.	*Mashed potato with grated cheese and broccoli* *Soaked dried fruit, mashed.*	*Hummus or other bean puree.* *Baked apple with oatmeal or wheat-germ.*	*Pureed cabbage with smooth peanut butter and pita bread.*

Your baby's main source of calories is still breast or formula milk, but you should also give drinks of water.

FEEDING AND NUTRITION

INTRODUCING CUPS

You can introduce your baby to drinking from a cup when he is about four months old. Aim to give up bottles by 12 months.

• *Cups with spouts are best as your baby will have to half suck and half drink to get anything. Soft spouts are the easiest to use*

• *As your baby progresses, he may prefer to move on to a two-handled cup that he can grasp easily. The kind with specially slanted lips are excellent because the contents will come out with very little tipping*

Two handles allow easy grip

Trainer cups
The lunchtime and late afternoon feedings are probably the best times to use the cup; these are times when your baby will be more likely to eat solids.

During his first year, your baby will move on from mere "tastes" of solids with his bottles, to three solid meals a day, with drinks of water, fruit juice (diluted if you wish), or milk.

Once he is happy with a couple of different solids, it is important to introduce a variety of tastes and textures. He will be able to deal with foods that have been pureed, mashed, or chopped, and to chew or suck on larger chunks of food (see **Finger foods**, opposite). Still, it is important to remember that every baby has different requirements and appetites. If in doubt, just feed your baby as much as he will happily take. The amount of milk or formula he requires will lessen as he increases the number of solid meals. Since he'll be getting most of his calories from solids rather than from milk, your baby will become thirsty. When he does, give him plain water or diluted fruit juice to drink (up to four ounces per day), rather than milk. Never give your baby a commercial drink containing sugar, artificial sweeteners, or colorings.

FEEDING YOUR CHILD

Until he's six months old, you will probably feed your baby on your lap or in a baby seat, but once his neck and back muscles are strong enough to support him, you may consider using a high chair or feeding table. With a feeding table you will have to bend down to feed the baby until he can feed himself and at first you may have to prop up your baby with cushions, so a high chair is probably the better option; make sure your baby is properly strapped in. Your child should always be supervised while he's eating. Almost all children gag on some food at some stage, and it is essential that you react quickly in such a situation. A new texture, taken for the first time, may make him gag out of surprise. If he does, pat him firmly on the back and encourage him to cough until the food is dislodged. Talk soothingly and gently rub his back, and he'll be more able to swallow the new food. Should your baby's choking happen to be severe (this is unlikely with the soft foods he eats at this age), you should know how to administer first aid (see p.333).

Your baby will soon look forward to mealtimes as an opportunity to play as well as to eat, so feeding will become messier. Keep your baby away from the walls and put newspapers on the floor in case he starts throwing food. Within a month or so of starting solids, your baby will be able to take food from the spoon.

SELF-FEEDING

Learning to feed himself is a huge step in your baby's physical and intellectual development, and you should encourage all attempts to do so. His manual dexterity and his hand–eye coordination will

Self-feeding
Allow your child to spoon-feed himself if he can. Choose foods that are not too runny, such as thick cereal.

Molded plastic bib to catch spills

Rubber suction pad keeps bowl firmly in place

Whole-wheat bread without whole grains is suitable

Pretty shapes will make food look appealing

Cut vegetables into shapes that are easy to grasp

greatly improve with self-feeding, so let him experiment if he shows an interest and be prepared to cope with the mess. Food provides your baby with the perfect motivation for speeding up muscle co-ordination and balance.

It may be several months before your baby becomes proficient at feeding himself. You can help by giving him non-runny foods that will stick to the spoon, such as oatmeal, scrambled eggs, or thick purees. If he finds trying to use a spoon frustrating, let him try finger foods. Food will be a plaything, most of which will land on the floor rather than in your baby's stomach. But there's no cause for concern; at the time a baby starts to self-feed, the initial growth spurt is beginning to slacken off, so he needs less food.

The best way to ensure that your baby gets at least some food is for both of you to have a spoon. Use two spoons of the same color and type so that you can swap your full spoon for his empty one when he has difficulty scooping up the food.

Finger foods
If your baby has difficulty using a spoon he will find finger foods easier to handle; even if the food is hard, he will suck it.

FOOD FOR SELF-FEEDING

FRUIT AND VEGETABLES

Any fresh fruit that is easy to hold, like bananas, cut into slices with the skin and pits removed

Soft-cooked vegetables, particularly zucchini cut into a shape that is easy to grasp. Don't cut vegetables too small

Mashed potato

CEREALS

Small pieces of dried, sugar-free cereal

Boiled rice

Whole-wheat bread or teething biscuits (without the complete grains)

Pasta shapes

PROTEIN

Whole-wheat bread

Pieces of soft cheese

Toast fingers with cheese

Small pieces of white meat

Low-fat cheese

Fileted fish in firm chunks

Sliced hard-boiled eggs

YOUR BABY'S NEEDS

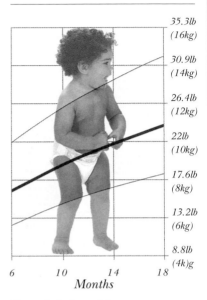

35.3lb
(16kg)

30.9lb
(14kg)

26.4lb
(12kg)

22lb
(10kg)

17.6lb
(8kg)

13.2lb
(6kg)

8.8lb
(4k)g

6   10   14   18
Months

Your baby's weight
The rapid weight gain of the
first few months slows down, but
your baby is still putting on
weight steadily. Any weight within the colored band is normal.
(For a full explanation of this
chart, see **Growth charts,** p.56.)

The food pyramid
This table shows the proportions in which the main food
groups should be eaten for your
baby to take in the right balance of nutrients. The two most
important groups are carbohydrates, and fruit and vegetables, followed by protein-rich
foods such as meat, legumes,
and dairy products. Sugars, fats,
and oils should form the small-
est part of your baby's diet – in
fact, the amounts of these that
occur naturally in other foods
will be more than enough. By
following these guidelines for
your baby, you will be helping
her form good habits for life.

Your baby will always take enough food to satisfy her needs. If she
doesn't want to eat, then she doesn't need to. This means that
there will be days when she will eat hardly anything, but these will
be followed by periods of eating a lot.

To eat a balanced diet, your baby should take in foods from all
the different food groups in the correct proportions (see below).
This doesn't have to be on a daily basis, though, so when you are
considering whether she is eating well, you need to think in the
long term: look at what she has eaten in the last week, not just
today. Viewed like this, a binge of eating nothing but bread for two
days is nothing to worry about, as your baby will probably take in
enough fruit and vegetables during the week to balance this out.
What is important is that she should be given a wide variety of
foods to choose from: she can't eat the foods she requires if they
are not made available to her.

Your baby will gradually come to eat many of the same foods as
you, prepared in a form that she can manage. It would be wrong,
however, to suppose that her needs are the same as yours or that
a diet that is recommended as healthy for you will be good for her.
You may aim to reduce your fat intake by using low-fat versions of
dairy products, for example, but you should give your child whole
milk until she is two years old; after that you can introduce low-fat
milk if you wish. The benefits to health of limiting sugar intake,
though, apply just as much to babies as to adults. You should never
add any salt to your baby's food.

Fats, oils, and sugars

Proteins: Meat, fish, eggs, dairy foods, and legumes

Fruit and vegetables

Carbohydrates: Bread, cereal, rice, and pasta

SUGGESTED MENUS – AGE 8–10 MONTHS

DAY 1	DAY 2	DAY 3
Breakfast	**Breakfast**	**Breakfast**
Rice cakes	Mashed banana	Cottage cheese or yogurt
Hard-boiled egg	Whole-wheat toast fingers	Whole-wheat toast fingers
Breast milk/formula	Breast milk/formula	Breast milk/formula
Lunch	**Lunch**	**Lunch**
Strained vegetable and chicken	Mashed potato and cheese	Strained lentils and mixed vegetables
Stewed apple	Pear slices	Banana and cottage cheese
Diluted fruit juice	Diluted fruit juice	Diluted fruit juice
Snack	**Snack**	**Snack**
Whole-wheat toast fingers	Rice cakes	Toast
Orange segments	Apple pieces	Fresh fruit
Breast milk/formula	Breast milk/formula	Breast milk/formula
Supper	**Supper**	**Supper**
Cauliflower and cheese	Pasta and tomato sauce	Tuna and mashed potato with steamed zucchini
Semolina and fruit puree	Yogurt with fruit puree	Rice pudding
Breast milk/formula	Breast milk/formula	Breast milk/formula

BOYS' WEIGHT

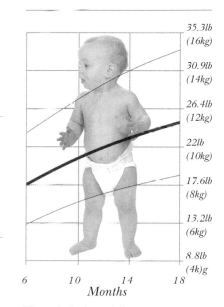

35.3lb (16kg)
30.9lb (14kg)
26.4lb (12kg)
22lb (10kg)
17.6lb (8kg)
13.2lb (6kg)
8.8lb (4k)g

6   10   14   18
Months

Your baby's weight
The rapid weight gain of the first few months is past now, but your boy is still getting steadily heavier. Any weight within the colored band is normal. (For a full explanation of this chart, see **Growth charts,** p.56.)

A FLEXIBLE ATTITUDE

The sample menus shown above are intended as a guide to your baby's main meals. Remember, a baby's stomach can't hold very much, and she will need to eat more often than an adult, so don't insist she finish her meals, and be prepared to give snacks in between times. Of course you should encourage your baby to have regular feeding times, but if you try to make her eat only at mealtimes, they'll become battlefields and she may end up not getting the food she needs when she needs it. If she shows that she's had enough, don't try to make her eat more.

Of course it is frustrating if you have spent a lot of time preparing a meal and your baby refuses it, or it ends up on the floor. The answer is to make feeding times as easy on yourself as possible: don't spend a lot of time preparing complicated dishes, and take precautions to protect the walls and the floor from thrown food.

• *Always wash hands with soap before handling food, especially after using the toilet or changing a diaper, and after playing with pets. Make sure your family does the same*

• *Be scrupulous about keeping the kitchen clean, especially work surfaces, chopping boards, and utensils used in food preparation. Never use wooden utensils; they harbor millions of germs*

• *Always use a clean tea towel or paper towels to dry dishes, or let them dry in a rack after rinsing them with hot water*

• *Keep the garbage can covered. Empty it often, and rinse it out with hot water and a little disinfectant each time you empty it*

• *Cover any food that is left out of the refrigerator*

• *Keep separate cloths for dirty tasks and for washing your child's high chair. Change or boil cloths at least once a week*

FOOD PREPARATION

Now that your baby's diet includes a range of foods, you need to take sensible precautions to protect him from the effects of harmful bacteria – salmonella and listeria poisoning, for example – so you should be well informed about safe storage and preparation.

BUYING AND STORING

The most important thing to look for when buying food is freshness. Shop often, and use food as quickly as possible. Bruised or damaged fruit and vegetables deteriorate quickly, so don't buy them. Always wash fruit if the skin is to be eaten, as there may be a residue of insecticides or other chemicals. Most packaged foods now carry a "sell by" or "best before" date, so check this and make sure that there are no signs of damage to packages, cans, or jars.

Food stored in the refrigerator should be in clean, covered containers. Store cooked and raw foods on separate shelves, and put raw meat and fish on a plate so the juices don't drip onto food on the shelf below. Check the packaging to see if food is suitable for freezing, and never freeze foods for longer than the time recommended by the manufacturer. Always defrost frozen foods thoroughly in the refrigerator before using, and never refreeze food once it has been defrosted.

COOKING AND REHEATING

Always cook your baby's food thoroughly; this applies especially to meat, poultry, and eggs. Never give raw or soft-cooked eggs to your baby, nor should you give soft cheeses or nut products. If you're

Coarse grater

Hand-held blender

Preparation methods
At first you will need to puree or grate foods for your baby. Steaming is a fast method of cooking that helps preserve nutrients.

Steamer

preparing food in bulk quantities, don't allow it to cool before putting it into the refrigerator, as this will just give the bacteria a chance to multiply; put it in a cold dish, cover it, and put it straight into the refrigerator or freezer. To avoid *E. coli* and other bacteria, cook hamburger thoroughly, to an internal temperature of at least 160°F (71°C). Make sure hamburger meat that you eat in restaurants is served well done, with no trace of pinkness or blood.

PREPARATION

At first you'll have to puree all your baby's food, but this stage won't last very long, so if you don't have a blender or food processor it's probably best just to get a cheap hand-operated food mill. At first a sieve will be perfectly adequate. As your baby gets older you can feed him coarser foods. By the time he is six months old he will be able to take a thicker puree, and at nine months he will enjoy a mash with chunks of meat or vegetables in it.

You can use a variety of liquids to thin home-prepared foods: the water you've used to steam fruit or vegetables is ideal. To thicken foods, you can use ground, whole-grain cereals like wheat germ, cottage cheese, yogurt, or mashed potato. If you feel you need to sweeten food, use naturally sweet fruit juice, not refined sugar. In general, however, young babies don't have a developed taste for sweets, so try foods unsweetened first, adding sweetener only if your baby absolutely refuses everything without it.

PREPARATION TIPS

DO	**DON'T**
• Use fruit and vegetables as soon as possible after buying	• Buy bruised or wrinkled fruit and vegetables
• Peel tough-skinned fruit and vegetables if the skin is likely to cause your baby problems	• Prepare vegetables a long time in advance or soak them in water, as this destroys the vitamins
• Cook soft-skinned fruit and vegetables in their skins; this helps retain the vitamins and provides additional fiber	• Crush or bruise fruit and vegetables; this destroys any vitamin C present
• Cook fruit and vegetables in a steamer or in a tightly covered pan with as little water as possible. This helps to retain the vitamins normally lost in cooking	• Give red meat more than twice a week as it has a high saturated fat content
• Give your baby cooked and pureed meat or fish. The puree can be thinned with vegetable water or soup	• Overcook canned foods, as this destroys the vitamins
• Use canola or corn oil. Limit butter and saturated fats	• Add salt or sugar to your child's food
	• Let freshly prepared food cool at room temperature; refrigerate it right away

USING PACKAGED FOODS

Packaged foods are more expensive than homemade ones, but they are convenient, especially if you are in a hurry or traveling. Always observe the following guidelines when using them.

• *Check the ingredients listed on the jar. They are listed in order of quantity, so anything that has water near the top of the list will not be very nutritious*

• *Avoid foods with added sugar, salt, or modified starch*

• *Make sure that the seal is intact; if it is damaged, the food could be contaminated*

• *Don't heat the food in the jar – the glass might crack*

• *Don't feed your baby from the jar if you intend to keep some of the food, as the leftovers will become contaminated with saliva. You can feed him from the jar if he's likely to eat the whole thing*

• *Don't keep opened jars in the refrigerator for longer than two days, and never beyond the "best before" date*

• *Never store food in an opened can; transfer it to a dish, cover, and refrigerate*

• *Check ingredients lists carefully if you are introducing food types gradually; many contain eggs, gluten, and dairy products. Some even contain nuts.*

FEEDING AND NUTRITION

As your child grows his nutritional needs increase proportionately; greater quantities are needed during growth spurts and when he's learning to walk. Your child should have a diet containing sufficient amounts of protein, carbohydrate, fats, vitamins, and minerals, and he will get all of these as long as you provide a wide variety of foods. Because he is growing, he still needs more protein and calories for his body weight than an adult.

Although, broadly speaking, a variety of foods from three of the four food groups (see p.62) – carbohydrates, fruit and vegetables (fiber), and protein-rich foods – will fulfill your child's needs, some foods within the groups have particular nutritional value. All fruit

GIRLS' WEIGHT

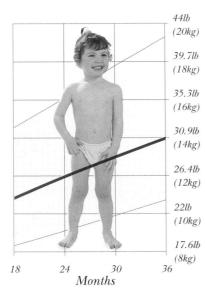

44lb (20kg)

39.7lb (18kg)

35.3lb (16kg)

30.9lb (14kg)

26.4lb (12kg)

22lb (10kg)

17.6lb (8kg)

18   24   30   36
Months

Your toddler's weight
Weight gain may be irregular during spurts of growth, but any weight within the colored band is normal. See **Growth charts**, p.56.)

A balanced diet
Variety is the key to a good diet. Choose foods from each of the groups in the chart.

FOOD GROUPS	NUTRIENTS
Breads and cereals *Whole-grain bread, noodles, pasta, rice*	*Protein, carbohydrates, B vitamins, iron and calcium*
Citrus fruits *Oranges, grapefruits, lemons, limes*	*Vitamins A and C*
Fats *Butter, margarine, vegetable oils, fish oils*	*Vitamins A and D, essential fatty acids*
Green and yellow vegetables *Cabbage, sprouts, spinach, kale, green beans, squash, lettuce, celery, zucchini*	*Minerals, including calcium, chlorine, fluorine, chromium, cobalt, copper, zinc, manganese, potassium, sodium, and magnesium*
High protein *Chicken, fish, lamb, beef, pork, liver, eggs, cheese, nuts, legumes*	*Protein, fat, iron, vitamins A and D, B vitamins, especially B$_{12}$ (naturally present in animal proteins only)*
Milk and dairy products *Milk, cream, yogurt, cottage cheese, cheese*	*Protein, fat, calcium, vitamins A and D, B vitamins*
Other vegetables and fruits *Potatoes, beets, corn, carrots, cauliflower, pineapples, apricots, nectarines, strawberries, plums, apples, bananas*	*Carbohydrates, vitamins A, B, and C*

and vegetables provide carbohydrates and fiber, for instance, but leafy green vegetables are particularly high in minerals, and citrus fruits are a good source of vitamins A and C (see chart, left).

SNACKS

Until the age of four or five, your child will prefer to eat frequently throughout the day. His stomach still can't cope with three adult-sized meals a day, so he is not ready to adopt an adult eating pattern. He may want to eat between three and fourteen times a day, but the typical range is five to seven times. What he eats is more important than how often he eats. As a rule, the more meals he has, the smaller they will be.

You may be accustomed to thinking of snacks as "extras," but they are an integral part of any child's diet, so should not be refused. As long as the snacks do not reduce your child's daily nutrition, and are not being used as substitutes for "meals," snacks can be wonderfully useful for introducing new foods gradually without disrupting your child's eating patterns. Avoid giving your child highly refined and processed foods like cookies, candy, cakes, and ice cream, which contain a lot of calories and very few nutrients. Fresh fruits and vegetables, cubes of cheese, peanut butter or cheese sandwiches with whole-grain bread or white bread with added vitamins, and fruit juice all make good, nutritious snacks.

Planning snacks Snack foods should contribute to the whole day's nutrition, so don't leave them to chance; plan them carefully, and coordinate meals and snacks so that you serve different foods in the snacks and in the meals.

- Milk and milk-based drinks make very good snacks, and contain protein, calcium, and many of the B vitamins. You should use whole milk until your child is at least two years old; then you can use low-fat but not skimmed milk unless your child is significantly overweight (see p.70). Citrus juices are also very nutritious, especially when fresh, and contain a lot of vitamin C. If you buy fruit juices, avoid those with added sugar.

- Your child may become bored with certain kinds of foods, so try to give him plenty of variety, and make snacks amusing if you can: you could use cookie cutters to cut cheese or bread into interesting shapes, or make a smiling face by arranging pieces of fruit on a slice of bread.

- A food that your child rejects in one form may be acceptable in another: yogurt can be frozen so that it becomes more like ice cream, and a child who rejects cheese sandwiches might enjoy eating cheese and tomato pieces out of an ice-cream cone.

- You can also increase your child's interest in food by involving him in planning or even preparing part of a snack. He will take great pride in eating a sandwich if he has helped you wash or tear the lettuce, for example, or if you allow him to assemble the bread and filling himself.

BOYS' WEIGHT

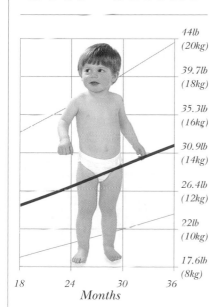

44lb
(20kg)

39.7lb
(18kg)

35.3lb
(16kg)

30.9lb
(14kg)

26.4lb
(12kg)

22lb
(10kg)

17.6lb
(8kg)

18   24   30   36
Months

Your toddler's weight
Your child may have spurts of growth, but these will balance out with periods of slower weight gain. Any weight within the colored band is normal. (For a full explanation of the chart, see **Growth charts**, p.56.)

Little and often
Your child will need more snacks than you do, as he can't eat large meals.

PORTABLE CHAIRS

Your child can eat at the table in her usual high chair, but there are other types of seats available that are more portable and will give her greater independence.

Clip-on chairs
These light collapsible chairs are suitable for babies over six months of age. Some will grip the table when your toddler sits in the chair; others are attached to the table by clamps. These are not necessarily suitable for all tables, so read the manufacturer's recommendations carefully before buying.

Booster seat
Help your child reach table height with a specially made seat, suitable for children over 18 months. It is more stable than a cushion and can be strapped to a chair.

FEEDING YOUR TODDLER

By the age of 18 months your baby will already be eating more or less the same foods as you, and she will probably take about one third to half an adult portion at meals. You should try to ensure that she has at least one protein food at each meal, and four servings of fruits and vegetables a day. Aim to give a good mixture of foods from the different food groups in the chart on p.66.

Don't give your child highly seasoned or sugary foods – fresh fruit or yogurt rather than sweetened desserts should be offered. You also should avoid any small, hard pieces of food that your child could choke on, like whole nuts or popcorn, fruits with pits or seeds, or very small pieces of raw fruit or vegetables.

FAMILY EATING
Now that your toddler is feeding herself, she will enjoy sitting at the table during family mealtimes. Although she's eating the same food as everyone else, you may need to mash or chop it so that she can eat it without much help. A very messy eater can be fed beforehand, then allowed to sit at the table with some finger foods. Difficult eaters feel encouraged to eat more at family meals.

It will be some time, however, before your child is ready to sit still during mealtimes. If she wants to get down from the table, let her go, and don't try to make her come back to finish her food if she has obviously lost interest in it; she will make up for it by eating more at the next meal.

MESSY EATERS
Your child may regard mealtimes as just another game and will see nothing wrong in getting food everywhere. Although it may seem to you that she is doing it on purpose, it's just a phase, and her coordination will improve eventually. Make mealtimes easier on yourself by surrounding the high chair with newspaper, which can be gathered up after each meal. Being tidy can be turned into a game: you could draw a circle on the tray of the high chair to show your toddler where her cup should go; if she keeps it there, reward her.

Keeping clean
Bibs and easy-to-wash plastic equipment help keep messy mealtimes manageable.

MENU PLANNING

The menus below assume that your toddler will eat three meals a day and several snacks. If you find in practice that she eats fewer meals and more snacks, just make sure you choose snack foods that you would have served at mealtimes.

SUGGESTED MENUS AGE 18 MONTHS

DAY 1	**DAY 2**	**DAY 3**
Breakfast	*Breakfast*	*Breakfast*
Whole grain toast	Cereal with milk	Fruit juice
Chopped hard-boiled egg	Fruit juice	Cereal with milk
Milk	Sliced pear, without skin	$1/2$ mashed banana
	Whole-grain toast	Small container of fruit yogurt
Lunch	*Lunch*	*Lunch*
Small piece white fish	Hamburger on a whole-grain roll	Cheese sandwich on whole-grain bread
Brown rice	Steamed broccoli	Pieces of raw carrot
1 tablespoon corn	1 medium tomato	Apple slices, without skin
Fruit juice	Milk	Milk
Snacks	*Snacks*	*Snacks*
Milk	Milk	1 orange in pieces
1 small yogurt	1 unsweetened whole-grain cookie	$1/2$ c. yogurt
1 banana	1 cup water	Fresh fruit juice
Whole-grain roll	1 rice cake	1 small package unsalted vegetable chips
Dinner	*Dinner*	*Dinner*
Cauliflower with grated cheese	Whole-grain roll	Tuna (not in oil)
String beans	Green peas	Chickpeas
Small chicken pieces, without skin	Chopped liver	Tomato pieces
$1/2$ banana blended with 1 cup milk	Whole-grain pasta (dry weight)	Milk
Small whole-grain roll		

MAKING FOOD FUN

Making mealtimes exciting for your toddler will encourage her to try new foods. Fun foods do not have to be difficult or time consuming; a little imagination is all it takes.

Smiley pizza face
Cheese, vegetables, and fresh fruit decoratively arranged on top of a plain pizza can be very appealing and makes a highly nutritious child's meal.

Obesity is one of the most common nutritional problems among children in prosperous Western societies. Most plump children, however, are not medically overweight, and no special action is needed as long as they are healthy and active.

If you think your child is over-weight – that is, markedly fatter than her friends – consult your doctor, who will be able to tell you if your child's weight is above the normal range for her height.

The most common causes of over-weight are a poor diet and lack of exercise. The best way to help the child is often for the whole family to adopt a healthier diet: less fat and sugar, more fresh fruit and vegetables, and more unrefined carbohydrates.

You should never aim to make your child actually lose weight; aim for her weight to remain stable while she grows in height. These guidelines may help:

• Bake, grill, and boil foods rather than roasting or frying

• Give water or diluted fruit juice when your child is thirsty. Never give sweetened drinks or soda

• Give whole-grain bread, raw vegetables, and fruit as snacks

• Whole-grain bread and pasta and brown rice are more filling than their refined equivalents

• Encourage your child to be active by playing lively games with her and her playmates

• Children 12–36 months old should drink 24 ounces of milk each day to meet their need for calcium. Low-fat or skim milk can be used for children over the age of two years if vitamin supplements are also given

FEEDING PROBLEMS

Some young children are "difficult eaters," but in many cases the real difficulty is with a parent who expects the child to conform to an eating pattern that doesn't suit her. If you approach feeding problems with sympathy and a flexible attitude, they will usually just disappear. In some cases, there may be a genuine problem, such as intolerance of or allergy to certain foods, and you should consult your doctor. Never try to isolate a food allergy yourself; your child could suffer if you deprive her of particular foods.

FOOD PREFERENCES

In the second year your child will start to show likes and dislikes for certain foods. It is very common for children to go through phases of eating only one kind of food and refusing everything else. For example, she may go for a week eating nothing but yogurt and fruit, then suddenly go off yogurt and start eating nothing but cheese and mashed potatoes. Don't get angry with your child about this, and don't insist that she eats certain foods. No one food is essential to your child, and there is always a nutritious substitute for any food she refuses to eat. As long as you offer your child a wide variety of foods, she will get a balanced diet, and it is far better for her to eat something that she likes – even if it's something you disapprove of – than to eat nothing at all. The one thing you must watch out for is your toddler refusing to eat any food from a particular group – refusing any kind of fruit or vegetables, for example. If she does, her diet will become unbalanced, so you will have to think of ways of tempting her to eat fruit and vegetables, perhaps by cooking the food in a different way or presenting it imaginatively (see p.69).

If you spend time cooking food that you know your toddler doesn't want, you will feel annoyed and resentful when she doesn't eat it, so give yourself and her a break by cooking food that you know she will enjoy.

Don't try to camouflage a disliked food by mixing it with some-thing else or bargain with your child by offering a favorite food if she eats the disliked one; she may very well end up refusing other foods as well. If you are introducing a new food, make sure your child is hungry; that way, she is more likely to take it. Never try to force her to take something she doesn't want; if she thinks it's very important to you, she will just use it as a way of manipulating you.

REFUSAL TO EAT

Not eating is an early indication that your child may be unwell, so observe her carefully. If she looks pale, and seems fretful and more clumsy than usual, check her temperature (see p.278) and speak to her doctor if you're worried.

Occasionally your child may have eaten a lot of snacks or a drink of milk before her meal, and she won't show her usual appetite. As long as the snacks are nutritious, this is nothing to worry about.

If your child refuses to eat for no reason that you can see, don't let yourself be bothered by it. She will always eat as much food as she really needs, and if you insist on her eating, mealtimes may become a battle that you will always lose.

FOOD INTOLERANCE

The inability to digest certain foods fully has to be distinguished from a true food allergy, which is quite different and very rare. Intolerance occurs when the digestive system fails to produce essential enzymes that break down food inside the body. One of the most common forms of food intolerance in children is lactose intolerance – the inability to digest the sugars in milk. The enzyme, in this case lactase, may be absent from birth or its production may be disrupted by an intestinal disorder such as gastroenteritis. Pale-colored, bulky, smelly stools are characteristic of the disorder. Sometimes food intolerance occurs for reasons that are not known. If your child habitually has symptoms such as diarrhea, nausea, or pain after eating a particular food, intolerance may be the cause. The best remedy is to avoid the food concerned, but don't try to identify it yourself; you will need medical advice to pin down the culprit food and to eliminate other causes.

FOOD ALLERGY

Most cases of suspected food allergy turn out to be no more than intolerance, or the combination of a fussy child and a fussy mother. A true food allergy is quite rare and occurs when the body's immune system undergoes an exaggerated reaction to a protein or chemical it interprets as "foreign." It is a protective mechanism, and symptoms can include headache, nausea, profuse vomiting, diarrhea, a rash, widespread red blotches on the skin, and swelling of the mouth, tongue, face, and eyes.

At first the allergen – the substance that causes the reaction – may produce only mild symptoms, but these may become more severe if the child is repeatedly exposed to the food concerned. Some foods that commonly cause allergic reactions are wheat, shell-fish, strawberries, chocolate, eggs, and cows' milk.

In the 1980s food allergies attracted a great deal of attention, and were blamed for behavioral disturbances in children, including hyperactivity. More recent studies have cast doubt on these claims: parents continued to report behavioral disturbance even when, unknown to them, the suspect food had been withdrawn from the child's diet. In a very small number of cases it has been proven that food was responsible for the behavior, but in very many more cases bad behavior is a way of seeking attention, love, and affection from parents and others. I feel very strongly that too many parents have been willing to blame foods for behavioral problems rather than look to their own attitudes as a cause. Meanwhile, many children have been needlessly deprived of nutritious foods.

You should never attempt to isolate a food allergy on your own without medical advice, and never assume an allergy is present without a clear diagnosis from a pediatric allergist.

WHEN YOUR CHILD IS ILL

Loss of appetite is often one of the first signs of illness in a child, but this need not be a cause for concern if the illness is brief.

- *Your child must drink plenty of fluids, especially if she has been vomiting or had diarrhea*

- *There is no need for a special invalid diet, though it is sensible to avoid rich or heavy foods if your child has an upset stomach*

- *Offer some of her favorite foods to cheer her up, and give smaller portions than usual. Because your child is resting, she will probably not want much*

Giving drinks
Your child's appetite may be poor when she is ill, but make sure she gets plenty of fluids by offering her favorite drink.

FEEDING AND NUTRITION

TREATS AND REWARDS

Every parent knows that there are times when it is important either to reward good behavior or to offer a bribe in return for some form of cooperation.

Candy might seem like the most suitable reward, as it is always appreciated by children. However, you may feel that to give candy routinely as a reward undermines the consistency of your approach to candy-eating in general. There is no hard and fast rule on this, and there is no reason why you shouldn't occasionally reward your child with candy as long as you make it clear that it is a one-time gift.

It's worth making an effort, though, to devise other forms of reward: a favorite yogurt flavor, a small toy or a new box of crayons, or a specially extended bathtime or bedtime story.

I don't believe in placing a total ban on candy, because this can encourage children to be obsessive.

I do believe in rationing candy, though, and this always worked with my own children. If you let your child have one piece of candy after lunch and one after supper, and encourage him to brush his teeth afterward, you will be encouraging self-control, good eating habits, and good oral hygiene.

Your preschooler will eat almost the same diet as you, and his dietary needs should be seen in the context of the eating habits of the whole family: you may even have taken the opportunity to improve your own diet as a result of considering the needs of your child. At this stage you will probably be concerned less about making sure your child is getting the right foods in the right amounts, and more about whether he is learning adult behavior and manners at mealtimes. This is a good time to teach him table manners that will last into adulthood.

FAMILY AND SOCIAL EATING

For many families, mealtimes are about much more than making sure everyone is fed; they are social occasions when all the members of the family sit down together, exchange news, and enjoy one another's company. For a small child these times form an important part of his learning process; he can appreciate this social aspect of mealtimes and will learn most of his behavior at the table from his experience of family eating rather than from any number of lectures at a later age. Every family has its own accepted standards of behavior and I am not going to lay down rules about what these should be. What is important, however, is that your child learns to fit in so that the family can enjoy their mealtimes together without repeated disruptions caused by bad manners and arguments about behavior.

As soon as your child first sat in his high chair at the family dining table, he was watching and learning. He will want at least to try the foods that you are eating and will often join in the conversation. Try to include your child in family meals as often as possible. Encourage him when he attempts to follow your (good) example. Give praise, for instance, when he asks for something to be passed to him instead of attempting to grab it from the other side of the table. Children learn most naturally and easily by example and will rapidly pick up the norms of behavior that the rest of the family observe. If yours is a family where everyone leaves the table when it suits them, for example, rather than waiting for the others to finish eating, it will be hard to persuade your child to sit still and wait.

There will be occasions when you want your child to behave especially well at mealtimes – usually because you are having visitors. Allow him to join in the excitement of a special meal by letting him help set the table, perhaps. If he understands that some occasions demand an extra effort, he will find it easier to understand why you want him to be particularly well behaved and will therefore react better to your wishes.

KEEPING MEALTIMES RELAXED

It is important to prevent family meals from becoming a battlefield for more generalized family conflict. The association between food and love can be very close, and arguments about food and eating can be associated with tensions over other issues. In such cases food and eating behavior – for example, refusal to eat – can become a weapon that the child uses either to gain attention or to express anger, distress, and many other emotions. It is best, therefore, to be fairly easygoing about table etiquette with your child, to make mealtimes as relaxed as possible, and not to be drawn into arguments. Insist only on those aspects of table manners that you consider essential; refinements can come later.

EATING AWAY FROM HOME

A small baby can eat only what you give him, but an older child will have pronounced preferences about what he wants to eat, and the opportunity to follow them. There are likely to be more occasions when your child is eating outside the home, and while you obviously can't account for every mouthful he eats, you should try to ensure that the good habits he has learned at home are not undermined once he starts to eat elsewhere.

If your child goes to playgroup, nursery school, or "real" school, try to make sure he has a good breakfast before he goes. If he doesn't, he will become hungry again long before lunchtime, and both his temper and his concentration will be affected. A healthy midmorning snack like a piece of fruit or a cup of cereal will help tide him over until lunchtime. If food is going to be provided for him, try to find out what will be offered; if you are not satisfied, or if there are no arrangements to feed your child, then provide him with a nutritious packed lunch instead. Lunch need not always be sandwiches; you could give chicken pieces and potato salad, pieces of raw vegetables with a yogurt dip, or other foods that your child can eat with his fingers.

Children are often encouraged to try new foods because they see their friends eat them, and you may find once your child starts at playgroup or school that he starts to eat foods that he previously rejected at home.

FAST FOODS

Try not to resort to fast food restaurants too often when you are out with your child and want to stop for something to eat. Most of the foods available in these restaurants – french fries, hamburgers, hot dogs, and sugary soft drinks – are high in salt, fats, or sugar, and low in nutrients. If you can, bring a supply of healthy snack foods with you, or choose somewhere that offers more healthy foods, such as sandwiches and salads. If your child particularly asks for hamburgers and fries, however, you may want to indulge him now and again – but make it clear that such foods are a special treat, to be eaten only occasionally. My family used to eat at a hamburger restaurant once a week for Saturday lunch. This satisfied everyone and is not so frequent as to damage good health.

EATING OUT

There will be many occasions when you'll take your child out to eat. Being prepared will make the experience more enjoyable.

• *Try to find out beforehand what facilities will be available at the restaurant you choose: if you are booking a table, mention that you will be bringing small children, and find out whether there will be room for your child's stroller, and whether a high chair can be provided if you need one*

• *Many children's menus are very limited and offer just hamburgers, hot dogs, or fish sticks – all with fries. If you really don't want your child to have these foods, ask whether you can order a small portion of a suitable dish from the main menu, and whether you will be charged full price for it*

• *Most children will enjoy the experience of eating out, and you should involve your child fully, allowing him to choose his own meal and to give his own order to the waiter if he is not too shy*

• *Bring along your child's booster seat if he normally uses one. If you think he will have difficulty drinking from a glass, you could also bring along his training cup*

• *Many restaurants positively encourage children, and will be happy to provide straws for drinks, bibs and high chairs for young babies, and even small gifts such as paper hats or pictures to color in*

HOLDING AND HANDLING

A newborn baby may appear very vulnerable and fragile, but she is more robust than you imagine. With this knowledge uppermost in your mind, you will be able to inspire confidence in your child rather than uncertainty. For the baby's comfort, and for your own peace of mind, it's important to feel at ease when you handle her; you must be able to hold your baby confidently in order to bathe, dress, and feed her successfully.

HANDLING YOUR BABY

When you move your baby, the action must be as slow, gentle, and quiet as possible. You'll find that you instinctively hold your baby close, look into her eyes, and talk soothingly to her. Not surprisingly it has been proven that all children benefit from intimate physical contact, particularly being in a position to hear the familiar sound of your heartbeat. Premature babies, for example, gain more weight when they are laid on fleecy sheets, which give them the sensation of being touched, than when they are laid on smooth ones. Your newborn baby will find comfort in any kind of skin-to-skin contact, but the best way to give her this is for both of you to lie naked in bed. Here she can smell and feel your skin, and hear your heart beating. In this way, too, you can make sure that she becomes familiar with the smell of her father's skin.

PICKING UP YOUR BABY

PUTTING YOUR BABY DOWN

For the first three months of her life, you should always lay your baby on her back.

Research in recent years has shown that babies who sleep on their fronts are at greater risk from crib death (SIDS) than those placed on their backs, and media publicity about this finding has resulted in a significant drop in crib death.

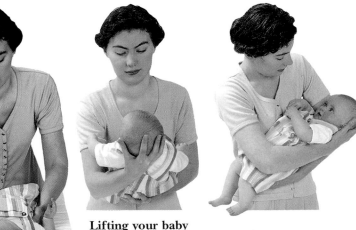

Lifting your baby
Slide one hand under your baby's neck and the other under her back and bottom to support her lower half securely. Pick her up gently and smoothly and transfer her to a carrying position.

Whenever you pick your baby up and put her down, do it in a way that supports her head; until she is about four weeks old she'll have little control over it. If her head flops back, she will think that she is going to fall, her body will jerk, and she'll stretch out both arms and legs in the Moro, or startle, reflex (see p.20).

Put your baby down and pick her up with your whole arm supporting her spine, neck, and head. You may want to try swaddling your baby: wrap her firmly in a shawl or blanket so that her head is supported and her arms held close against her body. Once she lies down in the crib, you can gently unwrap her. Swaddling your baby tightly makes her feel secure, so it's a useful way of comforting and calming a distressed baby.

CARRYING YOUR BABY

One way to carry your baby in your arms is to cradle her head in the crook of either arm, which is slightly inclined. The rest of her body will rest on the lower part of your arm, encircled by your wrist and hand, which support her back and bottom. Your other arm will provide additional support to her bottom and legs, and your baby can see your face as you talk to her and smile at her.

The second way to carry your baby is to hold her against the upper part of your chest with her head on your shoulder. Your forearm should be placed across her back and your hand should support her resting head, leaving your other hand free. This can be used to provide support for your baby's bottom or to help you balance. Your sense of balance will change at first as you get used to carrying your new baby.

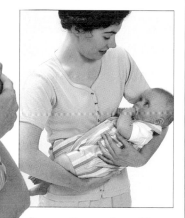

Supporting and cradling
Hold your baby's head and support the length of her body when carrying her. Holding her close will make your baby feel secure and relaxed, especially if she can see your face.

Newborns are best carried in slings worn on the chest, where they feel close to you and secure.

• *Look for a sling in a washable fabric, for it will get dirty as you carry your baby around*

• *It must be easy to put on and comfortable to wear for both you and your partner. Try it out with your baby before you buy it*

• *Your sling should support your baby's head and neck, and keep her secure; she must not be able to slip out the sides*

• *The shoulder straps must be wide enough to support your growing baby's weight. Wide shoulder straps will also make carrying more comfortable*

• *It has been said that a baby shouldn't be carried in a sling until she can support her own head. This is not true. Use a sling as soon as you and your baby are happy about it*

Slings
These light-weight fabric supports are a comfortable way to carry a young baby.

BABY MASSAGE

Massage can have all the benefits for a baby that it has for an adult: it is soothing and can calm a fretful baby, and it is a marvelous way of showing love. If you massage your baby every day he will learn to recognize the routine and will show pleasure as you begin. You can continue to massage your baby as he gets older; a massage is often the ideal way to calm an excited toddler.

Provide a relaxed atmosphere before you start. As this will be a new experience for you both, any distractions can spoil the mood and upset your baby, so choose a time when there is no one else around, and unplug the phone. Make sure the room is nice and warm and lay your baby on a warm towel or on your lap. Work from his head down, using light, even strokes, and ensure that both sides of his body are massaged symmetrically. Make eye contact with your baby throughout the massage and talk quietly, gently, and lovingly to him.

GIVING A MASSAGE

Head
Start off by lightly massaging the crown of your baby's head, using a circular motion, then stroke down the sides of his face. Gently massage his forehead, working from the center out and moving over the eyebrows and cheeks to finish around his ears.

Make sure you massage both sides of your baby's body symmetrically

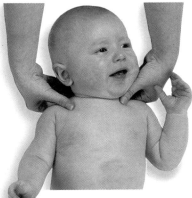

Neck and shoulders
Gently massage your baby's neck from his ears to his shoulders and from his chin to his chest. Then stroke his shoulders from his neck outward.

Arms
Stroke down his arms to his fingertips. Using your fingers and thumb, gently squeeze all along his arm, starting at the top.

76

Chest and abdomen
Gently stroke down your baby's chest, following the delicate curves of his ribs. Rub his abdomen in a circular motion, working outward from the navel.

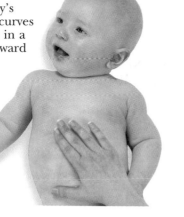

BENEFITS FOR BABY

Your baby can only gain from the pleasures and sensations of a loving massage.

• *Your baby loves being with you, and the intimate contact of massage enhances this. He will recognize it as a clear sign of your love*

• *If unsettled, your baby will be calmed by the soothing strokes of your hands, which will relieve anxiety and make him feel secure*

• *Massage can often ease minor digestive upsets, such as gas, which may well be making your baby fretful*

• *Babies need touch. Research has shown that they would rather be stroked than fed*

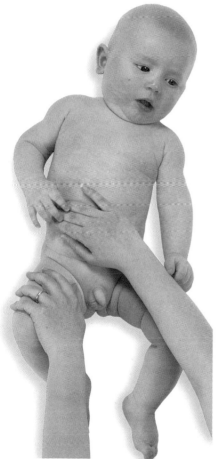

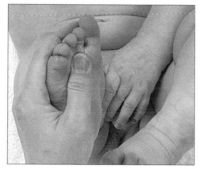

Feet and toes
Rub your baby's ankles and feet, stroking from heel to toe, and then concentrate on each toe individually. End your massage with some long, light strokes along the whole length of the front of your baby's body.

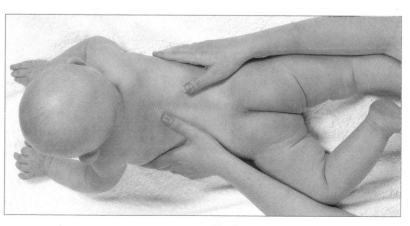

Legs
Now you can massage your baby's legs, working from his thighs down to his knees. Stroke down the shins and move around to his calves and ankles. Gently squeeze all the way down.

Back
Once you have massaged your baby on the front, turn him over and work on his back.

OLDER BABY

HOLDING AND HANDLING

HOW WE HANDLE GIRLS

According to research, we start preparing our girl babies from the day they are born to conform to a feminine sexual stereotype. When handling girls, we

• *Coo, whisper, and smile gently, and cradle them softly*

• *Don't handle them excitingly so they never know the sensation of flying through the air*

• *Make bathing times for girls much more sedate than for boys*

• *Give them soft, cuddly toys and discourage them from rough, dirty, or dangerous play*

• *Sympathize with slight injuries and make no attempts to stop them crying, so they grow up thinking shows of helplessness and emotion are all right*

If you would like your daughter to grow up tough, independent, and self-assured, you should adjust your behavior and encourage her independence (see opposite page).

By now you should be quite relaxed about carrying your baby. You will probably settle on a couple of favorite ways of carrying him, depending on whether he wants to be cuddled or to look at what is going on all around him. He is much heavier now, so make sure that you adopt a method of lifting him that won't strain your back.

PICKING UP AND CARRYING YOUR BABY

Your baby now can control his head, so there is no need to support his head as you did when he was newborn. Now you can pick him up simply by putting your hands under his armpits and lifting him forward toward you. This is also a very good way of putting him into a high chair: his legs will dangle and he can be slipped into the chair. Alternatively, you can lift him with one hand curled diagonally around his back and the other supporting his bottom.

You can carry your baby in the crook of your arm, against your shoulder so that he faces you, or with your arm stretched diagonally across his back and holding his thigh as he sits astride one hip. A sling can be used, although for longer journeys a backpack will give you more support.

CARRYING POSITIONS

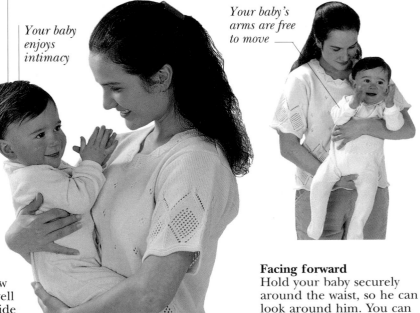

Your baby enjoys intimacy

Your baby's arms are free to move

On one hip
Your baby can now support himself well enough to sit astride your hip. This allows him to look all around.

Facing forward
Hold your baby securely around the waist, so he can look around him. You can use your other hand to support him, or keep it free.

Talk to your baby while bouncing him

Rocking
You can make this activity into a boisterous game by swinging your baby quite high, or just doing it gently to soothe him.

Bouncing
Lift your baby up and down on your knees rhythmically. You should always support him so he doesn't slip backward.

SWINGING AND BOUNCING GAMES
All babies love to be bounced and swung, but just how much they enjoy it will depend on how they're feeling. Being swung up in the air is exciting for your baby, as he can look at his surroundings – and see your face – from a whole new perspective. Sometimes he will prefer to be bounced on your knee or simply gently rocked. Always give your baby a chance to relax after boisterous games by cuddling him quietly for a few minutes.

Swinging
Raise your baby up high, then swoop him down between your legs. He will love looking down at your face from a height.

Hold your baby firmly so that he feels safe.

Your baby will love the sensation of flying through the air

HOW WE HANDLE BOYS

Experiments show that we handle baby boys quite differently from baby girls, and that we persist in this stereotyping even if we are merely fooled by, say, their wearing pink or blue clothes. When handling boys, we

- *Speak, laugh, even shout out loudly, and grasp them firmly*

- *Swing them around so that they get used to lots of action and physical movement*

- *Encourage them to splash and kick in the bath*

- *Give them tough, hard toys and praise adventurousness, even naughtiness, with encouraging words or phrases*

- *Are efficient rather than tender when a boy scrapes his knee, discouraging shows of emotion and applauding independence*

If you want your son to be more in touch with his gentler side, adjust your behavior to encourage greater gentleness (see opposite page).

79

TODDLER

HOLDING AND HANDLING

LIFTING UP YOUR TODDLER

Make sure you know how to handle heavy weights in a way that won't strain your back.

Once you have a baby, there are many opportunities for putting a strain on your back. Your child requires constant lifting and carrying, and carriages, strollers, and other equipment must be shifted. It's important you learn to lift without injury and strain. Keep your back straight, bend your knees, and, using the powerful thigh muscles to do all the work, lift. Never lift with your legs straight and your back curved forward.

Never refuse your toddler a hug; although she needs less holding now than when she was a young baby, she will often ask to be carried like she used to be when she's been out for a long walk or when she's generally tired and cranky. She will frequently be clingy when she feels pain or discomfort, or if she is feeling unwell. You should always respond to her signals and should not hesitate to give her a hug for comfort and affection. Your child will make it clear to you when she has had enough reassurance – she will get down and run off to play. Babies who are given love and cuddles when they need and ask for them usually grow into independent and self-confident individuals.

The desire for physical affection remains with us always. Parents should never scoff at their children's needs, and always respond. When my children were growing up, they liked a cuddle every now and then, especially when they were tired, had had a scolding from a teacher at school, if they were fearful about my departure or absence, or if the world simply didn't feel right.

"CLINGY" CHILDREN

Older children will still occasionally want to sit on your lap. When they feel ill at ease in strange circumstances, they may even want to eat sitting on your knee, particularly if strangers are present and they feel that they are being watched. Let them do so if it is convenient; you will find that just a few moments of intimacy will give a child the confidence to handle any situation.

Bedtimes are particularly important times for showing affection. In my opinion, a child should never have to go to bed without some cuddling. A hug and a kiss will provide a sense of security and the conviction that you really do care. The rule is that you should always be there with a comforting arm and a kind word when your child is hurt, worried, puzzled, or frightened. Not all children require physical reassurance, so be prepared to provide comfort in the form that your child wants.

THE UNRESPONSIVE CHILD

From a very early age some children stiffen their bodies and cry when you hold them. These usually grow up to be children who avoid physical contact – who turn away if you try to kiss them, for example, and make no physical advances themselves. Such children may never enjoy physical affection comfortably, and a parent may find this hard to cope with because it seems like rejection. If your child behaves in this way, don't insist on cuddles that she clearly does not want. Give your physical affection only when she shows you that she wants it, and respect her wishes.

SHOWING AFFECTION

By the age of three or four years your child will be much more independent, and you may assume that she needs fewer overt displays of affection. While this may be true, it would be a mistake to think that she wants to go without any physical affection at all. You should pay special attention to boys, who are often expected to give up hugs and kisses at a very young age because it is not considered to be proper "masculine" behavior.

It is all too easy to lose the habit of showing affection, so make a resolution to hold and touch your child as often as you can every day, whether it's letting her sit on your knee or putting an arm around her when you look at the paper, or giving her a kiss when you put her to bed. I always made it a rule to tell my children every day that I loved them.

Older children can be self-conscious about being kissed or hugged in public, so be sensitive to this. Choose private moments when they can enjoy your care, attention, and love.

HELPING CHILDREN GET ALONG

It can be very difficult to handle rivalry between siblings and their constant conflicting demands on you. You can foster feelings of warmth rather than competitiveness if you encourage these feelings from the beginning. Many hospitals and parent groups offer "sibling preparation" classes that can help ease anxieties before a new baby arrives. When the baby comes home, ask your older child for help in caring for the baby. Even toddlers can fetch diapers, hold bottles, or stroke the baby's hand. Always let the older child open presents for the baby, and be sure to have plenty of small presents stashed away for the older child.

COMFORT AND ENCOURAGEMENT

With any luck your child won't be averse to warmth and affection even after she's reached adulthood, but cuddles do change and get more grown-up, and you have to give the kind of affection your child needs rather than the kind you want to give. So adapt your style to what gives her most comfort.

Preschool children need lots of hugs every day, especially congratulatory ones, as when they've mastered something like getting their shoes on the right feet. Comfort hugs are essential at the first sign of tears. A child responds much better to a hug than a reprimand. Therapeutic hugs reduce the pain of a vaccination, a bump, or a cut in seconds. Never let your child go to sleep without a huge hug and an "I love you."

As your child gets older, hugs are transformed into other actions, but they have the same bolstering, encouraging effect. A hand on the shoulder, a caress, or taking your child's hand is a sign of love and her sense of security and confidence will soar. Your child craves your love and approval; never leave her in any doubt that she has both.

Giving comfort
Many of your child's troubles can be solved with a hug and a few sympathetic words from you.

DRESSING

GIRLS' CLOTHES

Unisex stretch suits and rompers are ideal for everyday wear, but you may prefer more feminine clothes for special occasions.

- *Make sure all clothes are machine washable, because they won't stay clean for long*

- *Avoid very fluffy or lacy cardigans. Fluffy ones will irritate your baby's skin, and tiny fingers catch in lacy ones*

- *Hats can be both practical and pretty. Choose one with ties or elastic and a wide brim for sun protection or for warmth in winter*

Dressing up
Your little girl will look very special in a pretty suit and hat. Elastic cuffs are comfortable provided they're not too tight.

Everyone loves dressing a baby, and your friends and family will all want to buy clothes for your baby as soon as she is born. You are bound to take great pride in her appearance, and might wish to buy some dressy clothes for special occasions, but there's no need to spend a lot of money – she will grow out of clothes very quickly. Remember that as far as your baby is concerned anything goes as long as it's soft and comfortable to wear, and can be put on and taken off without too much disturbance.

Your baby will spit up and drool on her clothes, and there are bound to be accidents and leaks from diapers, so buy only machine-washable, colorfast clothing, and avoid white – it quickly gets dirty, and frequent washing makes it drab.

Look for soft and comfortable clothes with no stiff seams or rough stitching. Toweling, cotton, or pure wool clothes will feel nicer on your baby's skin. If you buy clothes made of artificial fibers, check that they feel soft. By law, sleepwear must be flame retardant. Look for special labeling and washing instructions before buying.

Avoid open-weave knits, because your baby's fingers could get caught in the holes. Check the fastenings, too: snaps in the crotch allow easy access to the diaper area, and snaps at the neck mean

CHOOSING CLOTHES

Easy-fitting clothes will give your baby the most comfort and warmth. Pay special attention to the cuffs, ankles, and neck, where fastenings could cause discomfort.

All babies will feel snug and comfy in a stretchie

Fasteners that snap open and closed are very quick and easy

Loose-fitting shoes with soft soles allow movement

BASIC LAYETTE

6 wide-necked cotton undershirts or T-shirts	2 nightgowns with drawstring ends
1 hat	2 pairs socks and padders
1 blanket for swaddling	2 pairs mittens (for winter)
8 all-in-one stretch suits	1 quilted or fleecy all-in-one outer suit
2 woolen jackets or cardigans (4 in winter)	1 snowsuit (for winter)

your baby won't grow out of something too quickly just because her head is too big for the neck opening. Babies hate having their faces covered, so look for wide necks or clothes that fasten down the front. Front-fastening clothes also allow you to dress your baby without having to turn her over. This will make dressing much more comfortable for her and easier for you.

Make a note of your baby's measurements and bring it with you when you're shopping. Babies of the same age vary a great deal in size, so look at the height and weight given on the label rather than the age. If in doubt, buy the larger size: loose-fitting clothes are warmer and more comfortable than clothes that are too small, and your baby will soon grow into them.

Nightdress
Loose-fitting sleeping garments are comfortable for your new-born baby. A drawstring at the end prevents the night-gown from riding up around her body, and gives you easy access to her diaper.

Loose-fitting cuffs give your baby plenty of room to move

An envelope neck allows you to take the nightdress off more easily

A drawstring keeps your baby's feet inside and allows for easy diaper changing

BOYS' CLOTHES

Look for clothes that are practical as well as good-looking to dress your baby boy.

• *Strong primary colors look good on both sexes*

• *An overall and T-shirt set is comfortable and looks stylish. Look for overalls with snaps at the crotch so you can get at your baby's diaper easily*

• *Hats with tie-down ear flaps are cozy in winter*

• *Don't think tights are just for girls; babies lose socks and bootees very easily, so tights are practical as well as warm*

• *Sweatsuits are very comfortable and allow easy access to the diaper*

Everyday wear
All-in-one suits with snap fastenings are ideal for your little boy and very versatile. Match them with soft footwear.

KEEPING YOUR BABY WARM

You may worry that your new baby is not warm enough, but a few commonsense precautions will keep him comfortable and safe. Remember that babies can easily become too hot; this could lead to heat rash and is also a factor in crib death (SIDS).

• *A great deal of body heat is lost through a bare head; make sure your baby always wears a hat when you take him outdoors*

• *Very young babies have trouble regulating body heat, and should be undressed only in a well-heated room and out of drafts*

• *The baby's room should be at a constant temperature, and the amount of covering he needs will depend on this temperature (see p.122)*

• *If your baby is cold you may need to warm him up. Adding a layer of clothes is not enough in itself; you need to put him in a warmer place first so he can regain his normal body temperature, or hold him close to share your body heat*

• *Never leave your baby to sleep in the sun or close to a source of direct heat such as a radiator*

• *Wrap your baby up if you take him outdoors, but remove outdoor clothes once you bring him inside again; otherwise, he won't be able to cool down efficiently*

DRESSING YOUR BABY

At first you may be nervous about dressing your baby and trying to support him while manipulating the garments. Dressing will become easier with practice, so just be gentle and patient.

You should always dress and undress a young baby on a nonskid flat surface, as this allows you to keep both hands free – a changing pad is ideal. Your baby is very likely to cry as you take off his clothes. This is because young babies hate the feel of the air on their naked bodies; they like to feel snug and secure. It's not because you're hurting him, so don't get flustered by it.

DRESSING

Put undershirt over head
Lay your baby on a flat, nonskid surface and make sure his diaper is clean. Roll the undershirt up and pull the neck open with your thumbs. Put it over the baby's head so that it doesn't touch his face, raising his head slightly as you do so.

Undershirt armholes
Widen the left sleeve or armhole and guide your baby's arm through. Repeat with the other arm. Pull the undershirt down.

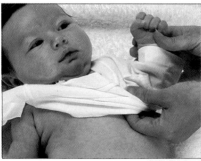

Gently guide your baby's arm through the sleeves

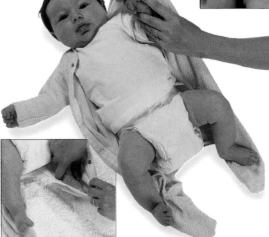

Put on stretch suit
Lay your baby on top of the open suit. Gather up each sleeve and guide his fists through, pulling the sleeve up the arm as you do so. Open up each leg and guide his foot in, making sure it reaches right into the toe. Finally, fasten the suit.

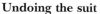

UNDRESSING

Undoing the suit
Put your baby on a flat surface and unfasten the suit. If his diaper needs changing, gently pull both legs out of the suit so that his top remains covered while you change him.

Keep your baby's top covered if you want to change his diaper

Bend his knee gently as you ease his foot out of the suit

Taking off the suit
Lift the baby's legs up while you slide the suit underneath his back as far as his shoulders.

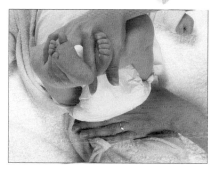

Roll the fabric and carefully slide the hand out

Hold the baby's elbow gently

Removing the top
Grasp each sleeve by the cuff and gently slide your baby's hand out. If he's wearing an undershirt, roll it up toward the neck and gently pull his arms from the sleeves, holding him by each elbow as you do so.

DRESSING ON YOUR LAP

When your baby is three or four months old he will have enough muscle control to sit on your lap while you take off his clothes.

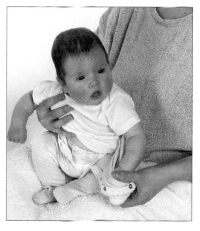

Sit with your legs crossed so that your baby will fit neatly in the hollow of your legs and cradle him with your arm, as his back will still need some support. You may find it easier to deal with the bottom half while he's lying flat.

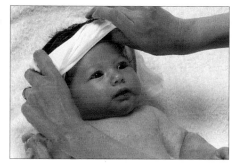

Taking off undershirt
Pull the neck wide open and lift the undershirt over your baby's head, keeping the fabric off his face.

85

OLDER BABY DRESSING

OUTDOOR CLOTHES FOR GIRLS

Your little girl is more active now, so she won't always be bundled up when she's outdoors. Look for outdoor clothes that are comfortable and won't restrict her movements.

• *Heavy tights are warm and comfortable, and can be bought in colors and patterns to match your daughter's dress*

• *In very cold weather, a short cape over your little girl's coat will keep her extra warm*

• *Mittens can be clipped to sleeves or joined with a ribbon and slipped through the sleeves*

• *Sun hats are not just pretty; they are essential if your child spends any length of time in the sunshine*

Choosing clothes
Be sure the knees are protected if your baby is crawling.

Once your baby has learned to crawl he'll be far less willing to sit or lie still while you dress him. On the other hand, he is now much more able to help you as you put on his clothes. For example, an 11-month-old baby can make a fist or stretch out an arm, if you ask him to, or hold his arm still while you pull his sleeve into place. If he's very restless you can sing a song to him or engage his attention with a toy, or involve him in the whole dressing process by naming each item of clothing as you put it on or take it off, and getting him to repeat the names after you, for example. You could also turn dressing into a peek-a-boo game: "Where's baby's foot? Oh, look, here it is!"

Here are some tips for dressing your baby if it's difficult to get him to hold still:

• Stand him between your legs so that he's immobilized while you pull up his pants.

• Sit him in his high chair so that you can put on his shoes.

• You can make a game out of putting on his shoes by placing them at the bottom of the stairs and getting him to step down into them carefully while you steady him.

CHOOSING CLOTHES

Now that your baby is more active, you will need to look for clothes that allow easy movement. He will be awake longer, and moving around, so his clothes are more likely to get dirty and you'll therefore need more of them. You'll also have to consider whether they are tough enough for the wear and tear that your child will give them: look for sturdy fabrics that last well and strong fastenings that won't break or fall off. If your baby is crawling, make sure his clothes protect his knees. Once he begins to walk he'll need shoes (see opposite page).

When you're buying clothes, check the label to see what kind of material they are made from. Natural fibers are both strong and comfortable, so look for pure cotton or a fabric with a high cotton content. Toweling, denim, and corduroy are all strong and hardwearing. Look, too, for clothes that can be easily pulled down or up once your child is learning how to use the potty, and avoid zippers or complicated fastenings; elastic waists are by far the easiest for him to manage.

Until he's walking, socks or woolen bootees are all your baby needs, even when he's crawling. Fabric bootees with elastic at the ankles stay on better. Ensure there's plenty of room for movement; the bones in your baby's feet are so soft and pliable that even tightly fitting socks could misshape the toes if worn regularly.

CHOOSING SHOES

When you are buying your child shoes, always go to a reputable store where the staff has been trained to measure and fit children's shoes. The salesperson should measure the length and the width of your child's foot before trying any shoes. Once your child tries on a pair of shoes, the salesperson should press the joints of the foot to make sure that it is not restricted in any way, and that the fastenings hold the shoe firmly in place and don't let your child's foot slip around. Make sure your child stands up and walks around in the shoes to check that the toe doesn't pinch and hurt when he's walking and to double-check that there's no slipping.

A sturdy, well-made pair of leather shoes is most suitable for general outdoor wear, especially once your child starts running and playing. You should, however, get a pair of rubber boots for wet or muddy conditions. Although leather shoes and sandals are solid and sensible and last well, there is nothing wrong with inexpensive canvas shoes or sneakers as long as you make sure that they fit properly. If your child suddenly becomes less steady on his feet it may be a sign that he is outgrowing his shoes. Well-fitting shoes are essential to ensure that your child has good feet in adult life. Don't try to save money by buying second-hand shoes; they will have molded to the first owner's feet.

SHOES FOR HEALTHY FEET

OUTDOOR CLOTHES FOR BOYS

Choose clothes that leave your little boy room for growth and allow him to move freely.

- *Always put a hat on your little boy if he's out in the sun. Baseball caps worn back to front protect the nape of the neck*

- *Buy outdoor clothes on the large side. This leaves room for extra layers underneath, and allows the child to grow into them*

- *Cut the sleeves off an outgrown jacket to make an outdoor vest*

Choose a sturdy leather pair for outdoor wear. Your child's feet must be unrestricted but held firmly in place and unable to slip out. The toes shouldn't curl up or hurt when he walks. Never buy secondhand shoes.

Make sure there are no seams or stitching on the upper that might rub your child's foot

The heel should be no higher than 1 1/2 inches (4 centimeters) from the sole

Wide toes allow your child's toes to fan out. Make sure the toe box is high enough so that it doesn't exert pressure on the toenails

Adjustable fastenings hold the foot firmly in the shoe. Buckles and Velcro are easier for young children to manage than laces

The sole should be light and flexible, and slip-resistant

Surfaces should be easy to clean or polish

There should be space between your child's big toe and the end of the shoe – at least 1/4 inch (0.5 centimeter), but no more than 1/2 inch (1.25 centimeters)

*Your little girl will try to dress
herself now, so choose clothes
that she can manage easily.*

• *Buy dresses with fastenings at
the front; ones that fasten at the
back are too difficult for toddlers
to manage*

• *Show her how to get her tights
the right way around, and how to
roll them up before she tries to
put them on*

• *Avoid very fitted clothes; they
don't leave much room for growth*

Room for growth
Loose-fitting
clothes with
adjustable
fastenings are
most suitable
now that your
child is grow-
ing fast.

SELF-DRESSING

As your child grows older, she'll develop the coordination required
to dress successfully. You should encourage her in her attempts at
dressing or undressing, however slow or awkward – they're a sign
of growing independence and maturity. Learning to manage by
herself will improve a child's coordination and increase her confidence, so be patient with her first clumsy efforts.

Lay out your child's clothes in such a way that she can maneuver
them on easily. For instance, you could drape a cardigan on the
back of a chair so that she just has to sit down and slide her arms
into the sleeves. Let her do as much as she is capable of, and don't
step in to help unless it's really necessary, though you will have to
deal with most of the fastenings yourself until your child is old
enough to manage them.

At 18 months she will already be trying to manage fastenings,
and by two and a half she will be able to close a button in a loose
buttonhole, and put on her own pants, T–shirt, and sweatshirt. By
the age of four she will probably be able to dress or undress herself completely and will have enough dexterity to put her clothes
away tidily. There are several things you can do to make getting
dressed easier for your child.

• Teach her how to button from the bottom up.

• Sew large buttons onto a toddler's clothes so that she can handle them easily.

• Velcro fastenings will be easy for her to manage, but don't use
them where they might chafe her skin.

Dressing himself
By the age of three your toddler
may be able to dress himself
completely, though it will take
him a long time. Allow him
his independence, and
don't step in to help unless
you're really needed.

*Dresses or pants with ties
or buckles can be
adjusted to fit your child
as she grows*

*Little hands
can grasp a
zipper more
easily if it has
a ring attached
to the tab*

• Buy pants with elastic waists to avoid zippers.

• Children find it difficult to put sweaters on the right way around, so explain to her that the label always goes at the back.

Choosing clothes As your child becomes more involved in dressing herself, she will become more conscious of the clothes themselves. Babies are largely unaware of what they are wearing as long as it is comfortable and does not impede their activities, but toddlers gradually begin to notice the colors and type of clothing they put on, and your child may develop preferences. Clothes that seem similar to those worn by mommy or daddy might be especially attractive. The feel of a garment will also be important to her – whether, for example, it is soft or itchy, tight or stretchy. If she takes a dislike to a garment, it may be because it doesn't fit properly and is therefore uncomfortable to wear.

Your child's concerns should be taken seriously when you are buying her clothing. Once your main requirements, which are practical ones – warmth, durability, washability, and cost – are met, there is no reason why you shouldn't indulge her; the image of a favorite cartoon character or a particular color may be the deciding factor as far as she is concerned. Allowing her to choose which clothes to wear each day is also important. You may want her to wear long pants on a cold day, but let her choose which pair.

She may develop seemingly irrational likes or dislikes for certain items of clothing – insisting on wearing a particular T-shirt every day, for example, or refusing to wear the hand-knitted pullover that Granny gave her for her birthday. The easiest policy is to go along with these preferences as far as possible, though occasionally bribery, or at least negotiation, may be in order: you could offer a special treat in return for wearing that pullover on the afternoon that Granny comes to dinner.

DRESSING A BOY

Help your little boy to dress himself by making sure his clothes don't have tricky fastenings.

• *Boys are usually slower than girls at learning to use the potty, so it is particularly important to avoid awkward fastenings on your little boy's pants*

• *Look for adjustable straps on overalls, or add a button so the straps can be lengthened*

• *Pants with elastic waists are easiest but, if he has trousers with zippers, show him how to pull the zipper away from him as he closes it to prevent it from catching*

• *Show your little boy how to sit down to put his feet into his pants legs, then stand up to pull them up*

Sliding buckles can be adjusted for the best fit

Choosing fastenings
Until your child has enough dexterity to manage buttons and zippers, you need to choose clothes and shoes with manageable fastenings.

Hooks are easier to manage than buttonholes

Shoes
Velcro fastenings rather than laces or buckles will allow your child to fasten his own shoes very easily.

BATHING AND HYGIENE

WASHING A GIRL

There is no need to open the lips of your baby girl's vulva to clean inside, and you should never try to do so. Just wash the skin of the diaper area and dry it carefully.

When you are washing your baby girl, take care to wipe from front to back – that is, toward the anus – when you clean the nappy area. This will avoid soiling the vulva, and minimize the risk of spreading bacteria from the bowels to the bladder or vagina, which could cause infection.

Part of your daily routine will be to keep your baby clean. Many new parents worry about handling a very small baby in the baby bath, but you will soon get used to bathtimes and look forward to it as an opportunity to have fun and play with your baby. Instead of feeling apprehensive, set aside half an hour, have everything you need around you, try to relax, and you will enjoy it.

A young baby doesn't need bathing very often because only her bottom, face and neck, and skin creases get dirty, so you only have to bathe her every two or three days, and even then you can wash only the dirt-prone parts instead of putting her in the bath (see below). This allows you to wash the parts that really need washing with the minimum of distress to her. Be sure the water you use is just warm to the touch. Avoid hot water, which could scald a baby's delicate skin, and cold water, which may give the baby a chill. Do wash your baby's hair fairly often; it gets dirty from sweat and other sources. A small squeeze of baby soap in the bath water will suffice for newborns; you don't want to leave soap residue on the skin.

Babies don't like having their skin exposed to the air, so you should keep your baby undressed for as short a time as possible. Warm a big, fluffy towel on a radiator (not too hot) and have it ready to wrap your baby in as soon as you are finished.

WASHING A BABY

Face and ears
Using fresh tepid water, moisten a cotton ball and gently wipe your baby's face. Wipe the eyes from the bridge of the nose outward. Clean outside and behind the ears.

Wipe from the inner part of the eye outward

Hands and feet
Clean with water and a new cotton ball, then dry with a towel. For an older baby you can use a washcloth.

BODY CARE

Once you have taken care of your baby's diaper area, and made sure that her skin is kept free from any traces of food or dirt that might cause irritation, the rest will take care of itself.

Eyes, nose, and ears Wash your baby's eyes with a couple of cotton balls and some fresh tepid water. Work from the inner part of the eye to the outer, and use a different cotton ball for each eye to avoid spreading any infection that may be present.

Don't poke around inside your baby's nose and ears; they are self-cleaning, so don't use nose or ear drops, except on your doctor's advice. Just clean ears using moist cotton balls. If you see wax in your baby's ears, don't try to scrape it out; it is a natural secretion of the canal of the outer ear, is antiseptic, and protects the eardrum from dust and grit. Removing it will only cause the ear to produce more. If you are concerned consult your doctor.

Nails Your newborn baby's nails should be kept short; otherwise, she may scratch her skin. The best time to cut them is after a bath, when they are soft; use a pair of small, blunt-ended scissors. If you are nervous about it, bite the nails off; your mouth is so sensitive that you will not hurt her.

Navel During the few days after birth, the umbilical stump (see p.15) dries and shrivels, and then drops off. Give your baby sponge baths before the stump has healed. Allow the area to stay open to the air as much as possible to help speed up the shrinking and healing process.

WASHING A BOY

If your baby is uncircumcised never pull his foreskin back for cleaning; it's tight and could get stuck. Wash the whole of the diaper area and dry carefully, particularly the skin creases. By the time your baby is three or four years of age, the foreskin will be loose and can retract without being forced.

If your baby has just been circumcised, you should watch carefully for any signs of bleeding. A few drops of blood are quite normal; so is swelling and slight inflammation, but this will settle down. If bleeding persists, however, or if there is any sign of infection, consult your baby's doctor. Make sure that you get advice about bathing your baby and special care of the penis, and what to do about the dressing if one has been applied.

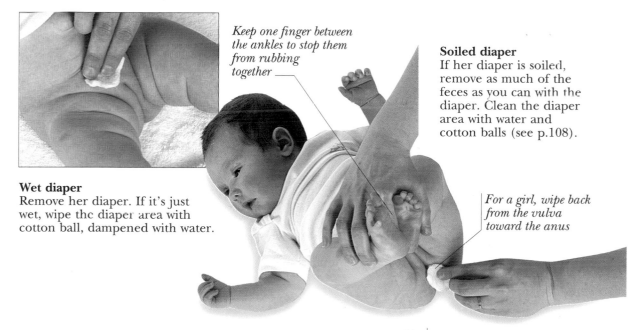

Keep one finger between the ankles to stop them from rubbing together

Soiled diaper
If her diaper is soiled, remove as much of the feces as you can with the diaper. Clean the diaper area with water and cotton balls (see p.108).

Wet diaper
Remove her diaper. If it's just wet, wipe the diaper area with cotton ball, dampened with water.

For a girl, wipe back from the vulva toward the anus

TOILETRIES

A newborn's skin is delicate. You should not use wipes until your baby is at least six weeks old; they remove the natural oils from her skin and can leave it dry and uncomfortable. Special baby toiletries are mild and won't irritate your baby's skin – many are hypoallergenic.

• *A little baby oil in your baby's bath water is a good moisturizer for very dry skin*

• *For delicate skin, like the diaper area, baby lotion makes an ideal moisturizer*

• *Baby powder can be drying to your baby's skin. If you use it, shake it onto your hand first, or it may be inhaled by your baby. Never use powder on the skin creases, where it can cake and cause irritation*

• *A + D ointment and petroleum jelly are waterproof and will protect your baby's skin from urine. Medicated diaper creams containing zinc oxide are good if your baby has diaper rash (see p.111)*

GIVING A SPONGE BATH

If your baby really hates being undressed, or if you are a bit daunted by giving her a bath, the best method is to give her a sponge bath. Hold your baby securely on your lap while removing only the minimum amount of clothing at any time. If you find it difficult to maneuver your baby while she is on your lap, put her on a changing pad and follow the same sponge bath method, taking care to keep one half covered while you wash the other.

SPONGE BATH

Upper body
Sit your baby on a towel on your lap. Undress her top half and wash her front with a sponge or cloth and warm water. Pat her dry. Lean her forward over your arm and wash her back.

Diaper area
Either wash your baby's hair at this stage, or put some clean clothes on her top half and remove her lower clothing and diaper. Clean the diaper area (see p.108).

Use cotton balls and water to clean your baby's diaper area

Lower body
Using the sponge or cloth, wash your baby's legs and feet. Gently pat her skin dry, put on a clean diaper, and dress her.

CARE OF THE HAIR

Wash your baby's hair frequently, with baby shampoo or plain water. After about 12 to 16 weeks, wash your baby's hair with water daily and once or twice a week with baby shampoo. Make sure that you use a tear-free variety of baby shampoo, but nevertheless take care to avoid getting it near her eyes. You can use a "football carry" (see picture, right) for a small baby, or you can sit on the edge of the bath with the baby across your legs, facing you. (She will feel secure this way, particularly if she's scared of the water.) Don't be nervous about the fontanels (see p.17); the membrane that covers them is very tough, and there is no need to scrub the hair, so you can do no harm as long as you are gentle.

Hair washing
Tuck the legs under your armpit. Support the back and cradle the head.

Apply the shampoo or bath lotion to your baby's hair, and gradually work it in until a lather forms. Wait about fifteen seconds before rinsing it off; there is no need to apply it a second time. To rinse the hair, just use a washcloth dipped in warm water to wipe the suds away. Try to remove every trace of soap. When drying your baby's hair, avoid covering her face or she may panic and start to cry. It is best just to use the end of the towel to avoid this.

DISLIKE OF HAIR WASHING

Many babies hate having their hair washed, even if they enjoy having a bath. If this is the case with your baby, it may be best to keep hair washing separate from bathtime; if your child associates the two she may start to fuss about taking baths as well.

The main reason for dislike of hair-washing is that babies hate getting water and soap in their eyes, so try to avoid this as far as you can. Specially designed shields are available that fit around the hairline and prevent water and suds running down your baby's face while you rinse her hair. You may also find that your baby will become less distressed if you hold her in your lap while washing her hair, and use a washcloth to wet and rinse it rather than pouring water over her head.

Never try to force the issue, and never forcibly hold your baby still while you wash her hair. If hairwashing is obviously very distressing for her, give up for two or three weeks before trying again. You can still keep her hair reasonably clean by sponging it to remove any food or dirt, or brushing it out with a soft, damp brush. The hair will probably become greasy after the first few days, but this will not do any harm.

CRADLE CAP

Occasionally, red scaly patches may appear on your baby's scalp. Cradle cap is extremely common, and is not caused by a lack of hygiene or by any shampoo you're using. It usually takes a few months to clear up.

Control cradle cap by gently washing your newborn baby's scalp with a very soft bristle brush and a little baby shampoo dissolved in warm water. You should comb through the hair, even if she has very little. If cradle cap does appear, smear a little baby oil on her scalp at night to soften and loosen the scales, making them easy to wash away the following morning. Don't be tempted to pick them off with your fingernail; that only encourages more scales to form. If the condition persists or spreads, consult your baby's doctor, who may recommend a special shampoo.

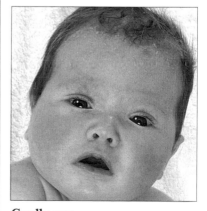

Cradle cap
Scaly patches on a baby's scalp are very common. They are harmless and usually clear up after a few months without any need for special treatment.

BATHING TIPS

Make bathtimes as pleasant as possible for you and your baby.

• *Before you start, make sure that you have everything that you need on hand*

• *Test the temperature of the water with your elbow or the inner side of your wrist*

• *Keep the bath water shallow – about 2–3 inches (5–8 centimeters) is deep enough*

• *Keep the time that your baby is undressed to a minimum; small babies quickly become cold*

• *Wear a waterproof apron to protect your clothing; a plastic-backed toweling one will feel nice against your baby's skin*

• *A hooded towel will make your older baby feel extra snug. Warm it on a radiator first, but don't let it get too hot*

GIVING A BATH

You can bathe your baby in any room that is warm, has no drafts, and has enough space to lay out all that you need. If necessary you can fill the baby's bath in the kitchen or bathroom and then carry it to the chosen room, provided it is not too heavy.

A small baby can be washed in a specially designed plastic baby bath. Place the bath on a worktop or table of a convenient height, usually about hip height, so that you don't have to bend too much. This will protect your back from any unnecessary strain. Some baby baths come complete with their own stands, or are designed to straddle the bathtub or sink, which makes bathing your baby a far more comfortable task.

GIVING YOUR BABY A BATH

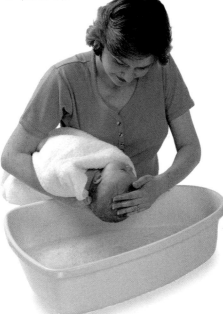

Testing the water
Use your elbow or the inner side of your wrist to test the temperature of the water. It should feel neither very hot nor very cold. Until you get a feel for the right temperature, you could use a bath thermometer, which should register 85°F (29.4°C).

Before the bath
Undress your baby, clean his diaper area (see p.109) and wrap him in a towel. Clean his face and ears gently with moistened cotton balls (see p.90).

Washing his head
Holding your baby in a football carry, as shown, lean over the bath and wash his head. Rinse well and pat dry. A gentle brushing is good for cradle cap.

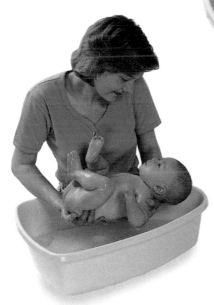

Putting him in the bath
Support your baby's shoulders with one hand, tucking your fingers under his armpit, and support his legs or bottom with the other. Keep smiling and talking to him as you place him in the bath.

Washing
Keep one hand underneath your baby's shoulders so that his head and shoulders are kept out of the water, and use your free hand to wash him.

Lifting him out
When he is clean and well rinsed, lift him gently onto the towel, supporting him as before.

Drying
Wrap your baby in a towel and dry him thoroughly. Don't use powder or cornstarch on the diaper area; it could irritate the delicate skin.

FEAR OF BATHING

Some babies are terrified of having a bath. Should your baby be frightened, don't ever force him to remain in the water; try again after a couple of days, using only a little water in the bath. You can give him sponge baths in the meantime to keep him clean.

If your baby continues to be frightened of water, try to introduce it in a play context. Fill a large bowl and place it in a warm room (not the bathroom). Place a towel next to it, and put some toys into the bowl. Undress your baby and encourage him to play with the toys. If he seems happy doing this, encourage him to paddle in the water, keeping a firm grip on him.

After you've done this a few times, swap the bowl for a baby bath and continue to let your baby play. When he tries to get into the water with the toys, you'll know he's lost his fear of water, but be patient; let him do this a couple of times before you start to wash him in the bath as well as letting him play.

95

OLDER BABY

BATHING AND HYGIENE

SAFETY CHECKLIST

Be very careful when bathing your child – there are several points to remember.

• *Place a nonskid bath mat in the bottom of the bath*

• *Always check the temperature of the water before putting your baby in the bath. Even older babies need considerably cooler bath water than adults use*

• *Turn the taps off tightly before putting your baby in the bath.*

• *Cover the taps with a washcloth so that your baby doesn't scald or hurt herself on the metal*

• *Don't let your baby stand or jump in the water unsupported. A fall, even if he isn't injured, could make him fear bathing*

• *If your child likes toys in the bath, choose light plastic ones with no sharp edges*

• *Don't let out the water while your baby is still in the bath. Many babies find the noise and the sensation of the water disappearing frightening*

• *When you lift your baby out of the bath, make sure that you are standing steadily. Take the strain with your legs, not your back*

• *Make sure you dry your baby well after a bath. Snuggling him in a warm towel can provide a comforting end to bathtime, even for older children*

Between three and six months old your baby will grow too big for a baby bath, so you will have to start using the bathtub. To make the transition easier for your baby, first place the baby bath inside the bathtub. Once he gets used to the big tub, he will probably spend many happy hours there enjoying his favorite toys and splashing in the water.

BATHTIME ROUTINE

Once your baby is mobile, he will get much dirtier than before and baths will become a regular feature of your day. Washing a baby is more awkward in the bathtub than in the baby bath. Spare your back by kneeling next to the bath and make sure that you have everything that you need at hand. Keep the water shallow – no deeper than 4–5 inches (10–13 centimeters) – and use a plastic suction mat on the bottom of the bath to keep the baby from sliding around. Specially made bath rings also give support, but they can tip over, so never leave the baby alone in the tub. Always, always keep a close watch and never leave him alone.

By about six months your baby will feel quite secure in the water and will no longer be scared of being undressed. Try to make bathtimes fun and as trouble-free as possible.

FEAR OF THE BATHTUB

If your child finds the bathtub frightening, you'll have to be patient and let him get used to it gradually. You could try filling the baby bath with water and put a few toys

The "big bath"
Your child will enjoy splashing around, so always use a nonslip mat.

in; then place it inside the bathtub and put a nonslip bath mat next to it. Put your baby in the bathtub where he can play with the toys and climb into the baby bath if he likes. Once he has got used to this, you could also add a couple of inches of water to the bathtub (keep a close watch). Your child can then climb in and out of the baby bath and get used to sitting in the shallow water in the bathtub. You can gradually increase the amount of water that you put in the bathtub; after a while you will probably find that your child doesn't notice whether the baby bath is there or not. If you feel he still needs reassurance, get into the bath with him and play water games with him in your lap.

BATHTIME PLAY

Once your baby is able to sit up, you can give him some extra time in the bath after he's been washed, and let him enjoy splashing and playing with toys. You don't have to provide special toys; sponges, bowls, and cups will keep him entertained. If you have two small children, you could try bathing them together. It will save time for you, and your older child will be able to share games with the baby. Suds are always a great favorite, so you could add bubble bath to the water (not too much, though – it can irritate the vulval area in little girls). Every now and then get into the bath with your baby and have fun together.

BATH TOYS

Your baby will get a great deal of fun out of playing with everyday household objects. Make sure that any bath toys you use are clean and waterproof, unbreakable, without sharp edges, and reasonably light. If you give your baby plastic bottles – for example, old shampoo bottles – make sure that they have been thoroughly washed to remove all traces of their previous contents and remove the lids; your baby will put all these "toys" into his mouth.

Many toys, particularly those made of hard plastic, such as rattles and stacking cups, are also suitable for the bath. If you want to invest in special bath toys, there are lots to choose from. The traditional boats and ducks are always big favorites, but you can also get waterproof books for the older baby, or elaborate activity centers that work when water is poured through them.

Traditional plastic ducks are always popular bathtime toys

Bathtime play
Simple floating toys will give your baby added enjoyment at bathtime.

EARLY DENTAL CARE

As early as possible, encourage your baby to form good habits with a toothbrushing game.

Let him see you brush your teeth so that he can see how it should be done, then offer him a soft toothbrush to play with. He will try to imitate you by putting the brush in his mouth and moving it around. You don't need to see that he's doing it properly; at this stage it's a game to introduce him to the idea of toothbrushing as something he likes. When you really want to clean his teeth, wet a handkerchief and smear on a pea-sized helping of toothpaste, then gently rub it across the gums and any teeth that your baby has. You should clean the gums even if there are no teeth; it gets rid of the bacteria that cause plaque, and gets small children used to the idea of brushing their teeth.

TAKE CARE

However secure your baby may seem playing with his toys, no baby of this age should be left in the bath unwatched, even for the shortest period of time. Also check that the water is not getting too cold; your baby may be distracted from his discomfort by play. Never add hot water while your baby's in the bath, and make sure your water heater is set lower than 120°F (49°C).

BATHING AND HYGIENE

BATHROOM SAFETY

Baths should be carefully super-vised as a child of this age is still at risk from slipping and falling under the water. Although your child is now old enough to sup-port himself in the bath, much of what has already been said about safety still applies (see p.96).

Toddlers are generally eager to start doing things for themselves – washing their own face, for exam-ple – and so there is the added risk that your child may turn on the hot water or grab the soap or shampoo and get it in his eyes. Cover the taps with a towel to soften any falls or bangs.

A child who has previously been happy in the bath may become set against it, especially if he gets frightened. Providing plenty of amusements in the bath and per-haps getting him to share the bath with a sibling can help. Allowing him to share a bath with you will resolve most difficulties.

Your toddler will probably regard bathtime primarily as playtime, and you can take advantage of this in teaching him to wash him-self by making a game of it. Let him have his own special sponge for bathtime and show him how to wash his face first, then his arms and legs, and so on. He won't be able to do a very good job of it yet, so you'll probably have to go over the same areas yourself with a washcloth. Soap your child's hands and show him how to spread the soap over his body and arms; then make a game of rinsing all the suds off.

WASHING ROUTINES

Children are often hungry when they wake up, so it's best to leave washing until after breakfast, when your child will be more willing to stand still to have his face and hands washed, teeth brushed (see p. 97), and hair combed. From the age of about 18 months he can start learning to rinse his hands under running water and, later on, he will learn to soap them, though he may make quite a mess with the soap and water.

CLEANLINESS

The younger you start teaching good hygiene the better. The best way to teach is by example. Wash your hands with your child: get your hands soapy together and wash each other's hands, then inspect each other's hands to see whose are the cleanest. If he finds the washcloth rough, let him use a sponge, which is softer.

Make it clear that hands should always be washed after using the toilet. You should start this at the potty stage (see p.113) and do it with your child every single time. Similarly, make sure your child washes his hands before meals or after handling pets.

Encourage your child to do this for himself. Make sure he can reach the sink and toilet easily by putting a stool in the bathroom for him to use, and make sure that he knows which is the hot tap and which the cold.

HAIR CARE

Your child will probably have a thick head of hair by now, and this will need regular washing to remove everyday grime. Unfortunately there are few children who enjoy this process. You will make life easier for both of you if you keep your child's hair short. You can also make washing as easy as possible for your child by using the following tips to help to reduce the potential for conflict.

• Use a tear-free baby shampoo and get a special halolike shield that will keep the water and suds away from his eyes.

- If your child really hates hair washing, try allowing him some control over it: choosing whether he holds his head back for washing or forward, for example, or holding a sprayer and wetting his own hair.

- You could also offer incentives to be good, such as the promise of a special game or story once hair washing is successfully completed, or even get in the bath yourself and allow your child to "wash" your hair in return for your doing his.

TOOTH CARE

You will have been brushing your baby's teeth from the time that they first appeared (see p.97) and you should continue to do so at least twice a day. Always brush his teeth after the evening meal so that food particles are not left in the mouth overnight. As your child gets older, he will probably want to hold the toothbrush and do it himself. While this should be encouraged, he will not be able to clean his own teeth effectively, and you should always follow up his efforts yourself with a thorough brushing.

When brushing your child's teeth, use a small, soft-bristled brush and a toothpaste containing fluoride. Use only a pea-sized amount of toothpaste, as an excess of fluorine (usually from a range of sources) while your child's teeth are growing can cause fluorosis (discoloration or mottling of the enamel). There are many "fun" flavors of toothpaste available, which may give your child an added incentive to brush his teeth. Sit your child sideways on your knee, holding him securely with one arm, and gently brush the teeth up and down. If he won't keep his head still, try gently resting your free hand on his forehead.

With any luck it will be years before your toddler will need any form of dental treatment. Nonetheless, it is important to get him used to the idea of going to the dentist. Make a point of taking him with you when you go for a checkup. Most dentists are sympathetic to the need to remove any possibility of fear in young patients, and will probably be happy for your child to sit in the "magic" chair and ask him to open his mouth so that his teeth can be checked and counted. At about two years, you can schedule an appointment with a pediatric dentist.

NAILS

Keep your child's fingernails and toenails cut short; it is more hygienic, and helps keep him from scratching himself or others accidentally. Long toenails may also make his shoes uncomfortable. You will probably still find it easiest to cut his nails when they are soft after a bath, and, as children's nails grow very quickly, it is a good idea to incorporate a nail-cutting session into your bath-time ritual once a week. Use blunt-ended scissors, specially designed to be safe for young children, or nail clippers. You will find it easier to restrain your wriggling child if you sit him on your lap. Follow the natural line of his fingernails and do not cut too close to the quick. Toenails should be cut straight across.

PETS AND HYGIENE

You may be concerned about the possible health risks to your toddler in having a pet. However, if you follow a few simple rules of hygiene, you should have no cause for concern, and the rewards to your child will be well worth the effort.

- *Ringworm (see p.101) is a contagious skin condition that can be caught from pets; it is commonly seen in children. If you suspect ringworm, consult your child's doctor promptly*

- *Always try to stop your child from kissing his pet, especially near its nose and mouth*

- *Encourage your child to wash his hands after playing with his pet – especially before touching or eating food*

- *Both fleas and worms are easily avoided by regular use of preventive treatments on the pet*

- *If an infestation occurs, treat it promptly and keep your child away from any pets until the treatment has worked*

BATHING AND HYGIENE

CLEANLINESS IN GIRLS

Many girls are naturally fastidious, and you can take advantage of this in teaching your child to keep herself clean.

• *Encourage good habits in your little girl from an early age by showing her how to wash herself and clean her teeth*

• *Let her brush her own hair; she will prefer it, and it means she can choose her own hairstyle, ribbons, barrettes, or hairband*

• *Let her have her own special washcloth, soap dish, and towel; she will be proud of her own things*

• *Allow her to rub baby lotion into her skin after bathing*

• *Teach her to change her underwear and socks daily*

• *Provide her own laundry basket so that she can discard her own dirty clothes*

By the time a child has reached the age of three years, she will have developed her own views on many aspects of her day-to-day life and will want increasing control over her daily routine. This is often expressed negatively in a reluctance or even refusal to co-operate with mundane tasks such as bathtime and hairbrushing, which are often seen as unwelcome interruptions to more exciting forms of play. The best way to avoid arguments is to turn washing and brushing into a game, or to incorporate a fun element into the task. Allowing your child to take increasing responsibility for carrying out a task, supervised if necessary, or giving her some element of choice about the activity – choosing which comb or which shampoo to use, for example, can make it more interesting and encourage cooperation. The following hints will make the daily routine easier and more enjoyable for both of you:

• Try not to rush your child to complete a task she is trying to manage by herself. It leads to tension and may make her less willing to help next time.

• Don't leave bathtime until last thing before bedtime, or your child may be too tired to enjoy it.

• Encourage interest in toothbrushing by using disclosing tablets once a week. The need to brush away the color is a great way to ensure that your child cleans her teeth really well.

• Make hair washing fun by letting your child see in a mirror all the silly hairstyles she can create from lathered hair.

• Offer the bribe of the use of some "special" grown-up toiletries such as perfumed soap or bubble bath in return for her co-operation at bathtime. (I believe in bribes for young children.)

EXPLAINING ABOUT HYGIENE

By the age of three your child is capable of understanding, reasoning, and comprehending why something is important. If you give her a reason why she shouldn't do something rather than pulling rank, she's likely to desist, and you'll gain her cooperation more readily if you present arguments in favor of certain actions. Explain to your child that if her hands are dirty they are covered in germs that could make her very ill, or that if she has handled the dog she might have germs on her hands that could give her a nasty tummy ache.

Once your child begins to understand the reasons for washing and toothbrushing, you must be consistent. Children are very logical, and if you have persuaded your child that it is essential to

Hair shield
Keep soap and water off your child's face with a specially designed shield.

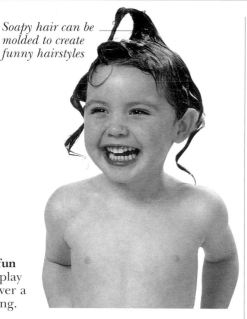

Soapy hair can be molded to create funny hairstyles

Make hair washing fun
Allow your child to play games to help get over a dislike of hair washing.

Boys are sometimes resistant to washing, and you may have to spend a lot of time reminding your son to wash and brush.

- *Make bathtimes as much fun as possible, with toys, games, and lots of suds*

- *Spend some time showing him how to wash, and do this several times if necessary*

- *Try not to be excessively fussy about cleanliness; if he's in the middle of a game, let handwashing wait until he's ready*

- *Let him wash himself as soon as he can make an attempt, then clean him thoroughly yourself at the last moment*

- *Enforce daily change of underpants and socks*

- *Give him his own laundry basket and encourage him to fill it*

wash her hands before meals, and brush her teeth afterward, she will probably question you if you overlook it. At the same time you should try not to be excessively fussy about cleanliness.

CONDITIONS PASSED BETWEEN CHILDREN

As soon as your child starts to socialize with other children, she is at risk from a variety of minor disorders that are commonly passed between children. Don't be unduly upset by these; they are not necessarily a result of poor hygiene, and all can easily be treated. (For more information see **Parasites and insects**, p.296.)

Ringworm A fungal infection affecting the scalp (tinea capitis) or the body (tinea corporis), ringworm appears as small bald areas on the scalp, or round, reddish or gray, scaly patches on the skin. These are usually oval in shape and the edges of the patch remain scaly while the center clears, leaving rings. Consult your child's doctor, as the condition is irritating and contagious.

Nits (head lice) Head lice are passed easily from child to child. The insects are hard to see. Most people first notice the pale, oval eggs (nits) attached to the hair; nits become more apparent as the hair grows. The scalp may be very itchy. Wash the child's hair with a doctor-recommended insecticidal shampoo, cover with a special conditioner available at a pharmacy, and comb with a nit comb. Repeat every two or three days for at least two weeks or until clear.

Pinworms and roundworms Pinworms are the most common form of intestinal worm. They live in the bowel and lay eggs around the anus, causing tickling or itching in the anal region, often at night; this may cause the child to scratch. Roundworms are rare in the U.S. Your child's doctor can prescribe a drug to treat either type.

DENTAL CARE

By the time your child reaches the age of three years, the basic routine of tooth care should be well established (see p.99). Morning and evening toothbrushing sessions need to be carefully supervised by an adult, even though a child of this age will probably be eager to carry out brushing herself. Six-monthly visits to the dentist, to check that the teeth are coming through normally, are also important. These "tooth-counting" sessions are also a good way of letting your child get used to visits to the dentist.

Most people are now aware of the damage caused to teeth by sugar in the diet. Sugary foods produce acids in the mouth that damage the enamel coating of the teeth by removing calcium. Once this has occurred, the tooth is vulnerable to decay and cavities will start to form. While fillings can repair cavities, the tooth is weakened and, if severely affected by decay, may need to be removed. This could endanger the positioning of second teeth.

PREVENTING CAVITIES

A baby eats only those foods offered by parents and caregivers. As she gets older and gains independence, she will begin to express her own food preferences more vigorously and will have increasing opportunities for choosing foods for herself – and sweet foods are often favorites. For this reason good eating habits cannot be started too soon. Above all, try to control your child's intake of sweets. No child needs sugar or candy and you can easily find less damaging treats in the form of fruit and healthy snacks. Explain to your friends and family that you would prefer that they did not give candy or cake to your child.

In the real world, of course, children do receive and eat a certain amount of sugary food. You can limit the damage these do to your child's teeth by incorporating them into mealtimes. Sugary snacks eaten between meals are the most damaging. If your child has eaten something particularly sweet, make sure she brushes her teeth as soon afterward as possible.

Drinking substantial amounts of fruit juice is another common cause of tooth decay, even among children who eat very little candy, so go easy on juices. Eating, or drinking anything other than water, at night after the teeth have been brushed, can cause problems. The acids that cause tooth decay will remain in the mouth, allowing the enamel-damaging process to continue for many hours. If your child is greatly attached to having a bottle at night, give it to her before she goes to sleep, then remove it so she can't drink any more.

Toothbrushing
Give your child a soft toothbrush and encourage her to use it after meals, especially once the molars are through (see p.175).

EATING FOR DENTAL HEALTH

Taking care that your child is eating the right foods is the most important contribution you can make to her dental health.

• *Never let your baby go to sleep with a bottle of juice or milk, as it means your baby's teeth are bathed continuously in sugar and results eventually in "baby bottle mouth" – a mouth of rotten teeth as early as three years old*

• *Giving sweet foods between meals increases the number of times the teeth are exposed to harmful acids, so give them at the end of a meal instead*

• *If you give candy, don't choose sticky caramels, as these remain on the teeth longer*

• *Giving cheese at the end of a meal makes saliva alkaline, and helps counteract the acid that erodes teeth*

• *It is better to give a piece of cake, which can be eaten in a few minutes, than a package of candy that will be eaten all afternoon*

• *Give your child fruit or unsweetened yogurt as treats to avoid encouraging a sweet tooth*

FIRST FILLINGS

If you are lucky, your child will need little or no dental treatment throughout childhood. Your dentist will notice any signs of decay at your regular six-monthly visits, but you should make an extra appointment if you notice any unusual tooth discoloration or if your child complains of pain.

A dentist who is used to treating children will usually have developed techniques for minimizing fear. Great care will be taken to prevent pain with the use of local anesthetic sprays and injections as appropriate.

ACCIDENTS INVOLVING TEETH

The need for dental treatment other than for cavities in the under-fives is rare. An injury to a tooth that damages the nerve can cause it to "die" even if it isn't dislodged. In this case the tooth will become discolored but no other ill effects will follow and it can be safely left in place until it is replaced by the adult tooth. If a tooth is chipped, you should seek the advice of your dentist. If a baby tooth is knocked out altogether, you will need immediate dental advice; take your child to the nearest emergency room, bringing the tooth with you in a container of milk. In some cases the tooth can be replaced in the jaw, depending on the child's age and the position of the tooth.

FLUORIDE

Fluoride is a mineral that has been shown to reduce the incidence of tooth decay by strengthening tooth enamel. It is added to many toothpastes and, in some areas, to the water supply.

* *Fluoride can also be taken by mouth in the form of drops or tablets. Dentists recommend toothpastes containing fluoride for both adults and children*

* *Many dentists would argue that fluoride toothpaste alone does not provide sufficient protection against dental decay*

* *If the water in your area is less than 0.7 parts fluoride per million (you can find this out from your local water authority), your child may benefit from fluoride supplements in tablet form*

* *Always consult your dentist or doctor before giving supplements, and follow his advice carefully*

* *It is important to avoid giving excessive fluoride. This can cause a condition known as fluorosis, in which the adult teeth that are developing become mottled*

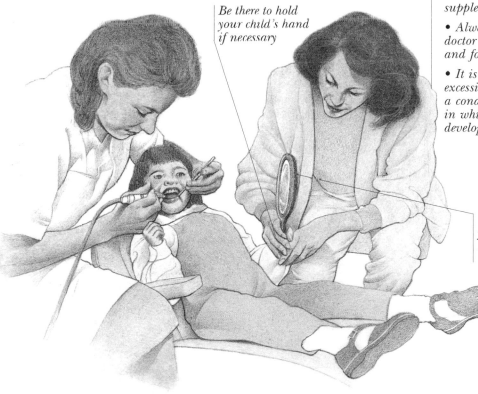

Be there to hold your child's hand if necessary

You may want to give your child a mirror to hold so she can see what the dentist is doing

Visiting the dentist
Always stay with your child during any dental treatment, or even a checkup; the reassurance of your presence is vital.

KIDNEY AND BLADDER FUNCTION

Once food has been absorbed into the bloodstream, waste has to be removed from the blood by the kidneys and eliminated as urine.

Production of urine *Waste chemicals in the blood are removed and dissolved in water by the kidneys. The urine then passes down the ureters and into the bladder.*

Voiding *Urine is temporarily stored in the bladder, which is periodically emptied through the urethra. Your baby will not be aware of passing urine until about 15–18 months (see pp.112–13). The sensation of wanting to pass urine does not come until several months later, because the infant bladder can hold urine for only a few minutes.*

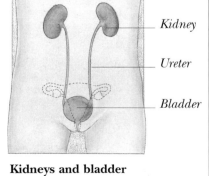

Kidney

Ureter

Bladder

Kidneys and bladder
The urinary and reproductive systems are closely linked; a girl's bladder is next to the uterus.

BOWEL AND BLADDER

A newborn baby can need up to ten diaper changes a day and, although the frequency of changes will decrease, most babies don't achieve any degree of bowel and bladder control until the second year. Although you can't speed up this process, your help and support will be very important to your child.

PASSING URINE

A young baby's bladder will empty itself automatically and frequently both day and night. As soon as it contains a little urine, the bladder wall stretches and the emptying action is stimulated. This is absolutely normal, and your baby cannot be expected to behave differently, at least until the bladder has developed sufficiently to hold urine for longer periods of time.

BOWEL MOVEMENTS

When your baby was in the womb, his intestines were filled with a sticky black substance called meconium. Usually meconium is passed in the first 24 hours after delivery, and once this has happened normal bowel movements will take over.

Once your baby settles into a regular routine, his stools will become firmer and paler. You don't need to pay much attention to them, and you certainly should never become obsessive or worried about them as long as your baby is content and thriving.

The number of stools a baby passes varies greatly, and initially many bottlefed babies pass a stool for every feeding. On the other hand, a breastfed baby may pass only one stool a day or less because there is little waste. The frequency of bowel movements gradually decreases as your baby gets older. It may be that, at the beginning, your baby passes five or six a day, but after three or four weeks he may be having only two movements a day. This is quite normal and should cause you no worry. Similarly, the odd loose, unformed stools or totally green stool are typical of a young baby's bowel movements and are no cause for concern unless unusual looseness persists beyond 24 hours; then seek your doctor's advice.

CHANGES IN BOWEL MOVEMENTS

Don't worry if your baby's stools change in appearance from one day to the next. It is quite normal for a stool to turn green or brown when left exposed to the air. If you are worried, consult your pediatrician, who will be able to advise and reassure you. As a rule, loose stools are not an indication of an infection. Watery stools, however, if accompanied by a sudden change in the color, smell, or frequency of passing stools, should be mentioned to your baby's doctor, especially if your baby seems unwell (see p.276).

Blood-streaked stools are never normal. The cause may be quite minor – a tiny crack in the skin around the anus, perhaps – but you must consult your baby's doctor. Larger amounts of blood, or the appearance of pus or mucus, may indicate an intestinal infection, so contact the doctor immediately.

The breastfed baby By the second day, the light yellow stools typical of the breastfed baby will appear. The stools are rarely hard or smelly and may be no thicker than pea soup. The food you eat will affect your baby and anything very spicy could upset digestion.

The bottlefed baby A baby fed on formula has a tendency to more frequent stools that are firmer, browner, and smellier than those of a breastfed baby. The most common tendency is for the stools to be rather hard. Discuss this problem with your pediatrician if it persists and seems to be causing your baby distress.

DIARRHEA

Diarrhea is a sign of irritation of the intestines resulting in loose, frequent, and watery stools. In small babies it is always potentially dangerous because of the risk of dehydration, which can develop very quickly. If your baby refuses food or has any of the following, contact your pediatrician immediately.

- Repeated watery stools.
- Green and smelly stools.
- A fever of 100°F (38°C) or more.
- Pus or blood in his stools.
- Listlessness with dark-ringed eyes.

If you think your baby is dehydrated, look at his fontanels. If they are depressed, your baby is dehydrated: contact your doctor immediately. If it is treated early, diarrhea can be cured quickly.

You can start treating your baby immediately yourself if his diarrhea is mild and he has no other symptoms. Continue to nurse your baby if you are breastfeeding; diarrhea usually clears up well on breast milk, but formula should be made up at half-strength, with half the regular formula to the usual amount of water. He may eat only small amounts of food, and will therefore be hungry more often. If mild diarrhea doesn't improve within two days, consult your baby's doctor.

When you start reintroducing food after a bout of diarrhea, it is best to start off with small portions of mild, milky ones like gelatin or yogurt; dried cereal with milk; mashed potatoes; white meat and egg yolks. Begin with less than half the normal amount on the first day, and on the second day, half to two-thirds of the usual amount. Drinks of mineral replacement salts formulated specifically for infants (Pedialyte, for example) are advisable at this stage. The drinks should be needed for only 4–12 hours. If all goes well you can return to your usual servings.

BOWEL FUNCTION

Food passes through the stomach into the small intestine, and from there to the large intestine. The waste products of food are stored in the rectum before finally being eliminated as feces.

Digestion The food is broken down by enzymes. Digestion starts in the mouth, then continues in the stomach and the upper part of the small intestine.

Absorption Once the food has been reduced to simple molecules, it is absorbed into the bloodstream as it continues its path through the small intestine. It then passes through the large intestine, where any water is absorbed by the body. The waste products pass on to the rectum as feces.

Elimination Feces are stored in the rectum and expelled through the anus. A baby cannot control the reflex that causes the rectum to empty – even for a second. Young babies generally have bowel movements with each feeding, due to the gastrocolic reflex, which stimulates the rectum to empty every time food enters the stomach.

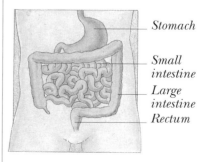

Stomach

Small intestine

Large intestine

Rectum

The bowel system
After food has been digested in the stomach and small intestine, the waste is passed as feces.

GIRLS'
DIAPERS

A girl will tend to wet the diaper at the center, or toward the back if she is lying down.

• *Disposable daytime and night-time diapers are designed differently to take this into account, with the padding at its thickest where it is needed most*

• *You may want to buy decorative or frilly pants to cover cloth diapers; these look pretty under a dress for a special occasion*

DIAPERS

Your first choice in diapers will be between cloth and disposable types. In recent years, the vast majority of parents have opted for disposables, though an increasing consciousness of environmental issues has led many parents to reconsider cloth diapers, which create less waste. Yet the issue is not clear cut: the detergents required to clean cloth diapers can be viewed as pollutants to the water supply, and the energy and water required to wash them might also be regarded as wasteful. While cloth diapers are cheaper than disposables in the long run, you need to consider the increased electricity bills for frequent machine washing, and the cost in your time. Providing that the diaper is changed as frequently as necessary, and that the basic rules of hygiene are observed, your baby will be happy whichever option you choose.

DISPOSABLE DIAPERS

Disposable diapers make diaper changing as simple as it can be. They are easy to put on – no folding, no pins, and no plastic pants – and can be discarded when they are wet or dirty. They are convenient when you're traveling as you need fewer diapers and less space to change in, and you don't have to carry wet, smelly diapers home to be washed. You will need a constant supply, so buy them in large batches.

Never flush disposable diapers down the toilet as they inevitably get stuck. Instead, put the soiled diaper in a strong plastic bag. The bag should be firmly secured at the neck before you throw it out.

CLOTH DIAPERS

Though cloth diapers are more expensive than disposables at first, they work out cheaper in the long run. Cloth diapers involve much more work than disposables because they have to be rinsed, washed thoroughly, rinsed free of detergent, and dried. You will need a minimum of 24 diapers to ensure that you always have enough

DISPOSABLE DIAPERS

Resealable tapes let you check if diaper is clean

Elastic leakage barriers provide extra protection

Elastic at legs gives a good fit with less chance of leaks

Absorbent inner layer has a plastic covering

clean ones, but the more diapers you can buy the less often you'll have to do the wash. When buying cloth diapers, choose the best that you can afford. They'll be good value in the long run because they'll last longer; they'll also be more absorbent, and therefore more comfortable for your baby

Shaped diapers are T-shaped, and have a triple-layered central panel for added absorbency. Their shape means that they are more straightforward to put on, and fit the baby more neatly.

If a diaper service is offered in your area, it could be a practical and time-saving alternative. Even if the cost seems high, the service will save you the trouble and expense of washing and drying the diapers – extra tasks you may not have the energy to cope with when caring for a new baby. Services provide prefolded diapers as well as diaper pails and deodorizers, and they often sell diaper wraps, plastic pants, pins, and clips. Prefolded diapers are the most commonly available. These square diapers have a thicker center panel for extra absorbency. Birdseye diapers are large, thin squares that must be folded to fit the baby. If you want to make your own diapers, toweling squares can be folded in various ways, depending on your baby's size and needs (see p.109). They are more absorbent than most disposables, so they are good at night.

With fabric diapers you may want diaper liners. Liners prevent the diaper from getting badly soiled; they can be lifted out with any feces and flushed away. You will also need at least 12 diaper pins or clips – these have locking heads to protect your baby's skin – and six pairs of plastic pants.

CLOTH DIAPERS

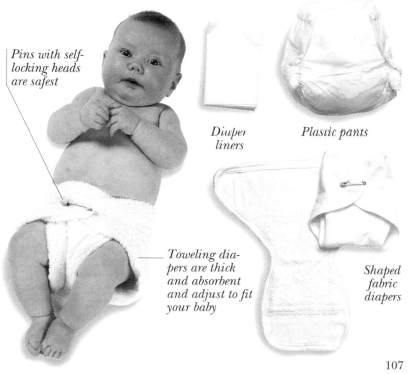

Pins with self-locking heads are safest

Diaper liners

Plastic pants

Toweling diapers are thick and absorbent and adjust to fit your baby

Shaped fabric diapers

BOYS' DIAPERS

Boys tend to wet the front of the diaper, and boys' disposables are designed to handle this, with extra padding toward the front.

• *Fold cloth diapers in such a way that more of the fabric is at the front, particularly at night*

• *Boys often urinate when they are being changed, so cover the penis with a spare clean diaper as you take the soiled one off*

• *Always tuck the penis down when putting on a clean diaper to avoid urine escaping from the top of the diaper*

CLEANING A GIRL

Always wipe your baby girl from front to back, and never clean inside the lips of the vulva.

Remove feces
Clean off as much feces as possible with the front of the soiled diaper.

Remove urine
Use a wet cloth or cotton balls to clean the genitals and surrounding skin.

Clean bottom
Lift up her legs as shown, and wipe from front to back. Dry thoroughly.

CHANGING A DIAPER

Your baby's diaper will need to be changed whenever it is soiled or wet. The number of changes will vary from one baby to the next. As a rule, though, you will probably change the diaper every morning when your baby wakes, before you put him to bed at night, after a bath, and after every feeding, including night feedings.

Changing disposables is straightforward, provided you choose the most appropriate diaper for your baby's size so that it fits him neatly. With cloth diapers you can choose the type of fold that suits you (see opposite page). You may want to use diaper liners, too.

DISPOSABLE DIAPER

Positioning your baby
Lay the diaper flat, with the tabs at the back. Slide the diaper under your baby so that the top aligns with her waist.

Hold the front firmly across the tummy

Fastening the front
Bring the front up between the legs and tuck it around the tummy. Unpeel the tabs.

Unpeel the adhesive tabs and pull over the front

A comfortable fit
Pull the tabs firmly over the front flap and fasten the diaper. It should fit snugly.

FOLDING CLOTH DIAPERS

Triple absorbent fold

This is the most suitable fold for your newborn; its central panel provides good absorbency and it is very small and neat. It is not suitable for larger babies, however. Start with a square diaper folded in four, with the open edges to the top and right.

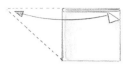

Pick up the top layer by the right-hand edge.

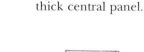

Pull it to the left to form an inverted triangle.

Turn the diaper over so the point is at the top right.

Fold in the middle layers twice to form a thick central panel.

Parallel and kite folds

These are suitable for a larger baby. You can adjust the depth of the kite to suit your baby's size. Both start with a diaper laid out in a diamond shape.

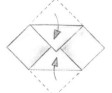

Fold the top and bottom points in to the center.

Pick up the left-hand point and align it to the top edge; do the same with the right.

Fold the sides in to the center to form a kite shape.

Fold the top point down to the center. Fold the bottom point up toward the center, varying the depth to fit.

CLOTH DIAPER

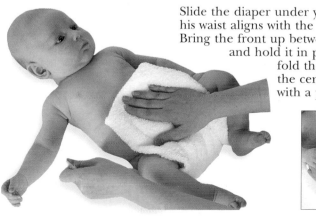

Slide the diaper under your baby so his waist aligns with the top edge. Bring the front up between his legs, and hold it in place while you fold the sides in to the center and fasten with a pin.

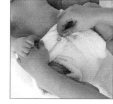

CLEANING A BOY

Boys often pass urine when released from their diaper. A diaper laid over the penis will minimize the mess.

Remove feces

Clean off any feces with oil or lotion and cotton balls, using a different piece for each wipe.

Remove urine

Using cotton balls, work from the leg creases in toward the penis. Never pull back the foreskin.

Clean bottom

Lift his legs to clean his bottom by holding both ankles as shown. Dry thoroughly.

*Washing diapers will take up a
lot of your time, so make life easy
for yourself by being as organized
as you can. The following tips are
designed to make your washing
routine easier.*

• *Rubber gloves or tongs will help
when handling dirty diapers*

• *Gadgets for holding soiled diapers firmly in the water while the
toilet is flushed can be helpful but
make sure the diaper is locked in
place*

• *Don't soak diapers in water
until diaper day – the standing
water is a drowning hazard, even
if your pail has a locking lid*

• *Don't put off doing the diapers
– they can mold or mildew if you
leave them too long*

• *Don't wash anything but diapers in a diaper load. Few baby
clothes can stand up to the hot
water and extra rinsing*

Diaper pail
Look for a pail with a locking
lid; be sure the pail is small
enough for you to lift easily.

DIAPER HYGIENE

It is important to wash diapers thoroughly; any traces of ammonia
will irritate your baby's skin, and fecal bacteria could cause infection. Strong detergents could also irritate your baby's skin, so start
by using soap flakes and test a new detergent with a single diaper
that you use and then isolate. Watch for irritation. If no irritation
develops, you may use that detergent. There is no need to boil diapers unless they are very stained or have become rather gray; just
use hot water for both rinsing and washing.

WASHING ROUTINE

Establishing a routine of washing will make life easier, especially if
you try to wash the diapers in large loads. To do this, of course,
you will need a large supply of diapers – at least 24. You'll use 8–12
diapers a day for a newborn, so two dozen diapers means diaper
washing every two or three days. The more diapers you have, the
less often you have to do the wash.

Choose a diaper pail with a locking lid, and make sure that the
pail is small enough to lift when it is full of wet diapers. Many pails
have a special compartment for a deodorizing disk, a useful feature. Make sure, however, that the disks you use are nontoxic; small
children have been known to eat them because they smell good.
You will also want to use a plastic garbage bag to line the pail.
Diaper services provide deodorizers and bags.

When you change a diaper, put wet diapers in the lined pail.
Shake feces off soiled diapers into the toilet, flush, and put the
diaper in the pail. When you are ready to do the wash, dump the
diapers into the machine and add detergent. (If you are using soap
flakes, they must go in first.) Let machine fill with hot water and
then add bleach if you wish. Bleach makes the diapers whiter, but
it weakens the fabric and may irritate the baby's skin. Test a sample diaper on the baby before using bleach on the whole load.

Run the full cycle and then run the machine again with just hot
water to rinse thoroughly. Diapers should be dried thoroughly in
a tumble dryer. Avoid fabric softeners, since they will make the
cloth less absorbent.

Plastic pants will become hard and unusable if you wash
them in water that is either too hot or too cold. Wash them
in warm water with a little dishwashing liquid, then pat them
dry and let them air before using. If they do become hard,
you can soften them in a tumble dryer with a load of towels.

DIAPER RASH

If urine is left too long in a diaper or on the skin, it is broken down
to ammonia by bacteria from your baby's stools. The ammonia
then irritates and burns the skin, and this is the most common
cause of diaper rash. A mild diaper rash will appear as small red
dots on your baby's bottom, but if it becomes more serious, you
will see an inflamed area of broken skin and possibly pus-filled

spots. The bacteria that produce ammonia dermatitis (diaper rash) thrive in an alkaline medium. Breastfed babies are less prone to diaper rash than bottlefed babies. If you follow the guidelines given (right), you will minimize the possibility of diaper rash. Not all skin conditions occurring in the diaper area are true diaper rash. It is important to identify a rash correctly so that you can take appropriate action.

If, despite your precautions, your baby develops a sore bottom, check the chart below to see if she needs treatment. If not, then continue your preventive measures (except for the use of barrier cream), as well as the following:

• Change your baby's diaper more often.

• Use a disposable pad inside a cloth diaper for extra absorbency at night, especially if your baby sleeps through the night.

• Once your baby has diaper rash it is important that her skin be aired between diaper changes for at least 15–20 minutes.

PREVENTING DIAPER RASH

The essentials are to keep your baby's skin dry and well aired, and to make sure that diapers are always thoroughly washed and well rinsed.

• *Start using a diaper rash cream at the first sign of broken skin. Ones that include zinc oxide are especially good. Stop using plastic pants, too, as they prevent evaporation of urine*

• *Keep your baby's bottom clean and dry, but go easy on soap – it can be drying*

• *Use diaper pads or extra absorbent disposables to keep your baby's skin dry*

• *Make sure all traces of ammonia are removed from the diaper by thorough washing and rinsing*

• *Never leave your baby lying in a wet diaper*

• *Leave your baby's bottom exposed to the air whenever you can*

APPEARANCE OF RASH	CAUSE AND TREATMENT
General redness that starts around the genitals rather than the anus. You will notice a strong smell of ammonia. In severe cases it may spread to the bottom, groin, and thighs, and can lead to ulceration if not attended to.	*Ammonia dermatitis, caused by irritation from ammonia. If the treatment outlined above doesn't work, consult your baby's doctor.*
Small blisters all over the diaper area in addition to a rash elsewhere on the body.	*Heat rash. Stop using plastic pants, and leave your baby's diaper off at every opportunity. Cool your baby down by using lighter clothes and blankets.*
Redness and broken skin in the leg folds.	*Inadequate drying. Dry your baby meticulously and do not use powder or cornstarch.*
Brownish red, scaly rash on the genitals and skin creases and anywhere the skin is oily – the scalp, for instance. Uncommon in diaper area.	*Seborrheic dermatitis. Your baby's doctor will prescribe an ointment for the rash, and perhaps a special lotion if the scalp is affected.*
Spotty rash that starts around the anus and spreads to the buttocks and inner thighs. You may also notice white patches inside your baby's mouth.	*Thrush, caused by a yeast infection. Consult your baby's doctor. She will probably prescribe antifungal treatments.*

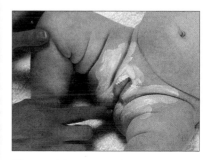

Zinc oxide cream
This protects your baby's skin from the irritant effects of ammonia.

OLDER BABY

BOWEL AND BLADDER

DEVELOPMENT IN GIRLS

Bowel and bladder control usually start earlier and are complete more quickly in girls. The age ranges given are approximate.

Early stages: 1–1 1/2 years

• *A sign that the bladder is maturing is when she gestures or makes a sound to indicate she's aware of passing urine*

• *There's usually no sign of bowel control at this stage*

Middle stages: 1 1/2–2 1/2 years

• *One day, between 15 and 18 months, she may bring the potty to you – and if you're quick you may catch her in time*

• *At about 18 months to two years you may find a stool in the potty after a meal. She may begin to come and tell you when she needs the potty and can wait for it. Once she can wait five minutes or so, try putting her in training pants during the day*

Later stages: 2 1/2–3 1/2 years

• *Girls achieve bowel control very quickly. She's clean day and night with occasional accidents*

• *She's dry all day. Try training pants for the afternoon nap; once she's dry for her nap you can try training pants at night*

• *She stays dry most nights. Bowel control is virtually complete. She*

Once your baby starts taking solids, you will find that he soils his diaper less often. You will continue to see changes in his bowel movements as his digestive system matures, right up to the age of five or six years. After the baby's taken solids for a few months, you may feel it is time he used the potty (see opposite).

CHANGES IN BOWEL MOVEMENTS

In general, you can expect your baby's stools to become firmer and less frequent with age. There are some pretty standard changes at some ages; I give them only to reassure you, not so that you will obsessively examine your child's stools. All dates are approximate.

0–6 months Depending on whether the baby is breast- or bottle-fed the stools are almost as frequent as the feedings, and are very soft. They go through color changes: first greenish black (meconium, see p.104), then yellow, then light brown.

6–12 months After your baby starts on solids the stools become drier, darker in color, and less frequent, say three times a day. Lots of drinks will keep the stools soft.

1–3 years As soon as your child is on the family diet he will probably pass only two stools a day.

3–5 years The stools are identical to adult stools, except in size, and many children pass only one a day.

MALABSORPTION AND CELIAC DISEASE

Malabsorption – impaired uptake of nutrients in the small intestine – can be caused by an enzyme deficiency, or celiac disease. This is an inflammation of the small bowel due to sensitivity to gluten, a substance found in wheat and rye. The inflamed bowel is incapable of absorbing many foods, so your baby can quickly become undernourished. Fortunately, this disease is quite rare.

In most cases of celiac disease symptoms develop before the age of two, although in some children the symptoms are mild and the disease may not be picked up until adulthood. Symptoms may include poor appetite, vomiting, and diarrhea; poor weight gain and growth; and the passing of pale, greasy, foul stools. Other problems, such as anemia, can develop due to deficiencies.

It's extremely important that a baby with celiac disease is properly diagnosed; otherwise, all development could be slowed down. Just as worrisome, many dietary deficiencies will develop, and his resistance to infection will be lowered. If you suspect celiac disease, ask your doctor about it immediately.

Celiac disease can be treated very simply; your baby will have to eat gluten-free foods. There are lots of gluten-free products available and foods cooked with gluten-free flour are delicious – I once attended the birthday party of a celiac child and couldn't tell the difference from the usual party treats.

THE CASE AGAINST "TRAINING"

Children who are allowed to achieve bowel and bladder control at their own pace learn to use the potty very quickly and have few accidents. It's only when parents interfere with their child's steady progress by expecting too much too soon that things go awry. I believe that babies are born wanting to be clean and dry; our job is simply to allow them to achieve this milestone happily.

An overly authoritarian parent can do untold harm, even at an early stage, and may be responsible for problems in later life. Imagine the scenario: an insistent mother is bending over her child, telling him that he can't get off his potty until he's performed. He can't understand what she means, because he is unaware of passing urine or stool – his bladder and nervous system are still too primitive. Even if he did understand he has no "control," as we think of it. He can't figure out why something so natural to him is so important to her. And so he has no idea how to please his normally loving mother. When he gets up the mother gets unusually rough, he can't cope, and he cries. If she goes on like this now he will certainly use her obsession with training as a weapon against her later. He sees his stools as something she wants and he will withold them when he is pitting his will against hers. The answer is to be flexible. At no point should you pressure or scold. Praise every success. Let little boys see their fathers passing urine. Children who are pressured into early training tend to be bedwetters, and more engage in pica (eating nonfood substances) and soiling than those children who develop at their own speed.

INTRODUCING THE POTTY

These are the ways to help your child be dry and clean, but only after he indicates to you by sound or gesture that he knows he's passed urine or stool. Allow him to find his own pace, without any pressure from you.

Step 1 *Start by giving him his own "potty" chair, which is like your toilet. Let him see his mother or his father using the toilet and let him see the results if he asks.*

Step 2 *Let him sit on the potty chair fully clothed while you read a story to him.*

Step 3 *Gradually let him get used to sitting without a diaper.*

Step 4 *When he soils or wets his diaper, sit him gently on the chair after you've cleaned him, while you collect fresh things.*

Step 5 *Once he's interested, let him sit two or three times a day.*

DEVELOPMENT IN BOYS

Boys are generally later than girls in developing bowel and bladder control, and bedwetting is more frequent in boys. The age ranges given are just a rough guide.

Early stages: 1 1/2–2 1/2 years

• *At this stage your little boy has no "control." His immature bladder cannot hold on to urine for even a second*

• *He still can't wait for you to get the potty after signaling that he's letting go of his urine*

Middle stages: 2 1/2–3 1/2 years

• *Your little boy may be able to bring the potty to you only after he can hold on to urine for a minute or two*

• *He'll come and tell you he needs the potty, but will still have frequent accidents*

• *When he's indicated he can wait several minutes and not before, try training pants during the day only*

Later stages: 3 1/2–6 years

• *He may be clean by day, with accidents, but wet at night*

• *He's clean, with accidents, day and night. When he's dry all day, try training pants during his nap, if he still takes one*

• *He's dry all day but needs a diaper at night*

• *He can stay dry through the night with very few accidents*

BOWEL AND BLADDER

AIDING A GIRL

Teach your little girl good habits of hygiene, like washing her hands and tidying the bathroom after her. You'll probably find that she responds well to this.

Girls are generally neater than boys, and will enjoy turning a cleanliness routine into a game: "Now we flush the toilet ... Now we wash the potty ... Now we wash our hands."

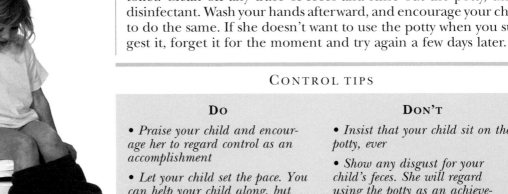

Toilet hygiene
Girls are generally more receptive than boys to being taught good habits of hygiene.

Once your child shows signs of being ready to use the potty, your aim should be to help and encourage her. If you do this, she is likely to achieve control quite quickly and without much trouble, and will remain happy and confident throughout. If you insist on her using the potty before she is ready, or try to force her, she will be unhappy at first at not being able to please you, and then guilty and resentful. Your relationship with your child will suffer and training will become a battle of wills that you can never win.

BOWEL CONTROL

Though a baby is aware first of her bladder emptying, she will probably achieve bowel control first as it's much easier to "hold on" with a full rectum than with a full bladder. You should, therefore, help her use the potty for bowel movements first; this is easier, in any case, because bowel movements are more predictable and take longer than passing urine. When your child indicates that she wants to pass a stool, suggest that she use the potty.

When she's finished, wipe her bottom (front-to-back for girls) then flush the toilet paper and the contents of the potty down the toilet. Clean off any trace of feces and rinse out the potty, using disinfectant. Wash your hands afterward, and encourage your child to do the same. If she doesn't want to use the potty when you suggest it, forget it for the moment and try again a few days later.

CONTROL TIPS

DO	DON'T
• *Praise your child and encourage her to regard control as an accomplishment*	• *Insist that your child sit on the potty, ever*
• *Let your child set the pace. You can help your child along, but you can't speed up the process*	• *Show any disgust for your child's feces. She will regard using the potty as an achievement and will be proud of them*
• *Suggest that your child sit on the potty, but let her decide*	• *Ask your child to wait once she has asked for the potty, even for a moment – she can only "hold on" for a very short time*
• *Let her be as independent as she likes, going to the toilet or using the potty, and praise her independence*	• *Scold mistakes and accidents*
• *Use training pants to give your child a sense of independence*	

BLADDER CONTROL

The first sign that your child's bladder control is developing is when she becomes aware of the passage of urine, and she may try to attract your attention and point to her diaper. As her bladder matures and is able to contain urine for longer, you may find that her diaper is dry after a nap. Once this is happening regularly, you can leave off the diaper during the nap and encourage her to empty her bladder beforehand. When she can do this and can let you know when she wants to use the potty, you can start leaving off diapers completely during the day, provided she is able to wait for a few minutes while you take down her clothes to let her use the potty. When you are out, you might find it useful to carry a portable potty; these come with disposable liners.

At this stage your child can't hold on to a full bladder for any length of time, and accidents are inevitable, so try to take them in stride, and never scold your toddler for them. Just clean up, change her clothing, and say, "Never mind. Better luck next time."

ACHIEVING NIGHT-TIME CONTROL

Control of the bladder during the night is the last to come, as a child of two or three can't hold on to urine for much more than four to five hours. Once your child wakes up regularly with a dry diaper, you can leave off the night-time diaper, but encourage her to empty her bladder before she goes to sleep. It is a good idea to keep a potty beside the bed for your child to use if necessary, but make sure that her nightclothes are easy for her to take down and that you leave a night light on so that she can see what she's doing. Be patient if she comes and asks for your help; its not easy for her to take responsibility for the potty herself. Try this for a week, but if your child has several wet nights, offer her diaper back for a while – otherwise, she will become very tired from disturbed sleep. If she does show signs of becoming more self-reliant, encourage her and boost her confidence. She will still have accidents, so it is a good idea to protect the mattress with a plastic sheet, putting the usual sheet on top. You could also put a small plastic sheet on top of the ordinary one, with a regular sheet over that. The top sheet can then be easily removed after an accident, and the undersheet will be protected by the plastic sheet.

USING THE TOILET

When your child starts to use the potty regularly throughout the day, encourage her to sit on the toilet; this will eliminate the inconvenience of taking a potty with you when you leave the house. Many children are nervous about sitting on the toilet seat because they feel they'll fall off or even fall in. To make your child more secure on the large toilet seat, you can use one of the specially designed child-size seats available that fit inside the rim of the seat. Suggest that she hold onto the sides so she feels balanced. You should also stay nearby until you are quite sure that she is comfortable on the seat. To help her to get up easily, put a small step or box in front of the toilet; she can also use this to reach the sink.

AIDING A BOY

Boys are often messier than girls in using the potty or the toilet, but there are some things that you can do to help.

Boys are more likely than girls to play with their feces. If this happens, don't show disgust; just wash your child's hands calmly, as you would if they were dirty with mud or paint.

Show your little boy how to stand in front of the toilet and teach him to aim at the bowl before he passes any urine. You could put a piece of toilet paper in the bowl for him to aim at. Let him see his father urinating so that he can imitate him.

Potties
Specially molded potties provide support and are suitable for both boys and girls.

BOWEL AND BLADDER

TRAINING PANTS

Before your child's bladder control is fully developed, you may want to use training pants.

• *Disposable training pants have easily tearable side seams so that they can be quickly removed in case of accidents*

• *Both nondisposable and disposable training pants can be left on at night. They are bulky, however, so some children find them uncomfortable.*

Training pants
Your child may prefer training pants to diapers since they seem more grown up.

By the age of three years most children have fairly reliable bladder and bowel control, but accidents will still be common. During the day accidents are most likely to happen when your child ignores the signals of a full bladder because he is engrossed in play or because he is reluctant to use the toilet in an unfamiliar place. You can help by reminding your child to go to the bathroom at regular intervals and by making a point of accompanying him to the bathroom when you visit new surroundings. Encourage your child to go independently in familiar places as soon as possible, but never insist on his going to a strange bathroom alone.

LATE DEVELOPERS

Some children achieve bowel and bladder control later because brain–bladder connections taken longer than average to form, so it is wrong and cruel to blame your child for accidents. Lateness in acquiring control is often hereditary; ask your parents and in-laws about this. If a doctor suspects there may be an underlying cause, including psychological causes, this will be investigated if appropriate. Otherwise no action is generally taken until after the age of three or four for daytime wetting or seven for bedwetting.

ACCIDENTS AND BEDWETTING

If your child wets himself, remember that however badly you feel about the inconvenience, it's likely that his embarrassment is much worse. Reassure him that you know it was an accident and that he hasn't failed you. Being prepared for accidents will help both of you; always carry spare underwear and pants on trips.

Bedwetting at night (see p.115) can happen to a child of any age and is very common in children up to the age of six, boys being especially prone. Most children grow out of it after this age without any special help. You will minimize your child's embarrassment if you keep him in diapers at night until you are confident that he has reached the point where he can stay dry all night. Once you let him go without diapers, be prepared for the occasional accident. Concern about the frequency of bedwetting should not be communicated to your child; it only increases his anxiety. Encourage him instead by giving special praise if he has a dry night.

CONSTIPATION

Should your child's stools become infrequent – that is, less often than once every three or four days – and hard enough to cause discomfort or pain, then he is constipated. Constipation without any other signs of illness is nothing to worry about, but if it causes your child discomfort, consult your doctor. Most doctors don't advise

CONTROL TIPS

DO	DON'T
• *Remind your child to go to the bathroom at regular intervals*	• *Scold or draw attention to any form of accident your child has*
• *Take a spare set of clothes with you when you go out*	• *Withhold fluids from a child in the evening*
• *Accompany your child to the bathroom in unfamiliar places*	• *Compare your child with others of the same age who may have better control*
• *Be sympathetic and make light of any accidents*	• *Make an issue out of any accident in front of friends*
• *Offer praise when your child has a dry night*	• *Be unsympathetic if your child needs to use the toilet at an inconvenient moment*
• *If wetting or soiling occurs after a long period of control, consider emotional stresses. If it persists, consult your child's doctor*	

REGRESSION

Regression to night- or daytime wetting in a child who has been reliably dry for some time is usually a sign of anxiety.

The arrival of a new baby is a typical reason for a child to regress to an earlier stage as a way of winning back attention, but any sort of upset such as a move to a new home or school can cause it. Occasionally regression can be caused by a urinary-tract infection. So when you visit the doctor for any urinary problem, take a sample of your child's urine for testing.

Bowel control, once developed, is usually much more reliable than urinary control. Bowel accidents are uncommon, and if they occur frequently, particularly after control has apparently been reliable for some time, it may indicate an underlying problem such as retention of stool or some form of emotional tension. Seek advice from your pediatrician.

using laxatives or purgatives for a small child. (Constipation is rare in very small babies and can nearly always be corrected by giving your baby drinks of water.) You should never try to treat constipation yourself without first consulting your child's doctor.

Once your child is on a varied diet, he shouldn't suffer from constipation if you are giving him enough fresh fruit, vegetables, and whole-grain breads; if he does, give more of these. The complex carbohydrates in root and green vegetables contain cellulose, which holds water in the stools and makes them more bulky and soft. Oatmeal is also a good source of fiber. A few stewed prunes or dried figs can help too, often producing a soft stool within 24 hours.

Although occasional constipation is not serious, chronic constipation can have implications for your child's health in later life. A child can become chronically constipated for several reasons. If you are a fussy parent and obsessive about the frequency of his bowel movements your child may withhold them as a means of getting attention. A child who has a crack in the skin around the anus may experience pain when trying to pass a stool, and hold on to the stools to prevent it from recurring. Some children retain stools because they are unwilling to use strange bathrooms.

Chronic constipation can also cause a condition called encopresis. Hard stools become impacted in the intestine, and loose, watery stools leak out past the blockage, sometimes causing the condition to be mistaken for diarrhea.

Illness with a high temperature may be followed by a few days of constipation, partly because your child has eaten very little, so there are no waste products to pass, and partly because he has lost water through sweating with the fever. This kind of constipation will correct itself when your child goes back on a normal diet.

NAME *Fanny Hughes*

AGE *32 years*

OBSTETRIC HISTORY *Son, Will, aged 5; normal delivery*

Daughter, Miranda, aged 7 months; normal delivery

PAST MEDICAL HISTORY *Usual childhood diseases*

FAMILY HISTORY *Husband, Chris, aged 35, was late in gaining bladder control and was a bedwetter up to the age of six years*

Fanny had expected Will to be a little late in mastering bowel and bladder control, since she knew boys were often later than girls in accomplishing complete control. She'd also read that the children of late developers are often late in gaining full bladder control, too, and her husband, Chris, had only achieved control well into childhood. She therefore remained very calm and cool when Will was developing control, and never pushed him. Will for his part was very cooperative and eager to please, and was fully toilet trained by three and a half years.

A CASE STUDY

REGRESSION

When Fanny started to grow big with Miranda, Will couldn't understand what was going on. He disowned his baby sister from the start. Fanny did everything she could to reassure him, showing him pictures of babies inside their mother's tummies, letting him feel the baby kick, and involving him in all the preparations. A month before the baby was due, Will started having disturbed sleep, during which he would babble about the baby, but he remembered nothing in the morning. Miranda was born at home. Will sat outside his mother's bedroom transfixed by all the activity but refused to go in and see his new sister. That night he wet the bed, which was something he hadn't done for a full year.

FEELING REJECTED

Chris was very angry with Will for not showing more interest in Miranda, scolded him, and sent him straight to bed. That night, because of all the upheaval in the house, Will did not get his usual bedtime story, and again in the morning the bed was wet. Chris, who was preoccupied with preparing breakfast for everyone and making Fanny comfortable, lost his temper with Will, who stood in the kitchen and wet himself again. "I don't know what we'll do with you," were Chris's last words to Will as he left for work.

Fanny realized that Will would never wet himself unless he was upset. The midwife immediately saw what the problem was when she arrived to find Will crying in the kitchen. She explained to Fanny that Will was suffering from dethronement. Having been the apple of Fanny's eye for five years, he felt knocked off his throne by Miranda, and Fanny would have to make him feel loved and secure again. She also suggested that Fanny ask the pediatrician to test Will's urine just to make sure an infection wasn't the cause of the bedwetting – the test result was negative.

SEEKING ADVICE

Fanny decided to have a heart-to-heart with her mother, who reminded her of a family rule – Dad always carried the new baby so that Mom had her arms free for the other children. She pointed out that Will wouldn't have felt left out if Chris had held the new baby so that Fanny's arms were empty for him. Then he'd have known that Fanny still had time for him and that she loved him. She reminded Fanny that when a new baby was born in their family, the older children always got a present from the new baby, so that they knew they were loved by her, too. She also suggested that on the first night Will should have been allowed to sleep on the couch in Fanny's room, so that he would feel special and included.

By now Fanny felt very guilty that she had taken none of these steps to make Will feel important and secure, and she went to her midwife for advice on how to restore Will's self-confidence. The midwife explained that a child who gets upset, for whatever cause – be it a new baby or starting nursery school – will regress to an earlier phase of development, exactly as Will had done. She pointed out that Will had no control over this and that, far from punishing Will for future accidents, the whole family must be very relaxed and play them down, saying things like: "It doesn't matter, Will. Let me clean you up, and then we can play a game, if you like." But Will was feeling far too insecure for a quick recovery, and the following morning he regressed even further and refused to feed himself: he demanded to be fed.

A PLAN OF ACTION

Fanny and Chris decided to take immediate positive action and, after talking to their midwife and pediatrician, started a program to rebuild Will's confidence.

- They told Will's nursery school teacher about the difficulties at home, and asked all the staff to be sympathetic and praise Will's efforts at every opportunity.

- Chris was to spend half an hour with Will when he came home each evening, when he would give Will his full attention and lots of hugs, and frequently tell Will he loved him.

- Fanny would also give Will half an hour of her time when he got home from school, with lots of hugs and expressions of love, taking a deep interest in his nursery school activities.

- Fanny would have regular sit-down breakfasts with Will, putting Miranda out of sight in her bassinet if possible. She would try not to bring Miranda into the room at these special times unless Will suggested it.

- Fanny would point out to Will all the things that he had mastered that Miranda, a tiny baby, couldn't do, and suggest that perhaps Will could teach Miranda, even protect her.

- Will would have his own private bathtime, and Fanny and Chris would take turns to read him a bedtime story each night.

- Fanny and Chris would alternate taking Will out for a treat on his own each week.

Fanny and Chris put this plan into operation immediately, and within three days Will was feeding himself happily. After a couple of weeks he asked to show Miranda his teddy bear, though he wouldn't let her touch it. He had no more daytime accidents after two weeks, and four weeks later he was staying dry through the night. Reassured by his parents' loving, caring attention, Will became more accepting of Miranda – in fact, three months later Will said that he'd marry Miranda if he couldn't marry Fanny.

NAME *Will Hughes*

AGE *5 years*

OBSTETRIC HISTORY *Normal birth, no complications*

PAST MEDICAL HISTORY *Minor ear infections in third year, cleared up after treatment*

SLEEP AND WAKEFULNESS

EVENINGS OUT

Because young babies are easy to carry and sleep a lot, they're very portable, so you can still enjoy going out by taking your baby with you.

In the early weeks it's a good thing for new parents, especially mothers, to get out of the house and relax with friends. It's easier to do this while your baby is young because she will sleep any- where. A car seat that doubles as a free-standing chair is ideal for this; it can be safely strapped in place in the car, then carried indoors when you reach your des- tination, while your baby sleeps.

Take advantage of this flexibility while you can; once your baby starts sleeping through the night, you will need to stick to a regular bedtime routine.

Sleeping
Ensure your baby is warm and covered, but not too warm (see p.123). A picture of a face will hold his attention.

A newborn baby tends to sleep a lot – unless she is hungry, cold, or uncomfortable, it is likely that she will spend at least 60 percent of her time asleep.

Your baby may fall asleep immediately after – and sometimes dur- ing – a feeding. She will probably be indifferent to noises such as doors shutting or the radio – in fact, she may find droning noises soothing. Babies' sleeping patterns do vary, though, so if your baby is wakeful after a feeding, don't insist that she stay in her crib.

It is important that your baby learn to distinguish between day and night. When it becomes dark outside, close the curtains and turn the lights very low. Make sure she is warm enough, and when she wakes during the night, feed her quickly and quietly without turning the lights up; don't play with her. In time, she'll learn the difference between a day- and a nighttime feeding.

WHERE SHOULD YOUR BABY SLEEP?

You will probably find it easiest to let your baby sleep in something that makes her portable. During the day, a car seat with a carry- ing handle is ideal if you drive. If you don't have a car, a portable bassinet is suitable both day and night since it is easily movable; some types can be attached to a wheeled chassis to become a car- riage. When she outgrows a bassinet she will need a proper crib.

With you Some parents opt to have their newborn sleep with them because night feedings are easier to cope with. It shouldn't be a difficult habit to break after a couple of weeks. If you do sleep with your baby, let her lie between you and your partner so she won't fall out of bed. There is little chance of rolling on top of her, but if you're worried you may prefer not to have her in your bed.

Your baby's bedroom Pay careful attention to the temperature of your baby's room. Babies cannot regulate their body temperatures as well as adults; to maintain the right level of warmth they need a constant temperature and enough blankets or sleeping clothes to keep them warm – but not too warm (see p.123). A night light or dimmer switch will mean that you can check your baby during the night without waking her.

Sleeping outdoors Except when it's chilly your baby will sleep quite happily outdoors, but make sure she's wrapped up and visible at all times and never place her in direct sunlight; choose a shady area or protect her with a canopy. If it is windy, put the hood up on the carriage or bassinet to act as a windbreak. A mesh net will protect her from insects.

Clothing Your newborn will need to be changed often, and while she is sleeping she should wear something that gives you easy access to her diaper. An all-in-one stretch suit or nightdress – one with a drawstring at the end so it doesn't ride up her back – is best.

It is important that your baby does not get too hot or too cold. In warm weather a diaper and an undershirt will be sufficient. In the winter, you can check that your baby is warm enough by touching the back of her neck with your hand. Her skin should feel about the same temperature as yours. If she feels too hot and clammy, dress her in a lighter sleeper or remove a blanket.

PROBLEMS

If your baby wakes you frequently during the night or she cries when you try to go back to bed, you'll be short of sleep and you'll find it difficult to cope. It is essential that you get enough rest and you should share the responsibility of night feedings with your partner – even if you are breastfeeding your partner could bottlefeed your baby with expressed milk on some nights. Alternatively, you can have your partner bring you the baby to feed and then he can change her diaper. If you're exhausted get help from a friend or relative, relax your routine, get up late, and take daytime naps.

Encourage your baby to sleep at night by tiring her out in the day with plenty of stimulation: talk to her, pick her up, and give her lots of different things to look at. If she wakes up a lot in the night because she is wet, use double diapers or diaper liners, and if she cries when you leave her, don't immediately return and pick her up. Rocking her cot, removing a blanket, or changing her position may be sufficient.

Early on swaddling or wrapping your baby in a shawl or blanket may help her sleep; the sensation of being tightly enclosed gives babies a great feeling of security. It is also a useful way of calming a distressed baby.

SWADDLING

To swaddle your baby, you need a shawl or small blanket. Fold the shawl in half to form a triangle and lay your baby on it, aligning her head with the longest edge. Then fold one point of the shawl across your baby and tuck it firmly behind her back. Do the same with the other point. Tuck the bottom of the shawl back underneath your baby's feet to keep them covered. The close wrapping holds your baby's arms in a comfortable position that feels safe and secure and may also help her sleep longer. If her limbs move while she is asleep, she is less likely to wake if swaddled.

Not all babies like swaddling and if yours doesn't, don't worry. It is safe to swaddle your baby in cold weather, but keep a check on her temperature by touching her skin. Unwrap her right away if she feels or looks too hot.

SETTLING YOUR BABY

Here are several things you can do to ensure that your baby settles down to sleep.

• *In the first month or so, wrap or swaddle your baby (see below) before you put her down*

• *Give your baby a comfort suck from breast or bottle*

• *Darken the room at night*

• *In cold weather put a hot-water bottle in the crib for a short time before you put your baby down – but never leave it in the crib*

• *Hang a musical mobile over the crib to soothe your baby*

• *If she doesn't seem to be settling down, rock her gently or stroke her back or limbs to soothe her*

• *Try carrying her around in a sling and jogging her up and down: your closeness and heartbeat will help her settle down*

121

By following these guidelines you will significantly reduce your baby's risk of crib death.

• *Always place your baby on his back or side to sleep*

• *Don't smoke, don't allow anyone in your house to smoke, and avoid smoky places*

• *When covering your baby, allow for room temperature – the higher the temperature, the fewer blankets and bedclothes your baby needs, and vice versa (see chart opposite)*

• *Avoid swaddling and tucking in so your baby can throw off bedclothes if hot*

• *If you think your baby is unwell, don't hesitate to contact your doctor*

• *If your baby has a fever don't increase the wrapping – reduce it so he can lose heat*

Protecting your baby
The most important thing you can do is put your baby to sleep on his back or side. You should also, make sure that he is not too warm.

PREVENTING CRIB DEATH

Sudden Infant Death Syndrome (SIDS), which is known colloquially as crib death, is the sudden and unexpected death of a baby for no obvious reason. It is estimated that about 5,000 babies die each year in the U.S. from SIDS. This has decreased from nearly 7,000 a decade ago.

The causes of crib death are unknown, and there is therefore no advice that can guarantee its prevention. There are, however, ways in which parents can vastly reduce the risk. Recent surveys have proved that immunization helps decrease the risk, as does keeping your baby in your room with you at night for the first six months. Falling asleep with your baby on the sofa greatly increases the risk.

SLEEPING POSITION

One of the most crucial risk factors is the position in which you put your baby down to sleep. In most countries, babies have traditionally slept on their backs. In the U.S. as well, most babies slept on their backs until the 1960s, and the number of crib deaths was low. In 1970, however, special-care baby units started to lay preterm babies face down because it seemed this position improved breathing and reduced vomiting, and eventually the practice was extended to full-term babies.

The significance of sleeping position in relation to SIDS was looked at in 1965, but the evidence was not convincing and it was not until 1986, when SIDS rates in different communities were compared, that it became clear that SIDS was less common where babies slept on their backs.

Quite by chance, when my first son was born in 1972, I avoided this risk by laying him down on his side, thinking that if he wanted to suck his thumb it would be easier for him to do so, and I kept him there with small soft pillows placed in front and behind him. Research in New Zealand since then has shown fewer crib deaths in babies placed on their sides, but without support they can roll onto their tummies. The safest position for your baby, therefore, is on his back. Some people will tell you that this position may allow inhalation of spit-up, but there is no evidence to support this.

SMOKING

A mother who smokes during pregnancy increases the risk of SIDS. (She also increases the risk of a premature or low birth-weight baby.) The risk is twice as great as for babies born to nonsmokers if the mother smokes after birth, and three times as great if she smoked during pregnancy and continues after giving birth. What's more, the risk increases with the number of cigarettes smoked, as well as when both parents smoke. Parents who smoke should quit – for their own health and that of their child.

TEMPERATURE

There's no doubt that overheating from too many night clothes, too many blankets, and too high a room temperature is a contributory factor, as SIDS is much more common in overheated babies. (The risk of overheating alone, however, is less than that from sleeping position and smoking.) Two-thirds of crib deaths occur in winter, when babies may be wrapped up too warmly.

Many parents increase the amount of bedding when a baby is unwell, but this is not what your baby needs. High temperature plus infection in babies over ten weeks old greatly increases the risk of crib death. If heat loss is prevented, the body temperature of a restless baby with an infection will rise by at least 1°C per hour. A baby loses most heat from its face, chest, and abdomen, so lying on the back allows body temperature to be better controlled.

Baby nests, sheepskins, quilts, and comforters are all heat insulators, and should not be used for young babies, because they prevent heat loss. You need not keep your baby's room warmer than the rest of your house; just make sure your baby has enough covering (see below). If you do have a separate heater in the nursery, use a thermostatically controlled one that will switch off if the room gets too warm and switch back on again as it cools down.

CONTINUING RESEARCH

To date, research has enabled the medical profession to identify the risk factors and educate parents and caregivers, leading to a very encouraging decrease in crib deaths. The causes, however, are still not understood. Current areas of research include the development of a baby's temperature control mechanisms and respiratory system in the first six months, and the recent discovery that an inherited enzyme deficiency may be responsible for about 1 percent of crib deaths. Two-thirds of crib deaths occur in winter.

60°F (15°C)   65°F (18°C)   70°F (21°C)   75°F (24°C)   80°F (27°C)

sheet and 4 blankets

sheet and 3 blankets

sheet and 2 blankets

sheet and 1 blanket

sheet

GETTING HELP

The unexpected death of an infant is a particularly painful bereavement, but support is available to help parents cope with their feelings of grief, bewilderment, and guilt (see Useful addresses, p.344–45).

• *Many parents seek help immediately after the death – sometimes within hours – and telephone support lines are available that can provide information and a sympathetic listener*

• *In the longer term, parents may seek professional help. The continued support of a visiting nurse, social worker, or religious adviser can be invaluable, so don't be afraid to ask*

• *Parents may be helped by being able to talk to someone who has been through a similar experience, either in support groups or on a one-to-one basis*

• *Support networks exist in some areas that continue long after professional help may have ceased, and these can be invaluable at times of particular grief, such as the anniversaries of the baby's birth and death*

• *Parents who have lost one baby through crib death are likely to be extremely anxious when another baby is born. Support networks exist that involve the parents and health care team in making sure the new baby receives the best possible care*

Controlling the temperature
Keep a thermometer in your baby's room so that you can see how much covering he needs. At 65°F (18°C), a sheet and 3 blankets is adequate.

SLEEP AND WAKEFULNESS

CAUSES OF WAKEFULNESS

Here are some of the things you can do if your baby is wakeful through the night.

• *Make sure that your baby is neither too hot nor too cold (see p.123)*

• *Check that your baby isn't in any discomfort from a soiled diaper or diaper rash*

• *Don't keep popping into your baby's room to see if he's asleep*

• *If your baby suddenly becomes sleepless, think about the possible causes, such as a change in routine, someone new staying with you, or your going out to work. Whatever the cause, he will need lots of your attention*

Restlessness
Put mirrors and noise-making toys on the side of the crib to amuse your restless baby.

Babies usually establish their sleep patterns within the first few months, and if you find that yours sleeps a lot in his first year, he will probably do the same in his second. At some time in the first 12 weeks he'll sleep through the night (though with some babies it can be much later), and once he starts to crawl he'll be using up so much energy during the day that he may sleep for 10 or 11 hours uninterruptedly. Even though he needs sleep, however, he's able to keep himself awake so that he can stay in your company. He may whimper and cry, become hot and bothered, and then so tense and unhappy that sleep becomes impossible. If your baby is clingy and sleepless and appears to be insecure, the best treatment for him is you. Stay with him, hold him close to you, rock him, sing to him, soothe him, and walk up and down with him until he feels that you are not going to leave him and is reassured by your closeness. This should only take about 10 minutes. If he rouses and whimpers when you put him back in his crib, wait a few minutes – he may settle himself to sleep.

WAKEFUL BABIES

There's no question that some babies need very little sleep. Wakeful babies, as I like to call them, are usually bright, curious, intelligent, and very affectionate. They quickly latch on to the fact that you're there all through the night and that they can attract your attention with crying or calling out to you. I firmly believe that no baby's crying should be ignored. A baby who is left to cry quickly learns that adults don't respond to his cries for help and love. He will stop asking for attention and may become solitary and withdrawn. Try not to get upset because your baby is wakeful; he's demonstrating his sociability and intelligence because he's learning all the time, and you'll find as he grows up that he's a very rewarding friend.

Solutions If your baby wakes before your bedtime, try carrying him around in a sling or put him in a baby bouncer so he can tire himself out. Wakeful babies very often need diversion, so as soon as your baby can sit up, leave some favorite soft toys or soft books in the crib. Put a mirror on the side of the crib so that he can look in it and talk to himself. A mobile above the crib that makes sounds can fascinate your baby for quite a long time, too.

I had two wakeful babies and I had to resort to extreme measures to get any sleep myself. I erected a camp bed alongside my baby's crib, and when he woke up in the middle of the night I would soothe him so that he went back to sleep without really waking up. This prevented him from getting upset with a crying bout.

If your baby only whimpers, don't get up immediately because he may go back to sleep without any soothing at all. If, however, the whimper becomes true crying and lasts more than a few minutes, you should go to him. The first time you go in, try soothing talk while patting him on the back. If this doesn't work, pick him up to soothe him, then put him back in his crib and leave the room. If he continues to cry, you may decide to go back every five minutes to calm your baby down. If you do, try to soothe your baby without lifting him up – say by rocking the crib or talking to him.

BEDTIME ROUTINES

As your baby gets older, he'll require more of your attention at bedtime and probably will have settled into some routine that he needs in order to sleep, such as a story, a song, or some kind of gentle game. Do everything you can to make your baby calm, tranquil, and happy before sleep. If necessary, forgo a scolding for a minor misdemeanor; you don't want your child to face bedtime feeling tearful and upset.

There's nothing magical about bedrooms or cribs. You are your child's favorite playmate, and he will be happiest if he goes to sleep in your company. If you have the energy, let him run around you until he actually drops asleep at your feet, curl up in the chair next to you, or put a pillow on your knee on the sofa and let him go to sleep with his head resting in your lap. As soon as he's asleep, you can take him to his crib; instead of a lonely child upstairs becoming upset and calling out to you, you'll have a secure, calm child who in all probability will sleep through the night.

Comfort habits Your child may become attached to a comfort item of some sort: a doll, a small handkerchief, or a tiny piece of torn blanket. Whatever it is, don't try to take it from your child and don't try to change it. You may also find that habits such as rocking, thumb-sucking, twisting his hair, or rubbing his top lip will become part of his bedtime routine. There's nothing wrong with any of these bedtime rituals. By using a comfort object to help him go to sleep, your baby is using his inner resources and becoming self-reliant. He will give up these habits in his own good time.

HOW NAPS CHANGE

Some babies sleep through the night from early on, some do not. As a rule, the more mobile your baby is and the more energy he uses, the more soundly he sleeps – sleep being divided between daytime naps and nighttime.

When your baby grows, night sleep usually becomes unbroken and naps are fairly regular – one in the morning and one in the afternoon for varying lengths of time.

Later, your baby's nap times will change: he may put off his morning nap until after lunch, and then need another nap at around 3:30 or 4:00 P.M. before sleeping for the night at around 7:00 P.M. Every day may be different.

Whatever time your baby is disposed to nap, take the lead from him; don't try to impose nap times on him. And try to clear your time so that you are able to take a nap with your baby; both of you will be recharged when you wake up.

Security objects
Your child may use a comfort object such as a soft toy or blanket to help him sleep. This is quite normal, so don't try to take it away from him.

Cotton under shirt

Fabric book

Silk hankerchief

Soft cotton blanket

Fleecy fabric rattle

TODDLER

SLEEP AND WAKEFULNESS

AWAY FROM HOME

It's quite reasonable for your child to be scared or refuse to get into a strange bed – when she goes to stay with friends or grandparents or when you go away on vacation.

• *Make the new bed into a playground: put lots of toys on the bed so that she associates it with pleasant activities*

• *Show your child that you are in easy reach. Get her to call out and then answer her back so she knows you are close by*

• *If she gets scared and refuses to use the bed, don't ridicule her, don't force her into bed, don't leave her alone, and don't lock the door – all of which will make things worse*

• *Try telling her that because she is being so grown-up in using a new bed she can have a treat, such as a new bedtime story or ten minutes' sitting on your knee watching television*

Many two-year-olds periodically wake up during the night. If your child is one of them, this may be distressing for you and your partner, but it is both usual and normal, and you should never deny your child love, comfort, and affection. There may be some obvious problem, but often you won't be able to find out a reason for your child's waking up. It could just be that she's a bit afraid of the dark, but she cannot explain to you what is wrong, nor can you reassure her with words. You have to comfort with actions, so give lots of kisses and hugs to show your child that she is loved.

Daytime napping As your child gets older, you will find she doesn't necessarily want to sleep at nap time, but she does need a rest. Try to make a routine out of nap time whether your child sleeps or not by, say, playing some music or reading. You may find your child goes to sleep at nap time if you allow her to sleep in your bed as an occasional special treat or if you give her some idea of how long nap time will be; one way of doing this is to put on her favorite tape and say that nap time isn't over until the tape is finished.

CRIB TO BED

When your child is strong and well coordinated enough to climb out of her crib and come into your room, it is time for her to start using a bed. Most children will be pleased and excited with their new bed, but if your child seems nervous, there are things you can do to help (see pp.128–29); the simplest is to let her take naps in the bed until she's ready to sleep in it at night. If you're worried that your child might fall out of the bed, install a guardrail on one or both sides as appropriate.

Naps
During the day, watch your child for signs of bad temper or fretfulness. Ensure that she rests or plays a quiet game.

126

PLEASANT BEDTIMES

From the age of three onward, your child may well use delaying tactics to put off going to bed. The way you handle this situation really depends on how much energy you have at the end of the day and what your previous bedtime routine has been.

If you have been looking after your child and managing household tasks all day, you'll be in need of private time and you may feel that you can insist on her going to bed. If you have been out at work all day, however, you will want to see your child, so you may feel very sympathetic to her pleas for your attention.

If you've always had quite a strict bedtime routine and your child suddenly departs from this, it's probably best for both of you if you firmly reinstitute the bedtime with loving fairness. If, on the other hand, you've been flexible about bedtimes, it's probably as well for your child's happiness and your serenity to let her stay with you and make herself comfortable. She will be asleep in a few minutes if she has the reassurance of your presence in the room.

KEEPING BEDTIME PEACEFUL

I'm convinced that bedtimes should be happy times, and with my own children I was always prepared to make concessions to this principle. I would do anything to avoid having my children going to bed unhappy. I would do my utmost to prevent any crying, and whereas during the day I might punish a small misdemeanor, it would go unremarked at night to make sure my child didn't go to sleep with the sound of an angry parent's voice in his ears.

If you have more than one child, let them enjoy their bedtimes in the same bedroom. Company is reassuring, and seeing a sister or brother in pajamas at the same time as her makes a child feel that bedtimes are fair, even if your older child is allowed to stay up slightly later. Until they get to an age where they require their own privacy, it's a good idea for children to share a bedroom.

FEAR OF THE DARK

As your child gets older and her imagination becomes more fertile, it's very easy to imagine frightening things in the shadows. A fear of the dark is entirely normal – even adults retain it. Leave a night light on in the room or leave a light on outside with a dimmer switch so your child can see her way to the bathroom if she needs it, or to your room if she's frightened. (If you use a night light, make sure it doesn't cast frightening shadows.) Never insist on her bedroom being completely dark, and never ridicule her fear; it's really a sign that your child is growing up and learning about the world around her. Tell her that if she wakes up in the night and is frightened, she can always come to you for a hug.

PRIVACY

You can teach your child to stay within her own space as early as two years, but certainly by three when she is open to reason. She'll learn that it's her responsibility not to disturb you thoughtlessly just because she feels like it.

Teaching her to respect your privacy is far better than shutting her out of your room, which you should never do. You can encourage mature behavior by providing her with her own private space, which is hers alone, in which her belongings reside and where she can find her favorite things. Children respond very quickly to the idea of privacy, particularly if they are given a private space of their own that they can tidy up, be proud of, and go to if they want to be quiet and play on their own.

You can affirm this sense of privacy by always pointing out to your child that certain things belong to her: this is her book, her toy, her dress, and they all have a proper place. In this way, she will become familiar with her belongings and where she can find them. By about the age of four, she's mature enough to realize that if she has her things, you have yours and that just as she doesn't like her possessions being disturbed, neither do you.

NAME   *Rachel Freiman*

AGE   *28 years*

MEDICAL
HISTORY   *Nothing abnormal*

OBSTETRIC
HISTORY   *One child, Hella, aged three years. Three months pregnant with second child*

There are several ways to lure a child from a crib to a bed, but the least tearful always involve a bit of preparation, so it's best to plan a few months in advance. Rachel and her husband Zak decided to move three-year-old Hella into a bed when Rachel was three months pregnant with their second child, and their decision was influenced as much by the need for extra space as by Hella's age.

CRIB TO BED

Rachel and Zak didn't think it was practical to have Hella in the small nursery with the new baby, nor did they want her to feel resentful that she was being pushed out of her own bedroom to make way for a new arrival. They decided to make the switch at the same time – a new bedroom and a new bed – before the baby arrived, so there seemed nothing unnatural about it. "With hindsight," says Rachel, "it may have been too much of a change all at once, because although Hella was excited about her new room, it was still an unfamiliar environment, which meant she was less settled at night."

Rachel and Zak involved Hella as much as possible, letting her choose the colors for her new room, and taking her shopping to buy her choice of Minnie Mouse comforter – a clever way of exciting her about her new bed. If you don't really need new bed clothes, it's just as effective to get your child a new toy – a teddy bear or a doll – that "lives" in the bed. This will make her feel secure.

LITTLE BY LITTLE

Rachel and Zak allowed Hella a few practice runs in her bed, which is a good idea. "As a treat," says Zak, "we would hide a little toy under the comforter and let her find it. Two weeks before we planned to move her in, we started letting her take her naps there – a good tip that Rachel picked up at a toddler playgroup. Because Hella had the naps during the day, she got used to her bed without the complication of night-time fears.

"I think it was a good idea to do this gradually, because children can have fears that adults never imagine. One of the new things we bought to go in Hella's room, for instance, was a Mickey Mouse alarm clock, to go with her comforter. On the second night in her new bed, we heard her crying and rushed into her room. She was obviously terrified and said there was a man there. We assured her there wasn't, but she insisted she could hear his footsteps quite clearly. Luckily, Rachel took her seriously and figured out it was the rather loud ticking of the alarm clock she could hear!"

Even though Rachel and Zak took the clock away, Hella refused to spend the rest of the night in her room. The night after was better, although there were several occasions during the following two weeks when she wet the bed. This seems to have been part of the adjustment process, as she hasn't done it since.

"It's difficult to see it from a child's point of view," explains Zak, "but I suppose it must be quite frightening to be put in a big bed in a new room. At first I thought Rachel was being pedantic when she said we should prepare Hella for the move, but in the light of experience I realize she was quite right."

WHEN IS THE RIGHT TIME?

There are no hard and fast rules for deciding when the time is right to make the switch. In general, it is between the age of two and a half to three and a half years, although this depends substantially on your child's temperament and your own personal circumstances; like Rachel and Zak, you may have little choice, or alternatively, your child might clearly outgrow her crib and refuse to stay in it. A child who can climb out of her crib can cause herself harm, and it is safer to put her in a low bed than run the risk of her toppling off the edge of a high crib.

Bear in mind that once your child is in a bed, she will be able to get out and investigate the nooks and crannies of her room when she wakes up in the morning. This means it is advisable to reassess safety measures to make sure that an unsupervised child won't come to any harm.

If, like Rachel and Zak, you are expecting another baby, don't move your first child out of her room or crib when the new baby arrives, as this will obviously fuel jealousy. As with everything else, it's best to give your child time to adapt to a new idea and involve her in the preparations wherever possible.

Unless you have to move your child, there is little point in trying to force the issue. While some children want to get out of their crib as soon as possible, others need a little more time and a bit more persuading. If all else fails, entice your child into bed by getting into it yourself – children are usually curious about what their parents are doing and will quickly imitate them.

MAKING A SMOOTH TRANSITION

Help your child make the switch to a big bed by recreating a secure environment like the one she had in her crib. If your child is scared or unsettled, she won't sleep, and that means you won't either, so it's worth preparing your child for the move. Start off, as Rachel and Zak did, by making it a positive and exciting change.

Tell your child that now she's a big girl, she's very lucky to get to sleep in a big bed, "like Mommy and Daddy do." Put lots of her favorite toys there and consider installing a night light or just leaving the bedroom door open so she can see the hall light. If music helps to soothe her, play some while she goes to sleep.

Once you have put your child to bed, don't make the mistake of disappearing suddenly, as this will unsettle her and you might find yourself back at square one. Instead, make sure she is comfortable: sing songs or read a story, leave a drink by the bed, then say goodbye more than once without closing the door so that she knows you are still there.

If your child is not changing rooms, put the new bed into the nursery for a few months before making the switch, so that it's familiar. Some children are scared they will fall out of their new bed because there is no barrier. If this is a problem, make a temporary barrier by lining up a few chairs next to the bed or putting a row of cushions between your child and the edge of the bed.

NAME *Hella Freiman*

AGE *3 years*

MEDICAL HISTORY *Minor childhood ailments. Bowel and bladder control now almost complete, wears training pants at night*

CRYING AND COMFORTING

WHAT TO DO

It is often not possible to know why a young baby is crying, so trial and error may be best.

• *Hold your baby as you try to discover why she's crying*

• *She may be hungry; if so try feeding her*

• *Check her diaper and, if necessary, change it*

• *She may be tired; try to soothe her to sleep*

• *She may be ill or in pain. If so, deal with it either with at-home measures or by calling the doctor*

All babies cry quite a lot and so will yours, so be prepared for it. There will be times when the reason for her crying is obvious: she's hungry, too hot, too cold, bored, uncomfortable because of a wet or a dirty diaper, or she might simply want your affection and closeness. One reason for crying that parents often fail to recognize is the desire for sleep. I well remember trying to console my newborn son in all kinds of ways before it occurred to me that he just wanted to be left alone to sleep.

Very young babies cry when they are disturbed, when they are roughly handled, such as at bathtimes, or when they get a shock, perhaps from feeling that they are going to be dropped, from a loud noise, or from a bright light. Most two-week-old babies respond to the security of being firmly wrapped in a blanket or held in strong, confident arms. Once you have investigated your baby's crying, don't worry too much about it – crying is practically her only way of communicating.

Recognizing different cries Within a few months, you will be able to distinguish between the different cries that mean your baby is hungry, is restless because she is bored, wants to be put down to sleep, or wants a hug. Of course, your baby is learning about you, too, and how to communicate with you. She cries out of need and you respond by giving her what she wants.

RESPONDING TO YOUR BABY

I believe you should respond quite quickly to your baby's cry. If you don't respond, your baby feels as you would if you were ignored in a conversation. There's quite a lot of research to show that your baby is affected by how you respond to crying. For instance, mothers who respond quickly to crying tend to have children with more advanced communication skills, including speaking and outgoing behavior. Babies who are ignored may cry more often and for longer in the first year than babies who are attended to quickly. It seems that parents cause their babies to settle into a pattern of crying often and persistently because they fail to respond, and a vicious circle is set up in which the baby cries, the parent fails to respond, the baby cries more, and the parent is even less inclined to act. A sensitive response from

Communication
Your baby can make his needs known only by crying, so always respond.

you promotes self-confidence and self-esteem in later life. Some parents are tempted not to respond, believing that it will spoil their babies. A baby has a limitless capacity for soaking up love, so there's no way you can spoil her with excess attention in her first year.

CRYING SPELLS

Most babies have crying spells. Often crying occurs in the late afternoon or early evening, when your baby may cry for as long as half an hour. If your baby has colic (see p.133), evening crying spells can last up to two hours. At one time it was believed that a child required this exercise to help develop healthy lungs and therefore felt they could leave their babies to cry. This is nonsense; you should always try to console your baby during a crying spell.

Once your child establishes a pattern of crying spells, they may go on for several weeks. It's understandable – it's your baby's way of becoming adjusted to being in a very different world from that experienced inside the uterus. The more sensitively you respond to her and take your lead from her, the more rapidly she will become acclimatized to her new lifestyle; the sooner you accommodate her likes and dislikes, the sooner crying spells will stop.

NIGHT-TIME CRYING

There is no doubt that every parent finds crying spells difficult to cope with, especially if they occur during the night. Don't get frustrated because your child doesn't respond to your attempts to soothe her. If walking up and down, singing songs, wrapping, or swaddling just don't seem to work, you could take her for a short drive; the gentle swaying motion of a car may send her to sleep.

During the night, crying will almost certainly make you feel impatient at the least, and at the worst, that you will do anything to stop your baby from crying. These feelings are normal, so don't become frightened and tense, otherwise the crying will simply get worse. If, however, your baby's crying during the night – or any time, for that matter – drives you to thoughts of harming her, that is a sign that you need emotional support. Talk with your pediatrician or other trusted professional before you reach a breaking point.

WHY DOES MY BABY CRY SO MUCH?

There is research that shows that a child may cry despite the best efforts to console her, regardless of whether or not she feels any discomfort. For instance, babies of mothers who have a general anesthetic during labor or who have been delivered by forceps tend to cry more in the first weeks of life. Similarly, babies born after a long labor are likely to sleep in short bursts and to cry quite a lot in between. There's no question that a mother communicates her mood to her baby, so if you are tense, irritable, and impatient, your baby will feel it and cry. There are individual and cultural differences between babies. Some cry a different amount even if they're given the same care and attention. For instance, researchers have observed that Chinese-American babies cry less than babies of other cultural backgrounds.

WHY BABIES CRY

Most of the time, young babies cry for one of four reasons: hunger, fatigue, discomfort, and pain. In addition, all babies benefit from a regular routine, especially in the early weeks; if the routine is disturbed, they often resort to crying.

It is natural, as a parent, to find your baby's crying unnerving, but perhaps it will comfort you to know that "difficult" babies – that is, babies who cry a lot – are no more likely to be more difficult later on than babies who cry less. This is especially true if parents have worked hard to console them, to help them feel loved and secure, and to enjoy them.

Newborn crying
Many newborns cry a lot at first, but then settle down after just a few weeks.

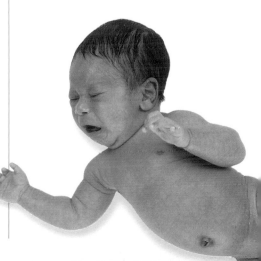

131

*Babies are born with a sucking
reflex. Without it they wouldn't
suckle and wouldn't nourish
themselves. I feel it's important
that babies are allowed to
indulge their desire to suck.*

*Some babies are more "sucky"
than others; I certainly had one
who wanted to suck all the time,
whether he was hungry or not.
With all four of my sons, I used
to gently put their thumbs into
their mouths so that they could
suck to soothe themselves. But at
the same time I see nothing wrong
with using pacifiers as comforters,
though very young babies will not
take to one readily.*

*While a baby is young, pacifiers
should be washed in exactly the
same way as you clean feeding
bottles and nipples. Once your
child is being weaned, however, and starts to use his
fingers for feeding himself,
rinsing is all that is needed.*

*Have several pacifiers so
they can be interchanged
when they get lost or
damaged.*

SOOTHING YOUR BABY

There are lots of remedies you can try to soothe and console your
baby if he's crying. As a general rule, most babies respond to movement and sound: hence the effectiveness of taking them out in the
car, where the motion of the vehicle and the steady humming
sound of the engine will usually quiet them. Your baby will probably find any of the following movements or sounds soothing:

- A movement that rocks him, whether it is you, a swing, a rocking cradle, or a rocking chair.

- Walking or dancing with an emphasis on rhythm, since it reminds
him of the time when he was being jogged inside the uterus.

- Bouncing him in your arms or in the crib.

- Putting him in a sling.

- Any form of music as long as it is not too loud but is rhythmic –
specially recorded sleeping tapes are available.

- A noisy toy that your baby can shake or rattle.

- A steady household noise such as the washing machine.

- Your own singing voice, especially if you sing a lullaby.

UNDERSTANDING THE CAUSE

You have to learn to read your baby's signals and gain insight
into his needs and desires. Once you recognize your baby's
cry you have to respond to it, otherwise he's bound to
scream even louder. Always be sensitive to your baby's
needs. Look, listen, and try to interpret what he is trying to say to you through his behavior. As you get to know
your baby, you will learn to understand what he really
wants. If you know, for example, that he's hungry, don't
delay his feeding by deciding to give him a bath first,
simply as a matter of sticking to your routine. Occasionally,
you have to ignore routines in order to respond to
your baby's crying.

There are all sorts of signs of small discomforts to
which you must be alert. When your baby has a cold,
for instance, his nose may become blocked, making it impossible for him to breathe and feed
at the same time, so he'll become angry and
frustrated and will almost certainly cry.

Undressing
Many young babies cry when
they are having a bath,
because they hate having
their skin exposed to the air.

CAUSE OF CRYING	WHAT TO DO
Hunger A hungry cry is usually the first cry that a parent recognizes, and it is the most common reason that young babies cry. They rarely cry after feeding. Babies love the sensation of a full stomach, more than being held or sucking.	Feed on demand. If you have a baby who wants to suck all the time, you don't need to feed; just give him a drink of boiled water. Use a pacifier, holding it in his mouth if necessary, so that he can suck on it.
Tiredness Until they're used to their new world, babies cry when they are tired; it takes an observant parent to realize this and put a baby down.	Lay your baby down where he is quiet, warm, and cozy. Wrapping or swaddling him before putting him down to sleep can help, too.
Lack of contact Some babies will stop crying as soon as you pick them up, because they want a hug. Babies brought up in cultures where they are constantly in a sling or swaddled rarely cry.	Always pick up your baby as soon as he cries. Carry him around in a shawl or a sling. Lay your baby tummy down across your lap and gently massage his back.
Startling A jerky movement, a sudden noise, or a bright light can upset your baby.	Hold your baby close, rock him gently, and sing to him. Avoid sudden jerky movements, noises, and bright lights.
Undressing Some babies dislike being undressed because it puts their bodies through movements that are neither familiar nor comforting and they hate air on their skin.	Undress your baby as little as possible in the first few weeks, and keep him wrapped or covered with a towel as you remove layers of clothing. Keep up a running commentary of reassuring talk as you undress him.
Temperature Babies tend to cry if they become too hot or too cold. They may cry if a wet or soiled diaper gets cold or if they are suffering from diaper rash.	Keep your baby's room between 61–68°F (16–20°C) with the coverings suggested on p.123. Remove blankets and clothing if your baby becomes too hot; add heavier clothing or a blanket if he's too cold. Change his diaper if necessary.
Pain Colic (in the first 3 months), an ear infection, or some other source of pain may cause your baby to cry. If it's colic, his legs will probably be drawn up to his abdomen.	Hold your baby close, hug him, and talk soothingly. If you can find the source of pain, such as a diaper pin, remove it immediately. If your baby seems ill, seek medical advice.

COLIC

Colic describes recurrent bouts of unexplained crying that usually happen in the late afternoon or evening but can be at any time. The crying may be very intense and brief or last for hours and is not generally pacified by the usual remedies. The baby's face becomes very red, the legs are drawn up to the abdomen, and the fists clenched. Colic is not due to pain.

Colic generally stops by the age of three or four months without your doing anything at all, is rarely serious, and needs no treatment but parents find it distressing. It is not known why it happens, but it usually starts in the first three weeks of a baby's life. It is well recognized that colicky babies are quite healthy and continue to thrive.

All sorts of causes have been put forward, such as constipation, diarrhea, overfeeding, underfeeding, gas in the bowel, being picked up too much or too little, indigestion, and tension.

As your baby is likely to cry every night for 12 weeks, I'm against using any kind of medicine to forestall the crying. Of course you should try to soothe your baby, but don't expect him to respond readily. Try to take comfort from the fact that these spells last for only three months and do not indicate a health problem, so there is light at the end of the tunnel.

OLDER BABY

CRYING AND COMFORTING

As your baby grows older and her world becomes more complex, the causes of crying change. In an older baby, the cause is nearly always illness or some form of emotional disturbance: mother leaving and the deprivation of her love, fear, anxiety, or separation.

BOREDOM

The older she gets, the longer your baby will spend being awake, and there is therefore greater scope for her getting bored. Many children cry out of sheer boredom, especially if left alone with no distractions, nothing to look at, and no one to play with. Your child of a year old enjoys your company more than anything else, and is constantly interested in what you are doing.

What to do Always leave toys in the crib, especially old color magazines or cloth books. Mobiles, baby gyms, or strings of interesting objects above the crib will help amuse and distract your baby. Though it may be tiresome for you, your baby will cry a great deal less from boredom if you keep her with you as much as you can.

FEAR OF SEPARATION

When your baby is about six to eight months, separation from a parent becomes the greatest source of distress to her and nearly always precipitates crying. Try to get your baby accustomed to separation over several months by leaving her for longer and longer periods, say 20 minutes, then an hour, then three hours. If you work outside the home, you will no doubt find your baby's fear upsetting, but this phase will soon pass as she gets used to seeing you go and always returning.

What to do While it lasts, be very careful about the way you take leave of your baby and ensure that she's familiar with her surroundings and the people she's with. If she finds separation very unpleasant the first time, she's likely to respond with crying the second time. It's up to you to make separation as easy as possible. Be sympathetic and supportive and never make fun of your child's fears. She will respond better to reassuring actions than words, so if you make a promise to her that you are coming back, always keep it. If you say that you're only going for five minutes, leave the room, get on with some job, and come back in exactly that time.

INSECURITY AND ANXIETY

As your baby gets older, she becomes increasingly aware of strangers. Those situations that cause her most anxiety are being in a strange place with you, or being with strangers. As long as you're there she

Dealing with anxiety
Unfamiliar people and places make your baby anxious, so reassure him with lots of hugs.

134

can cope, but being left in a strange place with strange people completely unnerves her. Never do it. Any source of anxiety makes your child clingy. She will turn to you for comfort. She may even lose her appetite. If you become aware that your child is anxious, you should respond to her immediately.

As your child searches for comfort she may become attached to an object, such as a blanket, or turn to thumb-sucking as consolation when you're not around. Nearly all children require some form of comfort that they control. Very often comfort objects are ones that they suck or stroke in moments of anxiety or stress, to simulate the effect of being stroked or being comforted.

What to do The best thing is extra reassurance, physical contact, hugs, love, and soothing talk. Your child will outgrow this period of anxiety, but it helps never to force her to go to a stranger if she doesn't really want to. Explain to strangers that she's shy and needs some time to get used to them. Your presence helps her to cope with new situations and experiences, even though she may feel fearful and uncomfortable. Whatever you do, let your baby have the comforter of her choice, and always give her lots of hugs.

This doesn't mean to say you can't gently encourage your child to be curious and adventurous. To grow up with a feeling of self-confidence, your child requires your approval, love, and praise, so give it every time she shows some independence.

FRUSTRATION

As your baby grows up, her desire to do things far outstrips her ability to do them, and so she becomes frustrated. This often results in crying. As she starts to crawl, then cruises along the furniture, then walks, you will almost certainly have to restrain her, which will result in added frustration, and crying every time you do it. By the time she gets to 18 months, your baby's spirit of adventure is in excess of her balance, coordination, and mobility. She is likely to attempt tasks that are beyond her and she'll become very frustrated as a result. Even though you know she is frustrated, you are going to have to stop her doing things simply to protect her.

What to do Make your home as childproof as possible (see pp.306–11): remove breakable objects from within her reach, and install safety plugs and guards around the house to make sure that she can't injure herself. Distraction is a good ploy for frustration, so always have a favorite toy on hand or be ready with a game.

Relaxed bedtimes
Spend time with your child just before bedtime in some quiet activity so he goes to bed calm and relaxed.

BEDTIME CRYING

Babies tend to cry at bedtime because they're tired, irritable, and don't wish to be separated from you. You can reassure them by establishing happy bedtime routines (see p.125).

• *Make the hour before bedtime a really happy one. Sit your child on your lap, read a story or book, play a quiet game, or sing a song to her*

• *A gentle, playful bathtime will make your baby slightly sleepy, as will a warm drink before being put to bed*

• *Your baby will almost certainly have a favorite game, song, or story, and for a baby repetition is happiness, so do as she requests. It increases her sense of security*

TODDLER

INJURIES

Toddlers tend to cry at even the most minor injury, such as a small scratch, an abrasion, or a tiny bruise.

In our house, I always had "the magic cream" (a mild antiseptic cream) on hand, and my children responded almost immediately to attention, reassurance, and a thin smear of the magic cream. Sometimes I had to sit down with them, hold them close, give them a big hug, and make very sympathetic sounds to show them that I knew how much it was hurting or how frightened they were – many young children are terrified by the sight of blood. Comfort and the magic cream nearly always had a calming effect.

Whenever your child comes to you in distress crying over a small injury, be sympathetic. Say you know how much it's hurting and don't try to make him be brave. In a few moments, he'll skip off your knee and return to his play after a kiss to make it better, a hug, and a favorite drink or snack.

If necessary, put some interesting idea into your child's mind to distract him from the injury, such as a special treat for snack, a special game with Dad, a picnic, or an outing to a favorite place.

CRYING AND COMFORTING

As your baby's thinking becomes more sophisticated, he gains a wider appreciation of what's going on in the world around him, and his reasons for crying become more difficult to figure out. He's starting to understand what you say, not only in terms of facts but of your answers, and he's beginning to use his own reason and respond to reasoned argument. He's becoming very aware of himself and other people, and of the will of others versus his own. His fears are therefore much more related to his daytime activities and any upset arising from them. Emotionally, he's developing very rapidly, too. He can feel guilt, shame, jealousy, and dislike, and be so upset that these emotions make him cry.

FEARS

The most common fears in this age group are of the dark and of thunder. Fear of the dark is so common as to be almost universal. It has no explanation, and reasoning with your child will not help. It's cruel to make fun of his fear, and you should never do that. Give your child an exciting night light – perhaps one with an interesting cover or one that plays a tune.

Fear of thunder and lightning is also very common, and the best way to deal with it is to distract your child while he can hear it. You can play loud music, turn on the television set, or take him into a quiet room and read him a story. You could also treat him by giving him the toy you had put aside for a rainy day.

DEALING WITH FEARS

One of the best ways to dispel fears is to talk about them, so get your child to be open and frank about what frightens him. Give him your full attention and ask questions, so he knows you are taking him seriously. Quite often fears are difficult to put into words, but hear your child out. Help him explain by supplying a few examples, and confess that you have similar fears, too. Never scold or ridicule your child about his fears. Do something simple and reassuring, like demonstrating to your child that it is fun in the swimming pool and the water is nothing to fear. Gradually your child will trust you and his fear will diminish. When he's old enough, try to explain how things work: for instance, that lightning is just like a giant spark.

If your child is afraid of going to a friend's house, talk him through it step by step: "First I'll drive you to Johnny's house, then you'll give Johnny his present and he'll ask you to play with him...." Most children have some irrational fears, such as fear of monsters, ghosts, or dragons. Remember, to your child a fear is serious, so you shouldn't try to tell him that his fears are unreal.

FEAR OF SEPARATION

Even when your child is three years old, he will still have fears about losing you. When he was younger, he worried about losing sight of you; now, he is fearful that you will not come back, that you will die while you are away from him, and that he will be deprived of you forever. Again, a very good way to reassure your child is to go step by step through what is going to happen when you leave him. The more details you can give, and the more you can confirm the details, the better. What you might say is, "When Daddy comes home from work, we are both going to get ready to go visit Aunt Sarah. I will have a bath, Daddy will shave, and we'll change our clothes. Then we'll put you to bed and we'll have our usual song, story, and game. Then Mommy will lie on your bed and cuddle you while we talk about your day and what you are going to do tomorrow. Mommy won't leave you until you are fast asleep, and the next thing you will know is that it is morning and Mommy will be there."

DETHRONEMENT

Your child is bound to feel pretty distressed at the thought of a new baby brother or sister and the "dethronement" that he thinks will follow. Take all the precautions you can to make him feel good about the baby. Refer to the baby as his new sister or brother, and let him feel your tummy as the baby grows and kicks. Show him where the baby is going to sleep, and teach him all kinds of helpful things he can do to look after her. If you are having the baby in a hospital, make sure your child is at ease with the person who is going to look after him while you're there. When you come home, have someone else carry the baby; you should have your arms free to scoop your child up and give him a big hug. Don't turn to the new baby until he asks to see her. Make sure that you bring home a present from the baby for him. If you have to stay in the hospital, let him visit you as often as you like, and when he does, make sure that the baby is not in your arms, but is lying in a crib at your side so you're free to hold your child.

OVERTIREDNESS

A child of this age very often becomes overexcited and overtired toward bedtime. He will try to put off his bedtime as long as possible and simply become more distressed. Your child might become so fragile that any small discomfort or frustration will make him cry inconsolably.

If you are expecting your child to have a late evening, or a special treat such as a party or a school play, make sure he has a nap during the day so that his energy will last. If he does become overexcited and overtired, it is especially important that you remain calm and quiet. Talk to him softly, give him lots of hugs, be infinitely patient, and take him gently to his bedroom. Sing him a song or read a story until he has become calm and quieted down.

TANTRUMS

Young children nearly always have tantrums out of frustration or because they are pitting their will against that of others.

Older children have tantrums because they can think of no other way of showing their determination. In the privacy of your own home, the best way to deal with a tantrum is simply to ignore it and leave the room.

It's slightly more difficult, however, if you're in public, but you can do several things. Don't fuss, shout, or get flustered. Take your child calmly into a quiet place and try to calm her. If you are in a store, take her out into the street or to your car. In a restaurant, you might try the restroom.

Fearful toddler
Always take your child's fears seriously and ask her to explain them if she can.

CRYING AND COMFORTING

FEARS

Three years is a highly anxious age, but by four years your child's fears are more clearly defined.

She will be easily frightened by sounds, for example, especially loud sounds outside, such as a fire engine. She may fear people of a different culture or appearance from herself, old people, "bogey men," the dark, animals, and your leaving her – especially at night. Children of this age may enjoy being mildly frightened by an adult in play, so long as it's clearly pretend.

By five years of age, your child will probably have more concrete, down-to-earth fears, like bodily harm, falling, dogs, sounds, thunder, lightning, rain storms (especially at night), and that a parent will not return home or be at home when she gets there.

Just as dislike of certain foods is suggested by chance remarks made by adults, fear of animals, cars, and thunder are suggested in a similar way. Gruesome tales and stories about ghosts, devils, and such may terrify a small child and lead to serious sleep disturbance. For this reason, you should choose bedtime stories carefully. Don't let your child watch scary television programs just before bedtime, and never deliberately frighten her with stories of "bogey men" to make her behave.

The four-year-old cries a great deal and may whine if her wants are not met or there's nothing interesting to play with. By the age of five, a child cries much less, though she may cry if she's angry, tired, or can't have her own way. Crying is now of shorter duration, and your child may be able to control it and hold her tears back. She is rarely moody and may be perfectly okay as soon as the crying is over. She may whine occasionally, though a lot less than she did at four years. This phase may pass, however, and give way to temper tantrums with loud angry crying and banging around. There may be a return of moodiness, whining, and expressions of resentment, but you can often get your child to laugh when she's crying by joking with her. Your child may become astonishingly brave about real injuries yet still cry at small hurts.

BAD DREAMS AND NIGHTMARES

Between the ages of three and five years, children quite often have bad dreams. Your child may walk or talk in her sleep, or have night terrors. This is normal because while her understanding of the world is growing, she cannot entirely make sense of it, and so she goes to sleep with unresolved questions. She's also getting more in touch with her feelings and she knows what it is to be afraid or feel something is not quite right. These feelings come out at night.

Often a child cannot explain her dreams and has difficulty in going back to sleep. Animals, especially wolves and bears, may chase your child during a nightmare, or she may dream of strange, bad, or odd-looking people, fires, and deep water. If your child wakes up, try to console her and take her in your arms.

Night terrors Sometimes you'll find your child in bed, terrified, and possibly thrashing and screaming. She may be angry or very upset. She may seem awake, but you'll be unable to get a response from her. This is a night terror rather than a nightmare, and can be very alarming. If she remains asleep, don't try to wake her; simply stay by her. If you find that she is sleepwalking periodically, put a gate across the stairs to prevent falls. You will feel quite anguished at your child's fear and pain, but all you can do is stay close and wait for the terror to pass. There is no point in trying to reassure your child specifically, because she is beyond reason. Don't leave her or scold her; that would simply make the terror worse.

PRESCHOOL NERVOUSNESS

A child who goes to nursery school without a backward glance, says good-bye to her mother, and gets straight into play at the sandbox is rather unusual. Most children harbor fears of a strange place with strange people and separation from you. You will need to give your child the time and the opportunity to adjust to this rather frightening change in her life.

You can do much to allay your child's fears by familiarizing her with the journey to school, the entrance to the school, her classroom, some of the children who will be in her class, her teacher, where the games are, and what some of the routines are. Most teachers will welcome your taking your child to the school several times before she starts so that she can feel comfortable in her new surroundings. Make the first visit as casual as possible. Stay for only a few minutes, so your child does not get bored or frightened and don't make her do anything she doesn't want to.

Making separation easy The first morning is likely to be difficult for both of you. You may have to stay with your child for the whole morning, but this shouldn't happen more than once. Don't forget that it is a great transition for her, so be patient. Many nursery schools will welcome your staying to give your child confidence. Once your child realizes you are not going to leave, she will be happy to get on with her classroom routines as long as you sit somewhere quietly and discreetly.

Maybe during the first morning, but certainly on the second, suggest that you are going out to buy a newspaper, but come back within five minutes, so your child is reassured. Don't go if your child gets very distressed at the prospect of your leaving. Once she's happy, suggest that you leave again, this time for about half an hour, and come back in exactly the time you promised. Over the next few days, leave for longer and longer periods according to how your child reacts. You'll find that in a short time you won't need to stay at all. A confident child may want to be self-reliant and suggest that you leave long before you think she is capable of being separated from you. Sometimes a teacher will advise you when it's time to go.

Starting nursery school
Once your child is engrossed in some activity she may hardly even notice when you leave.

FAMILY CONFLICTS

Your child will become very distressed if she thinks that the people dearest in the world to her, her mother and father, no longer love each other and that there's a danger that they may separate or leave her.

Children are extremely sensitive to atmospheres within the home, so if you and your partner are going through a bad time, behave caringly and affectionately in front of your child and show that you have concern for each other. Witnessing an argument is one of the most harmful experiences you can inflict on your child, so that thought should act as a deterrent.

On the other hand, I don't believe in a united front between parents on every question. Your child should understand that it's all right for Mom and Dad to have different opinions, as long as they are expressed without acrimony.

Children have to get used to conflict because they're going to meet it very quickly when they leave home. The best place for them to become familiar with it is in the security of their own home.

Most children will blame themselves for any conflict between their parents and will go to great lengths to make you friends again. Reassure your child that she is not to blame for any anger you feel toward your partner, and that you love her regardless.

139

TRAVEL AND OUTINGS

Time spent planning your outing or travel schedule is never time wasted. The younger your baby, the more you will have to plan. In the first few months, your baby's feeding schedule won't necessarily be very predictable, so you'll need at least one spare bottle if you're not breastfeeding and, of course, whatever changing equipment you normally use. Lightweight baby bags containing a portable changing mat are widely available. Plan your route so that you know where you can stop, where you can change your baby, and where you can feed him without embarrassment or inconvenience. If you're planning to shop, it is even worth calling up stores to find out if they have a mother-and-baby changing room and avoiding those that don't.

With a very young baby, it's simply not worth undertaking a very busy outing where you will have to walk a great deal, carry heavy loads, or make lots of changes of transport. Be easy on yourself. Try to take a friend or your partner with you if you can, so there is always an extra pair of hands and someone to help you should a problem come up. Your baby can go with you anywhere so long as you're well enough prepared and have something in which to carry him – a sling, stroller, or car seat.

USING A STROLLER

If you do not want to carry your baby in a sling, a collapsible stroller is ideal for a small baby, who will fit comfortably and snugly into its shape. Babies are interested in their surroundings from an early age, so as soon as your baby can sit up, angle the stroller so he can see what is going on around him.

You must become adept at collapsing and opening the stroller within a few seconds without any problems, so practice at home before your first outing. If you cannot fold up the stroller efficiently, you will find people jostling to get in front of you when you are in a line, which will only add to your frustration. At the very least, you should be able to open it with only one hand, kick it shut with your feet, and know how to operate the brakes – and don't forget you will have to do all these things while holding your baby. Here are a few safety tips:

• When you open your stroller, always make sure it is in the fully extended position with the brakes fully locked.

• Never put your baby in the stroller without a safety harness.

• Never, ever, leave your baby in a stroller unattended.

• Should your baby fall asleep in the stroller, adjust it to the lie-back position so he can sleep comfortably.

- Don't put shopping bags on the handles of the stroller; they can tip the stroller and your baby may be injured.

- When you stop, always put on the brakes because you could inadvertently take your hands off the stroller and it could roll away.

- Check your stroller regularly to make sure the brakes and catches work well and the wheels are in good condition.

PUBLIC TRANSPORTATION

Using public transportation can really be a trial, as neither buses nor trains are equipped or serviced for mothers and young children. Picture yourself with a stroller, a heavy and wriggling baby, the baby bag, your handbag, a coat, and possibly a toddler in tow – public transportation is the last thing you want to face.

Of course, you can make things easier by never traveling in the rush hour or, with a young baby, carrying him around in a sling. For an older baby, a backpack makes you much more independent, and you can manage everything more easily with your hands free. Always prepare yourself well ahead of time. I simply would not leave home with my children without some distracting toys, a favorite book, and a favorite snack. All your belongings, including the stroller, should be gathered together prior to leaving and in good enough time so you can check them over to make sure you have not forgotten anything. The same goes for when you are getting off a bus or train; be ready to get off in plenty of time for your stop. Don't hesitate to ask for help from fellow passengers.

SPECIAL OUTINGS

Your baby is never too young for an outing; indeed, with a young baby you can go just about anywhere and, provided he can look around him, he will enjoy the change of scene even if he doesn't understand much of what's going on. When planning an outing for an older child, always try to consider what your child's personality can cope with best. If you have a quiet child who has a long concentration span, you can take him to a flower show or museum, and point out the things around him. If, on the other hand, he's very active, he'll need more space to run around in and a trip to the zoo, a playground, or an outdoor event may be more appropriate. Wherever you go, be prepared to make endless stops to look at whatever catches your child's attention. Always take enough drinks and snacks to keep your child happy for the full duration of the trip. Don't take on a trip of any kind if you or your child are feeling out of sorts; the day is bound to be a disaster, so don't feel guilty about canceling the outing altogether.

WHAT TO TAKE: OLDER BABY

For an older baby, you'll need solid food and feeding and changing equipment.

- *Changing mat*
- *Fabric or disposable diapers*
- *Baby wipes*
- *Diaper cream*
- *Plastic bags or sealable container for dirty diapers*
- *Baby food, dish, and spoon*
- *Bib for feeding*
- *Snack, such as fruit*
- *Diluted fruit juice*
- *Sun hat or woolen hat*
- *Cardigan or sweater*
  - *Comfort objects*
  - *Favorite book*
  - *Favorite toys*

Handling a stroller
Make sure you can kick it shut, open it up one-handed, and operate the brakes.

When traveling with your baby, always plan all your movements and stops in detail, so you can use your time efficiently.

• *Try to fit in a shopping trip between feedings or, if you think it is going to be a longer trip than the usual interval between meals, take a snack with you*

• *Always bring basic changing equipment in case your child needs a clean diaper. Many stores these days have special areas set aside for mothers and babies*

• *If you are traveling by car, adjust your baby's seat to a reclining position so she can sleep*

Harness

Anchor straps

Reins

Harness and reins
Keep your child safe on busy streets with a harness and reins. The harness can also be used in a high chair with anchor straps.

SHOPPING TRIPS

Taking a baby shopping brings its own problems. Your baby can easily become bored, hungry, fretful, and difficult to manage, so it's worth planning ahead quite carefully to minimize stress. Taking a car will make a world of difference: you can feed and change your baby in it, you can stack your shopping in the trunk and not have to carry it, and you won't have to worry about catching buses and trains. If you don't own a car yourself, it might be worth asking a friend who does to join your shopping expedition or asking a relative if you can borrow a car. Try to shop fairly early in the day, because the streets and stores are less busy. Always try to give your baby a good meal before you leave home; that way you may have two or three hours in which to complete your purchases without her getting hungry.

Bring whatever equipment you would bring on any other trip. Toys may seem something of a burden, but they will more than pay their way, because you can attach them to the backpack, stroller, or supermarket cart for your child to play with without her being able to throw them onto the floor. Bring some kind of small snack, too, because shopping seems to make children either hungry or cranky, and a snack will deal with both.

CARRYING YOUR BABY

You need to have your hands free for shopping, so how you carry your baby is worth some thought and attention. Once your baby is able to sit up with good head and back control, you can put her into your shopping cart. Many supermarkets now have carts equipped with infant seats and harnesses, but with the older type of seats you need to strap your baby in with reins. A backpack is ideal for carrying your baby on shopping trips; her interest will always be engaged, she will feel very secure with such close physical contact, and she should be well behaved and cry very little. Best of all, your hands will be left free. Try to undertake a shopping trip accompanied by your partner and have him carry the baby on his back, leaving you free to make the purchases. Reins are a very good idea for an older child, because they give her a sense of freedom and independence, but she will never be able to get very far away from you; a wrist link that is securely attached to her reins will prevent the two of you from becoming separated.

KEEPING YOUR CHILD UNDER CONTROL

Because babies are always grasping and reaching for interesting objects, walk down the center of the aisle so your baby is not tempted to dislodge cans and boxes. One way to control your child is to keep her interested, and you can do this keeping up a running commentary, with observations or questions that engage your child. Your young child will love being involved in shopping decisions, and she will feel very important and needed if you act on her preferences. With items where brand is not important to you, ask your child to select products by pointing to the one she would like you to buy. As my children got older and could toddle around the shopping cart, I used to ask them to put all their choices into the cart themselves, so that they were constantly engaged in looking for their favorite things, feeling a great sense of pride in finally finding them, and a sense of achievement in filling up the cart. At the checkout, don't feel that you have to buy everything your child has put in the cart; without her seeing, you can take out those things you don't want.

One of the ways I used to distract and entertain my children on a shopping trip was to ask them if they were thirsty or hungry immediately on entering the supermarket, and buy them a drink or a healthful snack. That way they could munch or sip their way around the supermarket and feel quite happy and occupied the whole time. If, however, you have a wayward child who keeps on getting into mischief, the only way to handle the situation is to keep your child on reins or in the cart to prevent her wandering off and getting lost, or shop without her.

LEARNING

Use your shopping trips as opportunities to teach your child – about colors, for example: "This can is red; that box is blue; that jar has a yellow label." Your child will recognize the corn flakes box that she sees at breakfast every morning and will soon understand what the words mean, so that from quite an early age, say, 18 months, you can say to her, "Can you see the corn flakes? Now I wonder where the jam is?" Word recognition can be encouraged by associating the contents of a carton or can with things that your child actually eats at home. For example, if she drinks juice regularly, you only have to take the carton of the brand she sees every day from the shelf and ask "What does this word say?" for her to respond with "juice," because she has learned from experience that juice is what comes out of that carton. All my children began to read food labels before they read anything else.

An older child will also learn about the act of shopping itself, and the decision-making and choosing that are involved. You can introduce her to the value of money and to counting, and to some degree you can teach her about sociability and manners, because she will quickly learn the justice of allowing other people to get to the shelves when she has a great interest in doing so herself.

SHOPPING WITH YOUR TODDLER

Once your child can walk, losing her in a crowd can be a danger, so take precautions against this.

• *Dress your toddler in something brightly colored so you can spot her from a distance*

• *Have some sort of family code for your children to come back to you. I used to carry a small whistle around my neck*

• *Use reins or a wrist strap in busy places so she can't wander*

• *From as early an age as possible, make your child learn her name, address, and telephone number so she can repeat them if she gets lost*

• *Teach her never to walk off with a stranger*

• *Make sure your child recognizes her surroundings when she's near to home by pointing out landmarks on every journey: "There's the mailbox on the corner, and there's the blue gate, and our house is the next one"*

Wrist straps
An adjustable strap links you and your child together at the wrists to stop her from wandering.

CAR JOURNEYS

JOURNEY CHECKLIST

As with any kind of outing with your child, the essential thing is to plan and prepare well in advance. The following tips will help to make things go more smoothly for you:

• *Try to start traveling early in the day, or at night when the roads are empty*

• *Carry a bag of spare clothes for each child in the car, be philosophical about accidents, and change your child readily into dry clothes*

• *For safety, tape cutlery to the inside of food containers*

• *Take some soft clothing, like a jacket or sweater, that your child can use as a pillow*

• *Always have a supply of bags into which cartons, bottles, and wrappers can be placed after use*

• *Pack a box of baby wipes to clean dirty hands and faces*

Children can be very active on car journeys. They're learning and taking great pride in newly acquired physical skills, like jumping, skipping, hopping, climbing, and running, and it's very difficult for them to be confined in a small space. All this is intensified in hot weather because your child will become tired, cranky, and tearful more easily than when the temperature is cool. Never leave a child alone in a car in hot weather, because the temperature inside the car can rise much higher than the temperature outside, causing him to become quickly overheated and even dehydrated. Always screen your child from bright sunlight by putting a shade over the window through which the sun is shining. Alternatively, attach a sun shield to your baby's seat, which serves the same purpose.

In the cramped circumstances of a long journey, your child can't be expected to behave well, and it's your job to make sure that he's cool, fed, given a sufficient number of drinks, has enough to occupy and distract him, is taken to the bathroom without a fuss, and that accidents are accepted philosophically.

SAFETY

Whatever else, your baby must be transported safely in a car. A young baby should go in a rear-facing car seat, which is used most safely in the back of the car. Never travel with your baby held on your lap, whether in the back or front seat; if the car stops suddenly your baby will be flung out of your arms and will certainly be injured. An older baby should sit in a front-facing car seat installed in the backseat. After any accident, you should always replace your seat belts, your child's car seat, and the anchorage kit, because they will have been badly strained and may be damaged. For the same reason, you should never buy secondhand car seats, harnesses, or anchorage kits.

Misbehavior like shouting or kicking should not be tolerated; it is extremely distracting for the driver and could even be dangerous. If your child does behave badly, pull over to the side of the road at the first opportunity, stop the car, and deal with the difficulty. Tell your child that you are going no farther until he starts to behave himself properly.

LONGER JOURNEYS

Most children will become restless if they have to travel for longer than an hour and a half. Your child has no idea of time, so he'll be constantly asking you when you are going to arrive or whether you are nearly there. One way to cope with this is to allow your children to change seats so that they can get different views, but always pull the car over and stop completely first. Restlessness can also be alleviated by stopping the car every hour for about five minutes and allowing your children to run around and get rid of excess energy. Announce the stops a few minutes in advance so that they can get themselves ready by putting on coats if it's cold outside.

Feeding A car journey is when breastfeeding comes into its own because you have no preparations to make whatsoever. You cannot feed when the car is in motion, however, because your baby would be very unsafe. If, however, you are bottlefeeding, use disposable bottles and condensed or powdered formula, or make up a batch of bottles, cool them in the refrigerator, and then carry them in an insulated bag. Alternatively, mix the formula when you need it in a sterilized bottle with some boiled water from a thermos. Never try to keep made-up feedings warm because that will only allow germs to multiply. Once your baby is weaned, you'll have to carry food, a feeding dish, a plastic spoon, a bib, a cup with a spout, a supply of drinks, and something your baby can nibble on, such as crackers. You can feed your baby directly from the jar, but remember that whatever he does not finish out of a jar of baby food must be thrown away, because it is contaminated with saliva, and germs will grow in it very quickly.

Changing Even if you normally use fabric diapers, forget the expense and take disposable diapers with you on a journey: they're just so convenient, quick, and easy for both you and the baby. You can always change your baby on the back seat of the car or in the trunk if he lies on a blanket or a towel. There is no need to do any more than top and tail your baby while traveling, but be meticulous about cleaning the diaper area, and always have a supply of diaper cream to prevent diaper rash. Wipes are an essential, as is a sealable container for dirty diapers.

The older child Your child will get bored and hungry, so always have some nutritious snacks like raisins, sugarless dry cereal, or pieces of cheese in plastic bags, and take more drinks than you ever think you'll need – your child's capacity for liquid is greatly increased when he's traveling. Seedless grapes make a very useful snack, because they quench your child's thirst as well as satisfying his hunger. You will need toys to distract your child while traveling (books may be a bad idea, though, if he suffers from motion sickness), and these can be arranged in different ways for safety and convenience. Buy or make a special cover for the front headrest of your car with pockets in the back that can carry drinks, snacks, and toys, or tie toys to coat-hooks or handles so that they don't get lost under seats. Magnetized games are particularly useful in cars because the pieces won't roll off, and you can stick Velcro on certain toys so they will adhere to the car seat and stay in one place while your child is playing with them. I always found it best if I allowed my child to choose some of the toys that he wanted to take and to be responsible for putting them into his own suitcase or bag. Cassettes with music or children's stories may give you at least half an hour of peace, so always have one ready. "I spy" games are always a favorite, particularly if you join in, and will keep your children occupied for quite a long time if you make the object interesting. Keep a special treat tucked away in the glove compartment with which to relieve tension or tears.

MOTION SICKNESS

Some children suffer from motion sickness whenever they're in a car; others do so only occasionally. Most children eventually grow out of the tendency, but some do not. There are some things that you can do to help minimize motion sickness.

* *Don't give your child a rich or fatty meal before a journey*

* *Give a child's dose of motion-sickness drug, available without a prescription; always give it at least half an hour before you leave*

* *Stay calm. If you're anxious your children will become anxious, too. Car sickness may be worsened by anxiety and excitement*

* *Snacks that can be sucked are a good idea, because they do not create a mess, so let lollipops be a special treat for travelers only*

* *Keeping your child occupied or distracted will help prevent car sickness, but don't let him read, as this may bring it on*

* *If you notice your child becoming pale or quiet, ask him if he wants to stop. If possible, open a window a little bit to let in some fresh air until you reach a safe place to stop, then get him out of the car, and be very sympathetic if he actually vomits. Give him time to recover before you continue with your journey*

* *A supply of baby wipes will help you clean up your child (and the car, if necessary), should he vomit*

* *Give your child a drink after he's vomited to get rid of the taste in his mouth*

Use the following checklist to make sure you've got everything you need for your child.

• *Passport and immunization documents if you're traveling to another country*

• *Your baby bag*

• *Travel crib*

• *Stroller or sling*

• *A bouncing chair if used*

• *Changing equipment or potty*

• *Feeding equipment*

• *A vacuum bottle for cool drinks*

• *Toys and games*

• *Comfort objects*

• *Sun hat*

• *No-iron, drip-dry clothes*

• *Plenty of clothes to protect your child from heatstroke or sunburn*

Sun protection
Dress your child in a sun hat and T-shirt and apply sunscreen regularly when she's outside playing in the sun.

PLANNING A VACATION

Never think your baby is too young to travel. Children nearly always surprise us and rise to the occasion in ways we never think possible. Traveling with young babies is a hobby in my family; I am told that when I was only six weeks old, my mother and father took me camping, living in a tent for two weeks by the sea! When my third son was only ten weeks old, we took him to Italy, and while we were finding our lost luggage in Rome, he was by far the best behaved of all of us. He even philosophically accepted my efforts to find the right formula for him, which took three days.

BEFORE YOU GO

A golden rule for hotel vacations is to ensure there are facilities for children, and that children are really welcome. Things to look for in a hotel include such child facilities as a day-care center, a place where you can take your child for early supper, a children's menu, high chairs and cribs, a playroom, and an outdoor play area with trained attendants. It is worth going to some trouble to ensure that these things are available because if your child is not happy, you will not enjoy the vacation yourself. If you are going to the seaside, make sure the beaches are safe.

Immunizations If you are traveling outside the U.S., find out well ahead of time – six months at least – if additional immunizations are needed, though in most areas of the world, the same immunizations are required and your baby will be fine if his shots are up to date. The reason for starting early is that some vaccines need time to become effective, and for others, as with hepatitis, you may have to wait four to six weeks between injections or you may not be able to follow one vaccination immediately with another. You can get information from your pediatrician. Ask your pediatrician if water treatment tablets or liquid are recommended for the area you're going to.

Food Introduce your children to any exotic food at home so you can determine their likes and dislikes well in advance. If they like experimenting with food, there is no reason not to let them eat the local food, as long as it is well cooked and sanitary.

AIR TRAVEL

Most airlines make special facilities available to children if they are asked ahead of time. Try to book a flight that won't be crowded, and if you have a baby, ask for bulkhead seats, which have special folding tables for a bassinet or cradle. If these are not available, ask for any seat that might have more legroom. Travel cribs may be available. Ask the airline staff if they will heat up baby bottles for you. On some flights, children's meals may be available; if they are not, you will need to take your own. Most travel agents will make all these inquiries on your behalf. Given that children can be somewhat unpredictable, it is essential that you make careful plans and, if possible, not travel alone. Here are some things to think about before you travel:

- Aim to reach the airport early enough to avoid long check-in lines, and give yourself plenty of time to get there.

- Put all travel documents in a special bag, inside a loose, light-weight shoulder bag. If you can, fit in your baby bag, too, with spare diapers, spare clothing, and some snacks.

- Make sure that everything you take on board, including your baby bag, has an indestructible label.

- Take a few of your baby's favorite toys with you or see whether any of the games suggested for use in the car (see p.145) would work on a plane to entertain your child.

- Carry your baby in a sling so your hands are free.

- Change your baby's diaper just before getting on the plane.

- Take a folded stroller on the plane with you; the crew will take it from you as you enter and return it as you leave.

- Babies and children feel some pain during takeoff and landing, so keep aside a bottle or your baby's pacifier so she can suck on it to equalize the pressure in her ears.

SAFE SUNBATHING

Children can get heatstroke (see p.340) in a very short time, and this is a dangerous condition. Also dangerous is sunburn, which can injure a child's skin and greatly increase the risk of skin cancer later in life.

If your baby is under six months, never expose her skin to direct sunlight and do not use sunscreen of any type. The guidelines (below right) are for children over six months old with sunscreen of SPF 15 or more. Although the times in the sun seem short, please adhere to this schedule and dress your child in protective clothing the rest of the time. At all times, she should wear a wide-brimmed sun hat and sunscreen. Apply a generous coating of a sunscreen with an SPF of 15 or above to all exposed areas and reapply every hour, or sooner if she goes in the water.

Even if there have been no untoward effects after the first five days, do not extend the time in the sun beyond one half hour. Your child can remain outdoors, but should be protected by shade (trees, umbrellas), clothing, and a hat in addition to sunscreen.

A baby has to be kept as cool as possible, and this means a minimum of light cotton clothing, but something that covers all of her body, unless she is kept constantly under a sunshade and never exposed to direct sunlight. If you can, always make sure the carriage is placed where there is a light breeze to cool your baby's skin. Bear in mind that children lose a lot more body moisture than adults do in a hot climate, so always have water with you and give your child as much as she wants.

SUNSCREENS

There are many sunscreens available. Use one that protects against both UVA and UVB rays, with a sun protection factor (SPF) of at least 15.

Sunscreen is not recommended for use on babies under the age of six months.

What the SPF means is that one can stay in the sunshine that number of times longer without getting burned than one could have without the cream; if your child would normally burn after 10 minutes, a sunscreen with an SPF of 15 would allow her to stay in the sun for 150 minutes without getting burned.

Many sunscreens say that they are waterproof, but if your child is running in and out of the ocean or swimming pool, reapply sunscreen every half an hour or so.

Under other conditions reapply sunscreen to your child's skin every hour or so.

EXPOSURE TIMES

Expose your child to the sun for a very short time at first, and increase it gradually.

Day 1	5 minutes
Day 2	10 minutes
Day 3	15 minutes
Day 4	20 minutes
Day 5	30 minutes

30 minutes is the maximum exposure time for a child.

CHAPTER 3

PLAY
and Development

When your baby is born he becomes immersed in a confusing world of sights and sounds, none of which makes any sense to him. The process of identifying and memorizing the things around him begins immediately. As a parent, you can help him to make sense of his surroundings.

The starting point in your baby's social development is your physical presence. As soon as your baby is born he will become familiar with your smell and voice, and what you look like, and he will come to associate you with comfort and love. You can encourage his instinctive desire to communicate with talking, touching, eye contact, and play.

During the first year of life your baby's brain doubles in weight, not because he acquires any more brain cells, but because more and more connections are being made between existing brain cells. "Learning to think" is a complex process of building up associations that results from observing and interacting with the world.

Your child will not only mature socially and mentally, he will also become skilled phyically. He will learn to sit, then crawl, and later to walk and run, and he will develop fine manipulative skills. All of these things will open up new areas of experience for him.

CHOOSING TOYS

Your child will grow and learn very rapidly in the first three years, so your choice of toys should reflect his changing needs.

- *Simple toys are more versatile, so they have a longer life and are better for imaginative play*

- *A baby will need toys that stimulate all five senses. Introduce your baby to different colors, textures, shapes, and sounds*

- *Older babies enjoy games that involve building, particularly "put-in, take-out" toys, so blocks of different sizes are ideal*

- *As your child's manipulative skills develop, he will be able to manage interlocking blocks and more advanced shape-sorters*

- *Preschool children enjoy drawing, painting, and imaginative play, and simple games like picture dominoes, which improve concentration*

Painting
Give your child painting and drawing materials to allow him to develop his creativity.

PROMOTING DEVELOPMENT

The first six weeks of life are a critical learning period for your baby in which you should be actively engaged. Your role as teacher starts at your baby's birth and continues for many years; it's your job to make his world an interesting and exciting place in which he can grow and learn.

I firmly believe that the most important teacher in a baby's life is the person who most consistently looks after his health and well-being – ideally, this is you. From a very early age, your baby will recognize you, first by smell and sound, and enjoy a unique bond with you. That means you are best equipped to teach him about his world, for even as adults we learn best from people with whom we feel comfortable or have rapport. Your partner likewise has an important role to play. He should form a close and loving relationship with your baby as early as possible so that he becomes equally involved in teaching. Look for every opportunity to share in your baby's progress; much of his early development will be dependent on a secure and caring environment, so make sure you give him lots of attention.

PROVIDING THE RIGHT ENVIRONMENT

Although very young babies enjoy a fairly predictable environment, it is still possible to provide stimulation so he can experience many sensations at a time when he's dependent on his senses alone for learning. Do so by surrounding your baby in the first six months with a variety of sounds, smells, sights, and textures. In the early months, your baby cannot interact with his surroundings the way he will when he learns to move and speak. His intellectual and emotional development, therefore, will be improved only through the different experiences you introduce to him.

When your child begins to play and walk, pay attention to the way he uses his toys. Make his playthings appealing by arranging them imaginatively and, rather than buying your child new toys all the time, encourage him to interact with existing toys in different ways – for example, by showing him how to use a cardboard box as a car or a boat. Children don't always need store-bought toys to encourage them to play. Often your child will get stimulation from improvised toys: a tent made out of sheets, for instance, a balancing board, or a tunnel made from blankets and chairs, all provide the backdrop for imaginative play.

In practical terms, the area in which your child plays should be safe, with potential hazards removed so that he cannot hurt himself, or break or damage anything. Sandboxes in the yard are ideal (but must be covered to prevent fouling by animals), or a corner of a room can be set aside specifically as a play area.

WORKING WITH YOUR CHILD

In order to allow your child to achieve his full potential, you should set aside time to work with him, matching your efforts to your child's stages of development. Actively involved parents find the role of teacher comes effortlessly and naturally. Your child is always eager to learn new things, so make the experience fun and mutually rewarding. Take any opportunity that presents itself – intimate moments of play or storytelling, for example, to teach colors, textures, opposites, and so on.

Teaching your child is not a formal process with specific rules and targets. All teaching should be playful and be done with games. Feed your child's increasing curiosity and need for new experiences. Introduce new concepts, answer his queries but, most importantly, praise him at every stage so that the learning process becomes unself-conscious and enjoyable, and one he wants to repeat over and over with you.

When you work with your child, be sure to stop the moment he shows any sign of boredom and take care not to put him under any pressure. If he decides early on that learning is fun, he'll feel this way throughout his life and will thrive on knowledge.

THE IMPORTANCE OF PLAY

Your child's development will center around play, and this is the most natural way for him to learn. It is only in the last twenty years that the full value of development through play has been recognized, since playing was previously regarded as an empty activity, used to fill the time when children could not be usefully employed. We now recognize that play is an essential means of acquiring the majority of adult skills, particularly social ones. Your child will first learn to form relationships and to share with children his own age through play, and toys will have a significant educational role in all your child's developmental milestones.

Choose toys for their educational value. Reading, writing, and math proficiency requires certain basic skills that your child will acquire through building and construction toys, playing with puzzles, and matching colors, shapes, and textures. The best toys are the ones that children return to again and again because they are limitless in their appeal – usually ones that encourage inventiveness. For this reason, a household item like a strainer may give more lasting pleasure than many an expensive and elaborate toy. By sharing your child's games and encouraging him in his play, you'll strengthen the bond between you as he comes to see you as a giver of knowledge and fun.

Places to play It's nice to set aside a special activity space for your child – a sand tray, for example, or an area for messy play like painting or water games – but your child can play anywhere, as long as you take the proper safety measures (see pp.306–13). The kitchen is an ideal place, provided you are there to keep an eye on your child. You could set up a dolls' corner where the dolls can be put to bed each evening and awakened in the morning for breakfast.

TELEVISION

The average child watches an average of eight hours' television a day. One hour a day is more than enough for your young child.

More than this may prevent him from acquiring communication, imaginative, and coordination skills that could be more thoroughly developed through games and storytelling. You should, therefore, monitor the amount of television your child watches and be wary of using it as a convenient babysitting tool when you don't feel like amusing him. Used carefully, however, television can be a useful aid to acquiring new concepts, like telling time.

Research shows that your child could continue to live in the fantasy world of television long after he's stopped watching, causing nightmares if he's watched anything frightening or violent.

Swedish researchers have shown that bringing a child back into the real world – with a story, toothbrushing, or laying out tomorrow's clothes – can banish this unpleasant effect of television.

YOUNG BABY

LOCOMOTION

HEAD CONTROL

The most important physical change during your baby's first weeks will be the development of neck strength and head control.

A newborn's head is proportionately very large and heavy for his body, which means that before your baby can begin to control the rest of his body, he must first gain control of his head.

Once your baby can raise his head from the mattress he will begin to increase his strength, which will encourage him to further locomotive skills. Holding your baby in the air in a face-down position will encourage him to raise his head, something that he will try for himself when lying on his stomach.

As he becomes stronger, your baby's head control is steadier, and his spine will gradually take more of the weight of his torso. This is the first stage in his learning to sit, crawl, and walk.

The first few months of your baby's development is a very exciting time for you as a parent as you watch him first see the world, then move to become involved in it. As his coordination and muscle strength increase, your baby's body control will quickly improve. The gradual refinement of his movements and his growing curiosity about his surroundings are excellent stimulation for all aspects of development. Every child develops at his own speed, however, and the ages given below for the various stages of coordination and control are only approximations.

Newborn
Your baby will flex his limbs toward his body, which will remain curled up for several weeks as he gradually straightens out of the fetal position. His head will be very floppy at first, but you will notice that he turns it to his preferred side when lying down. Always support his head and neck when lifting him.

Your baby can lift his head only momentarily

If you hold your baby, he can keep his head up for a while

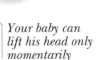

His neck muscles are getting stronger

1 month
Your baby will be able to lift his head slightly for a few seconds and will have lost his very newborn appearance. If you raise your baby from the mattress he may be able to keep his head in line with his body for a second or two. His knees and hips will become stronger and will begin to straighten even more.

2 months
Your baby can hold his head up for longer now. In a prone position, he'll hold his head in line with his body and will quickly develop to raising his face from the mattress to an angle of 45°.

3 months

Your baby can now lie quite flat and take the weight of his shoulders and head on outstretched arms. There is little head lag when he is held in a sitting or standing position.

Your baby can hold his head up when lying prone

YOUR BABY'S POSTURE

Although your baby's posture will mature as his muscles strengthen naturally, you may both enjoy bending and stretching exercises. As long as they are done gently, they will do no harm. And they are yet another way to spend pleasurable time with your baby – which will benefit you both!

Changing time is a good opportunity to do this; your baby will come to associate the pleasure of a clean, dry diaper with movement. Take your baby's feet gently by the ankles and bend and straighten his legs a few times. Take it slowly, and stop if your baby doesn't seem comfortable.

Your baby loves to be held in a sitting position

4 months

Your baby now concentrates on learning to sit up unsupported. Her head control continues to increase and she turns to the left and right when her attention is caught. She can support her chest and head weight on her forearms when lying prone, raise both legs off the mattress, and rock from side to side. She learns to roll over in whichever direction she chooses.

Your baby's head control continues to increase as he develops an interest in his surroundings

Your baby's head control and neck strength will increase with practice

5 months

Your baby has full head control even when propped in a sitting position. He may be able to take the full weight of his head, shoulders, and chest on outstretched hands. His rocking movements become stronger.

6 months

As your baby's limbs become stronger, he can take a lot of his weight on his arms. He'll sit with his hands forward for support and hold his hands out to you when he wants to be lifted.

He may even sit unsupported for a few seconds. If you gently bounce your baby up and down with his feet on your lap, he can take some of his own weight with his leg muscles.

Before he can crawl, your baby may work out his own highly individual way of moving around using the coordination he has mastered.

Some babies shuffle along on their bottoms, others use crablike, sideways movements, and others devise their own unique methods. It is not important what personal maneuver your baby works out: he has managed a great achievement in moving independently, and this is all that matters. You should never discourage your baby from his first attempts at being mobile. They are his tools for learning to control his body, and it is important that he is allowed to discover the limits of this control. Give his curiosity and spirit of adventure free rein.

ENCOURAGING MOVEMENT

Although your baby may appear to make crawling movements in his first weeks (see p.21), he'll stop this as his body straightens out from the fetal position. Before he can really begin to crawl, he must uncurl his body, control his head, lift his chest clear of the floor, and develop strength in his arms and legs.

Your encouragement and praise will make this an exciting and pleasurable time for both of you. As your baby gains head control, for instance, you may encourage him to lift his head by holding a brightly colored toy above him. As his back and shoulder muscles gain strength, you may wish to occasionally pull him into a sitting position when he is lying on his back. Once he can sit up, you can play games that make him swivel in this position; call "peek-a-boo" from his side so he has to turn to look at you. By about five months, when your baby has full head control, rocking and swinging games will help him practice keeping his head stable.

PROPPING

From as early as six weeks you should include your baby in daily life by propping him in an upright position with pillows. Since he can focus better by now, this will allow him to see what is going on and engage his interest in his surroundings. Once this stimulation begins, your baby will find the desire for involvement irresistible.

PREPARING TO CRAWL

Your baby has to be strong enough to hold his head and chest off the floor before he can crawl. By the time he's about six months old, he'll be able to push his chest clear of the floor and hold this position with his knees under him, but he will be around eight months old before he can pull himself forward along the floor.

It is impossible to pinpoint exactly the age at which your baby will crawl, if at all. If he's engrossed in watching what is going on around him he may hate lying on his stomach, and so leave crawling to a later stage. Some babies skip the crawling stage altogether, but go on to learn to walk perfectly.

You can encourage your baby to crawl in a number of ways, the best being to use yourself as an enticement. Praise any efforts your baby makes in order to divert him from feeling tired or frustrated by unsuccessful attempts. Your praise and support will be far more useful to him than will attempts to "teach" him to crawl by moving his arms and legs in a crawling movement.

A bouncing chair
The chair's springy responses to your baby's movements encourage him to move around. Always place the chair on the floor, never on a table.

PREPARING TO STAND

Before your baby can stand he must have strength and balance. Although he is unlikely to have strong leg muscles or control over them before he is 10 or 11 months old, a young baby will enjoy being bounced up and down on your knees. Hold your baby facing you with his feet touching your knees and gently raise and lower him, making sure that his neck is well supported. Your baby will enjoy the sensation of bearing his own weight, and it will strengthen his leg muscles in preparation for walking. From about 6 months he'll try to bend and straighten his legs in a jumping movement whenever he is held in a standing position. These movements are your baby's earliest attempts at walking.

EXERCISES

You can encourage your baby's physical development from a very early age by playing simple exercise games, which he should enjoy. You should dress him comfortably, but in a warm room with no drafts, his diaper will be all he needs.

STRENGTHENING ACTIVITIES

Flier
Lie on your back with your knees drawn up and balance your baby on his stomach, on your shins (knees). Stretch his arms out to the side – this should make him raise his head – and then bring his arms back to the original position and begin again.

Arm stretch
Lay your baby on his back and let him grasp your thumbs. Stretch one of his arms above his head. As you then lower the extended arm, raise his other arm above his head.

Your baby will be happier if he can see you and follow your movements

SAFETY

From the moment your baby becomes mobile, it is vital that your home is "childproof" (see pp.306–11) to prevent accidents.

• *Never leave your baby unattended. Even before he is mobile, your baby will need to be with you for reassurance and safety*

• *Once your baby learns to roll, never leave him lying anywhere except on the floor in an area clear of sharp or hard objects*

• *Even when he has mastered control over his head, continue to put pillows around your baby's bottom and lower spine*

• *Keep all poisonous substances out of your baby's reach*

• *Securely guard all fireplaces, cupboards, banisters, and stairs*

Crossovers
Holding your baby's hands, stretch his arms to the side, then back across his chest. Repeat.

FLOPPY INFANT SYNDROME

NAME *Catherine Dallas*

AGE *31 years*

OBSTETRIC HISTORY *First baby, normal delivery, no complications*

From about four months Catherine thought that Henry was a bit slow: he still didn't have control of his head, which tended to loll, and he hadn't made any attempts to sit up. If she tried to support him in a sitting position, he rolled to one side or the other.

When she was dressing Henry, Catherine noticed that his arms and legs flopped back onto the bed after she'd fitted them into a sleeve or legging.

As Henry was her first baby, Catherine was unsure whether or not Henry was late in developing but wisely decided to seek her doctor's opinion. When questioned by the doctor, Catherine could remember some other signs that all was not normal with Henry; when he was first born she had noticed that his eyes flicked back and forth quite quickly but hadn't known that this wasn't usual in newborn babies. Henry had seemed rather weak with his sucking, and had a tendency to drool, which indicated difficulty in swallowing – but she was told many newborns have the same trouble.

After carefully examining Henry and asking Catherine some questions, the doctor said Henry should see a pediatric neurologist for a full assessment. He used the phrase "floppy infant syndrome," saying it had many possible causes and might take a few months to discover the underlying problem in Henry's case.

Catherine was convulsed by fear and anxiety after hearing the doctor's opinion, and she desperately needed answers to her many questions. What is floppy infant syndrome? What causes it? Is it inherited? Would future babies be affected? What was the outlook for Henry? Would he ever be normal? How could she help him?

POSSIBLE CAUSES

I suggested to Catherine that we should take one step at a time: tests could answer all her questions. The list of possible causes of floppy infant syndrome is huge; the name simply describes the condition of a baby, not what's causing it. The "floppiness" can be caused by any one of hundreds of rare diseases, none of which can be diagnosed without extensive high-tech investigations. However, family history and careful clinical examination can narrow the list to one of three main categories.

Genetic This may be obvious if other family members have suffered, but may come to light only with chromosome testing, which can pick up gene abnormalities.

Muscular Muscular diseases such as muscular dystrophy may be tracked down with EMG (electromyography) and blood testing. The blood test measures levels of a chemical that is present in the blood when muscle tissue is being broken down. A muscle biopsy may also be carried out, so that a tiny piece of muscle can be studied under a microscope for abnormalities.

Brain The cerebellum, the part of the brain responsible for maintaining muscle tone, is situated at the back of the head and may not develop normally while the baby is in the uterus. CT (computed tomography) scanners and MRI (magnetic resonance imaging) are used to give pictures of the brain that can be examined in minute detail. Very rarely the brain may be damaged at birth, but usually only in a prolonged, difficult labor.

DIAGNOSTIC CLUES

Henry's Apgar score (see p.24) had been lowish at birth for muscle tone, an early clue to what happened later. Another clue was the nystagmus (flickering eye movements) that Catherine had noticed in Henry at birth. Nystagmus often originates from damage to or incorrect development of the cerebellum, so already we had an indication that this should be the first area to examine.

All the signs Catherine had noted but dismissed – weak sucking, drooling, poor swallowing, nystagmus, and poor muscle tone – are early symptoms of floppy infant syndrome, although it's not until they're all added together that their significance becomes obvious. I tried to reassure Catherine that she need not feel guilty about missing those early signs, since it would not have made any difference to Henry's future or his possible treatment.

LEARNING TO COPE

Before any tests were started, and with the cooperation of Henry's doctor, I encouraged Catherine and her husband, Mike, to see a psychiatric social worker rather than try to cope alone. It's a great help to talk constructively with an expert who can sympathize with conflicting emotions, and help couples to cope and plan. This turned out to be very comforting for Catherine and Mike, and they continued to see their social worker for many months.

HENRY'S DIAGNOSIS

When the tests were carried out, there was good news among the bad: the genetic tests were clear, meaning that Henry's disabilities were spontaneous and future babies would most likely be perfectly normal. As far as doctors could tell, his intelligence was not impaired and the muscle biopsy showed no dystrophy. It looked as if the lesion was in the brain, and MRI scans confirmed this with pictures showing a slightly small, underdeveloped cerebellum.

At 16 months Henry was behind in terms of development, but this was thought to be due to his weak muscles rather than mental retardation. He was a wonderfully sociable little boy, however, and very loving; he brought Catherine and Mike much pleasure. He was slow to speak, but made sounds so they knew he had the desire to communicate through conversation – a good sign. He had much better control over his body and was getting slowly stronger, though he would probably not walk till perhaps four or five years, and could have difficulty remaining steady. His vision and hearing are normal.

NAME *Henry Dallas*

AGE *18 months*

MEDICAL *Normal delivery.*
HISTORY *Nystagmus
(flickering eye
movements) at
birth and Apgar
score low for
muscle tone
(hypotonia).
Subsequent
motor develop-
ment slow*

Catherine has discovered from Henry's doctor, the social worker, and specialist that there is all kinds of help available for Henry (see Useful addresses, p.344–45). She knows she must be prepared for the fact that one day Henry might have to live in a special-care facility. In the meantime, she is taking Henry to physiotherapy sessions to strengthen his muscles and improve his physical co-ordination. The physiotherapist is very happy with his progress, and pleased, too, to see what a good teacher Catherine is becoming. Catherine is feeling more confident in her own strength and resourcefulness now that she realizes there is a great deal that she can do for Henry.

159

OLDER BABY   LOCOMOTION

As your baby learns to sit unsup-ported for longer periods of time, her sense of balance and her desire to walk will increase.

• *From about six or seven months, your baby will begin to take her full weight on her knees and hips, but she'll need to be balanced by you. She'll test her leg strength with a sort of dancing movement: a hop from one foot to another. As she becomes more confident she'll practice bending and stretching her legs*

• *By nine months, your baby's ability to balance will be greatly improved. She may be able to take all her own weight on her legs, but she'll still need to hold on to something. Any stable piece of furniture will support her, but she should never be left alone in this position; she'll find it difficult to sit from a standing position and a fall may seriously affect her con-fidence and pleasure in standing*

• *By about ten months, your baby will be able to lift one foot while she stands, provided she's supp-orted. She'll be able to pull herself into a standing position, but will still have trouble lowering herself*

During the first few months of life, your baby achieved head control and learned to coordinate and refine her movements in easily recognizable stages as her muscles became stronger and her balance improved. Now she is ready to start moving around, and the next year will be an exciting one for both of you as she learns to crawl and then to walk.

It's important to remember that all babies develop at their own speed, so the ages given here are the general times by which most babies have achieved these skills. A few babies walk by eight months; others show no interest in walking at all, but walk perfectly later on, so do not be too concerned if your baby's development doesn't match these stages exactly. Your baby may never crawl at all, going instead from shuffling (see p.156) to walking. Or she may move around on her hands and feet – a bearlike motion – rather than on her hands and knees.

Your baby can balance on three limbs while reach-ing out for an object

8 months
Your baby will stretch for things that are held beyond his reach. He'll sit unsupported, briefly at first, but gradually for longer periods of time. He'll master leaning, both forward and to the sides, and will test his own balance by rocking back and forth in a sitting position or twisting around, though he'll probably fall over.

10 months
Your baby may sit unaided for up to ten minutes. He's proba-bly mastered creeping. He can pull himself to his feet, but you'll still have to hold him in a standing position and help him sit down again.

Your baby's arms can now take some of his weight

1 year

Your baby can creep or crawl. When held in a standing position, he'll try stepping. He may try "cruising" – walking sideways while holding on to something.

Your baby will be able to turn and pick up an object behind him while sitting

14 months

After cruising, your baby will perfect standing alone and may even take his first independent step. Soon he'll be taking a few steps together in order to move between one stable support and another. He'll still need support to sit from standing.

16 months

Your baby's steps are high and unsteady, but her style will soon become more refined. She'll stand up and sit down without help, and can creep up stairs. You must be extra vigilant about safety; now that she's mobile she'll want to investigate everything she sees.

18 months

Your toddler can climb stairs unaided, although she needs support to keep balanced. Her steps are lower and more steady, and she rarely loses her balance. As her balance and coordination improve she'll progress to walking backward and running.

BALANCE

Between seven months and one year your baby will develop righting reflexes, which control her basic body movements.

These help her move from prone to standing positions and vice versa, to get on her hands and knees, and to sit up. They control the position and movement of her head and are responsible for the development of balance

- *By eight months, your baby will lean forward and backward in order to test her balance*

- *Between seven and nine months, your baby can lean forward and to the side without losing her balance. She can roll over and will try to crawl*

- *From ten months, she can twist her upper body while sitting. This strengthens her lateral trunk muscles and improves her balance*

Your baby's first attempts at walking will be unsteady and he'll hang on to objects for support, but in a couple of months he'll be independently mobile.

• *Your baby will "cruise" before he walks – that is, haul himself up on any large item and then sidle around it. Make sure that any unsteady or lightweight furniture is secured or removed from his path*

• *Next he'll start to move one hand over the other as he cruises rather than sliding them together and then moving both hands and feet at the same time. This is an important stage as your baby develops the confidence and balance to take all his weight, briefly, on one foot*

• *His next goal is to negotiate gaps between two supports. He'll hold on to both at once and let go of one support only when he's firmly holding on to the other*

• *He'll soon progress to crossing wider gaps. Still holding on to a support with one hand, he'll move into the center of the gap and, once he's got his balance, release one support and take a step toward the next one, grabbing for it with both hands*

• *Finally, your baby will begin to "toddle," staggering a couple of paces to reach the second support. He'll launch himself into the open and take several unsupported steps with confidence. He may soon lose his balance, sitting down with a thud, but he'll usually set off for his goal and waddle bowleggedly toward it with his arms held high and wide*

ENCOURAGING SKILLS

The transition your child makes from an uncoordinated baby to an independent toddler is a major turning point in his development, and you can help by encouraging him to stand and gently urging him on during his early attempts at walking.

He needs lots of room to move in and a soft covering under his feet so that he can fully enjoy his newfound freedom. Give him plenty of praise at every stage, but try not to push him to go faster than he feels he can – walking involves tricky techniques of balance and coordination and so is one of the most difficult skills your child will ever learn.

HELPING YOUR CHILD STAND

Let your baby take more and more of his own standing weight from the time he can control his head. His leg muscles, hips, and knees will gradually strengthen and he'll relish taking his own weight on them. When you hold his hands he'll bounce about and play standing and bouncing games. Hold him on your lap, on cushions, on a bed, or in the bath, and encourage these active games.

From around nine months, your baby will take nearly his entire weight on his legs, but will still need support to do so because his muscle strength is more advanced than his balance. You can encourage him by taking him to stable pieces of furniture and getting him to grip with his hands so that he is nicely balanced. Stay close while he holds on. He'll need to develop his balance in order to stand securely so, when he is sitting, urge him to lean forward and sideways by placing toys just out of reach in front and by his sides; this will strengthen his trunk muscles. He will find it difficult to sit down from a standing position, but you can make it a little easier by gently manipulating his hips and knees. At the age of ten months, your baby is far more mobile on his hands and knees. The muscles of his trunk are getting stronger all the time as he twists and turns while sitting or crawling. Offer your fingers to encourage him to pull himself up to sit and stand. He'll be delighted at his achievement, so always praise him well.

Learning to stand
Teach your baby the sensation of supporting his own weight by holding his hands and playing gentle leg-bending games.

HELPING YOUR CHILD WALK

Although your baby will learn to walk on his own – if there are no impediments to his doing so – you may help him practice if you both find it fun and you have the time. Put your baby on his hands and knees and sit a short distance away. This will impel him to move toward you. He'll come more eagerly if you hold out your arms, call his name, or offer a brightly colored toy. To prompt your baby to twist, place a toy behind his back and support him as he turns around. Soon your baby will be able to stand up if he is supported by furniture. While he is standing and firmly supported, bend one of his knees and lift his foot; this will help him learn to step and bear his weight momentarily on one foot.

Once your baby begins to cruise, help him practice walking forward by holding his hands and guiding him. You can help make cruising easier by positioning stable pieces of furniture close to one another around the room, but remove any items that could tip over easily when he pulls on them.

Call to your baby while he is cruising around the room. Give him the courage to launch himself by moving the pieces of furniture slightly farther apart. Sit a little way from him and, while he's holding on to the furniture, hold out your arms and call him to you – but always be close enough to catch him if he stumbles.

Once your baby can stand alone he may take his first independent step. A stable standing toy, like a push-along wagon, is ideal encouragement for him to practice walking alone. When your baby can kneel, lower his body without support, and stand up unaided, a chair with arms will allow him to sit down without falling and will provide good bending practice for his hips and knees.

Practice more leg movements with your baby, using a large soft ball that he can try to kick to you. This is also good for acquiring balance. Show him how to squat, and help him master hip and knee bends – which are all the more enjoyable if you do them together to music. Games that use backward or sideways steps will provide practice in walking and balancing skills. "Ring-around-a-Rosy," played by holding your baby's hands while walking, sitting, and standing, is a lot of fun and allows your baby to imitate you, making his sense of achievement even greater.

There's no right age for your baby to start to walk, but he is most likely to take his first unsupported steps between the ages of 9 and 15 months.

Toys for walking
Your toddler's mobility and independence will be enhanced by sturdy, wheeled walking toys.

SAFETY

As your baby's independence grows, safety in his environment becomes increasingly important.

• *Keep close by when your baby is taking his first unsteady steps and take particular care when he walks and creeps up stairs. Make sure the floor is not slippery and don't give him shoes until he is walking outdoors*

• *Give your baby plenty of clear space for his walking attempts. Trailing cords or small pieces of furniture might cause him to trip*

• *Install special protective edges on sharp-cornered furniture and door handles*

• *Remove glass-topped furniture or cover it with safety film*

• *Install safety gates at the top and bottom of your stairs. Gates at the top of the stairs should open onto the landing and should not have horizontal bars that your baby could climb*

• *Keep all poisonous substances well out of reach, and out of sight, in a lockable cupboard. Even vitamin pills are dangerous*

• *Don't leave sharp or hot objects within your baby's reach*

TODDLER

LOCOMOTION

LOCOMOTION IN GIRLS

The age at which a specific milestone in locomotion is achieved will differ from child to child.

In the preschool years, some girls may appear to be better than boys at jumping, hopping, rhythmic movement, and balance. Girls seem to enjoy games that involve these skills – hopscotch, jump rope, and dancing games – though undoubtedly differences in acculturation between the sexes accounts for this to a degree.

Between the ages of 18 months and three years your child will quickly progress in getting around. She will be very active on her feet, perfecting her walking and balancing skills, and you can encourage this development by involving her in your daily activities. She will begin to enjoy ball games, toys on wheels, and games that involve hopping, jumping, or climbing. Spend time with your child encouraging her in her new skills and building up her confidence: it will be vital in her continuing physical development.

21 months
Your child can now bend to pick up objects without toppling over. Walking becomes steadier, and he can walk with his arms by his sides instead of held out high. He can run quite well, but will have difficulty turning corners and may topple over if he stops suddenly. He may be able to kick a ball, but rather awkwardly, since he can't balance well on one leg.

2 years
Your child is more fluent at ball games, both catching and kicking, and can walk backward as well as forward. He can go up and down stairs without holding on, putting both his feet on each step. He can now veer and swerve while running and can stop running without falling over.

2 ½ years
Your child can now jump with both feet off the ground at the same time, walk on tiptoe, and is steady on her feet – with your guidance she can carry a breakable object or hold a baby brother or sister on her knee. She can now run quite well and can glance over her shoulder without losing balance.

HOW TO HELP

Your child's toddler years are a time of great activity for both of you. She'll be interested in everything she sees and is developing the skills that will allow her to take part in a number of activities for the first time. This provides a great opportunity for you to involve her in many daily tasks that will be both fun for her and important to her development.

Give your child plenty of chances to practice her walking skills by going up and down stairs with her or leaving the stroller behind on short trips. Hold her hand if she needs support or when you go out shopping. Don't put too many demands on her walking abilities at this stage – she won't be able to walk farther than a few hundred yards. She is bound to have some lapses in her learning, so don't worry if she experiences setbacks in her walking like a stumble or fall – she will soon regain her confidence.

Agility in walking and running may also be developed by playing games that involve jumping and walking on tiptoe. Encourage your child to dance to music with you. She'll need plenty of practice at balancing, and this can be developed with ball games and other suitable toys. Start with a large, soft ball. Let her try walking along the top of a low wall, holding her hand all the time in case she gets a bit wobbly. Your child is probably too young for a bicycle, but a toy with wheels that she can sit on and propel with her feet will develop her love of motion and strengthen her muscles. Indoors, give your child soft toys like a mattress or foam rubber pad on which to jump and somersault. An outdoor swing will help her develop strength and coordination skills, but make sure this large outdoor equipment is safe (see p.311).

The more you involve your child in daily activities such as cleaning and washing, and climbing the stairs, the more practice your child will receive. Always take sensible precautions against falls and other household dangers, but don't worry too much; toddlers are amazingly resilient and will be oblivious to most of the bruises they inevitably receive in these active and inquisitive years.

Wheeled toys
A scooter can be used indoors as well as out, and will improve your child's coordination and muscle strength.

LOCOMOTION IN BOYS

In the preschool years, there is little difference between boys and girls in terms of strength and speed.

Young boys may well have fewer opportunities than girls to hone jumping, hopping, rhythmic movement, and balancing skills at play. You can help by allowing your little boy as much freedom of movement as he wants. Games that involve kicking a ball, dancing, or jumping will give him practice in these skills.

PRESCHOOL LOCOMOTION

ENCOURAGING GIRLS

Girls are often considered to be less outgoing and adventurous than boys, but it is important that they be encouraged to be curious and active, and to let off steam with physical activity.

• *Don't be overly concerned about your little girl hurting herself or getting her clothes dirty; this attitude can inhibit your child from discovering her physical potential*

• *Girls tend to be more naturally sociable, so encourage her to play team or cooperative games, such as hopscotch or jumping rope*

• *Include more energetic movements with your child, in games such as "Simon says"*

• *Girls tend to be more gifted at imaginative role-playing games, so try to encourage your little girl to include more physical creativity, with constructional and spatial skills, into her fantasy games*

• *Never hamper your daughter's adventurousness and curiosity; encourage her to climb and swing as you would a son*

Dance will improve poise and balance

Dance
Many little girls love the idea of being a dancer, and lessons can be an enjoyable social occasion as well as honing physical skills.

During these two preschool years, your child is really developing his physical skills and taking a pride in acquiring each new ability. At three years, your child has become much more nimble, walking up stairs with confidence. He can jump off the bottom step and stand on one foot for a second. He can swing his arms when he walks and can ride a tricycle. At four, your child is very active and well coordinated. He races around hopping, jumping, and climbing, and can walk down stairs rapidly, with one foot per step. He can even carry a drink without spilling it. By five, your child's coordination is finely developed. He can walk a straight line, go down stairs on alternating feet, skip a rope with alternating feet, climb confidently, and enjoy fast-moving toys and games.

ENCOURAGING SKILLS

You can encourage your three-year-old's jumping skills by playing hopscotch or holding hands and hopping on one foot. This will work off excess energy. You can practice arm-swinging with him by marching to music. Letting him ride a tricycle will strengthen his calf muscles and encourage flexibility in his feet, while backyard equipment such as a swing, seesaw, or slide will boost his physical confidence.

At four, your child should have access to outside apparatus, such as a climbing frame in the yard, to provide scope to exercise his muscles. You can also help him to master jumping rope and to try a range of other physical games.

Five-year-olds can jump rope and some may even enjoy the challenge of learning to ride a two-wheeled bicycle.

Wheeled toys
A three-year-old will have enough coordination to manage pedaling.

Sturdy pedals are easy to maneuver

ADVENTUROUS PLAY

If your child is encouraged to be adventurous, he will be willing to push himself to the limit and develop his full potential. A child of three or four has a very clear sense of self and his abilities and is discovering the limits of what is safe and feasible. If you are over-protective and don't allow your child to test his abilities, master a new skill, and move on, you will hold him back and he will lack co-ordination and confidence as a result. You must separate his fears from yours; his fears will make him sensibly cautious, while your fears will cripple both his curiosity and spirit.

By the time your child is three years old, he can walk and run confidently. He has boundless energy, and is ready to tackle more demanding activities, so give him plenty of scope: running, climbing, and pedaling will improve his skills and help him burn off surplus energy. If you can afford it, set up a climbing frame, rope ladder, or swing in your yard where you can supervise him from the house. Depending on your child's skill and confidence, he may be ready to tackle roller skating and riding a bicycle with stabilizing wheels. Introducing your child to sports and other activities now could lay the foundations for a lifetime of enjoyment, so give him the opportunity to try lots of different things: swimming, dancing, soccer, or horse-riding. At the very least, try to make sure he has somewhere he can run, climb, or just kick a ball around.

You can always help your child tackle new and difficult tasks at first , holding his hand and guiding him through them so that you are secure in your own mind that he is competent and therefore safe. Extend adventurousness and curiosity across the board, not solely in physical development but with toys, music, painting, and books.

ENCOURAGING BOYS

Boys are assumed and encouraged to be adventurous in their play, but it is a mistake to assume that all boys are outgoing and active. Some have an obvious preference for boisterous games while others prefer quiet, contemplative activities.

• *Games on large soft cushions and foam-filled furniture are excellent fun and good for promoting balance and coordination*

• *Boys are usually considered to be better at "spatial relationships" – knowing, for example, how one object fits onto another. Encourage this skill by introducing construction toys as soon as he can fit them together*

• *Provide plenty of opportunities for your little boy to be creative; items such as toilet paper tubes, old egg boxes, and yogurt containers can be turned into anything his imagination can conjure up*

Balance and coordination
Encourage your child's adventurous spirit by providing equipment such as roller skates.

Adjustable roller skates are comfortable and allow for growth

Inflatable armbands give your child confidence

Swimming
Your child's muscular fitness and strength, particularly in the arms, will be developed by swimming.

167

YOUNG BABY

MANIPULATION

YOUR BABY'S HANDS

At first your baby has little interest in his hands, but as he becomes more aware of his body they'll begin to fascinate him more and more.

When he waves his arms around, his hand will accidentally touch his face and he'll put it in his mouth to suck. At two to three months, he finds the movements of his fingers fascinating and will watch them for ages. By about four months, he'll grab hold of objects to "test" them in his mouth. At six months, he refines his manual skills and feels with his fingers as much as his mouth.

Your baby was born with the reflex to grasp anything that is placed in his palm – such as your finger – and not let go; his grip is so strong he can support his own weight (though you should never actually let him do so). When he is not holding something, his hands will be tightly closed in a fist, although they'll probably open and close when he cries, and he will open them instinctively when he is startled (see p.20). The early reflex grasp must be lost if he is to learn to select an object, reach out, and pick it up with thumb and forefinger – the basic skill of manual dexterity. Most babies will develop a mature "pincer" grip by one year of age.

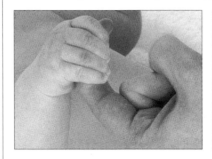 

Newborn
From birth, your baby has the ability to grasp an object and hold on. This grasping reflex is so strong it allows him to support his own weight.

2 months
Your baby is becoming more aware of his hands, and his reflex grasping action has almost gone. His hands are much more open now, too.

5 months
Your baby is eager to grab things with his whole hand. He will hold his feet, or a soft toy, and transfer them to his mouth to suck.

Your baby will love to suck his toes

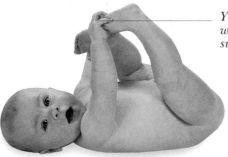

6 months
Your baby holds his bottle or cup, and he'll be able to hold between two hands an object that is given to him.

Your baby learns to feed himself

ENCOURAGING SKILLS

Even the most simple activities can add to your baby's feelings of confidence and achievement. He needs to feel that his hard work is noticed and appreciated by you, and that you are as pleased as he is about his cleverness and growing independence.

0–6 weeks Your baby must ignore his instinctive grasp reflex before he can manipulate objects. Test this reflex by letting him grasp your fingers and seeing how far you can pull him off the mattress. Encourage him to open his fingers by gently unfolding them one at a time as you play games like "This little piggy."

6 weeks Your baby's hands are opening and he is becoming aware of them. Help him take an interest in his hands by tickling his palms and fingertips with materials of different textures: soft, furry, smooth, or ridged – corduroy, for example. A gentle hand massage or rubbing of his palms will encourage him to open his hands.

2 months Your baby's hands are more open now, so continue to provide plenty of tactile stimulation by giving him objects of different textures to hold. Lay each object across his palm, following the horizontal creases, so he can wrap his hand around it.

3 months Your baby uses a wide open hand to grasp and reaches for things inaccurately. Encourage a mature grasp by giving him things to hold. Place a rattle in his hand and shake it a few times – he will be fascinated both by the feel and sound of it. Put a mobile above his crib to give him something to look at, and string toys across his carriage to swipe at (ensure they are safe; see p.310).

4 months As your baby starts to get his hand and arm movements under control, he'll reach out for things with increasing accuracy. Encourage him by presenting interesting objects while he is sitting propped up or lying down. He will still tend to overshoot when he reaches for something, so you'll need to compensate to ensure he does get the object.

5 months Your baby will be grabbing everything within reach, and he will particularly love crumpling paper, so give him white tissue paper to play with. He will love you to play with his feet where he can see them, so play "This little piggy" with his toes. Play giving and taking-away games to encourage him to open his fingers and let go. He will reach for a bottle to try to feed himself.

6 months His finger movements are becoming more precise all the time. You can let him hold his own bottle in two hands and give him a variety of finger foods (see p.61) for easy grasping and self-feeding. You can teach him how to feed himself with a spoon and how to pass an object from one hand to the other. As soon as this is mastered, he will joyfully start to practice his letting-go skill by throwing everything on the floor.

Self-feeding
At six months, your baby's hand-eye coordination is good enough to pick up finger foods and start feeding himself, although he is not yet very accurate at getting the food into his mouth.

OLDER BABY

MANIPULATION

By the age of six months, your baby will have learned to grasp objects voluntarily, and now she will gradually refine her handling skills as she learns to use them to eat, dress, wash, and pick things up. You'll find this time both rewarding and frustrating – your baby is learning to do more things for herself, but she won't be very adept at first so you'll have to be patient while she learns.

By 12 months, your baby will have the mature grasp that is a fine movement achieved by bringing the thumb and first finger together (opposition). She can give something to you by releasing her grip, and she will be able to roll a ball to you.

Your baby uses his whole hand to grip

9 months
Your baby can pick up small things by bringing his thumb and index finger together. He points with his index finger when reaching for something. He's eager to feed himself.

Your baby can grip objects between his thumb and index fingers

12 months
Your baby still enjoys throwing things as he practices "ungrasping." He can build a tower of two blocks and draw lines with a pencil. His coordination is improving so he spills less food.

18 months
Now your toddler can turn two or three pages of a book at a time and build a tower of three blocks. She is able to feed herself completely with a spoon and drink from a cup without spilling. She will put on some clothes, is fascinated by zippers, and enjoys finger painting and scribbling.

HOW YOU CAN HELP

Your baby's new skills can be encouraged as before in a variety of games that you can play together. Now that she's older, however, she'll be able to pursue some activities by herself; she'll also be able to apply herself to everyday tasks.

Everyday activities The business of getting food into her mouth will give your child a powerful motive to improve her hand–eye coordination. As soon as she is able – from about six months – let her hold her own bottle or cup while she drinks from it and give her finger foods to encourage fine finger movements. Before long she'll be able to feed herself with a spoon, a skill you can encourage by preparing semisolid foods that will stick to the spoon.

Dressing is another everyday activity that your baby will try increasingly to do for herself. She may be able to pull some of her clothes on and off, but won't be able to manage fastenings yet, though she will want to try.

Building blocks Once your baby is able to grasp a block, you can show her how to place one on top of another. At 6 or 7 months, she will have mastered this, but you can continue to stack blocks – three or four high or side by side – for her to see and copy. As her grasp develops (see right), she practices the novel skill of letting go and dropping things, and will throw blocks. By one year old, she'll be able to build a tower of two blocks by herself, and by 15 months she'll probably manage three.

Games There are all sorts of simple games your baby can play to develop her skills. She will love making noise with some pots and pans and a wooden spoon. Once she learns to let objects go, she will enjoy throwing them out of her stroller or high chair. You can make this into a game by showing her how to put objects into a container and take them out again.

Drawing Your baby won't be able to manage a pencil or crayon until she's about a year old, but once she starts, she will love to scribble. Give her lots of scrap paper – wallpaper remnants are good – and hang her pictures up where she can see them.

Building blocks
Help your child develop her grasp so she can let go as well as hold on, by introducing her to toy blocks.

YOUR BABY'S GRASP

The ability to grasp small objects precisely between thumb and finger – opposition – will be one of the great achievements of your baby's first year.

- *At about five months, your baby will grasp objects in her palm on the little finger side*

- *At about eight months, she will be able to grasp an object between her fingers, perhaps pushing it against the base of the thumb*

- *Next she learns to "ungrasp" and practices this by dropping and throwing things*

- *At about nine months, she will use her index finger to point – a step toward holding small objects with the thumb and index finger*

- *By the time she is one year old, she will have achieved a mature "pincer" grip, grasping objects between the thumb and index finger*

TODDLER

MANIPULATION

In terms of general development, the toddler stage marks a quite dramatic change from babyhood to childhood, and from 18 months onward you'll really notice this transformation, especially in manipulative skills. Over the next 18 months, your baby will be getting more independent as she learns to dress herself and to manage increasingly fine movements. Her creative skills also come to the fore at this stage as her building-block houses get more complicated and her drawings more recognizable.

Milestones
Your child may just be able to zip a zipper. He will try an "unscrewing" movement with jar tops and doorknobs by the age of two. He'll use crayons more deliberately and may be able to build a tower of four blocks.

Your child has a refined grip to clasp and twist objects

Your child can grip and pull fine materials

Thick yarn or shoelaces will be easy for your child to manage

Getting dressed
At two and a half, putting on and taking off clothes will become easier and your child will be eager to do these things for himself.

Fine movements
Your child will be able to thread large beads or spools on a string by two and a half years old.

Household items like thread spools can be threaded onto string

172

ENCOURAGING SKILLS

All sorts of everyday tasks are now becoming possible for your child to manage by herself, so give her every opportunity to do things by herself. More complicated toys, especially construction or craft toys, will help her practice and develop her skills.

Dressing By the age of two, your child will be able to cope with a number of dressing skills, though putting on her socks, shoes, and gloves will still be tricky, so let her choose her own clothes and practice getting dressed. Clothes with snaps and fairly large buttons, provided the holes are not too tight, will also help her to develop new finger skills. Continue to encourage her dressing ability and she will soon be able to put on and take off underpants, pants, and T-shirts. Once she can cope with all her buttons, including the smaller ones, she will be able to dress and undress herself completely.

Construction toys
Interlocking building blocks are always popular toys and are ideal for developing hand movements.

Improving dexterity As soon as your child can turn a doorknob with two hands and open a loose-fitting screw-top jar, give her toys that need to be fitted together. Washing and drying her hands will also be a favorite pastime so encourage her in this. Ensure that your two-year-old has plenty of colorful picture books on hand as she can now turn the pages of a book one at a time by herself. Your child can now build a tower of four blocks and with encouragement she'll make more complicated structures. Building blocks that need pressing and fitting together will help develop the small movements of her hands. Intricate tasks, such as threading large beads on a piece of string or fitting together jigsaw puzzles made of large pieces, will boost her manipulation skills.

Arts and crafts Children enjoy drawing at this age, so give your child plenty of drawing materials, including a range of different crayons, and start her off by showing the effect of all the different colors. She will also enjoy using paints, especially if you allow her to be messy and paint with her hands. You can also help her relate her drawings to the world around her by naming the colors of the crayons and then pointing out the same colors in everyday objects. She will soon be producing images of familiar objects, and by the age of two and a half, her pictures will become more recognizable.

ENCOURAGING INDEPENDENCE

With so many new skills to learn at this stage, it is important not to expect your child to develop at a rate that is too fast for her.

All children progress at their own pace, which is determined by the speed that their developing brain and nerves allow. Your child will want to please you and may try to do things that are more complicated than her development will allow. Failure is demoralizing because she feels she's let you down. A better approach is to give her all the help and encouragement she needs, showing her how pleased you are with every task she manages, without setting goals that are beyond her abilities.

Choosing clothes
Encourage your child's interest in dressing himself by letting him choose the clothes he is to wear.

PRESCHOOL

MANIPULATION

DRAWING

Your child's improving manual dexterity is clearly demonstrated by his ability to copy a circle.

2 ½ years
His earliest attempts at a circle may end up as a continuous round shape, like a spiral.

3 years
His attempts become more controlled, but the circle may not quite close or the lines may overshoot.

3 ½ years
Your child should be able to draw a closed figure, either a true circle or an oval shape.

Your three-year-old is maturing rapidly and by now can probably dress and undress himself completely, as long as the fasteners are all easy to reach. He can draw and color quite accurately and his drawings are becoming more recognizable. By the age of four he will have mastered the complicated action of using scissors. Building blocks are becoming too simple for him, so he is ready to move on to more sophisticated construction sets. He is already doing very simple tasks around the house, and from four years old he will get much better at jobs such as setting the table, washing his face and hands, making his bed, and putting his clothes tidily away.

Crafts
Your four- or five-year-old's ability to use scissors represents a huge step forward in manual dexterity and brain–muscle coordination. Give him simple models to make. Any scissors he uses should be blunt-ended.

Drawing
From three years on, your child becomes more skillful at drawing as she begins to master skills like copying two straight lines drawn at right angles. By four years, she begins to add more detail to her figures. You can make simple puzzles for her – draw an incomplete person and ask her to complete it.

174

TEETH

In the past it was thought that the primary teeth (milk teeth) were not very important because the adult teeth would come in to replace them in time. Now we know that they are vital because they guide the adult teeth so that they grow in the correct position. In addition, if the primary teeth are lost through decay this can spread to the bone beneath, eroding the support needed by the adult teeth.

Eruption time There is no standard time for your baby's first tooth to erupt. Some babies are born with one tooth, while others still have none at 12 months of age. (If a baby is born with a tooth, it is sometimes removed if it is crooked or badly positioned, for instance, or if it is loose and there is a risk of its falling out and causing the baby to choke.) As a general rule, however, teething starts at around six months, after which many teeth appear up to the end of his first year. If you are on the lookout, you will probably notice your baby's first tooth as it starts to push its way through the gum and form a small, pale bump. Your baby will be teething for most of the second year, and you should be prepared that the molars, which come through last, may be a bit upsetting.

Signs of teething Your baby may be somewhat irritable when he is cutting a tooth. The gum will be red and swollen, and you may be able to feel the tooth through the gum. Your baby's cheeks may be red, and he will probably drool more than usual. Giving your baby something to chew on can help. Symptoms such as fever, vomiting, or diarrhea are never caused by teething, so you should not dismiss them – inform your child's doctor.

USING THE TEETH

A raw carrot or a piece of toast will give your baby something firm to chew on when teething. This principle continues to hold good once she has all her teeth.

Crunchy foods, and particularly fresh fruit and raw vegetables, will encourage the development of strong jaw muscles. They also strengthen the teeth and cleanse them since the fibers within them are shredded during the chewing process. Your baby's diet should contain plenty of calcium and vitamin D (from dairy foods) to ensure the healthy formation of the permanent teeth that are already growing in the jawbones.

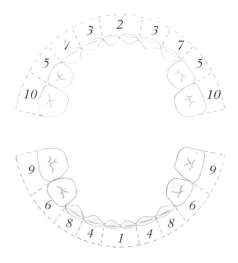

How the teeth come in
The numbers indicate the order in which the teeth arrive. The first to erupt are usually the lower front 2 teeth, then the upper 2 front teeth. Upper incisors come next, followed by the lower incisors. After this, the first upper molars erupt and then the first lower molars. The upper canines come in next, each side, followed by the lower canines. The second molars erupt first in the lower jaw, and then they appear in the upper jaw.

VISION

The development of normal vision requires two properly functioning eyes and plenty of visual stimulation. You can provide stimulation by:

• *From the day he is born, putting a photo of a face – yours or one cut from a magazine – at the side of the crib*

• *Hanging a mobile over the crib or stringing brightly colored objects across it to catch his eyes once color vision is more developed*

• *Taking your baby sightseeing. He's never too young, and if he's in a stroller, he'll be able to look all around him*

Recognizing faces
Give your baby an unbreakable mirror so that he can look at his own reflection.

A newborn baby is not blind; he simply cannot change focus yet. He can see everything at a fixed focus of 8–10 inches (20–25 centimeters) as plainly as you or I can. It used to be thought that a newborn baby's visual world need not be very stimulating because he could not see. We now know that the normal development of your baby's eyesight depends on visual stimulation right from birth. Nonetheless, a newborn baby's vision is more limited than an older child's, so you will have to fit his visual world into a range that he can perceive. The color-sensitive cells in a newborn's eyes are not fully developed so he will see the world in muted shades only.

Your newborn Although your baby's eyesight is limited, his eyes are very sensitive to the human face and anything that moves. At first he won't be able to focus on anything farther than 10 inches (25 centimeters) away, but if you bring your face to within about 8 inches (20 centimeters) of his, he will see you and you will notice that his eyes move in recognition and his expression changes.

Increasing recognition If you talk excitedly to your newborn, move your eyes, and open and close your mouth, your baby will respond from within a few minutes of birth by opening his mouth and sticking out his tongue. A baby of only a few hours old can bring his eyes to an object and follow it if it moves. At two weeks, a baby will automatically raise a hand to protect himself from something that is moving quickly toward him. At three weeks, his whole body may react with excited jerking movements when your face comes into focus. Your baby can fully focus by eight weeks, and he should recognize your face and respond to it with smiles and waving arms. He is also more conscious of other objects but, because your baby can focus only on nearby objects, the world appears rather flat and distant details are lost to him.

Depth of vision By three to four months, your baby can take in details and is able to build up a three-dimensional picture of the world – a necessary step before he becomes mobile, since he probably won't start crawling until his vision allows him to understand depth as well as height and width. He can tell the difference between pictures with two and three items, and can recognize patterns. This eye for detail improves until, by five to six months, he can discriminate between different facial expressions, such as sadness, fear, and joy, and will respond to them with his own expression. He will show excitement when he sees his food being prepared.

A sense of permanence From six months, he can identify objects and can adjust his position to see those that most interest him. From now on the biggest development in your baby's visual skill is the way his brain interprets the information his eyes see.

TESTING VISION

Your baby's doctor will check his eyes and vision routinely as part of all well-baby visits, and will advise you on any problems that may require treatment. But even at birth, you can get an idea of how well your baby's vision is working. Note your baby's reaction to your face when it is held 8–10 inches (25 centimeters) from his. If he sees your face, his facial expression should change; his eyes will dart to your face and he may open and shut his mouth. If you're in any doubt about your baby's vision, or if your child's eyes water a lot and bright lights cause him discomfort, consult your doctor.

Lazy eye (amblyopia) A child with lazy eye may turn his head so that the eye with better sight can more easily follow the action around him. This correctable condition results from a vision problem in one eye that is keeping it from receiving as much visual stimulation as the other. If your baby obviously favors one eye over the other, consult your doctor.

Crossed eyes (strabismus) If you notice that only one of your baby's eyes is focused on an object of interest and the other is pointing too far in or out, the problem may be strabismus, a treatable eye problem with several causes. He may tilt his head or hold it in an unusual position to get his vision in line. Find an interesting object, such as a toy and, keeping your child's head still (you may need someone to help you), move the toy to spell the letter H in the air. Check that both eyes follow the toy. (See **Crossed eyes**, p.287.)

Color blindness The most common form is the inability to distinguish between red and green (mostly, but not exclusively, found in boys). If your child is old enough, use colorful beads or blocks and ask him to pick out certain colors. If he hasn't learned his colors yet, ask him to match colors you pick out.

Peripheral vision To test whether your child has a normal field of vision choose a favorite toy and, with your child staring directly ahead, slowly move it from the outside to in front of his face until he sees it. His field of vision should extend to about 45° on either side.

Visual acuity If your child is old enough, test the accuracy of his vision with the following game. Stand about 20 feet (6 meters) away and hold up some fingers. Ask him how many fingers he sees, or get him to hold up the same number as you. If he fails, consult your doctor, although 20/30 vision is considered acceptable until five or six years of age.

OLDER BABY

VISION PROBLEMS

If your child has vision problems, make sure he has professional attention and regular checkups.

• *A child who is farsighted or has astigmatism may need to wear glasses for only two or three years before his eyesight develops normally. Farsighted children should have six-monthly checkups to see if their prescription for glasses needs changing*

• *The earlier children start wearing glasses, the more likely they are to accept them. At first a child may take them off and play with them, but he'll soon show a preference for seeing the world clearly*

• *A child with vision problems needs stimulation by touch, noise, and smell, so choose toys that have interesting textures and make different noises. Puzzles are particularly important; those with large, colorful pieces are best*

Brightly colored toys
Your child needs visual stimulation even if he has vision problems, so toys with a variety of shapes and colors are important.

HEARING

By explaining sounds and playing appropriate games with your baby, you can help him to listen in a discerning way to the confusion of sounds that he hears.

• *Be theatrical about explaining sounds. For example, put your finger to your lips and say, "Sssh, let's be quiet as mice," to explain the idea of quietness*

• *Describe sounds and music with appropriate adjectives such as "loud" or "soft"*

• *Teach the concept of high and low notes with songs*

• *Teach rhythm with rhymes and clapping songs – this will also help your child's speech*

• *Name every new sound, such as the cat purring, and imitate it*

Your baby needs to be able to hear the full range of sounds that are essential for speech if he is to be able to talk correctly. Only when your child shows, first that he can hear, later that he can imitate sound, and eventually that he can use different sounds correctly to form speech, can you be sure that he can discriminate between different sounds across the full normal range of hearing.

There are various clues to your child's hearing ability that you should be aware of, and several simple tests you can carry out to judge his progress. Carefully observe his reactions to different sounds and make a note of what you see. If anything about the way your baby responds to sounds concerns you, tell your pediatrician, who will conduct a more thorough test on your baby's hearing.

Your newborn baby reacts to noises without really understanding them. If he is startled by a sudden loud noise, such as a hand clap or a door slamming, he may throw out his arms and legs in a "startle" reflex action, as though to save himself from falling. A little later on, sudden sounds will make him blink or open his eyes wide in surprise. By four weeks, he will begin to notice noises of longer duration, such as the sound of your vacuum cleaner.

By the time he is four months old, your baby should be able to discriminate between certain sounds. For example, when he hears your voice, he will smile, or become quiet, and will turn his head and eyes toward your sound, even if he cannot see where you are.

After six months, your baby should turn at once to investigate soft noises made on each side of him, or at the sound of your voice from across the room. A nine-month-old baby should be babbling to hear his own voice, and will listen attentively to familiar sounds and search for softer sounds made out of sight.

EARLY TESTS

The first testing your child undergoes to measure his reaction to sound may well be in the maternity unit shortly after birth. This testing will use soft sounds to measure your baby's response to noise. Responses may vary from a slight movement of the head to a change in breathing rate. More extensive tests may be conducted during routine developmental assessments at about six weeks, and between six and ten months if there is cause for concern.

The problem with early testing is that, until about seven months, babies react inconsistently to noise and require careful monitoring with sophisticated machinery to achieve reliable results.

Parents with profoundly deaf children usually become aware of the problem fairly quickly. It is often more difficult to identify those with partial hearing loss because their symptoms can be mistaken for inattentiveness, slow learning, or shyness. If you are worried about your child's hearing, you should have him examined by his doctor as soon as possible so that he can receive proper help.

TESTING HEARING

There are simple tests you can do to check your baby's hearing from about six months of age. For the best results, the tests need to be carried out in a quiet room with no distractions.

You will need a high-pitched rattle, some hard tissue paper, and a china cup, a spoon, and a bell. Sit the baby on your lap, no closer than 4 feet from any wall, and ask another adult to take up a position to the side of your baby but outside his immediate range of vision.

The tester should stand 18 inches (45 centimeters) away for a six-month-old and 3 feet (1 meter) away for a nine-month-old, and make sounds at the level of the baby's ear in the following order:

- Produce low-pitched and high-pitched sounds with your voice

- Shake the rattle

- Tap the spoon against the cup

- Crumple the tissue paper

- Ring the handbell

If you get no response to any of the sounds, wait two seconds before repeating it. Wait a further two seconds and if there is still no response after three tries, go on to the next sound.

Children of nine months and upward should turn at once when they hear the sound and will often smile. Younger babies may be slower to react. A clear response to three of these sounds means your baby has enough hearing to speak. If your baby responds to fewer than three sounds, let your pediatrician know at once.

18 months to 2 years For an older baby or toddler, you should judge his response to spoken instructions. Sit him opposite you at a low table, with another familiar adult (such as his father or other family member) close by. Ask him to hand certain objects to Daddy, such as a ball, cup and spoon, doll, toy car, or building block, and see how he responds. Ask him again from different distances up to 10 feet (3 meters). For children up to three years, you could try the same test while partly covering your mouth with a piece of card to muffle the sound.

You shouldn't carry out these hearing tests too often, because even quite a young child will come to know what to expect and will turn toward the sound whether or not he is able to hear it.

OLDER BABY

HEARING PROBLEMS

Children must be able to hear in order to speak so it is essential to pick up any hearing problems early and seek professional help as soon as possible.

Temporary, partial hearing loss due to persistent ear infections can interfere with a child's acquisition of speech. Effective treatment is available and should always be sought (see pp.284–5).

Children with incurable hearing loss can function quite well with a hearing aid. In profoundly deaf children, however, comprehension of sound and language is significantly impaired.

There are many ways to approach communication for profoundly deaf children, and they are often used in combination. Among them are: cochlear implants, one of several signing languages, lip-reading, and oral language.

Simple hearing test
A six-month-old baby with normal hearing will turn his head if you ring a small bell near him, just outside his field of vision.

Even before your baby is born, all the essential brain structures have developed.

• *The cortex, which determines intellect, develops before birth*

• *The left half of the cortex controls thinking, and language centers are also located in the left side of the brain*

• *The corpus callosum connects the right lobe of the brain to the left lobe*

• *A boy's brain is about 10 to 15 percent larger and heavier than a girl's brain, though this has no bearing on intelligence or other mental functions*

MENTAL DEVELOPMENT

Your baby is born with a finite number of brain cells, yet his brain doubles in weight between birth and 12 months. The increase in weight is due to the growth of connections between the different cells used in thinking. When your baby sees a piece of bread, points to it, reaches for it, picks it up, puts it in his mouth, chews it, tastes it, and swallows it, he's built up many brain connections and slotted it all into his memory.

PREDICTING INTELLIGENCE

Although it's difficult to say what "normal" intelligence is, many experts in the field of development can define the sequence and rate of mental development in the average child and use this to predict intelligence. Remember that the average child doesn't exist: an average is theoretical, so you should never apply it to your own child, nor should you compare him with other children of his age.

There are major variations in the rate of development from child to child, and there is no correct age when any milestones should be reached. Most children experience growth spurts and pauses. Some show a temporary developmental pause and then go on to develop normally; others appear advanced in infancy but turn out to be average in later years. Then there is the well-known "slow starter," the child who is slightly behind in infancy, yet later does very well. A very few children show a progressive slowing in the rate of development. There are children in whom it is so difficult to predict the course of development that the outlook can only be guessed at cautiously and after repeated examinations. The conclusion is that you should not attempt to predict your baby's level of intelligence.

The great majority of babies turn out to be perfectly normal children. Sadly, a very small number lag seriously behind in all areas of development, with both physical (motor) and mental development being markedly delayed. Throughout the first three years, the developmentally delayed child shows below-average concentration and interest in his surroundings. He is late in aspects of development such as head control, sitting up, and grasping his toes, and in outgrowing his primitive birth reflexes, which may persist long after the usual age.

While there are clear indicators that a child is developmentally delayed, it is more difficult to spot the child with above-average abilities. A particularly intelligent baby may reach developmental milestones earlier than average, but the real indicators of his superior intelligence are more subtle: he'll display a greater variety of behavior, a greater interest in his surroundings, and more interaction with his environment than the average baby.

THE PARENT'S ROLE

Very few children are developmentally delayed, and equally few are especially gifted, so the chances are that your child falls within the normal range of intelligence. Your task as a parent is to accept his abilities and to help him develop his strengths by careful teaching. Remember, too, that there are many areas of ability: we tend to think of intelligence rather narrowly as verbal and arithmetic skills, but your child may have creative and artistic abilities that are just as valuable and just as much in need of nurturing. Never push your child: accept him for who he is, give him every opportunity to develop his talents; show him and let him know that you love and respect him just as he is.

INTELLIGENCE TESTING

Modern systems of intelligence testing were developed in 1905 by two Frenchmen. Originally they were intended to predict whether children were likely to do well at school, and concentrated on judgment, comprehension, and reasoning. Modern testing views intelligence as the ability to process information, and so the tests are devised to see how well a child is acquiring thinking skills and applying them to everyday life. They are limited to skills that are important at school, and don't take into account creativity or artistic talent. It is wrong to use IQ scores to predict how successful a child will be in later life, since thinking skills develop over time.

CREATIVITY

All children have some creative ability, and developing this in the preschool years is just as important as teaching letters and numbers. There is a whole range of skills and mental processes that you can encourage in your child to stimulate his creative abilities: point out the things happening around him, show him patterns, colors, flowers, animals, smells; act out empathy for other people; talk about feelings; invent stories; and imagine "What would happen if…?" Dressing up, painting and drawing, and making toys are all practical activities that can help your child develop his creativity and imagination.

Making costumes
Encourage your child to make his own dress-up toys with a variety of colored paper, crayons, scissors, and sticky tape.

AFTER BIRTH

After birth, the process of establishing connections within the brain takes place. These are the essential steps toward mental development.

• *The most productive period of mental development occurs during the first two to four years of life*

• *The greatest number of connections is made between birth and age two*

• *Once connections are established, the left and right sides of the brain "talk" to each other. Skills such as reading depend on this "cross-talk."*

MENTAL DEVELOPMENT

YOUR BABY'S SMILE

The first time your baby smiles at you is an exciting milestone in your relationship; it's also an important sign that she is developing mentally.

When your baby begins to smile, she is demonstrating that she can recognize you and that she wants to engage in an exchange with you – she's already being sociable. She will start to respond with smiles to your talking to her, because she has learned that this pleases you and makes you talk to her more – her first attempts at "conversation" (see p.198).

Smiling is an important indicator of a baby's maturity and desire for interaction with other people, and experts consider that a baby who smiles early in a sociable way may be showing the first signs of superior intelligence.

A colored rattle will catch your baby's attention

Stimulating your baby
Encourage your child to focus on objects by rattling and shaking toys in her line of vision.

Your baby's world is a confused blur of sights and sounds at first, and in the early weeks she is fully occupied with sorting out the things that have significance: your face and voice will be among the first things she recognizes. She will show her recognition with responses such as smiling, jerking her legs and arms, or cooing and gurgling. She demonstrates her good memory and hearing by becoming quiet if you play a recording of the human heartbeat – something that comforted her for nine months.

Newborn Within half an hour of birth your baby will flicker her eyes when spoken to. After one week, she knows your voice, and after two, she will show that she recognizes you. If spoken to from 8–10 inches (20–25 centimeters), where she can see your face, she will open and close her mouth in response.

1 month She will respond to the tone of your voice, becoming calm if you speak soothingly and distressed in response to rough tones. She gets very excited and her whole body jerks when she attempts to "speak." She follows a moving object with her eyes.

Recognizing mother
Your baby will recognize your voice and face, and show signs of this at a very early age.

2 months She smiles readily in response to your face and voice. She looks around in response to sounds, and stares at objects with intense interest.

3 months Your baby is becoming more aware of her body, and will look at her hands and move them. She responds to conversation by smiling, gurgling, and moving her body

4 months Your baby is curious about all sights, sounds, and people. She likes to sit propped against cushions so she can look around her. She now recognizes familiar objects and remembers routines; she'll get excited at the sight of a breast or bottle. She plays with her feet when lying on her back.

5 months Your baby now spends longer examining things, showing that her concentration is developing. She turns to sounds, and moves her arms and legs to attract your attention.

6 months She makes sounds to attract your attention, and puts out her arms to be picked up. She "speaks" to and smiles at her reflection in a mirror. She may show shyness with strangers.

WHAT YOU CAN DO

From the earliest days you should talk and sing to your baby. Her movements and sounds are her earliest attempts at speaking, so answer them to encourage her; make sure she can see your face clearly and make eye contact with her at all times, smile a lot, and exaggerate your mouth movements.

Feed her curiosity Everything is new and interesting to your baby, so show her objects and give her a chance to hold them. By the age of two months, she will like to sit propped up so she can look around; put lots of small, soft toys within her reach where she can see and touch them. Talk to her as much as possible.

Encourage awareness of herself Your baby's discovery of her own body is a gradual process. When she is about eight weeks old, you can start showing her her hands, and play simple physical games. By six months, she will smile at herself in the mirror.

PERCEPTION

Your baby experiences things through her senses just as you do, but she has to learn to single out what is important and what is not. Help her connect the information given by her different senses: show her a rattle, allow her to touch it, then shake it and draw her attention to the sound. Touch is one of the main ways that your baby explores her environment, so introduce her to lots of different textures.

Using a mirror
Point at your baby's reflection and say his name, so he starts to gain a sense of himself. You should use his name as often as possible to bolster his sense of individuality.

Make sure your child can see himself clearly in the mirror

PERCEPTION GAMES

From an early stage, your baby can make basic distinctions between big and small. She will also show interest in new sights and sounds, so the following game, which can be carried out from four months, may be fun.

- *Show your baby a card with a small circle above a large circle drawn on it*

- *Next show her a card with a small triangle above a large triangle. She is already starting to see the relationship between the small and large shapes*

- *Now show her a card with a small diamond above a large diamond. Because this fits the pattern set by the first two, she will likely show no interest in it*

- *If you show her a card with a large triangle above a small one she will likely show renewed interest because the pattern of small above large has changed*

Test cards
Your baby will be able to make quite sophisticated distinctions of pattern and shape.

183

LEARNING THROUGH PLAY

Babies and children learn through play, so play is a very serious business! Everything is a learning experience for your baby, and anything new is fun, so learning and playing are indistinguishable. If you are aware of the skills he's developing in his first six months, choosing games and toys that will interest him will provide enjoyment to you both.

Simple games Because your baby is fascinated by your face, "peek-a-boo" is one of the most successful games you can play with him. Hide your face in your hands or with a scarf or towel, then peek out at him, saying "peek-a-boo" as you do it. Babies develop a sense of humor quite early, and this is a game that they find endlessly amusing. When he's old enough to sit up without support, roll a large, soft ball gently toward him; he will eventually try to push it back to you with his hands; then you've got a real game going and he's acquiring early ball sense.

Rhymes and songs Your baby will love listening to rhymes, even when he's very young, because he likes to be talked to and rhythmic sounds are easier for him to listen to than normal speech. He will love to be sung to as well, whether it's a soothing lullaby or a more lively tune sung while you bounce him gently on your knee. Rhyming, rhythmic songs, and games encourage early speech.

Physical activities Even a very young baby will enjoy play activities such as gentle bouncing, swinging, and rocking. They will give him an awareness of his own body, which he will need as he begins to develop such motor skills as crawling and walking, as well as balance and coordination.

Feed his senses Your baby explores the world through his senses, and he will find anything new interesting (see **Perception games**, p.183). Allow him to spend as much time as possible propped up in a sitting position so that he can see what is going on around him, and leave small toys within his reach so he can handle them – toys that make noises or are made of differently textured materials are best. Catch his interest first by showing him the toys up close and demonstrating how the sound can be made – even something as simple as a plastic jar filled with fairly large beans and securely closed will serve as a toy. When he's older and able to grasp objects, you can give him stacking cups or rings – ones with large pieces are suitable while his grasp is still quite primitive. The kitchen is a good source of interesting toys for your child: small pans and lids, wooden spoons, spatulas, colanders and strainers, funnels, a set of measuring spoons, plastic cups, ice cube trays, and egg cartons. Let your baby create his own uses for them.

Look and learn
Color, shape, and sound are all interesting to your baby, so choose toys that give a variety of these things.

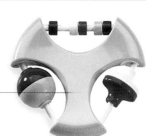

A rattle is an ideal toy as your baby gradually learns to grasp objects during the first six months

Toys that do different things are a good buy; this camera incorporates a mirror, makes clicking noises, and can be chewed

By about four months, your baby explores the world through his mouth, so provide toys that are safe to chew

Your baby will love toys that make a noise, so hang an easily operated music box over his crib or carriage

CHOOSING TOYS

Many parents find it difficult to choose toys for a new baby – relatives even more so. A young baby won't be able to interact with his toys much at first, so they should be soft, simple, sturdy, and attractive to look at and touch.

Soft toys Your baby will like soft toys that he is able to squeeze and that have nice textures for him to touch and cuddle.

Mobiles For a newborn baby, a coloured mobile hung 10 inches (25 centimeters) above a crib or carriage will provide visual stimulation. Hang it out of reach, but not so high that he can't focus on it. Change around the parts every few days to hold his interest.

Noisy toys Rattles, soft toys that squeak, and musical toys are all suitable for a young baby. By six months, he loves to play with a music box that he can operate himself – perhaps by pulling a string.

Books Your baby is never too young to be read to. From three to four months, choose books with large, brightly colored pictures; point to common objects and name them while he's sitting on your knee. Faces always attract him, so show him pictures in magazines and point out the parts of your face, then his face, and then the same parts in the pictures.

SAFETY

Safety is the most important consideration when choosing toys. With a young baby, bear in mind that he is likely to put everything into his mouth.

- *Toys such as rattles should be lightweight in case your baby hits himself with them*
- *Avoid toys with small holes that could trap your baby's fingers*
- *Avoid toys with long strings, which could be swallowed or wrapped around your baby's neck*
- *Soft toys should be made of flame-retardant material. Ensure they're washable and colorfast, because he'll keep putting them in his mouth*
- *Small parts that could choke him, like eyes on soft toys, should be firmly attached and checked often*

185

MENTAL DEVELOPMENT

LEARNING SPURTS

Your baby's mental development goes in spurts, rather than moving at a constant rate.

During a learning spurt, your child will latch onto new ideas and skills very quickly, and put them into practice immediately.

During these rapid learning phases, skills that your baby's already acquired may seem to slip a bit because his concentration is totally taken up with learning something new. Once a new skill has been mastered, he will regain any lost skills.

If your baby clearly enjoys certain activities, repeat them. Don't hesitate, however, to introduce him to new ideas, because he can absorb information very quickly and develop new skills at an astonishing speed. Aim to entertain him over as wide and interesting a range as possible. Your baby will latch onto what he wants and ignore the rest.

A learning spurt is usually followed by a period when development appears to slow down as your baby consolidates newly learned skills and prepares for the next spurt. This is a good time to help him practice skills he has just acquired until they are absorbed into his repertoire.

Your baby is developing new mental abilities at an amazing rate, most of it through play, and you can participate by giving him lots of interesting new experiences. Try to suppress any anxieties about what your child should be learning at this stage. Be guided by him and respond to his needs. He will develop much faster if you let him learn what he wants to, rather than what you think is best.

7 months Your baby is beginning to know the meaning of words and understands "no." He shows signs of determination by going for toys that are out of reach. Your baby takes an active interest in games and concentrates deeply on his toys. He will look around for a toy he has dropped, demonstrating a developing memory.

8 months Your baby's memory really takes a leap forward at eight months when he recognizes familiar games and rhymes, and will turn his head when he hears his name. He can anticipate movement and will hold out his hands to be washed, but turn his face away from a washcloth.

9 months Your baby is becoming familiar with routines, such as waving bye-bye and putting out his foot so you can put on his sock. He also knows "Pat-a-Cake" all the way through. Your baby knows what a doll or stuffed animal is and will pat it, and he'll look round corners for a toy, and for Daddy, if you say, "Where's Daddy?" This is a very important perceptual step: he's learned that things are still there even if he can't see them.

10 months Your baby may point out things in a book by the time he is ten months but he won't concentrate for long. He will be constantly dropping toys out of his stroller and wanting them picked up because he's learned the "letting go" skill. He may say one word with meaning. He is also starting to understand the concepts of *here* and *there, in* and *out, up* and *down.*

11 months Your baby's sense of humor really shows by now. He loves jokes and will repeat anything that makes you laugh. His interest in books is developing. He likes to have items pointed out, then he points them out if you ask him. He will repeat his name and shake his head for "no."

1 year Once your baby is a year old, he'll kiss and say two or three words with meaning. He'll pick up a toy and hand it to you, and may point spontaneously to an object that he recognizes in a picture. He starts to understand simple questions.

STYLES OF PERCEPTION

From about six months old, a child is developing his own "style of perception" – that is, the time and care he takes to look at a situation before making a decision. Broadly speaking, most people fall into one of two styles: reflective or impulsive. A reflective baby will look at something with fixed concentration and remain very still, whereas an impulsive baby will become excited and look away after only a short period of examination.

When your baby is 18 months old, you can get a sense of which style most closely describes him by trying a simple test: show your baby a card on which there is a picture and, below it, variations of this picture. Ask him to select the picture that exactly matches the picture at the top. A reflective child will look at all the options carefully before making a choice, and is usually right. An impulsive child is more likely to look at all the pictures quickly and then make a snap decision, which is often the wrong one.

Reflective children often do slightly better at school, especially in learning to read. An impulsive child may therefore need more help with schooling. Reflectiveness, however, is not always best. There are occasions when a child has to think fast, such as when playing games, and an impulsive child may be better able to make a good decision in the short time available.

YOUR CHILD'S MENTAL DEVELOPMENT

There is much you can do that will be fun for you and your baby as he develops mentally. Play hide-and-seek with a toy by placing it in front of your baby and letting him reach for it several times; then put a piece of paper in front to hide it. Your baby will move the paper to find the toy. Give him simple tasks, such as putting things in and taking them out of containers

Choose soft baby books with large colorful illustrations, and set aside a quiet time each day to read. Children enjoy tales about mother and baby animals, and such stories will help them learn about the sounds animals make. When reading illustrated books and magazines to your baby, try naming several items on a page, and then take your baby's hand and point to them. Name the items again.

At one year, your baby will begin to understand cause and effect. Describe your actions while, for example, putting his coat on him and taking it off, or dressing and undressing a doll. Describe what is happening when he plays. For instance, if he knocks over his bricks, say: "All fall down." Play lots of water games with him; give him pots, jars, and jugs that he can use to pour, empty, and fill. Put his toys just out of reach and retrieve them when he asks. Encourage independence with self-feeding.

An older child of around 15 months can be given simple tasks, such as putting things away or fetching something for you, to stimulate his sense of achievement and to encourage feelings of pride. Help him string words together to make simple sentences of three or four words. Introduce the concept of possession, particularly with his own things: "That's Michael's ball, your ball."

MEMORY

Now that your baby is older, his developing memory becomes more apparent. There are many things you can do, but don't push him: wait until he shows you that he's interested.

- *Repeat a short rhyme to your child over and over again, until he learns to say it himself*

- *Sing a brief song to your baby, accentuating the rhythm with handclaps, head nods, and gestures of your body*

- *Read aloud to your baby. If a story is repeated several times, he will anticipate events and say them before you get there. If you hesitate dramatically in mid-sentence, your baby will supply the missing word, such as* duck, tree, baby, *or* kitten

- *Reciting lists of numbers will call upon his developing memory, as will parroting the alphabet, especially if you give it a definite rhythm or rhyming pattern*

HOMEMADE TOYS

A baby under one year doesn't need store-bought toys. Use colorful, noisy household items to stimulate and fascinate her.

• *Anything that rolls: thread spools or cardboard paper towel and toilet paper tubes*

• *Interesting textures: pieces of felt, a string of beads, thick strands of yarn, or bean bags*

• *Interesting shapes: plastic ice cube trays, whisks, egg cartons, colanders and strainers, or plastic bottles of all shapes and sizes*

• *Anything that's noisy: wooden spoons and spatulas, small saucepans and lids, cake pans, or plastic cups*

• *Anything that rattles: plastic jars with seeds, beads, or paper clips inside (but make sure the lid's on tight)*

Noisy
A baby will love playing with pots, pans, and saucepan lids. The more noise she can make, the more fun she'll have.

LEARNING THROUGH PLAY

Your baby learns through play, and to develop fully she needs all her senses in use: sight, hearing, smell, touch, and taste. To provide the necessary stimulation, her toys and games should be full of variety so that they will appeal to all these senses. While you should obviously play with your baby as much as possible, it is also important that she learn to play by herself so that her senses of exploration and imagination are given full rein.

At seven months, your baby's mouth is still an important sense organ, and she'll want interesting objects that she can investigate safely. Her toys should be bright, colorful, and have an interesting shape to stimulate her perception of form and space as well as her sense of color. Primary colors are best at this age. Always name the color of an object she plays with.

Stimulate your child's hearing with toys that make ringing or rattling sounds when she shakes them. Music boxes provide endless fascination for young children, particularly ones with a string your baby can pull. As your baby's manipulative abilities improve, she'll become absorbed by touch as well as sound. She will love toys that make a noise when she squeezes them. Activity centers, which have a series of knobs and buttons that your baby can push or turn to make noises, can be attached to a crib or a bathtub. As well as stimulating both her hearing and sense of touch, they will help her understand the link between cause and effect. Rubber balls of all sizes are always a favorite.

Any fairly small objects with holes or handles into which your baby can poke her fingers or wrap them around are ideal. Look for objects that are brightly colored and, if possible, make a noise, like rings with bells on them. She'll love a large, specially designed baby mirror placed in her crib for her to stare into. Never put one of your own mirrors in the crib as it could easily break.

When she is ten months to one year old, your baby will pick up small objects like pencils, crayons, and eventually, paint brushes. She'll be more mobile now and will enjoy being able to push or pull toys like trains, cars, or wagons.

From one year to 18 months, having achieved some measure of dexterity, your baby will enjoy toys that challenge her manipulative abilities, such as puzzles. Nesting and stacking toys that can be built up or fitted together will encourage dexterity and spatial visualization. Now that she speaks and understands some words and ideas, she'll love stories and books. Those with brightly colored illustrations and different textures are best.

Toys that your baby can push or pull around build limbs and muscles

Books should have large, simple illustrations, and be made of a chewable material

Building with blocks gives your baby a sense of achievement

Musical or noisy toys will attract her attention

Coloring materials will satisfy your baby's need for scribbling

PLAYING TOGETHER

Your baby will enjoy playing games with you. To ensure she makes the most of new toys, show her how they can be used and encourage her to be imaginative with them. If you:

- *Roll a ball to her and encourage her to roll it back to you, she will exercise her hand-eye coordination*

- *Show her how to build a more complicated structure with blocks, such as a bridge, she'll practice her delicate manipulative skills*

- *Fill a container with water or sand and show her how to fill up measuring cups and containers, she'll experience the movement of different substances*

Water play
All babies enjoy splashing in water or floating a boat in a bowl. Provide unbreakable containers to pour and fill.

TOYS AND GAMES

As your baby grows, her developing skills and mental abilities will be reflected in toys that capture her imagination. Free-standing rattles that she can swipe at while eating, for example, will keep her amused at first. Large soft blocks are ideal for a six-month-old baby because they can be used for building and throwing, but an older baby will prefer hard blocks of wood or plastic, stable enough for more complicated structures. Puzzles and games that challenge your baby, such as simple jigsaws with knobs to make the pieces easier to pick up, are important for her development. Provide your baby with as wide a selection of toys as you can.

MENTAL DEVELOPMENT

IMAGINATION

Most children over the age of 15 months or so begin to develop a vivid imagination, and there are substantial individual differences. In general, the greater the intelligence, the greater the imagination.

Between 15 and 18 months, imagination begins to appear in doll play. At three years, your child will have imaginary playmates behind the sofa and will tell stories and play highly imaginative games. Her imagination may lead to the development of fears: of the dark, of noises, or of animals, for example.

At the toddler stage, your child starts to become an independent, person. Her speech will progress during this phase, and she'll be able to ask for what she wants and do some of the things you want her to do – if she so chooses. She'll have an insatiable curiosity about her world and everything in it, will be able to cope with increasingly complex ideas, and will be eager to put all she learns to good use.

MILESTONES

18 months Your baby will be able to ask for food, drinks, and toys. She may tell you she wants to go to the potty, but can't wait so has frequent accidents. She will carry out several simple requests and begin to understand more complex ones, such as, "Please get your hairbrush from the bathroom." She may also grab your arm or use other gestures to get your attention. Her vocabulary may consist of about 30 words.

2 years Your child's vocabulary of names and objects will increase rapidly, and she will describe and identify familiar items. She will obey complicated orders and find a toy that she played with before. She will talk nonstop and ask occasional questions.

Shortly after this, she will know who she is and say her own name. She'll try to build houses and castles with blocks, and repeat new words when encouraged. She'll begin to pit her will against yours and may become rather negative – saying "no" fairly often and not always going along with your wishes. She may know the difference between *one* and *several*, but she has little idea of the magnitude of numbers and so anything more than one may be "lots."

2½–3 years Your child will start to add detail to broad concepts, as in "A horse has a long tail," and be able to draw horizontal and vertical lines. She'll be able to say one or two nursery rhymes and find them in her book, and she'll know some colors. She will also ask "why?" and say "won't" and "can't." She may make an attempt to copy a circle that you have drawn for her (see p.174), but probably won't be able to complete it. Your child will now enjoy helping with household tasks. She will begin to grasp the concept of numbers and may be able to count to three. A boy will have noticed that his genitals stick out from his body, in contrast to those of little girls he has seen.

Chores
Your toddler enjoys helping you with some simple household tasks, such as sweeping.

Your child can understand prepositions, such as "in," "on," "under," "behind," and "after." At around three years old, she'll be able to form more complex sentences and her vocabulary may consist of 200–300 words. This, together with her ever-increasing curiosity, will lead her to ask incessant questions. She can distinguish between *now* and *then* and will also refer to the past. She knows her own gender. She'll become more sociable and like to play with others.

REASONING

As a toddler, your child may have satisfied her curiosity, absorbing a great deal of new information in the process, but rarely related it to anything else in her life. What happens in the third year, however, is that your child starts to think about her experiences and to learn from them. Information is sifted, matched up to other experiences to see if they fit together or if they differ greatly, and it is then put into similar or different pigeonholes. Your child is learning to reason.

Your child starts to plan ahead, and becomes much more creative and imaginative. Gradually all the information that she has absorbed so far becomes available to apply to a given situation. This new ability to think, imagine, and create changes your child's perception of the world considerably.

Many familiar things in the house or garden no longer contain the same interest. She needs wider horizons; she needs to explore, to push the frontiers of her experience and knowledge farther and farther. Your child becomes very interested in how things work. She is greedy for information and is constantly asking "why?"

A huge step is realizing that time is not just in the present: there is today, yesterday, and tomorrow. Planning for the future is one of the most critical aspects of our intellect, and it is during this third year that you will hear your child say for the first time, "I will eat that later" or "We can go tomorrow."

FORMING CONCEPTS

This is an important step forward for her. One way in which it will be obvious is when, between the ages of 18 months and two years, she starts sorting objects as a form of play; she might sort her building blocks out from her other toys, for example, or the different animals in a toy farmyard. You'll notice, too, that she's begun to understand how things are grouped: she knows, for instance, that her toy ball and an apple are similar in shape and that they roll; that sparrows and crows are alike because they have feathers and fly; that animals that bark and have four legs are dogs.

Some time before her third birthday, your toddler will begin to give these concepts names – round, bird, dog. She will use the names in all cases where they are appropriate – whether the dog in question, for instance, is a family pet, a dog she sees on television or in a book, or a toy dog. By the time she is three years old, she will describe things in a way that shows she also understands their differences: "our dog," "toy dog."

COLORS

To help your child grasp the notion of color, always mention the color of something that you are using or wanting.

• *Household items: "I'm looking for the green package"; "Where's that red can gone?"; "Oh, I've found the jar with the blue label"*

• *Your child's clothes: "That's a pretty pink dress"; "What a nice red sweater"*

• *Flowers, animals, and especially birds: "Can you see the robin's red breast?"*

• *Show your child how colors are made: "Look, if we mix a little bit of red with this white we will get pink; yellow mixed with blue will make green"*

• *Teach your child the colors of the rainbow and get her to pick them out if you see a real rainbow*

Concept of roundness
A toddler can begin to deal with sophisticated ideas. She will understand that roundness, for example, is a property of different objects.

LEARNING THROUGH PLAY

Play helps learning in many ways. It improves manual dexterity – building a tower of blocks or doing a jigsaw puzzle teaches a child how to make her hands work for her as tools. Playing with other children teaches her it's important to get along with others; she will discover friendship and learn to be kind and show consideration for other people.

Social play helps make a child's language more sophisticated because the more imaginative the play, the more complex the ideas that have to be put into words. Play aids physical development; the freedom to swing, climb, skip, run, and jump helps perfect muscular coordination and physical skills. Play also improves hearing and vision considerably.

TYPES OF PLAY

Girls and boys love dolls; dolls are children's pretend families, helping them create a make-believe world into which they can escape. While playing with dolls, your child is understanding human emotions. She will mother the doll, give it instructions, then dress it, put it to bed, and kiss it good-night. In this way your child is re-enacting the things that happen to her and learning to relate them to other people. Even action dolls for boys can bring out protective feelings. A child can also use dolls to get rid of feelings of aggression that might otherwise be directed against other children.

An important concept for a child to grasp is that of classification – whether things are the same or different. Farmyard animal figures can help form this idea; with a variety of sheep, horses, and chickens your child will be able to group the animals that look the same. You can help by showing her the differences and naming the animals as you put them into groups.

Children love playing with water, especially in the bath. Give your child empty plastic bottles and containers so she can create a variety of water effects. All children love blowing bubbles; put some dishwashing liquid in a cup and shape a pipecleaner with a circle at one end. Wading pools, such as the small inflatable kind, are ideal in the summer and needn't be expensive. Another summer game is to lay a sheet of plastic or tarpaulin on the ground and hose it with water; your child will enjoy sliding around on it.

Painting encourages your child's creative urges. She'll love finger painting and can produce a range of interesting prints and patterns with combs, pegs, sponges, thread spools, or cardboard tubes. Try cutting star shapes and other patterns out of pieces of potato so she can create unusual designs. Styrofoam egg cartons or baking trays will make good palettes for the aspiring painter. Give your child thick brushes so that she sees bold results immediately. Provide pastry brushes, cotton balls, corks, straws, and pipe cleaners for variety.

Costumes
Children love dressing up, so stock a box with old shoes, shirts, skirts, dresses, hats, and scarves, and include some cheap jewelry.

TOYS AND GAMES

Up to two years of age, your child will spend longer on toys that she can use independently, particularly those that imitate the adult world. Dolls, toy houses, and cars, for example, will enable her to act out the scenes she sees in real life. As she gets older, she will acquire new skills and enjoy anything that tests them – building and knocking down, or constructing and taking apart. Household items such as plastic containers and cardboard tubes will stimulate her creativity and imagination. Drawing, painting, making shapes with clay or colored dough, and fitting together puzzles encourage creativity. Long before she's able to write or draw formally, your child will love scribbling and using colors, so give her crayons and lots of paper. A box of colored chalks and a blackboard and easel, set up at her height, will be useful because she'll be able to draw, then rub out her work, and start again.

Children love being part of the domestic routine. A small child can be given a little bowl with some flour to mix each time you bake; she can help also with carrying, and use a small dustpan and brush to help with the cleaning.

A toy telephone will enable your child to imitate adults and feed the need for conversation and other wordplay

Your toddler is able to make increasingly complex use of building toys

Your child's picture books should now introduce simple vocabulary

Fuel your child's artistic talents with painting sets or play dough

OUTDOOR SAFETY

Once a child is old enough to have large toys to play with in the yard or playground, a whole new set of hazards can arise.

It is impossible to provide a totally safe environment for your child, but if you take precautions the risk of serious accidents can be greatly reduced. For example, ensure outdoor equipment is carefully installed and regularly checked for wear and damage.

- *Young children should always be carefully supervised, and never left alone to play outdoors, especially in wading pools*

- *Play equipment such as slides and swings should be checked regularly for strength, stability, and signs of corrosion. They should be installed on a soft, flat surface, such as grass or rubber padding – never on concrete*

- *Check all play equipment to ensure that there is no risk of scissoring, shearing, or pinching injuries and that surfaces are free from snags and splinters*

- *Instruct your children carefully on what they can and can't do on play equipment*

- *Ensure that tents, playhouses, and tunnels are made of flame-retardant material*

- *Ensure sandboxes are covered when not in use to stop animals from fouling them*

- *Fence off ponds and pools*

- *Always empty a wading pool after use*

PRESCHOOL

MENTAL DEVELOPMENT

GIFTEDNESS

It is tempting to think your child is gifted if he is farther ahead than others in one or two areas.

Truly gifted children, however, are advanced in most aspects of achievement and in the acquisition of skills. They will enjoy all kinds of brain exercises and may even find some of them very easy. A gifted child invariably learns quickly and is able to use that learning in a broad and flexible way. If this applies to your child, it will be important to provide him with plenty of stimulation, new games, new ideas for play, and plenty of creative opportunities. Otherwise he is liable to become bored and frustrated if he is not being stretched by his play (see pp.251–52).

Puzzles
You can aid your preschool child's mental development with some simple teasers.

The development of your child as an independent and reasoning individual really blossoms during the preschool years. His use of language will be much more fluent and he'll start to relate speech to the written word. His steadily improving grasp of shapes and understanding of sequences will mean he can solve more complex puzzles, such as rearranging pictures into the correct order or copying a design. He'll also be much more imaginative in his play so that he will be able to keep himself amused for longer periods without expecting you to join in.

A three-year-old child will want to help with simple household tasks, such as sweeping up or setting the table. His make-believe play will be more vivid, as he invents people and objects and puts them into more complex situations. He'll enjoy playing on the floor, alone or with siblings, for much longer periods. And he is beginning to understand that some enjoyable things must be put off to the future, such as a visit to a favorite relative or being able to buy an ice cream.

He is more independent and more self-centerd at the age of four. He may be fresh or even defiant, and more argumentative about getting his own way. He will have mastered the concepts of past, present, and future, though he may not understand how near or far off his birthday is.

By the age of five, he will be more sensible and controlled, and will be able to play games that have more complicated rules. He'll be able to appreciate clock time and it will help him relate to a daily routine. His sense of humor will also be more developed now, and he will be able to tell simple jokes and act out comical situations – anything for a laugh.

Ask your child which part is missing from this picture

Ask your child to put the pictures in the correct order

Use specially painted blocks to make patterns for your child to copy

Make a jigsaw puzzle by cutting up a post-card or photograph

PERCEPTION

Perceptual style – the way in which a child takes in a situation – depends on whether he is able to shut out what's going on in the background or takes a lot of notice of it. The former is called "field independency" and the latter is "field dependency."

Measurements of field independence or dependence show a strong difference between girls and boys. Boys are usually more field independent, and are therefore able to pick out a shape from a complicated background more easily than girls. This could be because, in general, boys are better at spatial visualization at an earlier age than girls.

It can be quite helpful to know if your child is field independent in his interests and personality. If he is, he will generally be able to focus on objects or tasks, while field-dependent children tend to focus more on people. This may account for the fact that baby girls, being more field dependent, are much more sociable from the outset than boys.

TESTING PERCEPTION

You can assess your child's field dependence or independence by seeing whether or not he is able to pick out a geometric shape from a complicated drawing. Show your child a simple shape, such as a circle, square, or triangle, and then ask him to find a figure exactly like that in a more complex drawing.

In order to find the figure, your child has to ignore the background detail (the field) and pay attention only to shapes. Generally speaking, children become increasingly field independent as they get older. After a while you will be able to introduce more complicated shapes – like a hidden animal – in increasingly complex backgrounds.

If your child is more field dependent, he'll rely more on outside clues, including your prompting and your encouragement. In contrast, however, a field-independent child, because of his greater ability to extract parts from the whole, will tend to be better at some cognitive tasks, such as those that require good spatial sense – playing chess, for example.

Jigsaws
Wooden jigsaw puzzles are easier to handle and don't bend like cardboard ones.

LEARNING DISABILITIES

Children learn at different rates, so apparent problems, such as a delay in learning to read, may simply be a normal variation in timing rather than a sign of any disability. But there may be other signs that might indicate a learning disability of which you should be aware.

• *Learning disabilities rarely occur alone. They are usually part of a broader picture including perhaps poor coordination, poor memory, and the inability to draw and to fit differently shaped blocks into matching holes in a board*

• *Dyslexia is a learning disability that should be spotted at an early stage. Sometimes called word-blindness, this condition is part of a wider spectrum of learning problems, including difficulty in spelling and writing. Early signs include delayed language development, apparent hearing problems, and clumsiness, but a proper diagnosis can be made only by a professional child psychologist, pediatrician, or specially trained teacher (see p.253)*

• *It is important to rule out or treat any vision or hearing problems that will interfere with learning before the preschool period*

Your child's insatiable curiosity needs a lot more stimulation than your home can offer, so go to the local park or playground regularly and plan outings to the countryside or zoo.

• *Let your child know in advance what to expect, say by reading a book with her, so she'll get the most out of the experience*

• *Talk about items of interest, and take crayons and paper, or a coloring book, and encourage her to draw what she sees*

• *The beach is full of new sights, sounds, and smells – don't forget a shovel and pail. Sand castles are a perennial favorite*

• *Provide a cheap camera to make a record of the trip and put her photos in an album*

LEARNING THROUGH PLAY

Play will continue to make a positive contribution to your preschool child's development. Once she has practiced her creative interests at play, she can apply them to the real world. Sometimes your child will be absorbed in a make-believe world of her own and won't need your involvement: at other times you can add to her enjoyment by suggesting new games or new ways to play with her toys.

Make-believe play Your child will create a little world of her own as part of her imitation of adults. An instant tent or playhouse can be made by draping a blanket over a couple of chairs or a small table. Children love playing with cardboard boxes, so long as they are big enough to climb into. Small ones become boats and cars; piles of them turn into houses and castles. Boxes laid on their sides are tunnels, and laid end to end become trains.

Dressing up is a favorite game at this age: a few simple props can transform your child into a doctor or firefighter. In her fantasy world, she is the adult and a teddy bear or doll serves as child. It often surprised me who my sons thought were family.

Messy play Any play involving water, sand, mud, or dough will stretch your child's intellect. Your child may build a wall in the sandbox that then becomes a castle, or she may simply enjoy playing with a bucket full of water and floating objects, which will keep popping up to the surface no matter how often she pushes them down. To make your supervision easier, set aside a time when messy play is allowed and a place where the mess can be contained and encourage your child to look forward to it.

Domestic play By now your child has mastered the coordination needed to help around the house. It's play rather than work because she's so eager to copy you. She helps in the kitchen by tearing lettuce leaves or arranging bread on a plate, and will enjoy setting the table, all of which improve manipulative and counting skills as well as independence and self-worth.

Musical play Any child with normal hearing can hear and enjoy musical sounds. She probably won't be able to play melodies, but she may be able to hum them and will enjoy banging out a rhythm. Rattles, wooden clappers, trumpets, and drums are all very good for this purpose, as are old pans or baking tins and wooden spoons. A xylophone will enable her to identify musical sounds and experiment with high and low notes. It's best not to buy a xylophone

Make-believe play
Your child will readily adopt a parents role toward her dolls and stuffed animals and may create a whole imaginary world around this relationship.

or other instrument until she's shown interest over an extended period of time and then it's worth investing in a well-made one, which will be better for your child's developing ear.

SHARING TOYS

Your child wants to be sociable so she has to learn the difficult skill of sharing. It's easiest if she learns to share with you first, so set her a good example: "Here's some of Mommy's ice cream"; "You can have half of my apple." Then introduce the concept of "One for you, one for me." Only then say, "May I have your pencil?"; "May I play with your dolly?"

A chalkboard with colored chalks and felt eraser is a good way of introducing your child to numbers and letters

A sturdy tape machine will enable your child to listen to her favorite songs and stories

Soft balls are safe for indoor play

Introduce your child to more complicated building sets

SIMPLE GAMES

Your child at four or five is old enough to understand simple board games. She will enjoy uncomplicated games involving a spinning wheel, dice, or moving pieces, as well as card games that rely on pictures, such as "Old Maid" and "Go Fish."

• *Many games will help her improve her counting skills and also her developing ability to concentrate. Games with rules that have to be followed can serve as an introduction to the concept that the real world is full of accepted standards*

• *She will have to learn to take her turn and to wait patiently while others take theirs. This will help her to realize that other people have rights and needs that sometimes take priority over hers*

• *The winning and losing element of games will teach her to understand and cope with disappointment and to try harder next time, as well as to enjoy the success of winning. Don't emphasize winning; it could make her unduly aggressive and competitive in later life*

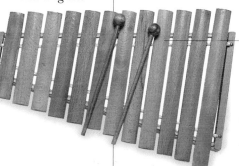

A musical toy, such as a xylophone, will allow your child to experiment with sounds

SPEECH AND LANGUAGE

FIRST SOUNDS

Your baby first starts to communicate with you at birth, but without sounds.

Within half an hour of birth, your baby moves her eyes at the sound of your voice, and when you're 10 inches (25 centimeters) away from her face, she will smile and mouth in imitation and recognition of hearing speech. She is born to talk!

Crying becomes the major way of saying she's discontented; burbles of contentment don't appear for another six weeks.

Social smiling at six weeks marks her desire to converse, and a few weeks later she'll start to make vowel sounds, such as "eh," "ah," "uh," "oh." By the time she's three or four months old, she will be making a variety of sounds: vocalizations, laughing, squealing, and blowing between her lips. Around five to six months, her first consonants appear –"m," "p," and "b" – and so she may say "ma" or "pa" very early on, though she will attach no meaning to these sounds.

Babies need and want to communicate from the very earliest days, and even before they begin to vocalize they will listen to and try to imitate sounds. The basics of languages are built into babies' brains. A deaf infant starts to babble at the same age as a child with normal hearing, so we know that auditory stimulation is not necessary for language development. Some theorists even say we have a "language acquisition device" somewhere in the brain that makes language inevitable.

Before your baby is six weeks old, she will have learned that if she smiles or makes sounds, you will respond. What is remarkable is that even at this early stage she realizes that she can call the shots: she smiles, you are pleased, and so talk to her more; and she can keep a two-way "conversation" going. By smiling and talking to your baby and showing your pleasure when she responds, you are giving her the very first lesson in communication.

Newborn Your baby will respond to human voices from the moment of birth, and she will try to imitate gestures and expressions. She will sense when you are talking to her and will respond with sounds and by moving her entire body.

4–6 weeks She can already recognize your voice. She'll respond to your smiles and speech by gurgling and wait for you to reply. Keep your face close to hers when you talk to her so that she can see you, and reward her sounds with more smiles and talking.

4 months Your baby now has a range of sounds, including squeals and blowing between her lips. She communicates with you through laughter, so always laugh and giggle a lot when you talk to her.

6 months There are many signs that your baby is beginning to understand what you say. She babbles and strings sounds together. Singing to her, repeating rhymes, and speaking rhythmically will all help her understand language and encourage early speaking.

Talking to your baby
Your earliest conversations with your baby will involve smiles rather than sounds.

BEGINNING TO TALK

OLDER BABY

For your baby to talk, she must first understand what you say. Her understanding will increase rapidly toward the end of the first year. From six months onward, she will understand when you say "no" firmly, and at nine months can follow simple orders like waving bye-bye. You can help her by making meanings clear with theatrical emphasis and gestures: read to her, show her pictures and repeat the names of the things she can see, and give her a clear, slow running commentary about everyday actions.

Children who are sung to, have nursery rhymes repeated to them, are spoken to in a rhythmical way, and are involved in singing and rhyming and clapping games speak earlier and better than children who don't, so you should do all these things from your child's earliest days. As soon as your child says her first word, or what you think might be a word, repeat it to her. Tell her she's a clever girl and show her how pleased you are with her.

7 months By now you will be able to discern clear syllables in your baby's sounds, such as "ba" or "ka." She will probably use a special sound to attract your attention, such as a cough or a squeal, and will have started to play games with her tongue and lips.

8–9 months Your baby's range of sounds is increasing, and she has added the consonants "t," "d," and "w" to her repertoire. She will start to imitate real speech sounds, and may use one word with meaning. She pays close attention to adult conversations.

11 months By now your baby is almost certainly using one word with meaning, and can understand a few simple words, such as "bath," "drink," and "dinner." Praise her for every new word, and repeat it; she will say it over and over when she sees your approval. You are your child's first model of good speech, so speak clearly and slowly to her.

15 months Your baby is breaking gradually into jargon – that is, strings of sounds with the occasional recognizable word and with the phrasing and inflections of real speech. This is a sign that she is just about to start talking. She may start to use some favorite phrase of yours, such as "oh dear," in appropriate situations.

18 months Your baby may be able to use about ten words with meaning. Her understanding is increasing all the time, and she can point out many objects in her picture books or in the world around her if you ask her to.

Teaching words
As your child begins to learn her first words, play a game of handing her objects and repeating their names.

FIRST WORDS

Acquiring speech is a complex process, and there are a few typical ways in which children simplify pronunciation.

Your child may acquire words a little at a time, so that "dog" starts out as "d," then "do," and finally "dog." Some difficulty with consonants is normal until four or five years of age.

Double consonants are especially difficult; your child might say "pay" for "play." She'll simplify words that contain sounds made in different parts of the mouth, so that "ball" becomes "baw." You can help her by stressing the last letter of words.

Make every effort to encourage and understand your child's attempts at communication.

SPEECH AND LANGUAGE

LANGUAGE IN GIRLS

Although language development varies from child to child, in general girls are more responsive to the human voice than boys, and they have better verbal skills throughout childhood.

Girls tend to be more verbal at an early age than boys, and begin to string words into sentences earlier. They have better articulation, pronunciation, and grammar, and are better at verbal reasoning.

Your baby is learning new words all the time now and he's also starting to put them together. His pronunciation will be indistinct, but this is no cause for worry; if he is using words with meaning and putting them together, then his language is developing. Mild speech defects, such as lisping, are very common in children and usually disappear without any treatment. There is great variation in the speed at which children acquire speech, so don't feel the need to compare your child with others of his age and don't worry if his development doesn't match the timetable outlined below. I give these dates merely as average guidelines; no child corresponds exactly to the average.

18 months – 2 years Your baby's speech will become more complex during this time. He will probably have a vocabulary of about 30 words, including possessives – "mine" – and negatives – "won't" – instead of simply "no." He is starting to combine words to make simple statements, such as "ball gone," or questions: "Where Daddy?" He understands that conversation is a two-way thing and will wait his turn to speak; he uses language to give information, to ask for things, to tell how he feels, and to relate to other people.

Remember that he can understand a lot more words than he can use, so you can continue to help him by teaching him new words. Use adjectives whenever you can, and combine them with nouns: "good boy," "hot water," "big dog." Introduce adverbs, too: "Run quickly," "Pat the dog gently." When you use prepositions – "on," "under," "behind" – always show him what you mean.

2–3 years Your toddler probably has a vocabulary of 200–300 words by now, and he can talk at some length. He is interested in learning new words. His attention span is longer, and he will listen to you when you explain things or give reasons. He will still mispronounce words and may lisp, but his fluency and confidence are improving all the time. He can connect two ideas in a single sentence – "I get teddy and play in garden" – and can use pronouns such as "I," "me," and "you" correctly.

You can help your child increase his vocabulary by using unfamiliar words in your speech in such a way that he can guess at their meaning, and repeat them frequently so that he can learn how they are used. Read to him often and explain new words as they arise. He will like to hear the same stories read over and over, and will be able to understand increasingly complicated narratives.

Your child's use of language is becoming more social now, and he will talk more to other children than to adults, so contact with children is the best way to help him develop his abilities.

TALKING TO YOUR CHILD

It is important that you continue to talk to your toddler, and go on introducing new words and making your meaning clear with gestures and facial expressions. It is just as important, however, to allow him to respond so he learns that conversation works two ways. If he initiates a conversation by showing you something or asking you a question, always give him your attention. If you are impatient, or just respond with "That's nice," without looking at him, he'll become discouraged and may give up trying to talk to you.

Talk about everything you are doing in detail. When you are dressing him, give a running commentary: "Now we'll button your buttons ... one, two, three." Describe objects you are using: "Let's put the apples in the glass bowl"; "Would you like a yellow crayon or a red crayon?"

Although you shouldn't correct your child when he makes mistakes, there is no reason why you should talk to him in his own baby language. If he makes a mistake in grammar or pronunciation – "Grandma goed" – just repeat his words giving the correct form: "Yes, Grandma went home."

LANGUAGE AND UNDERSTANDING

You will be able to observe the way your toddler gradually gains concepts in his use of language. He will often use the same word to describe similar things, so that apples, oranges, and peaches are all "apple," because they are all round and fruit; and horses, cows, and sheep are all "horse," because they are all large animals with four legs. This doesn't necessarily mean that he can't tell the difference; only that he doesn't have words to describe all of them so he uses the nearest one.

By the same token, the questions your child asks you may be very simple because he can't fully express what it is he wants to know. So when he says, "What's that?" he may be asking, "What is it? What is it called? What does it do? How does it work?" all at once. Give him as much information as you think he can understand: "This is laundry powder. It's just like soap, and I put it in the washing machine to make our clothes clean." Always try to answer the question he is really asking.

Socializing
During the third year, your child's verbal skills will be improved by talking to other children.

LANGUAGE IN BOYS

Although there are many individual differences, in general, boys tend to be slower than girls at developing language skills, and this discrepancy lasts right through childhood.

Many boys are later in talking than girls, are slower to put words together in sentences, and take longer to learn to read. Speech problems such as stuttering are far more common in boys than in girls.

Although this difference in linguistic ability levels out somewhat during the teenage years, you can help your son's language skills in the preschool years by reading aloud to him and playing lots of word games.

PRESCHOOL

SPEECH AND LANGUAGE

Studies of the way children use language have shown marked differences in the way girls and boys speak to each other, which can be seen even during the preschool years.

The reason for these differences has to do with the way the sexes behave in groups. Girls want to be part of the group, so their talk aims to promote unity and reach compromises. In general, girls:

• Use language as a way of forming close, intimate friendships

• Make suggestions when playing in groups – "Let's play house"

• Give reasons for their suggestions: "Let's play in the yard because there's more room there"

As your child's world becomes wider, her language will have to keep pace with new experiences and ideas. Her perception of the world is becoming more complex, and so is her vocabulary; for example, she will start to realize that violet is different from purple, and look for the words to express this difference.

3 years Your child will enjoy learning new words, so she listens to adult conversations carefully and her attention span is increasing. She can understand words that describe how she feels, such as "cold," "tired," "hungry." She is also beginning to understand words such as "on," "under," "behind," though this will take longer. She should be able to give her first and last name. Because her mind is racing ahead of her ability to form words at this stage, she may start to stutter, but this is likely to be temporary. If she hasn't overcome her stutter by about four and a half, or earlier if it is severe, ask your child's doctor about consulting a speech therapist.

4 years Children of this age talk a great deal: they boast, exaggerate, tell tall tales, and have conversations with imaginary friends. Your child will ask lots of questions, as much out of a desire to keep you talking as out of any real curiosity, because she loves conversation. She will enjoy inventing silly words, and may indulge in mildly obscene verbal play, especially to do with the bathroom and the toilet. She will probably start to use slang, and she may call you names and threaten you.

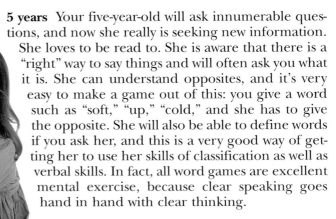

5 years Your five-year-old will ask innumerable questions, and now she really is seeking new information. She loves to be read to. She is aware that there is a "right" way to say things and will often ask you what it is. She can understand opposites, and it's very easy to make a game out of this: you give a word such as "soft," "up," "cold," and she has to give the opposite. She will also be able to define words if you ask her, and this is a very good way of getting her to use her skills of classification as well as verbal skills. In fact, all word games are excellent mental exercise, because clear speaking goes hand in hand with clear thinking.

Girls at play
Close friendships form the basis of a girl's social world, and this will be reflected in her choice of language.

BOOKS AND READING

Encouraging an interest in books is probably the best single thing you can do for your child, so read to her often; her attention span is increasing now, and she will be able to listen to stories with sustained interest. Words are crucial to the way our brains work; they are our main means of communicating, and they form the basis for everything your child will learn in school. Books will provide your child with new words and new ideas, and will explain to her how the world works.

Reading to your child
Even after your child has begun to read for herself, reading to her will be a very valuable time of sharing and learning.

Let your child know that you regard reading as a pleasure. Have plenty of books in the house and make it clear to your child that they are all available for her to look at. Store her own books on low shelves where she can easily browse through them.

Choose books for your child that are visually appealing; first reading books should be short, with only a few pages, and should have large illustrations, large print, and a simple vocabulary. Be willing to read your child's favorite books over and over again; she'll eventually memorize the words, and when she is ready to start reading herself, the familiar words will be easier to recognize.

TEACHING LETTERS AND NUMBERS

Take every opportunity to help your child become familiar with letters or numbers. Show your child how her own name is spelled, and let her try to copy it. As you read to her, pick out a simple word like "cat" and point it out every time it recurs. Then show her what it looks like, and ask her if she can find it on a certain page. When you are doing routine tasks, count out loud; buttoning the buttons on your child's cardigan, for instance, or setting the table. When you are out shopping, you could ask your child to get things for you: three packages of soup or two oranges.

Aids to learning
Give your child numbers and letters to play with. Magnetic ones can be attached to the refrigerator door.

BOYS' TALK

The way little boys talk to each other when at play is markedly different from the way little girls interact with one another, and this reflects attitudes that will continue all through adult life.

In any group situation, boys usually want to stand out from the crowd, so the things they say are intended to enhance their status in the eyes of their playmates. In general, boys:

• Tell jokes and stories far more than girls, as this allows them to be the center of attention; they will often interrupt a story being told by another boy

• Give orders and try to grab favorable positions for themselves: "Okay, we're going to play doctors. I'll be the doctor, you be the patient"

• Back up their suggestions by insisting, by appealing to the rules, or even by threats: "You have to be the patient because it's not your turn. I won't play with you if you don't"

GIRLS'
BEHAVIOR

*Girls tend to develop social skills
and enjoy the company of other
people earlier than boys do.
While not all children conform to
a stereotype, in general, girls:*

• *Are more sociable than boys,
and form closer friendships from
an earlier age*

• *Are more compliant with adult
requests than boys tend to be in
early childhood*

• *Show fewer competitive traits
and are less socially aggressive
and dominant than boys*

• *Cope more easily with
physical, emotional, and
intellectual stress than boys*

SOCIAL BEHAVIOR

Many features of your child's personality will have a vital bearing
on her development as well as her future prospects in life. Helpful
traits include the ability to get along well with other people, to concentrate, to profit from mistakes; willingness to work hard; good
powers of observation; thoroughness; creativity; an enquiring mind;
and determination. Less helpful traits are slowness of thought,
difficulty in expressing herself, overactivity, and diminished concentration, which may occur even in a highly intelligent child.

Your newborn baby needs to interact socially, especially with her
parents. She learns to be sociable by imitating you, first with facial
expressions, then with gestures and movements, and finally with
complete patterns of behavior. In this way the relationship between
parent and child forms the blueprint for all subsequent relationships, so it's your responsibility to be more aware of your behavior
and responses than ever before. From the moment you begin to
talk to your baby, she begins to develop into a social being because
she longs to converse with you.

Like all other development, social development has its own well-
defined stages. Everyone has heard of the Terrible Two's, when
children enter a stage of refusing to obey, and doing what they are
told not to. This is the child's way of asserting her independence
and, although at times you'll believe that it will go on forever, it's
simply a stage in learning to interact with other people.

PREDICTING PERSONALITY

It would be marvelous if we could predict the future personality
of a child when she was still an infant. Personality and character,
however, derive partly from heredity and partly from environment, so there remains the possibility that, as the result of
negative environmental factors or the lack of secure, loving relationships, a child may not have the opportunities she needs to grow
up as a loving and lovable adult.

In view of the profound effect of environment and family on
character, predictions during infancy are doomed to failure. However,
observant parents with several children can detect differences
in their personalities from the outset. Perhaps it's a good thing
that personality prediction is so difficult. From the point of view
of adoption it would be a pity if such predictions were possible.
Adoptive parents may wish to know the intelligence and
personality of an infant they are thinking of adopting, but such
predictions simply are not possible. All parents take a risk, whether
adopting or having children of their own. Whatever your child's
personality or ability, your task as parent is to value and nurture
your child's positive qualities, and love her for who she is.

INDIVIDUALITY

Your baby's individuality will gradually become more apparent as she grows and learns. You should treasure your baby's individuality and nurture her growth and strength.

The gradual insight you gain into your baby's personality is like watching a thrilling film in slow motion. All her preferences, the things that make her laugh and cry, the foods she likes, her favorite toys come together to create her unique personality.

Baby types There's much evidence now that within a week or so of birth infants show a primitive form of the traits they will show as they grow up and, probably, possess later in life. Undeniably environment has a profound effect on character formation, but much of the child's basic character is inherited from her parents, so it's fair to say that each baby will show basic personality traits that don't change much with age.

The traits that are easily recognizable by any parent are the amount of energy your child has, how well she can control her body (as opposed to being floppy), self-reliance, social responsiveness, family attachment, communicativeness, adaptability to various situations, exploitation of the environment, sense of humor, emotional expressiveness, reaction to success, reaction to restriction, readiness to smile, and readiness to cry. Between six weeks and three months, your baby will probably already fall into one of three main personality types.

She may be quite "good" or "easy," eating and sleeping and merging comfortably with her surroundings when awake, and seldom getting overenthusiastic in her responses.

She may be what is sometimes referred to as a high-keyed "sparkler," becoming as demanding in her bids for entertainment and companionship as she first was for food and comfort; the zest for living keeps her growing in self-play.

She may be an "in betweener," having up-days and hours and down-days and hours, asking only that you respond in kind to her moods of the moment.

While personality differences may be apparent very early on, it's in the first few months that you will notice your new baby starting to become more distinctly herself as you get to know her. Here are some traits you may observe as she grows:

- Easygoing, placid, daydreaming

- Cross and irritable

- Sociable

- Serious, determined

- Independent, often perverse

- Imaginative

BOYS' BEHAVIOR

Boys tend to be slower to develop social skills than girls. Although not all boys will show these traits to a marked degree, in general, boys:

- *Are more socially aggressive than girls*

- *Have more friendships than girls, but they tend to be superficial and short-lived*

- *Are more emotionally vulnerable than girls*

- *Tend to have more behavioral problems, particularly when around authority figures*

Social skills
Young children play alongside each other rather than together, but will enjoy the company.

YOUNG BABY

SOCIAL BEHAVIOR

BONDING

The relationship between you and your baby begins from the moment you give birth, and every aspect of your being becomes a comfort and joy to your baby.

He'll respond to your smell, the sound of your voice, the touch of your skin, and the sight of your face. This bond is so complete that your baby will be able to single you out from others in an astoundingly short time. The same will occur with your partner if he spends time alone with the baby.

Make every effort to ensure that the contact you and your partner have with your baby is pleasant, calm, and loving, even if at times this seems impossible.

An early start
By developing a close, loving relationship with your baby from birth, you are laying the foundations of a good relationship in future years.

Your baby's first six months are, surprisingly, a crucial time for his social development. It is during these early weeks that your baby comes to understand the pleasure of social interaction and the importance of communication. He grows beyond the basic requirements of warmth and feeding as he begins to enjoy the social aspects of being alive. Because you embody comfort, pleasure, and security for your baby, you are naturally the best person to teach him loving relationships, the basics of which are learned through the initial skin contact during the first few weeks.

Newborn From the very beginning, your baby will desire close contact with you. He'll appeal to you through head nodding, mouth and tongue movements, and jerks of his body. These are his earliest conversations; he's engaging with you and you should answer with noises, laughter, and bobbing head movements. He will learn quickly that he can make you respond.

3 months Your baby's conversational gestures are far more controlled. He'll turn toward the sound of your voice and wriggle with pleasure on seeing you. He understands that a smile is a happy greeting, his earliest "hello."

4 months By now your baby is such a social being he'll cry soon after being left alone, even if he has many toys around him. He'll be happy to respond to people who acknowledge him, but will have a special response for you and others in the family.

5 months At this age your baby has four main methods of communication: sounds, gestures, facial expressions, and crying. Unless he is asleep, he'll make the most of all four. He can tell the difference between an angry voice and a friendly one, and will react to each differently. He now shows a certain shyness with strangers, but will smile at a familiar face.

6 months Your baby's social advances are far more physical, even aggressive, but may be offset by a growing fear of strangers and a possessiveness over you. He'll explore much more with his hands, patting and touching your face and hands rather than just searching your face with his eyes.

RESPONDING TO YOUR BABY

Any response you make to your baby's attempts at conversation will further his understanding of communication, so you must try to be positive all the time. If a baby's gurgling is met with silence, he'll soon grow tired of such an unrewarding game and may well give up on all but the most basic communication. Always encourage a "two-way" conversation, either by imitating your baby's gestures and noises in an overt way or by chatting to him in order to elicit a response. Be theatrical with voice and gesture. The broader your gestures, the more he understands, the more fun he has, and the closer the bond becomes.

A young baby is sensitive to sudden noises, so bear in mind that although a wide variety of noises are calming for him, harsh or very loud noises will frighten and upset him.

Encourage your baby to cope with new faces by introducing him to any visitors he has not met before. This will allow him to get used to strangers in the security of your home. The more your baby enjoys social intercourse with you, the more likely he is to seek it actively as he grows older. Songs and rhythmic games will encourage him to equate joyful times with mixing with others.

YOUR BABY AS PART OF THE FAMILY

Your baby is longing to be a member of the family group with all its routines, rules, and customs. To become interested he needs to learn how to fit in. For this reason you should include him in family activities, outings, shopping, daily chores, and visiting friends from as early as possible.

The family group will be the basis of your baby's learning about the workings of groups in general. His behavior with family members will teach him about his expected behavior with strangers, and will open him to the social customs of his society. Your baby learns chiefly through imitation, so by copying your behavior he learns his own standards of social interaction.

DIFFICULT BABIES

A demanding baby – one who cries constantly and cannot be comforted – can be very difficult to cope with. It is vital that you share the responsibility with your partner and try very hard to control your temper. There are many causes of, and solutions to, a crying baby, and constant tears is a phase that is fortunately short-lived. If your baby is difficult it's important to understand why he is crying, keeping you awake, or ignoring you on purpose. Whatever his particular problem, your loving, and understanding approach will have a more positive effect on your baby than will chastising or ignoring him. Your pediatrician can offer advice and support.

If you have a baby who is discontented when hungry but never enjoys feeding or being held, you may feel rejected by him or responsible for his unhappiness. Try to keep these negative thoughts at bay. No matter how much he rejects you, keep trying to engage his interest. In all likelihood, this period will soon pass, so it's important to offer him warmth and affection now, and in the future, when he may welcome it.

One of the family
Try to include your baby in your activities, even if they do not directly involve him.

OLDER BABY

SOCIAL BEHAVIOR

From six months onward your baby will show his assertiveness in his demands and preferences. Your older baby is:

- *Very eager to show how grown up he is becoming*

- *Determined to be independent and to manage without help*

- *Demonstrating likes and dislikes with certainty and assertion, if not consistency*

- *Unable to consider consequences and gets very angry when he has to wait, often showing this with violent noises and actions*

- *Aware that he is a separate being from you and, as such, is determined to have his own way*

- *Often confused and unhappy at the conflict between his urge to be independent and his desire to love and please you*

- *More willful than his intellectual maturity will allow*

- *Extreme in his emotions, which range from great happiness to outbursts of temper tantrums*

- *Seemingly infatuated with saying the word "no"*

Your baby is becoming much more socially adept by now, and takes a great deal of pleasure in meeting and being with other people. His interactions with you are increasingly comprehensive as he learns to understand certain words and phrases, and uses the communication skills he has learned to mix with others in the world around him.

Touching, smiling, and all the contact of general company are vital to your baby's happiness at this stage, as he gradually learns to refine his conversational gestures and cries into recognizable signs of communication.

6–8 months Closeness to another baby will be a delight. He'll reach out and touch new friends and will enjoy social games like "Peek-a-boo" and "Pat-a-Cake." He will try to communicate with a series of shrieks, grunts, burbles, and coughs, and will mimic facial expressions and conversational gestures. You should "answer" him in order to stimulate these "conversations" and impress upon him that social interaction is a two-way activity.

8–12 months He will respond to his own name now and will understand that a firm "no" means that he should stop whatever he is doing. He is affectionate and will demand closeness with you, particularly big hugs and intimate smiles. Certain social rituals are common to him now – like saying "bye-bye" – which he'll imitate with little prompting. He'll no longer calmly allow a toy to be taken away; he'll show anger if this happens.

12–15 months His sociability is constantly expanding, and he enjoys being in groups, especially when he can follow conversations and join in whenever there's a lull. Despite his outgoing attitude, he will still need to be close to you for reassurance and security, and will often look to you when meeting new people – just holding hands will give him the confidence he needs. He can say a few words, ask for things, and show thanks when things are done for him in an individual way. He likes to be helpful, and enjoys sharing tasks with you.

15–18 months By now your baby is even more helpful with daily chores, and loves the independence of dressing and undressing himself. He is very affectionate, and shows love for his family, pets, and favorite toys. He imitates adult behavior and is fascinated by adult interaction and conversation. Despite being socially aware, he will tend to play alone and, although he will enjoy playing near another child, he will not tend to play with him.

HOW TO HELP

The concept of sharing is particularly difficult for your baby to grasp. It is unrealistic to expect your baby to give a toy to another baby if he is still playing with it. It is equally unfair to expect your baby to understand that he cannot take another baby's toy simply because he wants it. What you can do is demonstrate the basics of give and take. Your child of 18 months is generally able to comprehend reciprocity, but you must demonstrate it in a way that is reasonable to him; if he takes another baby's toy let him know that he must replace it with one of his own so that they can both play. Your baby is wholly capable of unselfishness and generosity, but any such act must be seen to be a pleasure for both parties. If your baby is willing to share his toys with other members of the family, encourage these small acts of generosity with others and try to build on them.

You should always include your baby in social gatherings and teach him the basic pleasantries from as early as possible. Introduce him to lots of new faces so he doesn't become dependent on you and the family alone for social stimulation. It will help him feel secure when he is away from you or his usual caregiver, although this shouldn't happen too frequently or for long periods of time.

INTRODUCING DISCIPLINE

Discipline should be applied first with the tone of the voice, later with the word "no," then by distraction, and only finally with very mild punishment. Spanking, threats, and withdrawal of pleasures have no place with small children. If you are too severe or too permissive your baby may become insecure. Before he is three, your child cannot respond to reason, and he still cannot grasp the connection between cause and effect. He will understand perfectly well that he has done wrong, or that you are angry, but it will take him some time to remember to connect a particular action with a particular outcome. For this reason it is vital that you point out a mistake to your child immediately so that he links the action with the punishment. You should also bear in mind that your baby's memory is very short, so if you brood over your anger and act later, he will not understand and will not learn from your attempts at correction. During a baby's first year, there are very few reasons for saying "no." I kept the rules for my children to a minimum, and I had only one unbreakable rule in their first year: when they were doing something that was unsafe for themselves or others, I would say "no" firmly while removing an object or stopping my child from performing a dangerous activity. I did not wait for my child to stop. As I was trying to teach what was unsafe, I always offered an explanation of why I was stopping him.

Your baby will be very receptive to justice and fair play, and to their opposites. He immediately recognizes inconsistency, so gently applied and consistent discipline will help your child develop self-control and a conscience, which in turn will help him in his decision making in later life. It will also give him a sense of responsibility toward others.

FEAR OF STRANGERS

It is not uncommon for a normally talkative and sociable child to become withdrawn, even tearful, when introduced to strangers or taken to a strange place. This is quite normal and should never be ridiculed or made into an issue.

Don't insist that he join in immediately with the group. A gentle introduction from you works by far the best, and your baby will soon forget his nervousness and find his place within the social gathering.

Even a very shy child, if gently encouraged, will join in with new friends after an hour or so, but rushing him may make him more insecure. A favorite toy will bolster his confidence, so don't take this security away. Once he feels relaxed, he'll play happily with his new playmates.

SOCIAL BEHAVIOR

IDENTIFYING WITH OTHERS

By the time your child reaches the age of three, she will begin the process of identification, both with herself and with other people around her.

You will start to see evidence of her self-awareness as she takes steps to command and control herself, showing that she can put herself in the position of others. You may overhear your child scolding herself when she thinks she has done something of which you would disapprove. She will begin to act out the part of the adults known to her, particularly you, often adopting phrases that you use regularly.

This will all become part of the process of her exploring and getting to know the way the world works and her own part in it. Now is the time to introduce her to the idea of a wider circle of people, teaching her to respect and be polite to them. Introduce her to visitors to the house – mail and other delivery people, window cleaner, et al. – as well as your own friends, and make meeting people part of her daily routine.

From her first moments, your baby looked to you as the center of her world – the main provider of affection and care. As she gets older and her self awareness and life experiences develop, however, she'll begin to see you as a separate person and will extend her interest to other people. Although you cannot make friends for her, you can help by introducing her to a few first companions. She will soon learn to adapt her skills and develop the social habits of older boys and girls.

18 months – 2 years At this age you should encourage your child to interact with other children. Invite children to the house and give her games and play material to facilitate socializing. Be patient; although her initial reaction may be self-centered, she will modify selfish behavior if it is played down and achievements praised.

2–2¹/₂ years As she is learning to share, encourage games that involve giving to others and respecting their wishes. She may demonstrate feelings of rivalry as a consequence and try to force her will on others. You will need to use discipline fairly while still encouraging and supporting all her efforts and achievements, since approval is more important at this stage.

2¹/₂–3 years As your child continues to socialize, she becomes more independent from you and more outgoing toward other children. She will start to be more generous and unselfish in play with others, and form stronger friendships with adults and children, showing signs of sympathy when others are in distress. Always encourage truthfulness and honesty in relationships with others.

RIGHT AND WRONG

Your child will learn the differences between right and wrong only if they are clearly pointed out. In the first year you can act out why hot or sharp things are dangerous by using sounds and actions. If your child understands why you want her to do something she is much more likely to do it willingly, so try to explain and then ask her opinion. There are situations that are non-negotiable: where your child's safety is threatened, when the thoughts and feelings of others should be considered, and where your child is tempted to tamper with the truth. You should be very firm on these points, and she will gradually learn a sense of responsibility for disciplining herself as she grows up. Freshness can often be mistaken for impertinence, but unless your child is imposing on the feelings of others, she may be displaying nothing more than a healthy resistance to authority, which can be useful, if sensibly directed.

A spoiled or over-indulged child will behave in a self-centered way, and this may be the result of the overprotectiveness, favoritism, or the high expectations of her parents. The best cure is to let her go to playgroup or preschool at two and a half to three to get her used to mixing with other children.

SHARING

Young children are naturally selfish and usually begin to think of others only when they're taught to do so. Your child has to understand that other children feel as she does before she is able to grasp the importance of thinking of other people's feelings. Do not worry if your child seems to be slow in learning to share; it's very difficult, but with your patience she will successfully acquire this skill.

MEETING OTHER CHILDREN

Just like all the other lessons she has to learn through life, your child's ability to make friends could be slow to develop, so introduce it to her gradually. Invite friends around, one at a time to begin with, to a familiar home environment where she is sure of herself. Be near at hand to give her help and support should she need it. She will then begin to build up a small circle of friends and gain confidence through her own place in it – an essential way to learn the ground rules for future friendships.

Shyness is something that affects many children. Common types of shy behavior include disliking new experiences, social gatherings, talking to unfamiliar people, and difficulty in making friends.

Toys for sharing
Encourage co-operation with others by getting your child to complete a puzzle such as this one with a friend.

Don't think of shyness as something wrong with your child; many well-adjusted adults are quite shy. The best way of dealing with it is not by criticism or forcing change, but by preparing your child for any situation she's likely to find difficult.

Excessive shyness does not mean that your child is retarded, and you should avoid becoming overprotective and overanxious. In most cases, time and patience are all that is needed.

TANTRUMS

Toddlers between the ages of one and a half and three often have temper tantrums as a means of giving vent to frustration when they do not get what they want.

This is quite normal because your child will not have sufficient judgment to control her strength of will or the language to express herself clearly, but as her knowledge and experience of the world broaden, the occasions when her will is pitched directly against yours become less frequent.

A tantrum may be brought on by such feelings as frustration, anger, jealousy, and dislike. Anger is brought on by not getting her own way; frustration by her not being sufficiently strong or well coordinated to do what she wants. It will usually involve your child throwing herself on the floor, kicking and screaming.

The best thing you can do is to stay calm, since any attention on your part will only prolong the attack. If she has one in public, take her away from too much attention, without fuss.

At home, an effective technique is simply to leave the room. Explain to your child that, while you still love her, you have to leave the room because you are getting angry. Never confine her in another room because this denies her the option of coming back and saying she's sorry.

PRESCHOOL

SOCIAL BEHAVIOR

GROWING UP LIKE MOM

By the age of three, your little girl is aware of the fact that she is female and that she'll grow up to be a woman.

This makes her very attentive to you – her mother. Her view of gender roles will be influenced by your attitudes. If you:

• Regard yourself as equal to your partner, your daughter will see this as normal

• Treat other women as close friends and confidantes, your daughter will see relationships with adult women in this way

• See working as integral to family life, your daughter will view a career as compatible with having a family

Your preschooler faces many changes in how she sees herself as her independence grows and her personality matures. Sudden upheavals can cause your child to exhibit quite violent changes of mood as she tries to relate her changing identity to her family life and the guidelines she has learned for social behavior, both of which are relatively constant. Be patient and allow her to mature in her own time. The difficult stages are easily outweighed by the thrilling ones, and your child must experience both in order to become a socially adept member of her community.

3 years If your child has been brought up to relate to new friends, she will separate from you easily from the age of three and a half onward, and at about the same time is learning to play interactive games such as tag. She is generous and usually quickly sympathetic when someone else is distressed.

4 years During the fourth year your child has an expanding sense of self, indicated by bragging, boasting, and misbehavior. She begins to realize that other children are separate entities. Your four-year-old wants to be grown-up. She becomes argumentative, and may be selfish, rough, or impatient, especially with younger friends or brothers and sisters. She'll express affection at bedtimes, but might be jealous of you and your partner together. Four-year-old boys, in particular, exhibit silly, boisterous humor.

5 years During the fifth year, your child may be serious, business-like, and realistic, and become excited in anticipation of the future. At this age, little girls are sympathetic, affectionate, and helpful. They have a strong feeling for the family, and appearance is very important. They're not afraid to call people by name. For little boys, mother is the center of the universe. They take others and themselves for granted and are interested in immediate experiences, but they show no interest in their own names or the names of others.

A role model
When your little girl starts to realize that she will grow up like her mother, she will take a special interest in your activities.

SEXUALITY AND GENDER

3 years By the time she is three years old, your child already has an interest in her own gender and the differentiation of herself from boys. At about the age of three and a half she'll express "I like" and then slightly later "I love," and she will affirm, if questioned, that she is a girl rather than a boy. She will begin to express interest in physiological differences between the genders and in boys' and girls' postures for urinating.

She makes no distinctions between gender at play and realizes that people touch out of friendship as well as out of love. She begins to become interested in babies and wants her family to have one. She will ask questions, such as "What can the baby do when it comes?" or "Where does it come from?" Most three-year-olds don't understand when they get the answer that the baby grows inside their mother. It is still vital, however, that you answer your child's questions as frankly and honestly as possible so that her trust in you is not undermined.

4 years By the age of four, children are extremely conscious of their navel, and under social stress, they may grasp their genitals and may need to urinate. They may show their genitals in play, indulge in verbal play or name-calling, and make jokes about urination or bowel movements. They have an interest in other people's bathrooms and may demand privacy for themselves but be extremely interested in the bathroom activities of others. They may begin to segregate themselves along gender lines. All your answers to your child's questions on sex should stress the aspects of loving, caring, and responsibility that an intimate relationship demands. Your child may also question how babies get out of their mother's tummies and may spontaneously think babies are born through the navel. This is a time when gender-stereotyped behavior is learned more from peers than parents.

5 years At five, your child will be familiar with, but not much interested in, physical differences between the genders. She'll be more modest and less self-exposing and will play less in the bathroom than earlier. She'll be aware of sex organs when she sees adults undressed and will wonder why her dad doesn't have breasts or her sister doesn't have a penis. Most children of five take the opposite sex for granted, and there's little distinction between the role of gender in play. There may be frequent boy-girl pairs. Girls' interest in babies continues: they may ask for a baby of their own and they may even dramatize this in games. Your five-year-old will constantly ask, "Where do babies come from?" and will accept "Mommy's tummy" as an answer, but some fix on the idea that you buy a baby at the hospital. She will make little connection between the size of a pregnant woman and the presence of a baby inside her.

GROWING UP LIKE DAD

Your little boy will have realized by the age of three that he will grow up to be a man, and he will become particularly interested in his father.

Your little boy will watch your partner and learn from him what it is to be a man. If your partner:

• Treats women, particularly you or his daughters, in a caring and considerate way, your little boy will believe that this is the correct way to treat women

• Sees other men as friends, your son will also find older men approachable

• Enjoys and participates in family life, your child will follow this example

• Resolves disputes with rudeness and violence, he will, too

A sense of identity
Your little boy will gain his idea of what it is to grow up as a man by observing his father.

It is all too easy to favor one child over an other, or at least to treat him in a way that seems like favoritism.

If a child is born several years after a previous one and is much wanted, for example, he may be treated preferentially. Sometimes it happens that the mother's favorite is the boy, the father's favorite is the girl, and the child born last is no one's favorite.

Favoritism reveals itself in many different ways, some of them apparently inconsequential, but very important in the mind of a child. A favored child may be:

- *Reprimanded less*

- *Allowed to do a greater variety of activities*

- *Given more treats, such as rides on father's back or candy*

- *Defended when he gets into trouble for being naughty*

- *Given more time and attention*

Of course, all children have different needs, and it is impossible to treat them absolutely equally, but you should beware of favoring one child, or even appearing to; children are very quick to notice such behavior, and a child who feels left out will suffer a blow to his confidence.

RELATIONSHIPS

Children who grow up in a stable, secure environment and feel loved by their parents are likely to become well-adjusted adults. Ideally, you and your partner will have equal but complementary roles: you have authority over some situations, your partner has authority over others, so that your child cannot play one of you against the other. The way a child interacts with his parents and siblings evolves gradually between the ages of three and five.

MOTHER AND CHILD

3 years At the age of three, children generally have good relationships with their mothers. Quite often the mother is the favorite parent with whom children like to discuss and relive past events. By three and a half, the mother-child relationship can sometimes become more difficult. Children can be simultaneously demanding and resistant. A child may refuse to eat, dress, or take a nap for his mother, but be quite compliant with someone else.

4 years By the age of four, your child will take pride in you, quote things that you say, and boast about you to friends, although at home he'll still resist your authority.

5 years The mother-child relationship is generally smoother by the age of five: the child likes to do things that you request, enjoys playing around you, and needs your presence, though not always your full attention. Children quite often express affection, such as: "I like you, Mommy," and although they accept punishment from you, it may not have a great impact on them. Boys may talk about marrying Mommy.

FATHER AND CHILD

3 years At three years, the mother tends to be the favorite parent, but the father can take over in many situations. For instance, a child may cling less at bedtime and go to sleep more quickly in the presence of the father. At the age of three and a half, girls may express closeness to their fathers.

4 years Children boast about their fathers outside the home and quote them as authorities. Some children may feel jealous of the time their fathers spend with their mothers and feel they are being deprived of maternal attention. If this is the case, a child may verbally express dislike for his father.

5 years By five years of age, children are likely to accept their father taking a caring role if mother is busy, ill, or away. Relationships with their father are generally smooth, pleasant, and undisturbed, and children often value special outings with their father. They often accept punishment better from mothers than fathers. Fathers may have more authority and tend to be disobeyed less.

Sibling relationships
Your child will enjoy the companionship of a sibling to play with, but don't be surprised by quarrels, since these are quite normal.

SIBLINGS

At the age of four, relationships with siblings can be turbulent. A child is old enough to be a nuisance to older siblings and can be selfish, rough, and impatient with younger siblings. Quarrels and physical fights over toys and possessions are common, as are complaints about fairness: "He's got more than me!"

A five-year-old child is usually good with younger brothers and sisters. Girls, especially, can be protective and kind toward younger members of the family, and are helpful rather than domineering. Having said this, a five-year-old is still too young to be responsible for younger siblings; although a child may take on a caring role while an adult is present, he may resort to teasing when left alone with a brother or sister. Five-year-olds usually interact well with older siblings, sometimes adopting a baby role in domestic play.

THE ONLY CHILD

Although there are benefits to being an only child, such as having lots of love and attention, there are also disadvantages. Without the presence of other children of a comparable age, the only child can sometimes feel lonely, and reluctant to join in groups. As long as you are aware of this, you can do things to compensate. It is important to introduce your child to other children at an early age. Encourage him to invite friends home and to visit other friends' houses, and arrange trips with other young children

Another problem associated with only children is the tendency that some parents have to be possessive and overprotective. This can be harmful for both parent and child. If you don't allow your child a sense of adventure and the freedom to experiment and explore, he may become timid and wary of new people and experiences. Parents, meanwhile, will have a more acute sense of loss when the child does become independent.

An only child needs the same amount of discipline as other children. Try not to be too indulgent and help your child realize that he cannot always expect to have your undivided attention.

REJECTION

Although it is unusual, some parents emotionally reject their children, and this can express itself in criticism and unfavorable comparisons with siblings.

The consequences of parental rejection can be acute. Signs of profound insecurity in a rejected child can be as follows:

- *Excessive fear or shyness*

- *Crying a lot*

- *Aggressiveness and tantrums*

- *Jealousy and attention-seeking*

- *Excessive clinging to mother, thumb-sucking, or masturbation*

- *Bedwetting or soiling*

- *Physical tics*

- *Head-banging*

- *Bullying, stealing, or lying*

- *Cruelty to animals*

MAKING FRIENDS

By the time your child reaches age four, he is likely to be able to play with other children in an interactive and sustained way. The members of your child's group may change rapidly and there may not be an allegiance to a special friend at this stage, though girls are more likely than boys to pair off with a particular friend. Although children may tease peers of the opposite sex, gender is not usually a criterion for selecting friends – neither is race.

By age five, children tend to select a single playmate, but their play is not necessarily interactive: children often "parallel play," occupying the same area but doing different things. The most frequent grouping is two children of the same gender, but even at this age, gender is not a major criterion for making new friends.

Although group play demands some cooperation from children, this is quite superficial, since children can often play with their own ends in mind and have little concern for the group as a whole.

SOCIAL GROUPS

Although children do not fit into rigid stereotypes, there are some common features in most groups of preschool children. Some children seem to be popular with everyone; others may be rejected by the group. Some children evoke neither strong negative nor positive feelings in others, leaving them with neither enemies nor friends. And even in preschool, children form cliques. The "star" is the child who is popular with everyone; the "rejectee" tends to be least popular; the "neglectee" doesn't evoke strong feelings in other children and, although he does not have any enemies, he probably has no friends; and the "clique" is a small group of children who repeatedly seek out each other's company.

The problems experienced by a child who is actively rejected are obvious and usually quickly spotted by teachers. Children who are ignored by their peers, however, may suffer a form of social isolation that is more subtle but equally damaging. Such children are typically quiet, reserved, and may blend into the background.

THE LONELY CHILD

Isolation in the early years of childhood can have several long-term negative effects. Studies have shown that children who have problems interacting with their peers not only suffer in the preschool years but have more emotional difficulties in later life than "sociable" children. It is important to intervene early by trying to discover the underlying problem and treating or correcting it. Encouragingly, preschoolers seem better able to learn new social skills than older children or adults.

Playing together
Children will often play next to each other even if they are not involved in the same game.

216

The first signs that a child is a loner may appear when he starts nursery school. Whereas other children pair off or form groups, this child remains solitary. When children are asked to find a partner, he will be the last one left without a partner, and when asked to stand in a line, he will find himself at the back.

If you think that your child is being left out of social situations it is important to take steps to help his social development. Fortunately, preschool children can learn new social skills easily if helped by sympathetic staff and you.

HOW TO HELP

If your child has poor social skills, there are various ways that you and your child's nursery school teacher can help. These include attaching a child to something or someone that raises their standing, or giving a child a responsibility that will boost confidence.

Opposite pairing This involves pairing a solitary child with a child who is outgoing and sociable. By being seen as the friend of a popular child, the less socially adept child will gain a significantly higher level of social acceptance in a short time – in some cases as little as three weeks.

Younger pairing Pairing a child with poor social skills with a younger child can be another way of conferring status. A study carried out in the 1980s showed that when unpopular children between the ages of four and five played with younger children, their level of popularity increased by at least 50 percent. Younger playmates offer positive social experiences to less socially adept children, which helps build their self-esteem and assertiveness.

Clique activities Although it might seem bad for children to form small, exclusive groups within a large group, allowing them to socialize in their preferred clique motivates them to get along with their peers outside the clique. Clique-based activities give children a sense of security and confidence about all social relationships.

Small groups It is sometimes mistakenly assumed that a child with poor social skills will socialize more easily when surrounded by a big group. In fact, small groupings are better at facilitating friendships because in a large group a child with poor social skills can remain very much in the background; in a small group, he can't be ignored as easily. A nursery school teacher can help by placing such a child in a small group – say three or four children – and then extending the size of the group gradually.

Star responsibility Establishing definite roles, such as giving the most popular children responsible tasks to do, appears to have a settling effect on all children of nursery-school age. Tasks could include giving out the straws for milk or organizing cleaning up. Children with less developed social skills appear to benefit from this strategy as much as other children.

YOUR CHILD'S NEW WORLD

Now that your child is socializing with children of his own age, whether at nursery school or at play, he will have new concerns of which you will become aware.

• *Clothes are one of the first ways of expressing individuality, and children may identify themselves with a particular peer group by the clothes they wear. By the time your child reaches nursery school age, he will probably want to select his clothes each day. Encourage his sense of identity and independence by having a flexible attitude toward clothes*

• *Toys, sports equipment, any sort of collection – such as a stamp or sticker collection – books, and comics are all powerful indicators of status among children. Even earning money for doing odd jobs is a sign of prowess*

• *Academic or athletic success and popularity also confer distinction. Some children also derive status from their parents – a high profile or professional career, affluence, or being well-traveled are all things that carry prestige*

• *If you feel that your child attaches too much value to a particular thing, or values something that is inappropriate, help him reassess priorities and perhaps reward him for some achievement that you consider worthy*

LYING

In order for a child to tell a lie he must have reached a stage in his psychological development where he can distinguish fantasy from reality. For example, if a 15-month-old is chastised by his mother for smearing poster paint on a wall and he shakes his head vigorously in denial, he is not lying – he may have genuinely forgotten the action, or may wish he hadn't done it, or may simply be unable to recognize the difference between fantasy and reality. Only when a child reaches the age of three or four years will he be capable of lying, and most children will lie if they find a situation sufficiently threatening.

HOW SERIOUS IS LYING?

Children lie for many different reasons and some types of lying are more serious than others. For instance, a make-believe lie is a natural part of a child's fantasy life, whereas a cover-up lie is a conscious attempt to avoid punishment.

Exploratory lying This is done simply to see your response. For example, a four-year-old child will tell his mother that he did not like his dinner even though he ate it all. This is designed to see how you will react. In most cases, your response to this kind of lying is enough to discourage him from doing it again. Some children, however, recognize that it wins attention, and they will employ it over and over again as they grow up. For this reason it is serious and must be discouraged.

Bragging This type of lying usually takes the form of a greatly exaggerated story and is done to boost the child's self-confidence. In an attempt to impress his friends, a five-year-old will state boldly that he has received many expensive birthday presents or that he lives in an enormous house. Although bragging is generally harmless, you can discourage your child from this type of lying by reinforcing his genuine achievements.

For a small number of children, bragging can become a permanent habit. Children who brag frequently do so because they desperately want to impress their friends and parents and they want to be loved. The danger is that people will come to view everything your child says with skepticism. Bragging lies can become a child's hallmark, and he may lose many friends as a result.

Make-believe lies These are lies that mix reality and fantasy, and they serve to add excitement to everyday experiences. For instance, a four-year-old may have a vivid imaginary world consisting of fairies,

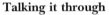

Talking it through
If you discover your child has been lying, explain what he has done wrong patiently but firmly, rather than getting angry.

218

monsters, and invisible friends, all of which he can describe in colorful detail. Childhood fantasies do not really constitute lies, and they should be seen as a normal phase of child development.

Cover-up lies Lies that aim to deliberately mislead are the type that parents worry about most. Children tell cover-up lies to avoid being punished, and they learn this tactic at a relatively early age. In one survey, mothers were asked to identify the most common reason for their four-year-olds lying to them. Nearly half of them said that it was a lie to escape a reprimand. Cover-up lies become more sophisticated and plausible as a child gets older.

Lies to avoid punishment can put parents in a difficult position. If you punish your child every time he does something wrong, he may learn to lie in response. On the other hand, if you don't reprimand your child he's likely to continue behaving in the same way. A balance needs to be struck between being too permissive and too punitive. I tried to encourage the truth with my children by saying that a child who told the truth would not be punished. They realized I was aware of the effort taken to be honest and promised not to lie; they rarely did.

DEALING WITH LYING

A study carried out several years ago investigated the impact of different parental responses on lying. It was found that children whose parents used moral principles to explain to their children why lying is wrong effectively reduced the frequency of lying. A parental response involving punishment increased the frequency of lying.

Children sometimes tell cover-up lies, not to escape punishment, but because they fear that their bad behavior will stop their parents from loving them. Therefore any punishment for lying should be accompanied by reassurance. A child needs to be aware that punishment and parental love are not mutually exclusive. There is much research to show that parents who are honest with their children receive honesty in return. Make it easy for your child to confess to his misdeeds by speaking to him calmly, rather than getting angry and making accusations.

Children often say things that are inaccurate or untrue; one important reason is that they hear their parents doing it: adults frequently tell "white lies" to avoid hurting other people's feelings unnecessarily. Your child may hear you saying something that contradicts what you normally say. If the reason for such tactful conversation is not explained to him, he can't understand why it is wrong for him to do the same.

Explaining about lying If your child continues to exaggerate the truth, it is important that you stress why telling lies is such a bad idea. If he is old enough to understand, you could try telling him the story of "The Boy Who Cried 'Wolf!'." Afterwards, talk about it and make sure that he understands that if you can't tell the difference between what is true and what is not true, you might not know when something really serious has happened to him.

HELPING A CHILD WHO LIES

Because children lie for different reasons, every child must be treated individually. There are, however, a number of do's and don'ts that apply to all children.

- *Act calmly – the child may genuinely be confusing reality and fantasy*

- *Try to understand the motive for a lie. Your child is not lying because he wants to be malicious; more likely he is afraid of the punishment he'll receive*

- *Explain to your child why it is wrong to lie. Use examples that he can understand*

- *Make punishments reasonable. If you punish your child too severely, he will be more determined to lie in the future*

- *Make your child aware that although you are angry with him, you still love him*

- *Don't ridicule the child who persists with bragging lies. Bragging indicates low self-esteem, and you should work to increase your child's self confidence with praise and affection*

- *Don't use physical punishment on a child who lies. Research shows that constant spanking for lies only encourages children to lie more, because they are afraid of being spanked again*

WHEN THINGS GO WRONG

There are two broad categories of abnormal social development: habit disorders and behavioral disorders. Habit disorders involve problems with eating, toileting, sleeping, or speaking, and behavior disorders involve problems with social conduct, such as aggressiveness (biting, hitting), angry and destructive behavior, poor

DEALING WITH PROBLEM BEHAVIOR

COMMON PROBLEMS

Toileting; bed-wetting, soiling

Eating problems: overeating, undereating, pica

Negativism

Inappropriate sexual behavior

Bullying

Biting

Aggressiveness

Lying

Stealing

Destructiveness

Severe shyness

Severe fearfulness

Obsessive behavior

Regardless of how loving and careful parents are in bringing up their children, sometimes things go wrong. The problems that arise may be temporary or of longer duration. For parents, such problems are frustrating since they may hear a great deal of contradictory "advice" from others, ranging from the need for more or less punishment, more affection or less indulgence to recommendations for various therapies. And often the child with behavior problems is shunned by her peers; hand in hand with that goes shunning of the child's parents by the parents of her peers. All in all, it is a painful and isolating experience for the entire family.

Problem behavior ranges from bedwetting to destructiveness and inappropriate sexual behavior. Although all children periodically behave in ways that are unacceptable, such behavior is worrisome only when it is extreme and/or persists over a long period of time. Parents may sometimes feel that a child with a behavioral problem is being manipulative or vindictive. It should be realized, however, that preschoolers are generally too young to behave in a calculated way. Rather than labeling the behavior, it is best to investigate what lies behind it.

It's not easy to pin down a cause or causes of problem behavior – many problems may result from multiple contributing factors. Sometimes inborn chemistry or genetics plays a part, sometimes it's a matter of environmental influences, and these may sometimes, but not always, be attributed to parenting shortcomings.

It is important that parents not take the full burden of responsibility on themselves, either for the cause or the cure. If your child is exhibiting problems that persist, seem very different from those of other children her age, or do not yield to your reasonable approach, discuss the issue with your child's doctor. You may be relieved to learn that your child's behavior actually falls within the "normal" range. The solution may simply be a matter of altering your own approach or certain aspects of home life. On the other hand, the problem may require more specialized professional attention.

It is equally important not to avoid the problem or deny that it exists. Although it is a natural impulse to wish such difficulties away – insisting they are just a "phase" the child is going through or a peculiarity of her "nature" – great harm can be done to a child by deferring action. There's a real possibility that the behavior is caused by an underlying factor that needs to be treated; it could be anything from bladder and bowel abnormalities, hearing or sight problems to a learning disability such as dyslexia, which may cause the child to behave inappropriately in school settings. And while her parents are hoping "it will pass," the child may suffer in her social, physical, and intellectual development.

The best thing to do is face the problem, consult the pediatrician (and, if need be, other professionals), and work on solutions. The happy fact is that most children can be helped with remarkable speed if appropriate action is taken early on.

control (stealing), and dishonesty. Although it may be tempting to seek simple causes and, hopefully, simple solutions to problem behavior, the fact is that it is often difficult to identify a cause or causes and prescribe an easy answer. Blaming the child – or the parents – and imposing a system of punishment rarely gets to the root of the problem. What is often more effective is positive reinforcement: praising and rewarding a child for success rather than criticizing or punishing the failures. For severe and persistent problem behavior, parents should seek professional guidance.

HABIT DISORDERS

Problems such as bedwetting, soiling bed or clothing, overeating, and faddish eating are found in most normal children and, as long as they occur occasionally only, they should not be perceived as disorders. However, when a child repeatedly wets her bed past the age when you would expect her to be dry, or overeats to the extent that she becomes obese, help should be sought. Habit disorders may result from parenting problems, emotional trauma or conflict (such as the arrival of a new baby in the family, a new home, or a change of school), or delayed development. Occasionally, there is a physiological basis for bedwetting; eliminate this possibility first.

Bedwetting Habitual bedwetting (enuresis) is the most common habit disorder and is never the child's fault. It is usually nocturnal; the most common reason is developmental delay. Most children are dry day and night by the age of five. Habitual bedwetting in a seven-year-old could be considered abnormal, but is probably the result of stress to the child; it will improve when the stress is removed. Occasional bedwetting is very common and is often caused by excitement, fear, illness, or a sense of threat, so it can be ignored.

Some families have a history of bedwetting, so a child should never be blamed for her slowness. Only about one in ten children suffering from enuresis has a physical or emotional disturbance, and these children usually suffer from enuresis during the day as well as the night. Possible physical causes include anatomical or physiological disturbance of bladder function, urinary infection, nocturnal epilepsy, and congenital abnormalities of the bladder.

Bedwetting is sometimes an emotional response to excessive parental pressure to be fully toilet trained. Insufficient or inconsistent encouragement or unrealistically high expectations before the child is developmentally ready are common reasons. Bedwetting is exacerbated by parental disapproval and teasing by siblings. Never scold or ridicule bedwetting, and always praise success.

Measures such as restricting fluid before bedtime and waking the child to urinate during the night occasionally help. The pad- and buzzer method of treatment, in which a buzzer sounds when the bedclothes become wet, is successful in some cases, but it shouldn't be used on children under seven. The best approach to bedwetting is to treat it as an accident or as lateness rather than illness and not to draw attention to it. Very young children may stop bedwetting if they are allowed to sleep in their parents' bedroom.

FECAL SOILING

Unlike bedwetting, soiling bed or clothing is unusual in toilet-trained children and almost always indicates stress or emotional disturbance.

Nevertheless, a physical cause should be ruled out first. There are three types: soiling that has been present from babyhood; regressive soiling, in which a toilet-trained child reverts to an earlier stage of development; and aggressive soiling, which is an emotional response to overly strict parenting, or overly severe or out-of-date toilet training (see p.113).

Aggressive soiling usually occurs in children who have been "toilet-trained" too early in life, because the parents place exaggerated emphasis on being clean. If a child feels stifled and isn't allowed to play and get dirty, she may express her frustration and anger through soiling.

The most effective way to deal with soiling is to reduce a child's anxiety. Overly strict parents should become more relaxed, and stressful or traumatic events need to be dealt with sympathetically.

DEPRESSION

Children become depressed when they face stress they can't cope with: moving to a new house or town, changing schools and leaving friends behind, separation from parents, divorce, or being abused are all examples.

In addition, it is now believed that any evaluation of learning disabilities in a child should include a check for depression, as the two often go hand in hand.

A depressed child may cry more than normal, lack interest in games and friends, and become irritable when efforts are made to rouse her from her apathy. Depression rarely occurs alone in children; it's usually combined with phobias, obsessions, and compulsive behavior. Sleep disturbance, loss of appetite, difficulty concentrating, which in turn causes difficulties at school, and tense, restless behavior are common features. As important as it is to recognize that depression can occur even in young children, it is equally important to realize that not every child who has an unhappy moment is depressed.

Parents who notice a marked change in their child's behavior in one or several of the ways described – and if it lasts for several weeks or more – should talk to their child's doctor. If the doctor finds no evidence of a physical problem, the next step is to consult a mental health professional.

There are many ways to help a depressed child. Psychotherapy – for the child or the family as a whole – can often be effective. For an older child (five and upward), medication might be an option if changes in body chemistry are a suspected cause.

Eating disorders Refusing to eat, overeating, being excessively fussy about food or eating only a few foods, and pica (eating things not usually considered edible, such as paper and plaster may all be classified as eating disorders if they occur more than occasionally.

Persistent refusal to eat or picking at food is common in children of preschool age. Poor appetite may be the result of anxiety or it may indicate a problem between parent and child. Parents may be overanxious, with exaggerated ideas about nutritional needs, or food may be used as a symbol of affection, with overfeeding resulting in undereating. Fortunately, food refusal in young children rarely leads to malnutrition – the best approach is to be more flexible about to meals and offer a wide range of foods.

Faddish or fussy eating is common in otherwise healthy children and many children go through phases of faddiness that pass. Faddish eating – eating only a very few foods – unless it is excessive, is not really a problem. But if you are concerned that your child's diet is nutritionally inadequate, consult your pediatrician.

Overeating is a more serious problem than food refusal or faddiness because it can lead to obesity. Obesity is not only bad for a child's health, it also means that she may be teased by her peers and suffer low self-esteem.

Children overeat for many different reasons; sometimes a child uses food to compensate for the fact that she feels unloved and insecure; sometimes a parent who feels inadequate will overfeed a child to make up for not giving enough love and affection. Attitudes about food and feeding may also be influenced by cultural factors. To prevent overeating, it is essential to identify the underlying reason, whether it is insecurity on the part of the child, or conscious or unconscious overfeeding on the part of the parent. A pediatrician will be able to suggest a suitable reducing diet.

Pica is the consumption of substances without any nutritional value, such as soil, gravel, chalk, paint, clothing, or even feces. It occurs most frequently among children from homes in which there are other problems as well. Children with pica may show other signs of disturbed behavior.

BEHAVIORAL DISORDERS

Antisocial behavior usually stems from a problem within the family or in the family's inability to adjust to society at large. A child may fail to identify herself as part of a family and to accept parental attitudes and standards of behavior. This is most likely to happen in homes lacking in consistent adult role-models, or where a child is constantly being moved around, scolded, punished, or mentally, physically, or socially abused. Common symptoms of behavioral disorders are bad language, temper tantrums, disobedience, aggression, stealing, and lying. As a child grows up she may stay out late, play truant from school, and take drugs.

Psychologists, child psychiatrists, and social workers can help explore the root causes of a behavioral disorder, and in some cases, psychotherapy is recommended for the child. Sometimes the whole family rather than the individual child may receive counseling.

OTHER PROBLEM BEHAVIOR

Most children at some stage will indulge in behavior that parents find worrying, unacceptable, or just annoying. In most cases, the reasons are quite innocent and the phase will soon pass.

Negativism Stubbornness, selfishness, and disobedience are all characteristics of negativism. To some extent, all preschoolers are negativistic. They may seem to delight in doing the opposite of what they are asked: when you want your child to go out she decides to stay in, or when you want her to eat her food she'll refuse it.

There are many reasons for resisting parental authority, and parents sometimes misinterpret them. A child may be negativistic, not because she wants to revolt against authority, but because she simply wants to continue with what she is doing. She has no conception of time, and sees no reason why she should stop playing an enjoyable game. Reasons such as a mealtime or going to bed are quite irrelevant if she is not hungry or tired.

Another explanation for negativism is that a young child cannot distinguish between two opposites. She is inexperienced, her life is charged with alternatives, and often she finds it impossible to differentiate between yes and no, give and take, or push and pull. Her interest in these double alternatives is so evenly balanced that she goes from one extreme to the other.

Flagrant negativism may result from insufficient parental encouragement. Even if your child is slow to perform a task or makes a mess, it is important to encourage learning early on.

Stealing Between the ages of two and five or six, a child may be so attracted to an object – a toy, coins left on a parent's dresser, or candy – that she takes it when she hopes no one is looking. Sometimes she will do it in such a way that her theft is discovered. Neither is a sign of a deep-rooted problem. Rather it is a normal overwhelming desire unbraked by social inhibitions, which you must help her to develop. Don't punish the act, but don't ignore it. Tell your child clearly and calmly that it is unacceptable and insist that the object be returned. In all likelihood, one or a few such interchanges are all that's required to end the behavior.

Resistance to school A child who says she doesn't want to go to school or, more commonly, complains of a stomach- or headache on school mornings may be coming down with a mild illness; she may be unhappy about something in school; or she may not wish to leave you because of shyness or something she is worried about at home. It's best not to force your child to go to school at first, unless this is a recognized and oft-repeated pattern. If an illness does not reveal itself in a day or two or if your child perks up once the threat of school is removed, you should talk with her teacher to help uncover any problems. If all is well at school and reluctance to leave home is the possible cause, try a loving but firm good-bye and a warm but restrained welcome home. If the behavior persists, consult your child's doctor.

SEXUAL MISBEHAVIOR

Adults tend to classify some aspects of normal development (such as games of "show") as prurient. They are quite normal stages of development, and it is only adult interference that leads to exaggerations of sexual play.

True sexual misbehavior may occur in isolation or together with other forms of antisocial behavior, such as truancy. Sexual curiosity and masturbation are common and normal features of childhood, and become abnormal only because of their frequency or the circumstances in which they occur. Unless you consider a child's sexual behavior completely unacceptable, it is important to retain a sensible attitude to this feature of childhood. Even if you consider behavior questionable, consult your child's doctor before labeling the behavior abnormal.

EARLY EDUCATION

DAY-CARE REALITIES

In our society at the present time, mothers of babies and young children often work outside the home. Without commenting on the implications for growing children, it can be said that this is a complicating factor of family life.

Options range from leaving the child with a relative or a hired caregiver in the child's own home to having the child cared for along with a small group of children in someone else's home or a larger group in a commercial day-care center.

For some children, day-care provides a transition from home to preschool. Under the best of circumstances, this is the case.

Determining if day-care is right for your child is a difficult issue. You must balance your child's needs and readiness with your own needs and those of other family members.

Whether or not you decide to send your child to preschool will depend largely upon the options available and whether or not they suit her needs and your own. Find out what's available in your area and spend what time you can visiting local nursery schools and talking to the teachers and other parents to get a good idea of what is being provided.

CHOOSING PRESCHOOL EDUCATION

There is no single kind of preschool that is best for every child. Each child should be in a school that fits her particular needs. All evaluations of preschool education show mixed results. One long-term assessment showed that boys in Montessori programs sustained gains in reading and math throughout their school careers. Other research shows that intellectual gains are found in all but the poorest of programs. But it's difficult to know how long these benefits last. Evaluations of Head Start programs in the U.S., for example, show that apparent IQ differences between children in Head Start and those who don't attend preschool at all diminish over time. Whatever the benefits of preschool education, there is no substitute for a loving and caring home environment.

Playgroups often take children from as early as two and a half years old. They provide the opportunity for interaction with other children of the same age and help develop early social skills, but in a less formal atmosphere than nursery school. Some day-care centers take children as young as six months, though of course they do not provide any educational or socialization programs for that age group.

Preschool may give your child a greater sense of confidence and therefore more self-control, as well as teaching her to share, be concerned for the needs of others, and take turns. Your child's skill in planning ahead and cooperating with others will improve through fantasy and group play.

The opportunities for play in preschool enhance the various ways that your child thinks – that is, imaginatively, speculatively, and inventively. Some preschools are designed to help disadvantaged children by building up their confidence. Children who attend such schools seem to be less likely to repeat a year than their peers who did not attend preschool, less in need of special education, and less likely to show delinquent behavior in adolescence.

I think there are very few risks to your child attending preschool, certainly no more than when she ventures outside the family; she'll just encounter them sooner. Risks may include minor health problems and exposure to behavior you find objectionable, such as swearing and rudeness.

SETTLING IN

You can help your child adjust to nursery school by taking her for one or two visits well in advance of her start date. Encourage her to play with the other children and to sit at one of the work tables or play with some of the equipment. But try not to push her to socialize with other children if she doesn't seem eager to at first. Some children are naturally more gregarious than others, and she will adjust in her own good time. The aim is to make her visits as enjoyable as possible. If you stress all the fun things she will do, her eager anticipation for school will be stronger than her worry about leaving you. If she is having trouble adjusting, most nursery schools will let you stay with her on the first day and for steadily decreasing periods of time on the following days. Make sure you pick her up yourself for the first week when she is most insecure. Once she is confident that she's not being abandoned, you'll be free to make other arrangements for pickup.

Your child's personality, maturity, place in the family, and willingness to leave home all will influence the way she settles down at preschool. In general, boys are more likely than girls of the same age to cry when their mothers first leave them at nursery school and they tend to cry when frustrated or angry with a teacher or helper. On the other hand, your child may enjoy being with other children as much as she does anything else about preschool. It's not unusual for two little boys or girls to rush eagerly toward each other when they meet at school.

Although your child is now attending nursery school, this doesn't mean that your part in her education is finished. Ask her what she has done at school and who she played with. By getting her to talk over her school experiences you will be consolidating the new words and skills she is learning. You can help her to improve her use of language by repeating what she says in the correct form, though not by directly correcting her. Your preschool child will be constantly seeking new information, and you should always try to answer her questions truthfully. If you don't know the answer it is best to suggest you both look it up in a book, or ask Daddy whether he knows, rather than just try to put her off.

HOW CHILDREN BEHAVE AT NURSERY SCHOOL

As a rule boys are more task-oriented in nursery school play while little girls talk more about being friends, recognizing similarities in each other, admiring one another's clothes, discussing who's friends with whom, and so on.

Dominant and aggressive behavior in little boys is very much in evidence in a preschool setting. Intelligence and ability to get along with others are as important to popularity in preschool as a boy's size or physical prowess. Popularity fluctuates from day to day. Hitting is a common form of aggressiveness in preschool groups. A few girls strike out at others, but this behavior is more common among boys. Boys take longer to learn not to hit others and make unprovoked, if rather mild, attacks on girls. Some may, for example, push little girls or gesture menacingly at them.

APPROACHES TO PRESCHOOL

No single method of preschool has proved to be significantly better for every child. Many parents send their children to preschool to give them an opportunity to play and be sociable; others simply because it allows their children physical outlets that won't damage the furniture. And still others do so because it provides a few hours respite and eases the burden when both parents work outside the home.

Structured classes are better suited to the needs of most small children. A chaotic environment may cause some boys to react in a way that some teachers describe as hyperactive. Structures vary within preschools. Some nursery schools follow a timetable for certain activities each day along the lines advocated by Maria Montessori, organizing the school around an orderly child-sized environment with specific behavioral guidelines such as putting things away after use.

A child who finds tasks easy and has lots of local friends may be suited to a traditional school. A child who has few local playmates and wants to socialize, on the other hand, may enjoy a less structured preschool.

CHOOSING A SCHOOL

When she's three or four, your child will be able to go to nursery school, if you choose. Whether you feel this is the correct step will largely depend on her nature. For example, is she still shy and clinging, or naturally outgoing? Only you can know whether she is ready.

The age at which children start kindergarten varies from community to community, but most children begin at around age five. When making a decision about preschool and, if you have a choice, of kindergarten, try to narrow the choices to a manageable few and then make visits.

Prepare a checklist of important points so you do not forget any of them. For example, are the teachers relaxed or formal? Is it a happy environment? What is the standard of facilities? How many children are there, and are they well supervised? What subjects are taught? Does the school feel safe? Are the children happy?

Sit in on a few classes and spend a whole morning or afternoon there, and also speak to mothers whose children already attend. You will then have much of the information you need to decide.

GOING TO SCHOOL

Starting school will be a great milestone for your child, and for you, too. You'll both have to make adjustments: your child will discover a new and exciting world, and you will have to adjust to his newfound independence.

IS YOUR CHILD READY?

The age at which a child is legally required to attend school varies among communities, but many parents are eager to send their children earlier if spaces are available, to give them a "head start." It is biology and not the calendar that determines your child's readiness for school. Certain physical skills are usually taken as signs that he has reached the level of mental development necessary for school success. (See checklist below.) Your child must be capable of taking care of many of his bodily needs, as well. He should also know his full name and be able to ask clear and concise questions. Many five-year-olds are proud of learning numbers and their ability to count. They also demonstrate their maturity by making strong efforts to keep themselves under control. You can introduce all these things to your child before he starts school.

You may feel pressure to send your child to school because most of the other parents in your social circle are doing so. Although it is difficult to resist such "peer pressure," parents must make the decision based on their individual child's readiness, not the prevailing custom in the neighborhood. If you are unsure whether your child is ready, ask a nursery school teacher, who will probably be accurate at predicting whether your child will do well.

SCHOOL READINESS CHECKLIST

Your child need not have mastered every skill on this list before beginning. If he has acquired several in each of three areas of development – cognitive, motor, and emotional – he is probably ready.

- *Join in the shared activities of a group*
- *Listen to a story and retell events in sequence*
- *Join in and readily follow instructions for games or new activities*
- *Express ideas and needs clearly to others*
- *Hop, skip, and jump*
- *Help around the house doing simple tasks*
- *Recognize primary colors and basic shapes – circle, square, triangle*
- *Recognize similarities and differences in sound*
- *Join in songs and know some simple ones by heart*
- *Cope with buttons, shoelaces, and zippers, and cut with scissors*
- *Attend to personal toiletry needs*

HELPING YOUR CHILD LIKE SCHOOL

Your child is more likely to succeed at school if he has the right frame of mind to begin with. You can achieve this by preparing your child before he starts so that he is physically and mentally ready for the demands that school will make on him. Encourage him to carry out simple tasks so that he understands the concept of responsibility. Make sure his play involves imagination and creativity, as well as opportunities for learning and developing his memory. It is important, too, that the school provide the right environment for your child's education, with motivated teachers who have a good relationship with their pupils.

Your child will undoubtedly benefit if you take an interest in his schoolwork and can continue his education at home. There is a real danger, however, that you will do more harm than good if your methods are very different from those being taught at school. Teaching methods change over the years so the current system probably bears little relation to the way you were taught. To avoid this, talk to your child's teacher about the school's particular methods and find out first hand about the subjects they are teaching and the books that are in use. You may be able to borrow books and equipment overnight. Some schools actively encourage parents to sit in as observers, or you may even be able to help out in the classroom. But don't overdo the schoolwork. Home should also be a place of comfort and refuge so you will need to strike a balance between helping your child progress with his education and overloading him with work.

YOUR CHANGING RELATIONSHIP

Your child's first days at school mark a change in his relationship with you. Until now he has been dependent on you for everything, but now he'll have to begin to learn to become independent, responsible for many of his own decisions and actions. This change doesn't happen overnight, but it is important to begin the process by encouraging your child to take on gradually increasing responsibility. By now he should already wash and dress himself, and he might be expected to keep track of his bookbag, books, and other equipment, and to lay his things out each night for the next day.

He'll feel very grown up and will not want to be fussed over, but you should always be ready to give him a hug whenever he shows he needs one. It is hard for your child to accept that he is not fully grown-up, and the emotional drain of daily social interaction may occasionally be too much for him. As with most things, a hug from you is the best remedy and will help him face the next day.

You may find that your child will object to such public displays of affection, particularly in front of his new friends. Don't feel snubbed. He is simply asserting himself as independent – grown-up enough not to need a kiss from Mom.

More than anything else it's important not to push too hard, even in asking what happened during his day. Clever prompting may elicit information about his time at school, but prying will only make him secretive.

OTHER ACTIVITIES

Once your child is in school, be it nursery school or kindergarten, it is likely that you will be spending a great deal less time with him. You may find yourself trying to fill the after-school hours with the sorts of activities you had before. Care should be taken, however, not to overload your child's day with "busyness." Too often children are dragged from classroom to museum to play date to organized activity as parents attempt to "make up" for time their child was in the care of others.

A child who has spent even a few hours of his day among other children in an intensely active learning environment may simply want to relax at home, spending unstructured time alone or with his parent. A snack, a hug, and story time on Mom's lap will be of greater value than a frantic round of activities. And it will do more to maintain the bond you have developed over the previous years.

CHAPTER 4

Family LIFE

If you have never had a child you may imagine that you can incorporate a baby into your life with minimal disruption. This is rarely the case. A new baby is a 24-hour-a-day commitment and you will find that, at least for a few months, your normal lifestyle will have to be greatly modified. This will be all the more true if you have twins or even triplets.

Your relationship with your partner will also be different. There will be less time for intimacy and companionship and you may find you need to stop and take stock of your joint responsiblities. Child care is often thought of as a woman's job, but there is no biological reason why this should be so. Shared parenting will reap benefits for you and your partner, as well as your child.

You may want to involve other members of your family in helping to bring up your baby, especially if you are a single parent, or if you and your partner both go out to work. Alternatively, you may decide to employ a nanny, au pair, or childminder, or enroll your child in a daycare program. Whichever choice you make, planning ahead and organizing your time is of paramount importance.

BECOMING A FAMILY

No matter how many baby books you read, and no matter how well prepared you are, you can still be knocked sideways by the impact of a newborn baby on your life. In addition to the physical requirements of looking after a baby, your normal domestic work will at least quadruple. Instead of doing the laundry once a week, you may find you have to do it every day. Such repetitive chores can create a heavy, tiring work load.

After the first few weeks, when relatives and neighbors stop dropping by to offer congratulations, the novelty of being home alone with a new baby can wear off rapidly. Mothers who have given up a job or a career may find that what they miss is not their work, but their work environment. They miss social interaction with their friends and colleagues. In particular, they miss the difference between work and home. With a young baby, you do not have the luxury of leaving your work behind.

Many people also find that making the transition from being a couple to being a family can prove more traumatic than they imagine. The dynamics in a relationship need to adapt to a new addition. Problems can arise when a couple finds it difficult to fit another person into the complex equation of human emotions that makes up a relationship.

NEW RESPONSIBILITIES

The arrival of a child means that choices become stark: beforehand, for instance, if neither partner wanted to clean the bathroom floor, it could be left until later. But a baby can never be left until later. His needs take priority, and somebody has to take immediate responsibility for meeting them. Time that was previously spent on other things must now be given to the baby.

Ideally these lifestyle changes are shared equally within a partnership, but in practice women very often end up taking on the main burden. Depending on individual expectations, this can lead to deep resentment within a relationship, causing a couple to move apart after the birth of their baby.

Research has shown that one in every two marriages in the U.S. goes into decline after the birth of the first child. All couples in the study, no matter how well adjusted they were, experienced on

Shared parenting
Spend time with your partner getting to know your child and learning to be parents together.

average a 20 percent increase in conflict within their marriage during the first year of parenthood. Although conflict can sometimes be healthy, it is often not what new parents expect.

To reduce the stress placed on a partnership, it is vital that each partner has at least some idea of what to expect and is able to compromise. Having a baby means rearranging your life.

EQUAL PARENTING

Although the role of men in parenting has changed over the last few decades, the attitude that child care is primarily a woman's responsibility still persists. Ideally, you and your partner should discuss your respective roles before your baby is born. Women should make their partners aware that being a good father doesn't just mean helping: it means fathering the child as well.

In a recent survey, 74 percent of fathers said they believed that child care should be shared equally. But when asked, "Do you share child care equally with your partner?" 87 percent replied "no". In other words, almost nine out of ten women will not receive equal help from their partners.

This isn't just damaging for women, it is also very limiting for men in two ways. First, a father's relationship with his partner may suffer if she feels resentment at a lack of help and support. Second, if a father doesn't play an active role in the early months and years of his baby's life, he may lose the chance to form a close childhood bond with his son or daughter. A detached father will have a negative effect on his child. Girls may have trouble interacting with men and boys will be deprived of a male role model.

FATHERING

Many of us remember our fathers seeming more distant and unapproachable than our mothers, but there is no reason why a child cannot enjoy an equally close relationship with both parents. A baby's relationships do not operate on an either/or basis, and you should never worry that if a baby spends an equal amount of time with his father, he may love his mother less. All young children need as much love as they can get, and both parents should do their utmost to provide it.

For a father to take on an equal role as a parent, he will have to overcome cultural pressures and perhaps change his own attitudes, too. He will also have to recognize his role as a caregiver rather than just a provider. Some men confuse parenthood with taking care of the bills, because that is what their own fathers did.

Today it may be economic factors that determine who is left holding the baby. If a woman earns more than her partner, or if he is unemployed, many couples can't afford to let misplaced male pride reduce their weekly income. While the rise of the house-husband has undoubtedly benefited lots of families, it is important to bear in mind that the man left at home with a small child suffers from the same problems as a woman: isolation and boredom.

Parental bonding
Your child cannot have too much love and attention, so both of you should give as much as possible.

A FATHER'S STORY

Anna and Henry Ewington experienced a bad few months after their son Alexander was born. Anna was exhausted, depressed, and overwhelmed, and Henry didn't feel very paternal.

Henry attributes this to the fact that he measured fatherhood in terms of doing things, and that Anna quickly took all responsibility for the baby.

Henry's frustration intensified Anna's difficulties. For the first three months, she experienced periods of postpartum depression. Their sex life deteriorated, and Henry started to feel rejected by Anna, both physically and emotionally. In just a few months, they decided it was make or break.

"We decided it had to be 'make' instead of break when we found out Anna was pregnant with Leora only ten months after the birth of Alex. I realized then that I had to give Anna enormous credit for being able to cope with it all. I half expected her to cave in, but instead she became stronger, perhaps because of having to cope with Alex."

During the third month of Anna's pregnancy, she had a threatened miscarriage. She was advised to stay in bed, and Henry decided to take unpaid leave from work so he could look after her.

"For the first time since the birth, Anna felt as though I was doing my part, and I felt, for once, that I was the linchpin of our family unit. Despite the emotional strain, I'm glad we went through it. It has made me an equal parent with Anna, whereas before I felt like an observer."

GRANDPARENTS

With the arrival of a first child, grandparents can be supportive or they can be the source of increased tension, especially if family relations are already strained. You will probably find that you see more of your in-laws once your baby is born, and ideally this will contribute to a happier family life.

Sometimes, however, the intimacy and interdependency of family relations means there is a fine line between helpfulness and interference. Ideally, you and your partner will have discussed the role you want grandparents to play. Once both of you have decided how much help you do or don't want, you will find it easier to establish your authority by setting out the rules in advance.

It is understandable that many grandparents, particularly grandmothers, want to show you how they coped with a crying baby or a disobedient toddler. This advice is usually well-intended and may be welcome. If it isn't, say so. Point out that it is your baby and that discipline – or any other matter – is therefore your responsibility. If you occasionally make mistakes, they will be your own.

It certainly is worth persevering to overcome problems with parents so your child will be able to reap the benefits of a secure and loving relationship with her grandparents.

A SPECIAL RELATIONSHIP

A good relationship between a grandparent and grandchild is rewarding for the whole family. Grandparents can offer a more relaxed perspective about your children, parents can rest secure in the knowledge that when grandparents are in attendance their baby will be well looked after, and a baby can learn to form an important emotional bond beyond her mother and father.

Grandparents can form special relationships with their grandchildren for several reasons. First, they see them less frequently than their parents do, which alleviates the strain of day-to-day care. Second, ultimate responsibility for a child rests with her parents. This frees grandparents to

Second time around
Your parents and your partner's parents are likely to have a relaxed attitude toward child care.

enjoy the thrill of parenthood without the accompanying worries and stresses. Third, a grandparent has already brought up at least one child, and problems are always easier to cope with the second time around. Grandparents are also likely to have more quality time to spend with their grandchildren.

As children become young adults with problems of their own, grandparents can offer a broader perspective on the difficulties facing them. A grandparent is likely to be the oldest person your child will ever know as a friend and can give your child an insight into how things were in the past, as well as being a lot more interesting and loving than history books.

Not all families, however, can enjoy the benefits of an extended family. This is particularly true today, as financial pressures force couples to move to where they can find work. Divorce can limit grandparents' access to their grandchildren. This can be terribly upsetting for grandparents and grandchildren alike, and it helps if a child continues to see her grandparents regularly.

LOVE AND SECURITY

The most basic needs of any young child are physical care and emotional love and security. If a child feels well cared for, she will develop into a more outgoing and relaxed person. A child who is given enough love and security at an early age is likely to become less demanding as she grows older. Conversely, a child who is emotionally neglected may grow up insecure, clingy, and fearful.

It is important that parents not shy away from giving their child adequate love and security for fear of "spoiling" her. Although it is true that a child should not get into the habit of thinking she can have anything she wants, it is even more important that she not get into the habit of thinking she is not loved.

Remember, your child's way of seeing things is very different from yours. Small and apparently trivial displays of affection (a hug, a pat, a kiss) will do much more to shape the personality of your young child than anything else. It is no good loving your child and trying not to show it, in the mistaken assumption that this will make her a "stronger" person. In fact, the opposite is true.

Affection produces emotional and physical results. For instance, when young babies are held in their mother's arms, they breathe more slowly, have a steadier respiration, cry less, and sleep more. This isn't so surprising, since cuddling takes a child back to the comforting sensation of the uterus when she was warm and secure. Hugging is also the best way of communicating to a young child that you love and care for her. If your child sees her parents hugging each other she will know that, in spite of any arguments you might have, you still love each other.

Even if your child can feel that you love her through your physical affection, it is also important that she hear it. Toddlers especially need to hear that you love them. They have reached the stage where they can tell you that they love you, and they need this affection to be reciprocated. Never be shy about showing your love – it is the most important thing you will ever share.

GIVING AFFECTION

Loving touch is crucial to our well-being and, in the case of babies, has even been shown to promote physical development.

If you're not sure how to increase the amount of physical affection you show your child, consider some of the following suggestions. These combine physical attention with love and companionship – exactly what every child needs.

• *Try carrying a young baby in a sling; almost all newborn babies love the sensation of being strapped close to you*

• *Every so often, give your baby a soothing rub with baby lotion or a massage (see pp. 76–77)*

• *Share a bath together, or take your baby swimming at the local pool. Hold her tightly in the water so she feels warm and secure*

• *As she gets older, do some exercise together – this doesn't have to be anything more complicated than putting on a record and dancing around the room*

• *Have a few rough-and-tumble games; many mothers leave this to the father or to other children, and particularly neglect to do so with girls*

• *Curl up in bed with your child, so that your child starts and ends the day knowing she is well loved*

NAME *Nicole Killen*

AGE *34 years*

OCCUPATION *Department manager in clothing store*

OBSTETRIC HISTORY *Normal pregnancy. Matthew born two days after due date*

Nicole was convinced that one day she would meet a wonderful man who loved her completely, and that they would have a caring relationship in a loving home. But it didn't happen.

"Whether it was circumstance or coincidence I don't know, but when I found out I was pregnant with Matthew, it seemed as though I were being given a chance actively to take control of my life, instead of waiting for someone else – who might never arrive – to do it for me."

THE SINGLE PARENT

When Nicole became pregnant with Matthew three years ago, she found herself in a difficult and unexpected situation. At the time she was having a noncommittal affair with a work colleague.

"I found myself in a quandary because throughout my whole life I never once envisioned myself as a single mother. I had grown up thinking a child should be the product of a loving relationship. But I knew that this wasn't a relationship I wanted to remain permanent."

FIRST REACTIONS

"The thought of becoming an unmarried single mother took a lot of getting used to. Initially, my own mother, who is quite conservative, reacted very badly, which made things even harder. She's come around to the idea now, but that's because Matthew is a lovable toddler whom she adores madly."

Nicole took three months' maternity leave after Matthew was born, then she was offered three further months on half pay. The first three months went quite smoothly – Matthew was quite a placid baby, and by the eighth week he usually slept five hours each night. "In fact, although I was exhausted, Matthew gave me so much joy that I took an unexpected delight in having him all to myself."

UNEXPECTED PROBLEMS

After three months, Nicole was torn between staying at home and going back to work, but in the end, despite financial pressures, she decided to stay at home. "I felt Matthew was just too young to leave with an unknown baby-sitter. It was only toward the end of the fifth month that I started to experience problems.

"The worst part was never having anyone to moan to at the end of the day. You can't moan to a six-month-old. Little problems and nagging worries soon developed into overblown crises that kept me awake for hours at night. The week before my six-month maternity leave was up, Matthew got a mild chest infection. Although it wasn't serious, I became so worried that I developed severe insomnia and was prescribed tranquilizers."

Matthew's chest infection lasted three weeks, and the doctor then diagnosed asthma. Nicole was immediately convinced that Matthew was a "sickly" baby who would be ill for the rest of his life. "If there had been someone else to share the worry with, I'm sure that I wouldn't have reacted so badly," she recalls.

RETURNING TO WORK

"I felt I had to postpone returning to work for another month. Then, when the day finally arrived, I was surprised by my own anxiety – not so much because I had to leave Matthew (I left him asleep with my mother), but because halfway to work I started to wonder if I could still do my job. The job I have is quite high pressured – part of my salary is based on commission – and things have to be up and running from 9:00 A.M. to 6:30 P.M. without a break. I worked four days a week, and it wasn't easy worrying all day at work and then worrying all night at home."

At this point, Nicole's mother moved in with her for five weeks so that she could have some time to adjust to being a single working mother. Having her there made Nicole realize that, although she couldn't afford it, she had to consider full-time help at least until the end of the first year. She began to explore the idea of hiring a nanny or mother's helper.

EMPLOYING A NANNY

When Matthew was eight months old, Nicole hired her first full-time nanny. The cost, for someone on her salary, was appalling. She also realized that, although she got a bit more sleep, most of the time she found it impossible to stay in bed and leave it to the nanny when she heard Matthew crying. "It may have been that his asthma made me overprotective, or it may simply have been that I didn't like sharing my home with a relative stranger – whatever the reason, after two months I asked the nanny to leave and decided to look after Matthew on my own."

This helped ease the financial situation, which by that point had become quite critical. It was still hard for Nicole to go out, because she couldn't afford to spend money on a baby-sitter and an evening's entertainment. She realized, nearly a year after the birth, that she hadn't been out socially since having the baby.

A LIFE OF HER OWN

"That was when I had the idea of having my first post-Matthew dinner party. About eight friends came around, each with a home-made dish, and we had a fabulous evening without waking Matthew once. Having the dinner party made an enormous difference to me. It was the first time I felt as though I was a social being again, rather than just a single mother. About a week later, I managed to stop taking the tranquilizers permanently."

Two months after Matthew's first birthday, Nicole arranged child care so that a sitter looked after him three days a week and he stayed with his grandmother one day a week. "This was the first time that things seemed to calm down enough for me to enjoy being a parent. I got used to the asthma attacks and no longer panicked unduly. My job was more under control, and I even began to nurture an infrequent social life. I no longer feel any guilt about having Matthew on my own, because I know he is well looked after and that he receives a huge amount of love."

NAME *Matthew Killen*

AGE *18 months*

MEDICAL HISTORY *Asthma diagnosed at 6 months of age*

ORGANIZING YOUR LIFE

Learning to look after your new baby in the first weeks can be overwhelming, so look after yourself, too.

• *Get your partner to help out with the baby so you can have some time to yourself*

• *Don't expect to be a perfect mother right away. You have a lot to learn, and your baby is learning, too*

• *Let the housework go. Do only the essential tasks, or get someone else to do them if possible*

• *Low potassium levels can contribute to a feeling of exhaustion. Eat plenty of potassium-rich foods, such as bananas, tomatoes, dried apricots, and plain low-fat yogurt*

• *Don't be surprised if you get the "baby blues" – up to 80 percent of mothers do, and it will pass after about ten days. If depression persists, however, you should seek help very quickly*

As any mother knows, the physical, emotional, and social demands on your life seem to multiply unendingly with the arrival of a new baby. Interrupted nights and hectic days coupled with the psychological pressure of taking responsibility for a complete new person combine to heap unexpected stresses on a new mother.

Organization can be the key to survival. Pregnancy is the ideal time to sit down and take stock of the situation before you are swept away by the joys and traumas of parenthood. No matter what stage you are at, however, it is never too late to organize your time so you get more out of it.

When you are planning your post-baby life, try dividing up things you have to think about into three or four areas: baby-related, work-related (house and/or office), partner-related, and you. This fourth category is usually undervalued, but happens to be one of the most important. If you aren't happy, your baby won't be happy. There are certain things that you will find helpful to think about in advance. For instance, if you are a working mother, have you spoken to your employer about if and when you want to return to work? Have you considered going back but at reduced hours? Is it possible for you to job-share?

If you will be working part time, will any of your employment rights be affected? They shouldn't be, but you should check now rather than finding out later on. You don't want to discover that you might be facing a salary cut when you've already committed yourself to expensive child care.

Establishing a routine A lot of the work you do in caring for your baby involves repetitive tasks, and these will be much easier to manage if you can work out some sort of timetable. Your routine should follow your baby's needs, not vice versa, so you won't be able to establish it right away; it will take your baby three to six weeks or longer to settle into a pattern of feeding and sleeping.

Time out
Make sure that you allow a little time every day to relax and indulge yourself; it's in everyone's interests that you do.

Be careful not to confuse organization with regimentation. You don't want your life to be inflexible, as the needs of a young child can change hourly. What is important is that the routine you create for yourself doesn't either bore you or ignore you.

TIME FOR YOURSELF

You are your child's universe, so it's best for him if you're not irritable, grumpy, and bored. While you must make every effort to meet your baby's needs, you must also look after your own needs.

Schedule at least half an hour each day to devote entirely to yourself – you may want to have a bath, read a book, watch television, write a letter, meditate, exercise, listen to music, manicure your nails, or give yourself a facial. Before the baby arrives, finding half an hour for yourself seems simple, but once he is born it can seem like an impossible task.

If you are to make some space for yourself, the first thing you must do is learn to accept offers of help graciously. Too many mothers feel they are failures if they don't personally attend to their child's every need. This can be a dangerous route to go down. It is based on unrealistic expectations and eventually leads to nervous exhaustion or even breakdown.

GETTING AWAY

If you and your partner have already discussed how you are going to share the new work load (see **Equal parenting**, p.231), the next stage is discussing how you can make some time for each other once the baby has arrived. Try to arrange for a baby-sitter to come at least once a month, or better still once a week, so parenting doesn't take over every single waking second of your lives.

Look into the possibilities of nanny sharing (see p.241) or, if you are not working full time, see if you can arrange a "baby-swap" with another mother. Find out about courses or activities that offer child care. This is an ideal way to meet friends, take up an interest, or increase your qualifications while your child is cared for and socializes with other children his own age.

Spending time apart from your child doesn't necessarily make you a worse parent – in fact, in most cases it makes you a better one. If you spend all your time with your child, he will develop unrealistic expectations of relationships in general and is likely to become overly demanding of friends and teachers alike.

Moreover, although your child needs a close and loving relationship with you, it is a mistake to think that he needs your company every second of the day. He will gain confidence and valuable social skills by learning to interact with other adults and children.

Handing over
Your baby doesn't need you every minute of the day, so let someone else take care of him now and then while you go out.

YOU AND YOUR PARTNER

When your baby arrives, your relationship with your partner changes immediately. All the common interests and experiences that previously held you together (your social life, your sex life, hobbies, vacations, and so on) suddenly go out the window overnight. You are likely to be so exhausted that your partner's needs are the last thing on your mind.

The discipline that a new baby imposes on your life makes keeping excitement and sparkle in a relationship a great effort. That's why many couples feel it's just never the same – and they're right. Sometimes it's better than it ever was before, but problems arise when one partner, inevitably the father, feels excluded.

YOUR PARTNER'S FEELINGS

Although it is widely acknowledged that a mother undergoes huge upheavals during and after pregnancy, there is less appreciation of the effects a new baby has on a father. Most fathers who accompany their partners through labor are in some state of shock after the birth. They are often traumatized by seeing their partners in considerable pain and distress. In fact, research has shown that nearly one in ten fathers suffers serious postpartum depression. One of the reasons suggested is that parental roles have changed so much in the last 20 or 30 years, making it more difficult than ever for fathers to adjust to parenthood.

Unless you make an effort with your partner, he may start to feel that "three's a crowd" and that he's being pushed out of the picture. It is unwise to let this type of situation develop, not just because you need your partner's help, but because he should spend as much time as possible with your baby at an early age. This will help him build a close and loving relationship that lasts throughout your baby's childhood.

THE "REJECTED" FATHER

Be aware that barriers between you and your partner are likely to spring from the fact that, as one psychologist put it, "although men and women become parents at the same time, they don't become parents in the same way." There are many sociological, financial, and environmental reasons for this, but the result is often straightforward resentment or jealousy.

A man can quickly feel isolated within the family unit. He suddenly finds his partner's time monopolized by the new addition, and unless he is taking an active role in caring for the baby, he's no longer sure where he fits in. It is quite common to find a father becoming jealous of his own child. This situation may be exacerbated if there were differences of opinion about having the child in the first place (men often complain of being "pressured" into having a baby).

TIPS FOR MOTHERS

Your partner will quickly start to feel he is nither wanted nor needed if you give all your attention to the baby.

- *Always ask your partner for help – you can't expect him to know how much you need it unless you tell him*

- *Involve him with the day-to-day care of the baby as early on and as much as possible*

- *Don't refuse help when it's offered – it's his child, too*

- *Do your best, no matter how unsociable you feel, to give your partner some of your attention and your affection*

- *If, despite these efforts and "talking it out," he is proving to be a reluctant father and you are at the end of your tether, leave him a phone number, hand him the baby, and go out for the evening – he'll soon realize what hard work it is!*

Sharing feelings
Always make time to talk to your partner so you can avoid misunderstandings.

Your partner may find these feelings particularly difficult to deal with if he also feels rejected on a sexual level. Often men take a new mother's diminished sex drive as a personal rebuff. If it's not too late, discuss the effects this may have on your relationship before the baby arrives.

POSTPARTUM SEX

If you haven't lost your desire for sex, that's wonderful and you should make the most of it. There is no reason to wait for your first six-week checkup to have sex if you feel physically fit enough. For some women, however, especially those who have had episiotomies, sex is not on the agenda.

After the baby arrives, your partner may share your lack of interest in sex, but if he doesn't, one sure way to make him understand your reluctance is to let him feel your episiotomy scar – most men will be very sympathetic.

A reduced sex drive is natural in that nature is doing her best to furnish you with the most reliable contraceptive of all – abstinence. After all, the last thing any new mother wants is to find that she's pregnant – imagine trying to cope with an eight-week-old baby and morning sickness.

Try to impress upon your partner, however, that there may be emotional as well as physiological reasons for your not wishing to have sex, and he needs to respect these equally.

COMMUNICATION

During the initial months of parenthood, both of you should make real efforts to keep the lines of communication open between you. No matter how exhausted or disorientated you may be, it is essential that you find the time to explain your feelings to each other.

Having a child changes things forever. If you are the one to spend most time with your new baby, you will be distracted from the fact that you have temporarily lost your lover. The same cannot necessarily be said for your partner – if he is not so involved in the day-to-day care of your baby, it is only natural that he feels the change in your relationship more strongly.

Let your partner help as much as possible in the care of your child (see **Tips for mothers,** left). Too often women involve their partners by giving them tasks that are only indirectly linked to the child. For example, when a mother says "I'll get Samantha ready while you run the bath," or "You heat up the food and I'll feed her," she is sharing some of the work, but not the child. Try reversing some of these options so your partner spends sufficient time with the baby, and make sure that both of you consider the advice given in the columns on the left and right.

An active father
A father who helps care for his child will feel needed by both his partner and the baby.

TIPS FOR FATHERS

Once your baby is born, you need to be sensitive to the needs of your partner and prepared for the physical and emotional difficulties she may experience after the pregnancy.

• *Don't leave the entire care of your child to your partner even if she doesn't seem to mind: first, there will be hidden resentment, and second, you will lose the chance to be a real father*

• *Spend at least some time alone with the baby; this will increase your own confidence and give your partner a break*

• *If you are working, talk to your employer about the new addition to your family. Consider taking at least two weeks off work when the baby is born, and see if you can change some of your working hours*

FEEDING

You must decide how you want your baby to be fed while you are away at work.

If you begin working before he is four to six months old – that is, before solids are introduced – you will need to plan. Introduce a routine so feeding times are predictable and constant. If you feed your baby at breakfast and around 6:00 P.M., the person who looks after him during the day need give only the expressed milk or formula for the other two daytime feedings.

If you don't want your baby to take any milk substitutes, freeze expressed breast milk; it will keep for up to six months in the freezer. It should take around two weeks to get into this routine. You will need to decrease your daytime milk production before returning to work or you will be uncomfortable during the day.

RETURNING TO WORK

When it's time to return to work – this will vary with employers – you may realize that you have not given yourself enough time to readjust after pregnancy. It is always a good idea to consult your doctor, as there are health factors to consider about which she can advise you. Some mothers find that they cannot bring themselves to leave the baby, while others – even though they adore the baby – are climbing the walls and have to "escape."

If you have decided to return to work, be assured that as long as you arrange good child care (see below), you will not be neglecting your child. There is no danger of your young baby forgetting who you are or transferring his affection to his daytime caregiver. The really important thing is that when you get home you spend quality time with your child.

I know from my own experience as a working mother that guilt pangs are inevitable. I felt certain, however, that my baby would instinctively know I was his mother. I was reassured when I later came across research showing that very young babies are quite able to single out their parents (whether biological or adoptive) due to the loving, interested attention that only parents can give. Similarly, it has been shown that premature babies can distinguish between the touch of their parents' hands through an incubator and the more matter-of-fact handling of nursing staff.

The important point is that it is the quality of the time you spend that counts more than the quantity. Love isn't measured in time: love is what you put into time, no matter how short.

CHILD AND CAREER

The job you face at home is twice as demanding as the one you face at work, and your terms of employment are worse. After all, you are expected to work seven days a week, 365 days a year. You will be frowned upon if you don't cook, clean, iron, entertain, and provide advice, nursing care, and sympathy continuously for at least 18 years, if not indefinitely. Your efforts will go largely unnoticed by society and, of course, you won't get paid a penny. In fact, you will have to pay for the privilege of being a parent – but as most parents will tell you, despite the job description, it's a privilege worth paying for!

Your child's first step, first smile, and first word are all priceless personal achievements. Helping to mold a tiny baby into a thoughtful, well-adjusted adult is a task requiring sacrifice, responsibility, and, above all, love. It also yields huge emotional dividends. To my mind this makes parenting one of the most important and rewarding jobs in the world. If we are able to provide better parenting for our children today, there will be far fewer problems for the adults of tomorrow

Given this, it is disturbing to see the low status attached to parenting, particularly for women, who shoulder much of the burden. Being a good parent involves helping your child's personality to develop in a positive sense and being a good role model. If you want your children to grow up and work hard, the fact that you work hard at your own job sets them an excellent example. Having to combine the role of principal parent with full-time career is not easy, but women are doing it with imagination and sheer hard work. The rise of the mythical "super mom" has meant that we are often expected to do it all without any help. There *are* a lot of "super moms" around: they are the ones who manage everything day after day, at home and in the office, without failing to give love and energy to their children.

CHILD CARE

You should start looking for reliable child care about six weeks before you plan to return to work. Currently both the public and private sectors have not given child-care issues the priority they should have, which makes things more difficult.

Unfortunately, the U.S. has fewer nursery places for preschool children than there are children who need it. Nonetheless, things are gradually changing. Some companies now provide workplace day-care centers.

Friends and relatives Letting a relative help can be the perfect solution for many mothers, but consider the situation carefully before asking someone. You can start to feel uncomfortably indebted, or conversely, they can feel taken for granted.

Because you don't have a "professional" relationship, it may be difficult to stipulate rules and guidelines that they don't take quite as seriously as you; disciplining problems, for example, can soon become frustrating, particularly if your views on childrearing diverge. On the other hand, if these problems are confronted early on, you can benefit immeasurably from the security, flexibility, and low cost of this type of arrangement. If you ask a friend, rather than a close relative, to help on a regular basis and you pay her, you will have to pay social security tax.

Childminders
You will be able to tell from your child's reaction whether he feels loved and secure with his childminder.

CHOOSING CHILD CARE

Your baby doesn't need only to be changed and fed: he needs the kind of loving attention that you would give him yourself if he is to learn to interact and become a sociable child.

Baby-sitters These care for your child during the day in your home or theirs. They may care for more than one child. Depending on local regulations, they may or may not be licensed by a public agency.

Nanny or mother's helper You can find one through agencies, by advertising locally, or in a newspaper or magazine. Although this kind of help can be expensive, you might consider sharing a nanny with another family. Parents' groups may be able to put you in touch with other mothers interested in sharing a nanny.

Day-care centers Run privately or by local authorities, these often have long waiting lists and usually only a small number of places for babies. Put your name down as soon as you know you are pregnant if you want your child to go to a particular nursery school.

Day-care centers (workplace) Perhaps you are very lucky and have enlightened employers who make it possible to take your baby to work with you. This means you can continue breastfeeding and have your baby close by all day. If there's a day-care center at your workplace, make sure you reserve a space well before your baby is born.

EFFECT ON YOUR CHILDREN

Children's lives can be seriously affected both by families that remain together in spite of turmoil and by angry and difficult divorce. It is not divorce in and of itself that is injurious to a child.

An amicable divorce may be barely damaging and its effect entirely different from that of an acrimonious divorce. The main reason for this is that in an acrimonious situation, each parent usually does his or her best to turn the children against the other parent. This has a very negative and damaging effect on children, and should be avoided at all costs.

SEPARATION AND DIVORCE

At some stage in every relationship, problems arise. In rare cases, couples live happily ever after, but the vast majority don't. This doesn't necessarily reflect a lowering of moral values; it is more an indication of the complexities and pressures of modern life. Support systems are weaker and expectations higher.

Statistics show that today two in three divorces are initiated by women, many of whom feel they are asked to do too much without adequate support from their partners. The average marriage lasts eight years – a depressing fact of life for growing numbers of children brought up without two parents.

PERIODS OF CHANGE

The problem for most couples is that in the long term people change. Although this can be difficult, it can also be invigorating and constructive. If you learn to develop together, you will prevent boredom and stagnation from building up in your relationship.

At the end of periods of change, which are often fraught with emotional insecurity, you will either grow together or grow apart. Whatever happens, it is vital that your children feel secure about their future at all times. For young children, change within a family unit (or fear of that change) is very damaging. Children do not have the defense mechanisms to protect themselves from the severe emotional insecurity that a breakup can cause.

EXPLAINING TO YOUR CHILDREN

A young child soaks up emotional signals like a sponge, whether or not they are directed at her. If you are happy, the chances are your child will be happy; if you are sad, she will be sad. Although it is always worth making an effort "for the sake of the children," don't fall into the trap of thinking they won't know what is going on. They usually sense when something is wrong, whether or not you have a smile on your face.

Because of this, it's always best to explain, at least partially, what is going on. If you don't, children will invent their own explanations, mistakenly blaming themselves for problems in the family. This is because children under five conceive the world only in relation to themselves. If you don't give a plausible explanation why you and your partner are arguing or splitting up, they may come up with explanations that are inconceivable to an adult, but make perfect sense to a child, such as: "Daddy has left because I don't clean my room properly," or "Mommy is upset because I wet the bed/I'm clumsy/I lost my pocket money." Feelings of guilt are severely damaging, especially for a child already struggling to come to terms with the emotional turmoil and insecurity that marital breakups can trigger. Doubt is one of the worst fears in a child's mind, so never leave your child in any doubt that you love her and that you will continue to look after her.

DIVORCE

If you reach the point where the only option left is divorce or separation, do not assume automatically that your children will be devastated. Some will be, but the effect on your child will depend greatly on age, personality, the circumstances of the divorce, and the prevailing social attitudes in the school and community.

I know of one primary school class, for instance, where out of 35 children, only 5 had parents who were still together. They were regularly teased by the others from "broken homes," who saw these five children as materially disadvantaged. the children whose parents were still together got only one set of presents on their birthday or at holidays and they had only one house.

Although having divorced parents is nothing to boast about, many of these children did. This may be deeply shocking to a lot of people, but it is just one more indication of the different times that our children are growing up in.

MOVING OUT

If the time comes when you have to leave, it is vital to let your child know that you are not taking your love with you, and that you will continue to be an active parent. Let your child know specifically when you plan to see her and, no matter how difficult it is, try never to break these arrangements.

If you are the parent left with full-time responsibility for your child when your partner has moved out, try not to be upset if she misses her father or mother. Don't try to make her forget that the other parent exists, and don't speak abusively about the other parent as this will only confuse your child further.

Even if your child appears to be unaffected by a marital split, keep a close eye on her and ask her teachers if they notice any difference in her behavior at school. Some children have fewer questions than others and keep their feelings of insecurity to themselves, but they may still need extra attention and love. Increased bedwetting, thumb-sucking, and general "clinginess" are all signs that your child is in need of reassurance and special care.

Grandparents can be a great boon at the time of the divorce. If possible, do encourage your child to see both sets. Don't let bad feeling act as a cutoff. Think of your child first – she needs continuity, security, and reassurance, and grandparents are second to none at providing these, as long as they don't bad-mouth either parent. Grandparents will also act as a mainstay during access periods and will show your child the unconditional love that every child needs if her parents are divorcing or separating.

Ask your child about her worries and anxieties, and give her space to voice them. Listen and take them seriously. Act upon them. They will almost certainly be things of which you haven't thought or would dismiss as trivial if you did.

ACCESS

Whatever your feelings are about your partner, it's best for your child if you're easygoing and generous about access.

Don't be stingy or confrontational – it causes your child such anguish. Hand her over somewhere civilized like one of your homes, not somewhere neutral like a park or shopping mall, or your child will feel like a commodity.

Plan well ahead, don't break promises at the last minute, and if your partner is late, be breezy about it, otherwise your child will worry about both of you. Don't make it an opportunity to denigrate her father or mother; be offhand, and keep your child calm: "Oh, I expect the traffic's bad," or "Shall we play a game of go-fish till he gets here?"

If your partner is consistently late or unreasonable, arrange a separate meeting to discuss this, out of earshot of your child. The only time to consider preventing your ex-partner having any access to your child is if you think she is at risk of being kidnapped or otherwise harmed. In such cases, it is best to seek professional advice, either through counseling services or a lawyer.

MULTIPLE BIRTHS

New parents are often surprised at the amount of work involved in caring for a newborn, and this is clearly even more true for parents who have multiple births.

Twins are by far the most common multiple births. Identical (monozygotic) twins are formed by the splitting of a single fertilized egg: the two babies develop from one egg and one sperm, and share a placenta. Twins that develop from the fertilization of two eggs by two sperm and have a placenta each are called nonidentical, fraternal, or dizygotic. Multiples of more than two can occur in any combination of identical and fraternal.

PREGNANCY AND BIRTH

Early rapid weight gain is a common sign of multiple pregnancy. The minor complaints of pregnancy can become more uncomfortable, and there are a few clinical conditions that are relatively more common in multiple pregnancies, such as anemia or fluid retention. Make sure you eat well and get plenty of rest.

A twin birth follows the same course as the birth of a single baby except there's a gap between the delivery of the first and second babies, which may be anything from a minute or so to a half an hour or more. The first stage is the same as for a single birth but, depending on the time lag between the two births, you may have to go through pushing twice. Multiple births are more likely to be premature than single babies.

* *Many parents of twins don't realize how much help they will need, though mothers who have already had one baby tend to be more realistic about this. Don't underestimate the task of caring for twins, and don't for one minute imagine that asking for help reflects badly on your adequacy as parents*

* *Helpers can create extra work. This is particularly true of a friend or relative who moves in to "help" you and then expects you to cook for her every evening, so consider this carefully before accepting long-term help*

* *You may find that everyone wants to help with the babies and no one wants to do the housework. They're your twins, and you must learn to mother them yourself, so don't be afraid to be firm about what help you need*

* *See **Useful addresses** (pp. 344–45) to find a support group for mothers of twins*

FEEDING

There are some special considerations if you are trying to feed twin babies and, whereas I would always advocate breastfeeding, you may want to consider the pros and cons set out in the chart below.

BREAST	BOTTLE
• *You can feed both at once*	• *Difficult to feed both babies simultaneously unless they are propped up on chairs*
• *You need to devote time to eating and resting to produce enough milk*	• *Being tired and busy does not affect supply*
• *Difficult to feed two babies discreetly in public*	• *Babies can be fed anywhere and by anyone*
• *Physically tiring, but you can express and let someone else feed*	• *Tiring, but others can help*
• *Eating well may cost a little more than your normal diet*	• *Cost of formula for two babies can add up*
• *Requires planning if you want to wean babies from breast to bottle to go back to work*	• *No physical adjustment is needed for you or babies if you are going back to work*

When you come to establishing daily routines, there are several ways in which you can try to get your twins to eat and sleep at similar times, though initially one may wake early and want feeding and the other may simply sleep on. You could feed the baby who wakes first while waiting for the second, then reverse them; or feed both at once and spend time talking or playing afterward.

SHOULD THEY SLEEP TOGETHER?

Twins are sometimes put in the same incubator after the birth, with the idea that they have been together since conception and would miss one another if apart. You could try putting your twins together in the same crib to help them settle and sleep. Some twins do seem to sleep better this way – perhaps they derive security from each other's presence – but others simply kick and keep each other awake. Twins can usually be left to sleep in the same room together or side by side in cribs or bassinets. They rarely wake or disturb one another; it seems as if they are immune to each other's crying. For twins who have been tightly pressed together before birth, swaddling (see p.121) may give them a greater sense of security.

DIAPER CHANGING

When twins are small they may seem fragile, and it may take longer to build up enough confidence to care for them efficiently and speedily. You do a very great deal of diaper changing with twins so you want to make the maximum use of disposable diapers. If you have a good supply of fabric diapers left over from an older child, it can make economic sense to stick with them, though you may decide that you do not want to add washing and drying to the task of changing two sets of diapers. With a diaper service, it's just a matter of ordering a larger quantity each week. Your twins may fit into the newborn disposable size for some months. Some parents cut ordinary fabric diapers in two, using one half on each baby.

IMPORTANCE OF PLAY

Because of the demands on your time, your twins may get less adult stimulation through play and physical contact than singletons, but more peer stimulation and company. Loving interaction, however, is not a luxury – it's essential to their physical, mental, and social development.

Pick a set time for play every afternoon, or plan the babies' sleeping times so they are awake in the evening when both parents can play with them. If one twin is asleep, give your other baby complete attention. Even five minutes of intimate play will be of great value to him. If you have older children, you may have even less time to play with your babies, but your older children can take your place.

THE FATHER'S ROLE

Most fathers want to be closely concerned with the care of their babies and so will enjoy looking after either or both of them to give you a break.

A father can help with feeding, changing, bathing, playing, reading the twins bedtime stories, and taking them out. Many fathers assume responsibility for shopping, and sometimes for cooking and housework, too. He can take time off work if necessary for doctor's appointments, checkups, visits to the dentist, and so on, and should be able to relieve you so you can catch up on sleep or have time to yourself.

Helping out
With the amount of work involved in looking after twins, your partner's help will be indispensable.

BEING A TWIN

Twins have a close and intuitive understanding of each other and enjoy the companionship of a child of the same age. Having the support and approval of another person can be very reassuring as they grow and encounter new experiences.

PHYSICAL DEVELOPMENT

If twins are premature, their growth and development will lag somewhat behind full-term babies. Don't make the mistake of expecting them to do too much too soon and, whatever you do, don't compare them to other babies of the same age.

There's no way of knowing how much more slowly your babies will develop, but if, for instance, they are five weeks premature, you can probably expect them to focus some weeks later than if they'd been full-term. They may sit up, walk, and talk as much as three months late depending on how prematurely they were born, but they will still reach milestones in the same order as other babies (see pp.150–203). Don't worry that your babies will never catch up. A large study of twins carried out in the U.S. showed that twin babies had caught up in height by four years and weight by eight.

Other factors affect the rate at which children develop. If your twins are identical, they'll probably grow to much the same weight and height; if they are nonidentical, and especially if they are boy and girl twins, one of them may grow and develop more quickly than the other.

TWINS AS INDIVIDUALS

When twins are hungry, it's often easiest to sit them next to one another and feed them together with the same food; they may sleep in the same crib (see p.245) when they are small, and they may prefer to play at the same time with the same toys. When your twins are of the same sex, look alike, or have similar temperaments, it's easier to treat them very much alike, but I think it's best to treat twins as individuals right from the start. Don't choose names that sound alike, and try to distinguish your babies' differing needs and responses. It can be particularly difficult for people outside the immediate family to treat identical twins as separate individuals, but it's very important that they should. It's easier when the twins themselves show their different personalities and you encourage them to do so.

DRESSING TWINS

Many parents wish to dress twins alike, especially if they are identical, and this can look very appealing.

You should, however, think of your twins as individuals from the start. Being recognized for one-self and being called by one's own name are powerful ways in which our sense of identity is established. If you dress your twins differently you can help ensure that they are treated as individuals. Relatives, friends, and teachers can get to know who wears what.

As your twins get older, I think it's much better to let them decide for themselves what to wear, and if you've always dressed them differently they will probably continue to do so themselves.

Individuality
Encourage each twin's sense of identity and individuality by dressing them differently.

THE SPECIAL BOND

Being one of a close-knit pair of twins has advantages and disadvantages. Twins often become very close to each other and are central figures in each other's lives. The relationship between them can seem far stronger and more influential than any other. It is based on many feelings and experiences in common and a profound, intimate knowledge of each other. Their closeness gives twins an unusual opportunity to see how things look to someone else – an opportunity that singletons have only rarely. These close ties can give twins great security and are in many ways a source of strength. On the other hand, some twins struggle very hard for separateness and seem actively to reject one another, despite having abilities and attitudes in common.

TALKING TO TWINS

When single babies start to talk, adults or older children notice and encourage them. With twins, each child is given less attention so twins usually talk and listen to one another and may even invent a private language. Although twins' speech may start late and then develop slowly, in time their ability to hold a conversation improves. If you want to speed that improvement, it probably helps if you talk to your babies separately. It's easy to forget to talk to young children if you are very tired and feeling overworked, and peace and quiet may be precious. It's through taking part in play and learning to talk with you and your partner, however, that children learn language and how to use it.

BECOMING SOCIABLE

Because twins have each other for company, they seem to be quite happy not mixing with other children. For the same reason, your twins will be quite happy left alone together with comparative strangers, or at a playgroup. The more twins play exclusively with each other, however, the more difficult it is for them to make friends and play with other children. They may be overconfident and rough in a new group, appear to want to take over the group, and upset the balance of relationships. Some may tend to remain apart from groups formed by other children. These difficulties sometimes arise when twins first go to school and have to adjust to other children in the class. Make sure your twins feel at home with any social group, be it family, friends, or toddlers, from a very early age.

Because they have each other, twins are usually less afraid when first separated from you, and this gives everyone the impression that they are confident children. But when one twin is left without the other, she may suddenly appear to be anxious and worried. This is because twins often mask each other's vulnerability. Twins, however, are just as much in need of your support and presence in new situations as a single child. A local playgroup can help your twins develop separate identities and learn the skills of making and keeping friends. The ideal would be for your twins to attend different playgroups or the same one on different days. Alternatively, ask the staff to encourage the twins to play separately.

SIBLINGS

Older children may feel doubly displaced by the arrival of twins. The needs of twins, especially if they are demanding, can drain the rest of the family and leave you with little time or energy.

If you have had to go into the hospital several times during your pregnancy, it may take quite a long time to get to know your children again and to regain their trust and security. They may feel angry and upset that you left them and then came home with two new babies.

Older siblings can become more grown up when twins arrive. Others may feel the need to revert to babyhood, and a child who was dry may need diapers once more. Your children are upset. They feel dethroned and don't understand why you have less time for them than before. From the age of about two, they miss having your full attention and resent your preoccupation with the two newcomers.

Do whatever you have to do to ensure that each of your children has at least half an hour a day of your undivided attention without any distractions. Then they will feel valued members of the family. It's a good idea for you and your partner to take the children out on their own so they have you entirely to themselves, and feel secure in your love despite the two new interlopers.

CHAPTER 5

Children with SPECIAL NEEDS

There are many reasons why a child may need more care and attention than his peers. Your child may have a chronic condition such as asthma; a learning disorder, such as dyslexia; a developmental disorder, such as autism; or he may simply be very advanced for his years. Whatever the case, he will need extra support and consideration in order to maximize his potential. This may take the form of special medical treatment, home care, or special education. The same goes for a very bright child who might outstrip older brothers and sisters and even parents. This can put a unique strain on your family, so get specialized help so that your child is given the chance to fulfill her potential.

Early identification of special needs is very important. A severe condition such as cerebral palsy will be apparent soon after birth, but others, such as dyslexia, can go unnoticed for years. Never be afraid to act on your suspicions; seek professional advice if you are at all worried. Diagnosis of a chronic condition or learning disorder may nevertheless come as a shock. Make sure you seek out any help or advice that is available; you are still your child's main caregiver, whatever his needs, and the better informed you are, the more you can do for him.

THE SPECIAL CHILD

Although all children develop at different rates and the range of what doctors and psychologists consider "normal" is wide, a small number of children fall at either end of the developmental spectrum. At one end of the spectrum are children who are unusually advanced for their age, in terms of both motor and intellectual skills; at the other end are children who haven't acquired basic skills such as language and children who learn very slowly. In between there are also children with specific developmental or learning disorders such as autism and dyslexia.

Perhaps surprisingly, very advanced children have similar needs to children who have a learning disorder – lots of stimulation, attention, and love. You might say that all children need these things – and you'd be right – but without them, children with special needs will suffer more. If such children do not receive the correct stimulation, they may not turn out to be "just average"; they could develop serious behavioral problems.

RECOGNIZING THE SIGNS

If your child does have special needs, an early diagnosis is very important so that he can have help. Some learning disorders are difficult to spot, especially if they are characterized by behavior that may be considered positive, such as quietness, little crying, or excessive sleeping. Autistic children, for example, are often described by their parents as well-behaved before other signs of their illness emerge. A gifted child, on the other hand, may be disruptive and not do well at school, making it hard for teachers to recognize his potential.

The lists below give some of the signs that might indicate that your child has special needs. Bear in mind, however, that children vary enormously in their rate of development and in personality, so what you regard as delayed speech in your child, for example, could be just a normal variation in development. If you are at all concerned, you should consult your child's doctor.

Developmentally delayed child
• Not speaking by the age of 18 months.

• Failure to interact with other people – to join in appropriately in conversation, for instance.

• Repetitive routines or habits beyond the normal age, such as asking the same question over and over again without responding to the answer.

• Problems with simple age-appropriate puzzles, and poor coordination of both large and small muscles.

• Overactivity and short concentration span.

Gifted child
• Very early and fluent language skills.

• Very independent behavior, or a preference for the company of adults.

• Tendency to be bored by repetitive tasks.

• Precocious development sometimes accompanied by socially inappropriate behavior.

• Unusually long concentration span.

If your child has special needs, don't think that he is incapable of learning, or – if he's gifted – that he can just wait until the other children "catch up." He requires teaching methods tailored to his individual needs, whether he is gifted or slow to learn.

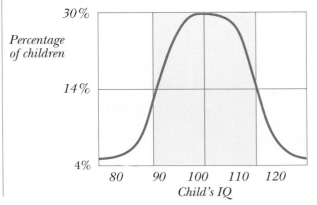

IQ chart
Very gifted children appear at the extreme right; children with impaired mental abilities are at left. Most children fall between these extremes.

Percentage of children

30%

14%

4%

80   90   100   110   120

Child's IQ

GIFTEDNESS

A gifted child is one who has advanced cognitive (understanding) skills and motor skills for her age. She can walk, talk, and reason earlier than average. She will be a high achiever in most areas, and she may have an IQ over 150.

Having a gifted child is rare. Although many children may be advanced for their age in a particular skill at a particular time, only about 2 percent of the population are truly gifted. If your child is gifted, however, you will probably be the first to notice.

DIAGNOSIS

Diagnosing a gifted child becomes easier as the child gets older, but one of the first signs that your child is more able than her peers is early language acquisition, particularly speaking fluently before the age of two. Early reading may be another sign of giftedness: some able children learn to read at four years, although environmental influences are obviously a factor. Other possible qualities of a gifted child are as follows:

• Good powers of reasoning and observation.

• A good memory for places and names.

• A strong creative and imaginative drive.

• Sharp powers of observation

• Being curious and always asking questions.

• More at home with adults than with children.

• An ability to grasp abstract ideas.

• Independence.

• Ability to solve problems or puzzles.

• Having an extensive vocabulary.

• Assimilating facts very quickly.

• Long concentration span.

• Ability to describe events, people, and situations accurately and vividly.

• Eagerness to spend time studying or learning.

• A specific talent, such as artistic ability.

• A high IQ.

SPECIAL NEEDS

Although you may perceive giftedness as an asset rather than a problem, your gifted child may not always be provided for adequately at school and she will have specific emotional needs that are different from those of the average child.

The gifted child may find it hard to relate to her peers. She may be impatient with other children for being slow and this may make her unpopular. Although your child may be condescending toward other children she will probably still want to be part of their group, and this may lead to frustration and isolation. Alternatively, your child may try to conceal her talents in order not to seem different and thus be more readily accepted by other children.

Interacting with adults can also be a problem. Teachers may treat gifted children as arrogant, precocious, or defiant. Gifted children are likely always to know the answers to questions and to be able to point out inconsistencies and question the reasons for doing something. The gifted child does not mean to be attention-seeking or trouble-making, and the negative response she gets from adults can make her withdrawn and antisocial.

A gifted child who is denied the chance to exploit her potential may show a confusing mixture of intellectual prowess and immaturity. She may sulk and have temper tantrums; she may be bored by basic school subjects; and, if she's restless and inattentive, her teachers, far from recognizing her talents, may believe that she is of low ability. You may have to intervene and discuss with your child's teacher the kind of specialized or accelerated learning your child requires and make sure that she gets it.

CAN GIFTEDNESS BE CULTIVATED?
Intelligence is wholly innate and overrides all cultures and backgrounds; cleverness is partly innate and partly environmental.

Although you can provide an environment conducive to intellectual development, it is unlikely that you can "create" a gifted child. Evidence suggests that some gifted children come from relatively affluent homes with educated parents who spend time stimulating and encouraging their children; it is debatable whether the extra boost can turn a very bright child into a gifted one. Being overly pushy as a parent will not help cultivate giftedness in a child, however. You can help your child fulfill her potential, but you cannot change that potential.

WHAT PARENTS CAN DO

It is important to know that your child is gifted since it may help to explain a lot of her behavior, especially behavior that is construed as deviant: social withdrawal, aggressiveness, tantrums, moodiness, and so on. It is also important in that it means you can start to cater to your child's specific needs. If you have a gifted child, don't adopt the attitude that she can simply wait until others reach her level. Gifted children need lots of intellectual stimulation and they will be deprived if they don't get it.

If your child is of school age, you should enlist the help of her teacher. If a teacher doesn't understand that your child is gifted, then he or she may perceive her as a threat or a problem. A sensitive teacher, however, will help your child to integrate with other children and will prevent her becoming isolated. Some schools have provisions for gifted children and in some areas there are enrichment programs that will supplement your child's learning (see **Useful addresses** p.344–45).

As a parent, it is important that you treat your child sympathetically. Although she may be very advanced in some ways, she will still be emotionally immature, so avoid treating her as a "little adult." Take care not to push your child as the resultant stress will harm her. You can provide plenty of stress-free intellectual stimulation for your child in the following ways:

- Provide toys that promote interactive learning. Limit television viewing, as it is a very passive way for your child to learn.

- Give your child freedom to play and try not to intervene too much, unless she asks for your help.

- Encourage any specific talents, such as painting.

- If you have a particular talent of your own, share it with your child and try to communicate your enthusiasm to her.

- Introduce your child to other gifted children.

- Encourage her to ask questions and, if you don't know the answer to a question, help her to look up the information in a book.

- Read her stories that will enrich her imagination.

- Involve her in your everyday tasks.

UNDER-ACHIEVEMENT

Whereas gifted children acquire skills very early, underachievers or developmentally delayed children acquire skills at an unusually slow rate. Some of the first indications that a baby is "behind" are not making much noise, not interacting with the environment in the same way as the average child, and lateness in smiling, responding to sounds, and learning to chew.

When parents try to engage their child in activities they may notice he has a short attention span, and he will spend brief periods doing lots of different things rather than devoting all his energy to one task or game. As he grows older, he may demonstrate a tendency to be overactive and he may have a lower than average IQ.

DIAGNOSIS

A developmentally delayed child will be later than usual in achieving some of the important developmental milestones (see below). It is important, however, to eliminate the possibility that a child has a physiological problem such as partial deafness or blindness. You should also find out whether the child has a severe developmental disorder, such as autism (see p.258–59), or whether he is simply developing at a rate that is below average. If you are concerned, ask your pediatrician to refer your child to a psychologist for assessment. Whatever the diagnosis, your child may need remedial help.

BEHAVIORAL MILESTONES

There are various clues or signs that a baby or child is developmentally delayed or underachieving. Although children vary in the speed at which they develop, behavioral milestones do exist – if a child has not reached the following stages then he may have a learning or developmental disorder.

Hand regard Your baby becomes aware of his hands at about the age of eight weeks, shortly after he begins to play with his feet. Between the age of 12 and 16 weeks, your baby will stare at his hands and waggle his fingers – he's discovering that he can control his hand movements. Hand regard may go on for as long as 20 weeks, however, in developmentally delayed children.

The grasp reflex If you put your finger (or any object) into a baby's palm, he will close his fingers around it in a tight grip. This reflex usually lasts about six weeks after birth, but will persist longer in a child who is developmentally delayed.

Mouthing At about six months, your baby will put everything that he can into his mouth. This behavior will last until around a year in a normal child and longer in a developmentally delayed child.

Casting Children up to the age of 16 months will throw objects out of the stroller – a behavior called casting. Developmentally delayed children may continue to do this for much longer.

Dribbling Slobbering and dribbling should stop at around one year. Developmentally delayed children may still be dribbling at the age of 18 months.

WHAT PARENTS CAN DO

Intellectual development is determined by both nature (inherited qualities) and nurture (things such as physical and social environment, and diet). Your child's potential IQ is decided before birth, but it can flower through the stimuli that your child is exposed to after birth. If your child is not encouraged to interact with other people from an early age and not encouraged to engage his senses in the world around him, the chances are he will not reach his full potential, even if that potential is limited.

If you suspect that your child is lagging behind, spend lots of time reading aloud and talking to him, playing with him, taking him out, showing him new things and new people, and encouraging him to play imaginative games with his toys. Give him toys that are educational and plenty of colorful books and pictures to look at.

Behavior modification techniques may be helpful. Put simply, this means rewarding your child's responses with praise and affection and being patient with his efforts, however slow they are. If you punish him for slowness, he may become discouraged and lose his incentive to learn.

DYSLEXIA

This is a learning disorder that affects reading, spelling, and written language. These difficulties may be accompanied by problems with numbers, poor short-term memory, and clumsiness. Although dyslexia particularly affects a child's mastery of written symbols – letters, numbers, and musical notation – she may have difficulties with spoken language, too. Dyslexia is a specific neurological disorder, not the result of poor hearing or vision, or low intelligence. One in seven children is dyslexic. Three times more boys than girls are diagnosed, but many authorities believe it affects as many girls as boys and that girls are simply underdiagnosed.

DIAGNOSIS

Many bright children are dyslexic, and the condition is often diagnosed earlier in these children since parents become aware of the gap between their child's obvious intelligence and her level of achievement in specific areas. The main symptoms of dyslexia are difficulty in reading and writing. A child may have problems perceiving letters in the correct order, or she may confuse similarly shaped letters such as b and d, and p and q. The following may help parents recognize dyslexia in their child:

• Poor spelling.

• Poor coordination.

• Difficulty in remembering lists of words, numbers, or letters, such as the alphabet or tables.

• Difficulty in remembering the order of everyday things, such as days of the week.

• Problems telling left from right.

• Jumbled phrases, such as "tebby dare" instead of "teddy bear."

• Difficulty learning nursery rhymes.

Many of these signs will not be apparent until a child begins school, but it is possible to test for dyslexia in the preschool years.

Labeling a child dyslexic if she is not is just as harmful as failing to recognize it if she is. No child should be labeled as dyslexic without receiving expert advice and professional testing.

EFFECTS OF DYSLEXIA

The problems listed above may occur in children who don't have dyslexia. The difference is that dyslexic children will suffer more severe symptoms and won't grow out of them.

Recent research suggests that as well as having problems with literacy, dyslexic children also have problems with distinguishing different sounds, and with memory and balance. For example, dyslexic children will find it much more difficult to balance on one leg than children who are not dyslexic.

A dyslexic child's strengths are likely to be sensitivity, intuition, and impulsiveness. Skills associated with the left side of the brain, such as dealing with written symbols, responding to instructions, and putting things in order, are weak in the dyslexic child. Some dyslexic children may be very creative and have an aptitude for drawing and painting.

SPECIAL NEEDS

One of the main problems that dyslexic children face is incorrect diagnosis. It is common for children to attempt to learn to read and write, fail to do so, and then be labeled "slow" or even disabled. This is very demoralizing for the child and is bound to affect her school performance overall. Parents and teachers often confuse dyslexia with a low IQ, but in fact most dyslexic children have an average or above-average IQ.

If dyslexia is recognized early, remedial education is very effective. A child diagnosed as dyslexic at the age of four or five, when she goes to school, will probably need only one half-hour of special lessons a day for about six months to bring her reading and writing up to normal standards. If it is not diagnosed until the age of seven or eight, however, the child will have a lot of catching up to do.

WHAT PARENTS CAN DO

You can do three things to help your dyslexic child at home. First, acknowledge that your child actually has a problem. If you are told that your child will catch up or will learn to read eventually, don't listen – dyslexia is a specific learning disorder that will respond only to the appropriate remedial treatment. Second, be supportive and positive, especially if your child is having problems at school. Third, play lots of learning games with your child, but keep it fun – pressure will worsen the situation.

Emotional support If your child is at school and is lagging behind other children, her self-confidence may be low, so it is very important that you help her feel successful at home. Don't show any impatience. Encourage her to do things she is good at and help her do things for herself.

Give her self-help aids, such as left and right stickers on her tricycle, and if she finds a particular task difficult, encourage her to take it slowly. The Orton Dyslexia Society (see **Useful addresses,** p.344–45) gives advice on coping strategies and remedial education for children with dyslexia.

Home learning games Playing games with letters, words, and sounds can be very useful. The following are all ways in which you can have fun and enhance your child's learning:

- Say nursery rhymes aloud together or make up rhyming poems or limericks. This will familiarize your child with the concept of rhyming words.

- Teach your child rhymes or songs that involve sequences of things such as days of the week.

- Play "Simon Says." This will help your child to follow instructions.

- Play "Hide the Button." This will encourage your child to ask questions involving spatial relationships, such as under, on, and inside.

- Introduce the concept of left and right.

- Ask your child to set the table at mealtimes.

- Play clapping games. Give one clap for each syllable of a word and ask your child to repeat it. Clap a rhythm to her name.

- Give your child groups of words and ask her to pick the one that doesn't fit.

- Ask your child to think of as many words beginning with a particular letter as she can.

- Play "I Spy." If your child has difficulty with letter names, make the sound of the letter instead.

- Encourage your child to trace words and letters, or to make letters out of clay or dough.

ADHD
(ATTENTION DEFICIT HYPERACTIVITY DISORDER)

This is one of the most common childhood disorders seen by psychologists. Children with ADHD may be hyperactive. Although they are not noted to be "overactive" from birth as such, they are likely to have been colicky, demanding babies. They become frustrated easily and are susceptible to mood changes. They are often perceived as ill behaved and possessing poor social skills. Four times as many boys as girls are diagnosed with ADHD, but some experts believe girls are underdiagnosed.

Because ADHD is so commonly seen in the United States at the present time, some people wonder whether this "epidemic" is the result of faulty diagnosis. On the other hand, some suggest it is merely "bad" behavior as a result of poor parenting; others suggest it is a normal personality variant that should not be regarded as a disorder at all.

WHAT CAUSES ADHD?

Although there have been many theories, no one knows for certain what causes ADHD. It was at one time believed that diet, especially a diet high in sugar or food additives, was a cause, but this is no longer considered valid. It is most likely that one of the causes is genetic, and research is ongoing to discover whether certain chemicals in the brain contribute to the condition. Although it was previously believed that a child with ADHD would outgrow it during or after adolescence, it is now thought to persist into adulthood.

If you are concerned that your child's behavior might be caused by ADHD, you should discuss it with your pediatrician, who may recommend medication, testing, and/or consultation with a specialist. Medication (usually Ritalin), supportive educational programs, and therapy to teach behavior modification and coping strategies can help.

EFFECTS OF ADHD

A child with ADHD may be unpredictable and disruptive. Even before he goes to school, he may have problematic relationships with adults and have acquired a reputation for rebelliousness. This has a negative effect on his self-esteem; when he does go to school he starts off on an unequal footing with other children. The performance of a child with ADHD may be variable: one day he might be quite compliant; the next he won't be able to sit still and will fidget incessantly. He may become a low achiever at school, with a reputation for poor concentration, and he may be thought to have a low IQ, even though he doesn't.

Boys with ADHD seem to suffer more than girls with ADHD, in that girls are likely to be better adjusted socially and more achievement-oriented. Boys in particular may be criticized for overactivity, and this can make the problem worse.

SPECIAL NEEDS

If your child is having problems at school – if he is irresponsible, careless, disorganized, and suffers from poor concentration and motivation – you need to eliminate other causes. Is he dyslexic (see p.253–54) or gifted (see p.251–52)? If his behavior has started recently, has he experienced a traumatic event?

Your child may need to be referred to an educational psychologist who will be able to diagnose ADHD and decide on appropriate action to meet your child's individual needs. Discuss your child's problems with his teacher and doctor.

WHAT PARENTS CAN DO

It is important for a child with ADHD to have an orderly home life and a structured, well-disciplined routine. If a child knows that he has to do certain things at set times of the day, he is less likely to be unruly. Parents should also remember that a child who has problems with self-control probably suffers from low self-esteem, because he meets with adult disapproval all the time. If he is praised for good behavior, he will learn that certain types of behavior gain your approval, while others don't.

Parenting a child with ADHD can be very demoralizing, since he may acquire a reputation as a troublemaker. Many parents feel isolated because their child is rejected by playgroups and nursery schools, and even banned from friends' and relatives' homes. Parents should not blame themselves for their child's behavior. Organizations such as CHADD (Children and Adults with Attention Deficit Disorders) (see **Useful addresses**, p.344–45) offer help and advice.

STUTTERING

When your child is learning to talk it is normal for him to stumble over words, repeat words, and hesitate. It is only when hesitations dominate a child's speech and cause him considerable distress that he is said to have a stutter. Whereas normal hesitation is the relaxed repetition of a word at the beginning or the end of a phrase, a child with a stutter will get stuck on a word and repeat one of its syllables over and over again.

IS IT SERIOUS?

When children are learning language, they are not always able to convey their thoughts in words as quickly as they would like to. Your child lives very much in the present, and he will want to convey the intensity of his feelings immediately – when his vocabulary is not wide enough or his language skills aren't advanced enough, he may stutter in his rush to get the words out.

Most children stutter at some stage. Your child may stutter on some days and not others; he may stutter when he is tired, excited, or in a particular situation or environment. It doesn't matter, though, unless he stutters in a lot of situations and gets very upset because of it.

Occasional stuttering is a natural part of language acquisition that will disappear and should never be made an issue or treated as a problem. Making a fuss about it may cause your child to become anxious and so lead to a true stutter.

WHAT PARENTS CAN DO

You can influence your child's speech by the way you talk to him. If you speak very quickly and appear distracted, your child may feel that he has to keep up and that you are not interested in what he has to say. Always try to speak slowly and appear attentive and interested. Look at your child and, if possible, talk to him on the same physical level. Use simple language and talk about very immediate things that can be seen. Avoid asking too many questions; describing your own feelings or experiences instead will encourage your child to contribute. Above all, never react negatively to your child's stutter or he will become more selfconscious and the stutter will worsen. When your child is struggling with a sentence, do not complete it for him or supply a word.

The speech pathology department of most hospitals is one source of help for evaluation and speech training. If your child is very anxious about stuttering, talk to him about it. If he knows that you understand, this will lessen his sense of suffering alone. If you don't talk about it, he may feel that it is something to be ashamed of. If he is very young and is having problems with speech, return to games and activities that involve looking or listening rather than speaking. If he is at school, discuss the following strategies with his teacher:

- Your child may need extra help with reading. If he is worried about particular words this can cause him to stutter. Reading aloud in unison with another child may reduce stuttering.

- Children tend to be more fluent when they are talking about something personal or a subject that they know a lot about. This should be encouraged whenever possible.

- If a teacher is observant about what encourages fluency and what increases stuttering, she can prevent your child from feeling embarrassed. When she needs information from your child it may help if she asks questions that require a "yes" or a "no" answer, particularly if your child is distressed.

- Some methods of speech promote fluency and should be encouraged. These include saying words that have a rhyme or a rhythm, saying words that have actions to go with them, reciting lists or counting, acting, or singing.

- It may be a good idea for your child's teacher to broach the subject of his stuttering with him in a matter-of-fact way, since your child will then feel that it has been noticed by a sympathetic adult and that he doesn't have to hide it.

WHAT CAUSES STUTTERING?

If your child is to become a fluent speaker then he needs to be supported and encouraged to boost his confidence. A combination of the following three conditions can cause a stutter to develop:

- Parental demands that overestimate the child's ability, such as asking lots of questions; insisting on clear speech; and expecting fast replies and grown-up behavior.

- A child's desire to impress people before his vocabulary is large enough.

- Stressful situations in which your child is tired, anxious, or frightened, or where people are talking very fast or there are lots of interruptions.

Stuttering is not inherited. A stuttering child believes that speaking hesitantly is in some way wrong or bad. The child becomes acutely self-conscious and focuses on the way he speaks, and this leads to worse stuttering. He may avoid situations that involve speaking, especially to new people. If the child is of school age, he may pretend he doesn't know answers to questions to avoid having to speak in front of other children.

SPECIAL NEEDS

A child who has a severe stutter may need the help of a speech or language therapist. A therapist might visit the child at school or may work with parents and teachers. The Stuttering Foundation of America (see **Useful addresses**, p.344–45) can be a helpful resource.

DELAYED SPEECH

At about 11 months of age, your baby will probably say simple words, such as "mama," "dada," "dog," and "cat," and by 18 months he will probably be forming simple sentences, such as "daddy in garden." Speech will become more sophisticated during the third and fourth year. As with all aspects of development, the age at which milestones are achieved varies, but if your child is very far behind others his age, there may be something wrong.

There are many causes of delayed speech, the most common being deafness. Ideally, this will have been diagnosed in the newborn period, but if you suspect your child may be deaf, have him tested immediately. Chronic glue ear (see p.285) can cause problems with hearing. A child may be late in speaking if he has not received enough stimulation – this can happen to children who have been institutionalized or whose parents simply don't talk to them enough. Boys are more prone to delayed speech than girls, and twins may speak later than average.

Other causes of speech delay are cerebral palsy, certain chromosomal abnormalities, and organic brain disease. Very occasionally, delayed speech is due to a physiological defect or a disease of the speech muscles, larynx, or mouth. Some disorders of the brain affect speech.

Children vary in the age at which they begin to speak, but if your child is not talking at all by 18 months, seek medical help. If your child is deaf, he may need to wear a hearing aid; if he has a severe speech defect, he may need speech therapy.

Tambourines or maracas can be used to beat out a rhythm

Improving fluency
Singing, or any kind of rhythmic speech, can reduce stuttering, so tapping out a rhythm to rhymes and songs can help your child feel more confident.

AUTISM

This is a condition in which a child has problems relating to people and situations and may show an obsessive resistance to any change in routine. A complex disorder that varies from mild to severe, it typically appears within the first three years of life and can be associated with other problems, including learning disabilities such as dyslexia and physical disorders such as epilepsy. Until quite recently, little was known about autism and there was a tendency to blame emotional deprivation or some negative aspect of the child's background or upbringing. We now know that autism has a physiological origin: an abnormality in the brain that may arise before, during, or after birth and almost always before the age of three years. It may be caused by an illness during pregnancy, such as rubella, a deficiency of oxygen at birth, or a childhood illness, such as measles. The cause may also be genetic. Autism is four times more common in boys than in girls.

DIAGNOSIS

Because autism is a developmental disorder it may take a while for parents to become aware that their child is different from other children. They may notice that their baby is uncommunicative in the first year of his life, but they may not attach any significance to this fact until later, when other signs become apparent. Most parents know that their child is autistic or that "something is wrong" by the time he is about three years old.

EFFECTS OF AUTISM

Children with autism vary considerably in their abilities, but there are three main traits that all autistic children share: problems with social interaction and communication, and impaired imagination. Many autistic children display repetitive behavior, and some have very sophisticated memories.

Social interaction If autism is severe, the child will be indifferent to other people. In babies this manifests itself as crying that can't be appeased by holding and cuddling, quietness, poor eye contact, and failure to return or respond to gestures such as smiling, waving, or facial expressions.

Autistic children show a lack of interest in interacting with other people, particularly children. They don't make friends and, when they do approach people socially, they may behave inappropriately: they may repeat snatches of conversation that have just been spoken, be aggressive, or use confusing language. In less severe forms of autism, the child may accept social contact but will not be very responsive or respond in a stilted, and repetitive way.

Communication From an early age most children show a desire to communicate with other people. Even before they can form words they will communicate nonverbally using facial expressions and body language. Autistic children seem to lack this desire. Even if an autistic child does speak he will tend to speak at people, rather than with them, or restrict his speech to conveying his immediate needs. The child may exhibit echolalia (repetition of words that he has just heard), and he may use specific words or phrases in a repetitive or inappropriate way. It is common for autistic children to be confused about when to use "I," "you," or "he."

Fixation An autistic child doesn't use his imagination when he is playing with toys and, rather than perceiving things in their entirety, he may become fixated by a small detail of a toy, person, or object. When playing with a toy train, for example, he might concentrate on just one small part of it, such as a wheel, rather than using it as a make-believe train.

Some autistic children do pursue activities that engage the imagination, such as reading, but these tend to be repetitive and stereotyped. For instance, the child may read one book again and again.

Repetitive behavior Repeated tapping, rocking, head banging, teeth grinding, grunting, screaming, finger flicking, spinning objects, and standing up and jumping from the back foot to the front foot are some of the behaviors that can occur. The type of repetitive activity depends on the child's level of ability. More sophisticated behaviors include arranging objects in complex, repeating patterns and collecting large numbers of an object. An autistic child may be interested in a topic, asking the same questions about it and demanding the same answers. A child may want repetitive routines, even inappropriate ones, to be observed without fail. For example, when he goes to bed he may want exactly the same sequence of activities each night.

Memory Some autistic children are able to store a memory and retrieve it exactly as it was first perceived, and the results can be very impressive. An autistic child may, for example, draw perfectly from memory a building he has seen or to repeat whole conversations or lists of information.

SPECIAL NEEDS

The severity of the child's condition depends on whether he has any other learning disorders (such as dyslexia, see p.253–54); whether he has any accompanying physical disorders (such as epilepsy, see p.270–71), the type of education he has access to; and his personality or disposition, which will affect how he reacts to his disabilities. It is important to diagnose autism and associated disorders as early as possible to meet his individual needs.

The National Society for Autistic Children (see **Useful addresses**, p.344–45) helps parents with autistic children, offers various publications on care and education and organizes conferences and workshops. Depending on the severity of the child's autism, he may be able to go to an ordinary school where he may receive extra help (about one in six autistic children go to an ordinary school), or will need to go to a special school for children with learning or developmental disorders.

Using sign language
If your child finds talking a problem, you can use a sign language or picture symbols to communicate – it can help to clarify your language to her.

Signs can be used to complement speech but not replace it

WHAT PARENTS CAN DO

Most commonly an autistic child's behavior is most problematic between the ages of two and five, and there may be an improvement between the ages of 6 and 12. As he grows up, the autistic child will probably become more responsive and sociable. Although no cure exists for autism, there are many different therapies designed to improve the behavior and adjustment of the autistic child:

Behavior modification This therapy concentrates on replacing dysfunctional behavior (tantrums, head banging, aggressiveness, and so on) with desirable behavior, using a system of rewards.

Relaxation and massage The child is taught how to relax using massage, music, touching, and verbal cues. Later, the verbal cues can be used on their own when the child shows signs of tension; because he associates them with feeling relaxed, they should dissipate the tension. Massage helps autistic children bond to people through touch.

Holding therapy This involves giving the autistic child plenty of hugs and cuddles, regardless of his indifference. The theory is that if one insists on holding the child, he will be comforted and reassured without the problem of having to initiate the interaction in the first place.

Speech therapy Some cases of autism are diagnosed by speech therapists, because poor language development is the first sign that parents notice. Speech therapy can also improve an autistic child's communication skills. If the child doesn't speak or his speech is very limited, he may be helped with a system called Total Communication, which includes signing as a language facilitator.

Psychotherapy This involves working with all the family so that parents understand the behavior of the autistic child. In some cases, the child might receive individual psychotherapy.

LIVING WITH CHRONIC CONDITIONS

The word "chronic" is used to describe an illness, such as diabetes or asthma, that is long-lasting, and whose symptoms are present on a daily basis or flare up occasionally. In contrast, an acute illness, such as tonsillitis, comes on suddenly and the duration of symptoms is quite short. Chronic conditions may be lifelong and you, your family, and your child will need to make some changes in your lifestyle in order to cope with the condition on a day-to-day basis.

DEALING WITH ILLNESS

The most common emotional reaction to the news that your child has a chronic condition is anxiety, combined with fear, bitterness, and possibly guilt that you yourself have done something to cause the condition. After the initial shock, many parents become very involved in learning about their child's condition and how to manage it. The first thing you need to know is what the treatment program entails – this may be daily injections, occasional blood transfusions, or just making sure that your child always carries an inhaler. You will also need to familiarize yourself with the symptoms of an attack or the possible dangers to your child, and learn what to do in an emergency.

When your child first starts to show signs of a chronic condition, apart from the physical unpleasantness of being ill, he will more than likely find the experience of visiting doctors and hospitals quite stressful. Stay calm in front of your child and don't worry or panic. He will see your anxiety and interpret it in his own way; he may even become terrified that he is going to die. Talk to your child rationally about his condition and explain what is happening to him. If he does not understand what is wrong with him this can be more frightening than the illness itself.

Because you are worried about your child's health it is quite natural for you to pay special attention to him. Be careful, however, not to exclude other members of your family, especially if you have any other children.

Research is conducted into chronic conditions, and management programs are becoming more advanced – in most cases your child will be able to live a near-normal life. (For self-help groups, see **Useful addresses**, p.344–45.)

ASTHMA

About 4 million children under the age of 18 in the U.S. suffer from asthma. It is responsible for 100,000 hospital admissions each year in the U.S. Boys are twice as likely as girls to suffer from asthma.

The symptoms of asthma – coughing, wheezing, and shortness of breath – are caused by narrowing of the airways, and episodes can be brought on by various triggers. They vary greatly in severity, but even a mild attack can be frightening in a young child. There may be a family history of asthma or the allergic conditions eczema and hay fever. The condition may improve as a child gets older. Over 50 percent of children affected by asthma outgrow the condition by adulthood.

Risk factors The reasons for the increase in rates of asthma are not entirely known; parental smoking, pollution, viruses, and low birth-weight are possible factors. Smoking is the only proven one, especially if a woman smokes during pregnancy, and if she or her partner smokes during their child's early years.

Research suggests that children who are not exposed to a wide variety of viruses and bacteria in early childhood and therefore fail to have their immune system challenged are more vulnerable to developing asthma. Children who are raised on farms are ess likely to have asthma than city dwellers.

Rising levels of air pollution caused by factories and vehicles are being blamed for the growing numbers of asthma sufferers. Vchicle exhaust fumes have increased by 75 percent since 1980, although all new cars have catalytic converters to reduce fumes.

DIAGNOSIS

Many young children may have wheezing episodes, but this doesn't mean they're asthmatic. It's the pattern of symptoms that develops over time that shows whether a child has asthma or not. It can be quite difficult to spot asthma in very young children for three reasons. First, a third of all children will have at least one attack of wheezing during their first five years. Most of these children will never have breathing problems again, so doctors probably will not use the term asthma. Second, doctors use a variety of words to describe asthma, such as wheezing, wheezy bronchitis, chesty coughs, or colds. Third, a "peak-flow meter," the device normally used to measure how well the lungs work, can usually be used only with children who are over five years of age.

Before reaching a diagnosis the doctor should wait to see how the pattern of the child's symptoms develops. It is this pattern, not the individual symptoms, that dictates a diagnosis of asthma. Typical symptom patterns are as follows:

- Repeated attacks of wheezing and coughing, usually with colds.

- A persistent cough over a period of weeks to months may be the only symptom in small children.

- Many restless nights caused by attacks of wheezing or coughing.

- Wheezing or coughing between colds, especially after exercise or excitement, or when the child is exposed to cigarette smoke and allergens such as pollen or house-dust mite droppings.

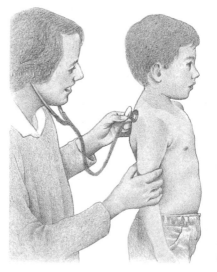

Diagnosing asthma
A doctor will need to monitor the pattern of a child's symptoms over time before he can diagnose asthma.

Many people believe that wheezing is the only symptom of asthma, but for young children a dry and irritating cough may be the only symptom. Healthy children do not cough persistently.

Children under the age of one year are most likely to suffer from wheezing, which is set off by virus infections such as with a cold or a runny nose. In fact, viruses are an almost universal trigger for young children. Breastfeeding may help improve a child's resistance to viruses.

TRIGGERS

If your child does suffer from asthma, you will find that certain substances or activities can trigger an attack. Once you have identified triggers, you should take measures to protect your child from coming into contact with them.

Smoking Help your child avoid cigarette smoke because it's especially harmful to growing lungs and can trigger asthma attacks. Never smoke around children and encourage visitors to your home not to do so.

Cold air You may notice that your child coughs or wheezes initially on going outdoors. Keeping your child indoors, however, is not the answer. A dose of medication (see p.262) just before going out may be all that's needed.

Activity If laughter, excitement, or exercise trigger asthma in your child, it is a sign that the asthma is not properly controlled. Consult your child's doctor, since it is very important for children to join in the fun and enjoy themselves. The symptoms of activity-induced asthma may be prevented if your child takes a dose of asthma medicine beforehand. Your child should warm up before playing games – several 30-second sprints over five to ten minutes will allow her to exercise for up to an hour or so. Swimming provides an excellent form of exercise for children who are suffering from asthma and it seldom provokes an attack unless the water is very cold or heavily chlorinated.

Allergies Minimize your child's exposure to potential allergens, such as mites, pollen, and fur. Complete avoidance of house dust is impossible, but it is helpful to avoid feather pillows, duvets, and shag rugs; cover your child's mattress with a plastic sheet; and clean and vacuum your child's room regularly.

TREATMENT

A doctor can prescribe medicine that will control the child's symptoms, though not actually cure asthma itself. There are two different types of medication available: anti-inflammatories, which prevent attacks, and bronchodilators, which relieve attacks. Most medications come in an inhaler. Children should always use their inhalers with a device called a spacer, which delivers the drug directly to the airways.

Bronchodilators A bronchodilator eases breathing during an attack by relaxing the tiny muscles around the narrowed airways, allowing them to open. It may also be used several times a day to stop symptoms from developing. Even if the attacks are infrequent, bronchodilator medicine must always be on hand.

Anti-inflammatories A child will probably have to take anti-inflammatory medication if she usually needs to use a bronchodilator more than once a day. These stop asthma from starting by reducing any inflammation of the airways and making them less sensitive to irritants. Anti-inflammatories must be taken regularly, even if the child is well. They take about 7–14 days to become effective from the time they are first taken. Once the symptoms are under good control, your child's doctor may decide to reduce the dosage. If your child needs to use both types of medication, it is always a good idea to label the inhalers clearly.

Treatment devices The drugs can be given in different ways, depending on the age of the child and her ability to coordinate her breathing with the use of the inhaler. The following is a general guide, but children vary as to which they can master:

up to 2	Nebulizer or spacer with face mask
2–4	Aerosol inhaler with spacer
5–8	Powder inhalers
8 up	Powder inhaler or aerosol inhaler

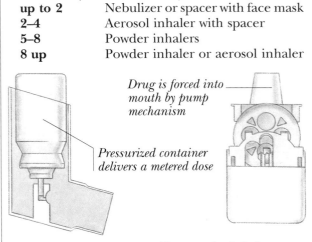

Drug is forced into mouth by pump mechanism

Pressurized container delivers a metered dose

Aerosol inhaler
A metered dose is inhaled directly into the lungs. This requires good coordination, thorough instruction, and a careful assessment of the technique with each type.

Dry-powder inhalers
These are good for giving anti-inflammatory medicines, but they cannot be inhaled very well when the child is wheezing or is tight chested because a good breath in is needed to drigger the device. An aerosol may still be needed for relieving these symptoms.

Vents around the mouthpiece allow exhaled air to escape

Valve opens as the child inhales and shuts as she exhales

A metered dose is sprayed into the spacer

Asthma medicines
Young children very quickly get used to the routine of taking their asthma medicine.

Spacer
An aerosol inhaler delivers the drug into the spacer and the child inhales it over several breaths. This ensures that the medication reaches the lungs. Even young infants can use a spacer if a mask is attached.

For most children, spacers are best. If your child finds it hard to take inhaled medicine, try using the spacer when she is asleep. If she knocks it away, wrap her arms around her chest. Some young children need a nebulizer; it emits a fine mist of medicine.

For an older child, turn the spacer into a toy by putting stickers on it, or play games in which you count out loud as your child takes five breaths from the spacer.. For severe attacks, nebulizers may be used; steroid tablets are also often recommended

WHAT PARENTS CAN DO

Although there is no known cure for asthma, modern asthma management can effectively reduce a child's symptoms and allow her to lead a full and active life. Regular contact with your doctor and close monitoring of your child are important.

Your doctor will develop an asthma management plan with you, and explain when to use the medication and what to do if symptoms get worse. This should be written down for you to keep at home. A vital part of any plan is a review meeting with a doctor or nurse every few months. You should monitor your child's symptoms closely and consult your doctor if you notice any of the following:

- Wheezing and coughing in the early morning.

- Increased symptoms after exercise or exertion.

- Waking at night with a cough or a wheeze.

- Increased use of bronchodilator therapy.

An emergency plan Any asthma attack can be life-threatening, so have an emergency plan agreed with your doctor for very severe attacks. Make sure all adults in whose care your child will be – baby-sitters, relatives, teachers, parents of children your child may visit – are informed about the plan.

- At the start of the attack, give your child her usual bronchodilator. Wait about ten minutes.

- If there is no improvement, call 911.

- Repeat the treatment until the breathing symptoms improve or help arrives.

- Give your child steroid tablets if they've been prescribed by your doctor.

- Keep your child in an upright position.

CYSTIC FIBROSIS

An inherited condition that affects mainly the lungs and the pancreas, cystic fibrosis (CF) is also known as mucoviscidosis because it produces thick and sticky mucus in the lungs and the pancreas. CF is the number one genetic killer of children in the U.S., affecting approximately one in every 2,500 children, though in differing degrees. The gene responsible for CF has been discovered and there is now a chance that there will be a cure by the time your child reaches adulthood.

WHAT CAUSES CF?

The disease occurs when both parents carry a gene for the disorder. One person in every 20 is a carrier of CF, but an affected gene will be masked by a normal gene from the other parent, and even where two carriers of CF have a baby, there is only a one-in-four chance that the baby will have CF. These chances apply anew for each pregnancy. They do not change the more pregnancies one has. CF affects girls and boys in equal numbers.

DIAGNOSIS

CF can be detected through a blood test. In the U.S., only six states routinely include CF in the newborn blood test required by law.

Another test, carried out when a child is at least three months old, measures the amount of salt in the sweat; children with CF have more salt in their sweat than normal children. (Some parents comment that their child tastes salty when they kiss him or her, even though children with CF do not sweat more than other children.) This sweat test is carried out on any baby who has recurrent bouts of pneumonia or fails to thrive, and on the brothers and sisters of a child with CF.

Parents' feelings Once the diagnosis is made, parents may have trouble accepting it, especially if their child seems well. They may feel angry, or guilty, but very soon they will realize that no one is to blame. Recriminations are not only pointless, they will do great harm to relationships within the family and to the child with CF. Although CF is a fatal disease, many who have it live into adulthood.

Parents may seek a second opinion. Doctors will be

happy to provide a second opinion, particularly for parents who have not yet had the chance to visit a special clinic for CF.

Some people find complementary therapies helpful, but they must be taken in addition to conventional therapy and should be discussed with the child's doctor. To ensure the child's future health, give conventional medicines exactly as prescribed.

Try not to overprotect a child with CF and remember she is a normal child who happens to have CF. She will be naughty and have all the same emotions as other children, and there's no reason to treat her differently in relation to discipline, education, or physical activities. Parents who do will not only be doing her a disservice, but also be creating problems for themselves in the long run. A child with a chronic illness can greatly strain a relationship, and parents need to talk openly with each other.

Learning about CF Much of the treatment for CF is carried out at home, and to be as effective as possible, parents should try to understand as much as they can about the disorder. CF is a complicated condition, however, and each child will be differently affected, so other people's experiences may differ. Parents should bear in mind that they can't expect to know everything immediately and no one will expect them to. Moreover, they will be given a huge amount of information and advice from various sources, some of which will be conflicting. (see **Useful addresses**, p.344–35.)

DIGESTIVE PROBLEMS

The pancreas, a gland in the abdomen, produces insulin, which passes directly into the blood, and digestive juices containing enzymes, which pass into the intestines, where they help with the digestion of food. In CF, the small channels down which these juices flow to reach the intestine become blocked with sticky mucus and the enzymes can't reach the intestines to digest food. The children often have large appetites but fail to thrive and pass large pale greasy stools because food cannot be absorbed properly.

Treatment Most of the missing digestive enzymes can be replaced with pancreatin, which is given in a powder or capsule form. For a young baby, the powder can be mixed with water or milk and given before each feeding from a spoon or feeding bottle. It should not be mixed with a whole bottle of

milk, because it will curdle the milk. Once the baby is on solids, she should eat whatever the rest of the family is having. Vitamins are not well absorbed in CF, so the child will need a dose of vitamin drops each day. The child's managing physician or pediatrician can recommend an appropriate type.

RESPIRATORY PROBLEMS

Inside the lungs are lots of tiny tubes, the bronchioles, down which air passes to reach specialized air sacs, the alveoli; here, oxygen enters the bloodstream and carbon dioxide leaves the blood to be exhaled. CF children have normal lungs at birth, but the mucus produced in them is abnormally thick, so it blocks some of the smaller airways and leads to infection and, later, to lung damage.

Treatment The aim of treatment is to keep the lungs as normal as possible, and there are two components to this:

- Clearing the sticky mucus from the airways with physiotherapy, breathing exercises, physical exercise, and medication.

- Prevention and prompt treatment of chest infections, usually with antibiotics.

WHAT PARENTS CAN DO

Even with pancreatic supplements, a child with CF may not absorb all the nourishment she needs in order to grow normally. The child will therefore need more calories, so high-energy snacks between meals, such as milkshakes, are helpful. Monitor the child's growth to ensure she is gaining height and weight as she should. (See the charts on pp. 318–325, which can be used to plot measurements.)

The only way to learn how to clear the thick mucus from the child's chest is from a physiotherapist and with lots of practice, so parents should not be afraid to ask for help. Physiotherapy should be started at the time of the diagnosis, and it's important to get into a routine early on. It will need to be done twice a day when the child is well, and more often when she has a chest infection.

Parents should work very closely with a doctor on the prevention and treatment of chest infections. Should an infection occur, the child will need extra physiotherapy and antibiotics.

WHEN TO SEE THE DOCTOR
Your CF child is very vulnerable to chest infections, so it's important to seek medical help promptly, either from the child's doctor or hospital clinic, if there is a suspicion that something is wrong. The following symptoms may indicate that a doctor's visit is needed:

• Decreased or poor appetite

• Weight loss

• Stomach aches

• Frequent or loose stools

• Increased or frequent cough

• Vomiting

• Increased sputum

• Change in the color of sputum

• Breathlessness

• Unwillingness to exercise

• Fever

• Cold symptoms

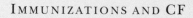

IMMUNIZATIONS AND CF
Babies with CF are particularly at risk from the common childhood infectious diseases, especially those that may affect the lungs.

A child with CF must stick rigidly to the normal immunization schedule (see p.283), and injections should be postponed only in very exceptional circumstances and after consultation with the child's doctor. Having a cold or a cough is not sufficient reason to delay immunization. CF children should also be immunized against flu every winter.

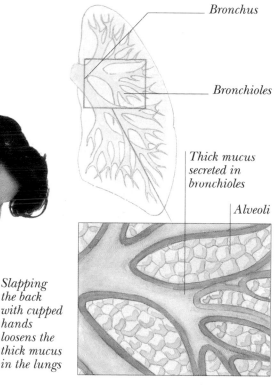

Bronchus

Bronchioles

Thick mucus secreted in bronchioles

Alveoli

Physiotherapy
To clear the thick mucus from the child's chest, use physiotherapy twice a day, and more often during chest infections.

Slapping the back with cupped hands loosens the thick mucus in the lungs

Blocked airways
Thick mucus blocks the airways, starving them of oxygen and ultimately causing parts of the lung to collapse.

Your child should lie on a comfortable support during physiotherapy

DIABETES MELLITUS

A chronic disease, insulin-dependent diabetes mellitus (Type I) in children is due to a lack of insulin. Insufficient insulin results in an increase in blood glucose concentration (hyperglycemia), causing excessive urination and constant thirst and hunger. An accumulation in the body of chemicals called ketones occurs when there is a severe lack of insulin. A high sugar level is not in itself dangerous, but high ketone levels are.

The onset of diabetes can be swift and may take some time to stabilize. Most diabetic children need insulin injections and a strictly controlled diet.

IS THERE A CURE?

Not at the present time. Type I diabetes occurs because cells of the immune system attack the insulin-producing islet tissue in the pancreas. Any cure must therefore replace the damaged tissue in some way. For this reason, transplantation offers the only viable therapeutic approach, but rejection of the transplanted tissue poses a serious problem.

There is promising research being carried out that suggests it might be possible to graft tissue into the body that will not be recognized as foreign. Already this approach has worked experimentally and has been used to reverse diabetes in a number of laboratory animals, without the need for anti-rejection therapy. It is quite possible that diabetes will be cured with transplants in your child's life-time. Progress has also been made with genetic research and the recent discovery of two new genes has opened up the possibility that the condition could be prevented.

ADJUSTING TO DIABETES

It can be quite frightening to be told your child has insulin-dependent diabetes, but the disease will not prevent a child from leading a full and active life.

How the family handles a child's diabetes helps determine the way in which the child accepts or denies the disease and becomes a balanced, mature person. Parents will soon know a lot about diabetes, the need for insulin, the technique for injection, and the importance of proper food intake and exercise. They will also need to know how to recognize signs of a low or high blood sugar level.

Subcutaneous injection
Pinch the skin gently and insert the needle at 90° to deliver the insulin to the layer of fat just below the skin.

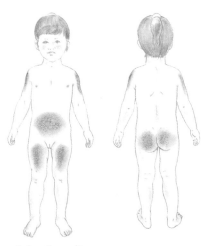

Injection sites
To avoid scarring, vary the injection sites. Suitable sites include the upper arms, thighs, buttocks, and abdomen.

CONTROLLING DIABETES

The aim of treatment is to keep blood sugar levels as near normal as possible. Too high a level (hyperglycemia) can lead to fatigue, excessive urination, constant thirst, weight loss, and an increased level of ketones in the body. Too little blood sugar (hypoglycemia) can lead to weakness, dizziness, confusion, and sometimes even seizures. Proper levels are achieved by a combination of dietary control and regular meals, with attention paid to the intake of sugar and carbohydrates, insulin injections, and regular physical exercise. Discuss home blood glucose monitoring (see right) with the doctor, as frequent and accurate measurement of blood sugar levels will help in managing the child's disease.

Perfect control is too much to hope for. Even if a child is completely trustworthy about insulin and food, he will still occasionally have a raised blood sugar. If a child eats candy occasionally, this act of breaking the rules isn't life-threatening, so too much fuss should not be made.

One bite of chocolate will not make any child sick, not even a child with diabetes. Even if the child has followed dietary advice, blood sugars can sometimes be a little high or a little low. Parents should always try to be be realistic.

WHAT PARENTS CAN DO

Parents will need to exercise skill to help their child accept his condition with the minimum of fuss. They should supervise invisibly while giving him responsibility to learn self-care and control.

Children with diabetes tend to worry more than children without the disease, and this is only to be expected; they have to assume important responsibilities and they know, or will come to know, that diabetes can do some very unpleasant things. Diabetes makes children feel tired and confused, and can make them lose consciousness. A child who is diabetic has to plan ahead when leaving home and remember to take along some candy or sugar and insulin and syringes if the trip is a long one. A child is threatened both physically and psychologically by diabetes, so it is important to be sympathetic without becoming overly protective. As the child grows older, however, he will gain mastery over the situation, learn self-care, and understand what needs to be done.

BLOOD GLUCOSE MONITORING

A system is available that enables parents to measure blood sugar level accurately at any time. Precise monitoring and testing of blood sugar may reduce and even reverse some of the complications of diabetes.

Begin by obtaining a drop of blood from a tiny finger-prick. The blood is dropped onto a chemically sensitive strip The strip is inserted into a machine that measures the blood glucose and shows it on a digital display. Another method relies on comparing the strip with a color-coded chart. Each gives accurate results.

Blood glucose monitoring makes it possible to measure blood sugar levels frequently and accurately without visiting the doctor and waiting for lab results; it enables parents to respond promptly to a low blood sugar count by giving high-carbohydrate foods, or to a high blood sugar count by injecting insulin. The child's doctor can recommend the proper insulin dosages or other medications according to glucose levels.

While it involves some degree of discomfort, blood testing is more accurate than urine tests, since there is a delay between the rise of blood sugar and the time that it takes before it shows up in the urine. Also, urine tests show high readings only when glucose is well above acceptable limits.

Blood samples
Use lancets and a machine for pricking the child's finger to obtain a drop of blood. You may prefer to use the sides, rather than the tips of the fingers as they're less sensitive. Place a drop of blood on the pad on the strip.

Testing strips
The strip will change color to indicate the glucose level. Compare the strip with the color chart on the side of the container.

CEREBRAL PALSY

In the U.S. each year roughly 5,000 babies are born with cerebral palsy and another 1,500 develop it after birth. It is a disorder that affects both boys and girls from all races and social backgrounds.

WHAT CAUSES CEREBRAL PALSY?

Cerebral palsy is caused by an injury to the brain, usually before, around, or soon after the time of birth. Causes of such injury include a difficult or preterm birth, perhaps because the baby fails to breathe properly; cerebral bleeding, which may occur in preterm babies; or bleeding into cavities of the brain (intraventricular hemorrhage), which may also occur in preterm babies; or an infection in the mother during the first weeks of pregnancy – German measles or cytomegalovirus, for example. Occasionally, the brain is formed abnormally for no obvious reason, or the disorder is inherited even if both parents are healthy.

TYPES OF CEREBRAL PALSY

If a child has cerebral palsy, it means that part of his brain either is not working properly or has not developed normally. The affected area is usually one of the parts of the brain that control the muscles and certain body movements; the disease interferes with the messages that normally pass from the brain to the body. In some children, cerebral palsy is hardly noticeable at all; others are more severely affected. No two children will be affected in quite the same way. There are three main types of cerebral palsy:

Spastic cerebral palsy Here, the cortex, which is the outer layer of the brain and controls thought, movement, and sensation, is affected. Tight and sometimes jerky muscle movements result.

Athetoid cerebral palsy This type involves the basal ganglia, groups of cells lying deep within the brain. The basal ganglia promote organized, graceful, and economical movement, so an abnormality can cause movements that are bending and wavelike.

WHAT PARENTS CAN DO

It's difficult to predict the effects of cerebral palsy, especially on a young child. It doesn't become more severe as the child gets older, though some difficulties may become more noticeable, and priorities will change: when a baby is young, for example, parents might concentrate on helping her sit up, but later they will be more concerned with communication skills and talking.

There is no cure for cerebral palsy, but if children are lifted, held, and positioned well from an early age, and encouraged to play in a way that helps them to improve their posture and muscle control, they can learn a lot and lead fulfilling lives.

There's no question that parents will have to work very hard with their child and there will be difficult moments when they feel that it's all too much. These feelings are natural, and most parents feel that they gradually get less severe. Indeed, many parents say they find bringing up a child with cerebral palsy a challenging and fulfilling task.

Children with cerebral palsy often tend to lie or sit in certain ways; their muscles are sometimes in spasm and they can have problems with their joints.

Having physiotherapy as soon as cerebral palsy is suspected can help reduce the risks of these complications developing.

- The child may get stiffer and have more muscle spasm when she's lying on her back, so she should lie on her side or tummy instead, supported with a cushion if necessary. It's also a good idea to change her position every 20 minutes or so.

- The child should be helped to learn to use her hands right from the start by being allowed to feel things with different textures and encouraged to hold toys and other objects. Toys securely strung over her chair can be useful.

- The child should be enabled to learn shapes by being shown different simple-shaped objects and encouraged to handle and play with them.

- A child of three or four years with cerebral palsy may want to help around the house like any child her age. Parents should explain what they're doing, let her watch and, if possible, join in.

Ataxic cerebral palsy This indicates that the cerebellum, which is located at the base of the brain, is affected. Because the cerebellum is responsible for coordinating fine movement, posture, and balance, an abnormality can result in an uneven gait and difficulty in walking.

EFFECTS OF CEREBRAL PALSY

Some children with cerebral palsy will have difficulty talking, walking, or using their hands, and most will need help with everyday tasks. Often, vision or hearing is affected. The child may suffer slightly or severely from slow, awkward, or jerky movements, stiffness, weakness, floppiness, or muscle spasms, and be prone to involuntary movements.

There are a number of disorders associated with cerebral palsy, due either to poor muscle control or to other abnormalities in the brain.

Eyesight The most common eye problem is crossed eyes, which may need correction with glasses or, in severe cases, an operation.

Hearing Children with athetoid cerebral palsy are more likely to have severe hearing difficulties than other children. This is not so for children with other forms of cerebral palsy. It is important that hearing difficulties be diagnosed early (see p.178–79). An affected child may be able to wear a hearing aid.

Speech The ability to control the tiny muscles in the mouth, tongue, palate, and voice box is necessary for speech. Difficulty in speaking, chewing, and swallowing often occur together in children with cerebral palsy. Speech therapists can help with both sorts of difficulty and ease communication.

Spatial perception Some children with cerebral palsy cannot perceive space and relate it to their own bodies; for instance, they're not able to judge distances or think in three dimensions. This is due to an abnormality in a part of the brain that is not related to intelligence.

Epilepsy About one-third of children with cerebral palsy are affected by epilepsy (see p.270–71), but it is impossible to predict whether, or when, a child may develop seizures. In some children, they start in infancy; in others, not until adulthood. If a child does develop epilepsy, it can be controlled with medication.

Learning difficulties People who are unable to control their movements very well or to talk are often assumed to have a mental disability. Some people with cerebral palsy do have learning difficulties or a severe mental handicap, but this is by no means always the case; many people with cerebral palsy actually have a higher than average intelligence.

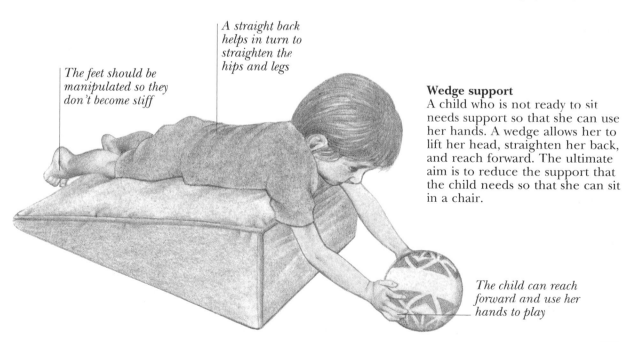

The feet should be manipulated so they don't become stiff

A straight back helps in turn to straighten the hips and legs

Wedge support
A child who is not ready to sit needs support so that she can use her hands. A wedge allows her to lift her head, straighten her back, and reach forward. The ultimate aim is to reduce the support that the child needs so that she can sit in a chair.

The child can reach forward and use her hands to play

269

CHOOSING AND USING TOYS

Despite their difficulties with movement, children with cerebral palsy need stimulating play as much as any child, but choosing toys can be problematic. Most toy companies make goods suitable for children with cerebral palsy. Parents planning to buy an expensive toy should ask a physiotherapist or occupational therapist for advice. Better still, they should join a toy library and experiment to find out which toys the child will find most rewarding. Wedges (see p.269) and standing frames can greatly help children with cerebral palsy to enjoy their toys. Once again, an occupational therapist will be able to help.

• When the child is playing let her choose from two or three toys, then put away the ones she doesn't want. If she's surrounded by lots of toys, she will easily be distracted.

• The child should always be shown how a new toy works, not once but many times.

• The child should be helped to use her imagination by telling her stories about her cuddly toys while playing with her, for example.

• If the child doesn't seem to want to play, parents should start showing her how much fun it is by starting to play with her toys themselves, and asking her to join in.

WHAT CAN BE DONE

Depending on the degree of disability, a child with cerebral palsy can be helped to achieve a degree of independence through a combination of means.

• *Physical therapy Can begin soon after diagnosis; it aims to improve motor development and prevent the weakening of disused muscles. In conjunction with special braces, it can help avoid contracture of the muscles into fixed, rigid positions*

• *Speech therapy To develop the child's communication skills*

• *Occupational therapy To enable the child to develop feeding, dressing, and toileting skills*

• *Drugs To prevent seizures and spasticity*

• *Surgery Sometimes used to correct severe contractures*

• *Mechanical aids From wheelchairs and Velcro fasteners and wheelchairs to computers and voice synthesizers*

EPILEPSY

The most common brain disease in children, epilepsy affects 1 in 100 births in the U.S. The normal electrical impulses in the brain are disturbed, causing periodic seizures that can be minor or severe.

EPILEPTIC SEIZURES

There are several forms of epileptic seizure. One, called "grand mal," involves recurring attacks of convulsions and difficulty breathing with loss of consciouness followed by stiffening of the body lasting a minute or less, and then a series of rhythmic jerks of the limbs, clenching of the teeth (when the child might bite his tongue), possible urination or double incontinence, and frothing at the mouth. When the convulsion is over the child will lapse into sleep and wake up without any memory of the fit.

In another form, called "petit mal," there are no abnormal movements, only a second or two of unconsciousness, very much like daydreaming. The child's eyes will glaze over and he appears not to see or hear anything. This kind of epilepsy is not easily recognized, and may go undiagnosed. Although not so dramatic as grand mal, petit mal seizures can interfere with a child's normal life, particularly with paying attention, school attendance and performance, and with certain physical activities where loss of control could pose a danger.

Epilepsy is not to be confused with febrile convulsions (see p.281), which are fairly harmless and are caused by a high temperature preceding or during an infectious illness.

HOW SERIOUS IS IT?

Epilepsy is not life-threatening. Most children grow out of the petit mal form by late adolescence. Those who suffer from the grand mal form can also improve with age and some grow out of it, but others may always need special attention, even though the condition is controlled by drugs. There must be supervision during activities like swimming or cycling.

It takes time to establish the level of medication needed and sometimes the epilepsy is not absolutely controlled by drugs. A doctor should be consulted to change the dose or the medication itself for better control. If your child has a convulsion of any kind, consult his doctor immediately.

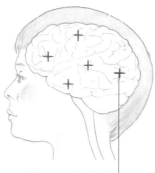

Electrical activity

Normal brain activity
The level of electrical
activity in the brain is
relatively low.

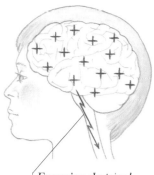

*Excessive electrical
activity causes fit*

Brain activity in a seizure
When an excessive level of
electrical energy builds up,
signals are sent to the body
which cause a seizure.

WHAT TO DO DURING A SEIZURE

• Don't try to restrain the limbs.

• Loosen the clothing around his neck and chest.

• Don't try to hold the child's teeth apart if they are
clenched, or put anything into his mouth.

• As soon as the child stops moving violently, put
him in the recovery position (see p.329).

• During a petit mal seizure, guide the child to
safety and stay with him until it has passed.

• Make a note of what happens during the child's
seizure so you can tell the doctor.

TREATMENT

If your child has a seizure, your doctor will ask you
about it and examine him to decide what form of
seizure he's had. If his seizures are recurrent, he'll
be referred to a hospital for an examination that
may include an EEG (electroencephalogram) and
other tests.

Epilepsy can be controlled, but not cured.
Anticonvulsive drugs taken daily will reduce the
frequency of grand mal seizures and eventually eradicate them in most children. Selective drugs can
now target a precise area of the brain and do not
cause the side effects associated with older drugs.

The child's condition will be reviewed periodically by his doctor, and if there are no seizures for
a year or two, he may try phasing out the drugs.

Surgery may be used on occasion if drugs are not
effective and if damage to a single area of the brain
is thought to be the cause. The child's doctor will
advise parents if this might be appropriate.

WHAT PARENTS CAN DO

It could be a shock to realize that one's child has
epilepsy, but parents must try to remain calm. Both
parents and child will need to get their confidence
back. A doctor can help by advising on how to cope
with the seizures.

It is important to observe the child's condition so
it can be reported to the doctor. Notes should be
made of the frequency of the seizures. If he is on
any medication, he should be watched carefully and
any mental or personality differences should be reported to the doctor. Parents should never stop the
child's medication without seeking medical advice
first. To do so could result in a severe, prolonged
convulsion after a few days.

The child should always be treated as normally as
possible. His friends and teachers should be told
about the condition so that they are not frightened
if the child suddenly starts having a convulsion. The
child should always wear a bracelet or medallion
engraved with information about his epilepsy.

When the child is old enough, you should teach
him to recognize the signs of an oncoming attack.
Many sufferers of epilepsy experience sensations
like an unpleasant smell, distorted vision, or an odd
feeling in the stomach just before a convulsion. If
the child can identify these sensations as warning
signs, he may be able to avoid having an accident.

THE OUTLOOK FOR THE CHILD

The aim of caring for a child with epilepsy is to control the seizures with a minimum of side effects and
enhance his quality of life as he grows up. Seizure
control should never be established at the cost of
drug side effects, as they may result in cramping of
important brain functions that allow the child to
develop normally.

Monitoring the child's condition is very important. Parents should not rely on a doctor to do this;
they should establish a plan that involves regular
visits; if the child has more than one or two seizures,
he should see his doctor immediately; the medication may need to be adjusted or changed.

SICKLE CELL DISEASE

This inherited disease is most common in people of African or West Indian descent, but may also occur in people from the Indian subcontinent, the Middle East, and the eastern Mediterranean. A child with sickle cell disease (SCD) will be prone to bouts of pain and may be at risk from other disorders, but most of the time he will be quite well.

TYPES OF SCD

Sickle cell disease is caused by an abnormality of hemoglobin, the oxygen-carrying substance in red blood cells. There are three main types: sickle cell anemia (the most common and severe form), hemoglobin SC disease, and sickle beta-thalassemia.

Sickle cell anemia When oxygen levels are low, the abnormal hemoglobin (known as type S) becomes crystallized, making the red cell fragile and ridged. These sickle cells – so called because of their characteristic sickle or crescent shape – can then become trapped in the blood vessels, causing a blockage that prevents blood flow. This accounts for the excruciating pain characteristic of an SCD attack. Sickle cells last only about 20 days in the body, not the usual 120 days for normal red cells, and the early death of red cells leads to anemia.

Sometimes aplastic crises occur, where the blood-forming activity in the bone marrow is reduced temporarily, decreasing the level of red-cell production and shortening the life of the red cells. As a result, the bone marrow may become inactive, which can be life-threatening.

Hemoglobin SC disease In this form of SCD, there are two abnormal hemoglobins – type S and type C. The disease appears later, and in a milder form, than sickle cell anemia.

There are other inherited anemias that are considerably rarer than sickle cell disease. Thalassemia is one; a subtype called Cooley's anemia often begins to show symptoms in childhood. A condition called G6PD deficiency is another, though it is very rare and rarely serious.

SICKLE CELL TRAIT

Sickle cell trait is found in areas where malaria was or is endemic, and offers some protection against malaria during the first years of life. It's not surprising, therefore, that between 8 and 13 percent of Americans of African descent, and a smaller but significant number with Middle Eastern and Mediterranean ancestry, have the trait.

A child can inherit sickle cell disease only if both parents pass on the abnormal trait, and even then the chances are only one in four. If only one parent passes on the trait the sickle cell gene will be masked by a healthy gene from the other parent. A carrier is unaffected, but the trait does show up in blood tests.

EFFECTS OF SCD

Apart from causing anemia and acute pain attacks called "crises," SCD can cause other problems, including infections and jaundice. There is also a small risk of a stroke occurring during a crisis.

Infections Children with SCD are particularly vulnerable to infections, especially of the lungs and bones, to salmonella infection, which is especially dangerous in SCD because it can spread to the bones and blood, and to meningitis. An overwhelming infection can cause a dramatic loss of blood cells in the spleen or liver, resulting in a massive drop in hemoglobin levels, which is potentially fatal if treatment is not given immediately.

Pain crises When sickle cells block a blood vessel oxygen starvation of tissue supplied by that blood vessel may result nearly anywhere in the body; the feet and hands are particularly vulnerable.

These crises are one of the most distressing aspects of SCD; the pain is violent and unpredictable, and it is very difficult for parents to watch their child in pain and be unable to help him. The crisis can be treated with pain-killing drugs, however. Sometimes crises are brought on by infections, strenuous exercise, low temperatures, or dehydration caused by vomiting or diarrhea.

Jaundice The rapid breakdown of red cells can result in increased levels of a pigment called bilirubin (see **Jaundice**, p.25). This causes a yellowish appearance in the whites of the eyes, which often increases with the severity of the crises. Skin may also have a yellowish tinge.

Development Children with SCD may experience slowing down of their growth (both height and weight) and puberty may also be delayed. They may exist in a permanent state of chronic anemia, leading to a rapid decline in their condition when ill.

SCREENING

Genetic and support counseling are essential for couples at risk for or with SCD in their families. In some areas all babies are screened for hemoglobin abnormalities regardless of ethnic origin. Early detection means that SCD can be managed properly, and in particular, that long-term treatment with penicillin can begin promptly to minimize the risk of lung infections.

Prenatal screening is available to find out if a baby's hemoglobin is normal and can be carried out at the time of amniocentesis (usually about 16 weeks into the pregnancy). Screening is advisable for pregnant women who are aware that they have sickle cell trait. Couples will be offered counseling to clarify the risks of having a baby.

TREATMENT

A child who has SCD will need frequent doses of penicillin to nip bacterial infections in the bud. This should be given from the time of diagnosis throughout life. All affected children need folic acid supplements. They should drink plenty of fluids to prevent

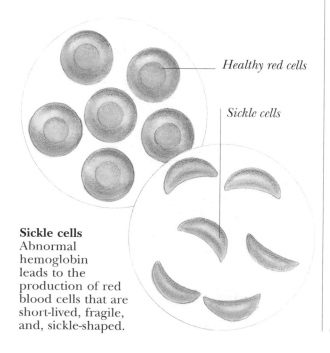

Sickle cells
Abnormal hemoglobin leads to the production of red blood cells that are short-lived, fragile, and, sickle-shaped.

Healthy red cells

Sickle cells

dehydration – approximately 1 quart (1 liter) daily – and should always keep warm, to encourage normal circulation. Although overexertion can cause problems, children should exercise and find their own energy tolerance level – exercise will improve the health of the heart and circulation. Pain and symptoms of infection should be treated promptly.

Where millions of red blood cells have been destroyed, exchange transfusion in the hospital will be necessary. Sometimes many exchange transfusions will have to be given. Although this is a lengthy procedure, it is well worthwhile since it will allow the child to lead a near-normal life. Painkillers, fluids, and possibly inhaled oxygen and antibiotics may be given too.

WHAT PARENTS CAN DO

Although knowledge about the disease is incomplete, it's important for parents to be as well informed as possible, so that they can help their child avoid pain crises. Counseling will give them a safe, confidential way of exploring their feelings, and provide a source of encouragement and support (see **Useful addresses**, p.344–45). With experience, parents can learn to manage mild crises at home.

When the child starts school, parents should inform his teachers of his condition, making sure they are aware of the problems it can impose on his education. The child might have to miss some classes, for example, because of hospital admissions or a crisis. The child should be reassured and encouraged to express his anxieties freely.

The child's feelings must be given great consideration. Many children with SCD can experience difficulties with their classmates at preschool and school. The child's teachers should educate the other children about SCD so that the child does not suffer from feelings of alienation or isolation – as he might if, for example, they thought they could catch the disease from him.

Once they can speak, many children with SCD express a fear of dying or being deformed. Others feel different and alienated, thinking they are the only ones who are suffering from this condition and that nobody understands them. Yet others are afraid of expressing when they are in pain in case nobody believes them. Parents can help greatly by making sure that the child feels assured of their understanding, sympathy, and care whenever he needs it.

CHAPTER 6

MEDICINE
and Healthcare

Most childhood illnesses are minor and others are easily preventable; immunizations are effective against most infectious diseases. In a baby, however, seemingly minor illnesses can cause complications: a cold that develops into a throat infection, for instance, may cause breathing difficulties.

You will be understandably anxious if your child is getting sick, is ill, or has had an accident. Sometimes deciding whether to seek medical help can be equally stressful. Even if your child's symptoms appear minor, you may worry that they are indicative of something more serious. You should never worry that you are being too cautious – if you find yourself wondering whether it is worth consulting a doctor, then you probably should.

The main cause of death in young children is accidents, but fortunately many injuries are preventable. You can reduce the likelihood of accidents by making your home safe and taking precautions when your child is away from home. You should also learn first aid so that you know how to help your child in an emergency. Don't just read this book; attend an approved first aid training course (see p.327) and learn the emergency procedures on pp.326–33 by heart.

TEMPERATURE

Whenever you suspect that your child is ill you should take his temperature. A raised temperature shows that the body is fighting off an infection. When your child's temperature is over 100.4°F (38°C), he has a fever (see p.281), which you should try to reduce.

TAKE CARE

Don't put a mercury thermometer in your child's mouth until he is at least seven; he may bite it and swallow mercury, which is a poison. Digital thermometers are harder to break and are easy to use with children of all ages. They are battery-operated, so be sure to keep spare batteries on hand.

THERMOMETERS

The most accurate way to take your child's temperature is with a digital thermometer, which can safely be used in the mouth (see below).

Mercury thermometers are made of glass and register the temperature when the mercury expands up the tube to a point on the scale. They should be used under the armpit.

Digital ear thermometers are easy and quick to use and very accurate. Strip thermometers are less accurate than others, but simple and safe to use.

Digital thermometer

Mercury thermometer

Digital ear thermometer

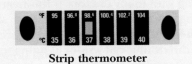
Strip thermometer

Digital thermometer (window shows temperature reading)

Mercury thermometer (to be used under the armpit)

Ear thermometer (window shows temperature reading)

Strip thermometer (a glowing panel indicates your child's temperature)

TAKING YOUR CHILD'S TEMPERATURE

Using a digital thermometer
Ask your child to open his mouth and raise his tongue. Place the thermometer under his tongue. Ask your child to place the tip of his tongue firmly behind his lower front teeth; this will hold the thermometer in place. Then ask him to close his lips, but not his teeth, over it. Leave for two minutes, remove, and read the number in the window.

Using a mercury thermometer
Position the bulb of a mercury in your child's armpit and fold his arm over his chest. Hold the thermometer in place for about three minutes. The armpit temperature is 1°F (0.6°C) below actual body temperature.

Using an ear thermometer
Digital ear thermometers are a quick, safe method of taking a child's temperature. Gently insert the tip into your child's ear and read the temperature from the display. The ear thermometer has a hygienic disposable tip.

Using a strip thermometer
The strip thermometer is easy to use. Carefully position the heat-sensitive side on your child's forehead and hold it there for a minute or so. The temperature should light up on the outside of the strip.

MEDICINES

Most medicines for children come in syrup form with a spoon, dropper, or syringe to administer them. Your child may be quite compliant when it comes to taking medicine, but he may resist.

If your baby refuses medicine, get your partner to help you, or wrap him up in a blanket so that you can hold him steady. Droppers and syringes are the best ways to give medicine if your child can't yet swallow from a spoon. Older children may be cajoled into taking medicine by the promise of a favourite food or drink to take the taste away.

GIVING MEDICINE

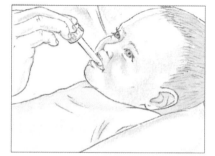

Dropper
Hold your baby in the crook of your arm, put the dropper into the medicine and draw up the right amount by squeezing the teat at the top. Place the dropper in the corner of your baby's mouth and gently release the medicine by squeezing the teat.

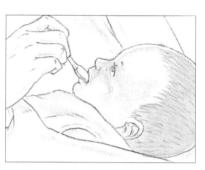

Spoon
The spoon should be sterilized with boiling water or sterilizing solution. Hold your baby in a semi-reclining position, pull his chin down with your finger, and place the spoon on his lower lip. Raise the angle of the spoon so that the medicine trickles into his mouth.

Finger
Measure out the correct dose of medicine into a small container. Dip your finger in it and allow your baby to suck it off your finger. Continue until he has taken the whole dose.

APPLYING DROPS

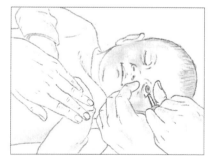

Eye drops
Lay your baby on his back and tilt his head in the direction of the affected eye. Gently pull his lower eyelid down with your finger and raise his upper lid. Let the drops fall into the corner of his eye. Get someone to help if necessary.

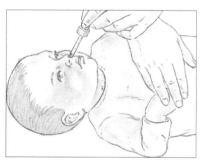

Nose drops
Lay your baby on his back with his head tilted backwards. Let two or three drops fall into the nostrils.

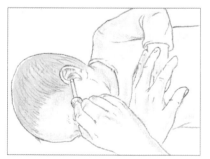

Ear drops
Lay your baby on his side. Using a dropper, let the eardrops fall into the centre of his ear.

HOSPITAL

At some point in your child's life, she may have to go into a hospital. This could be because she has an accident, a childhood illness, a chronic condition such as sickle cell disease (see p.272), which necessitates regular blood transfusions, or she needs an operation. With a little forethought by you, a stay in hospital does not have to be upsetting or frightening for your child.

TEACHING YOUR CHILD

If you don't like hospitals and you convey this attitude to your child, you may inadvertently make her stay in the hospital more difficult than it has to be. Try to teach her that a hospital is a friendly place where people go to get better. Some hospitals have open houses, ice-cream parties, and other events to introduce children in a positive and cheery way. If a child's first experience of a hospital is when she's sick, it'll seem more alien than it would otherwise.

If you know that your child is going to the hospital, read her a story about a child who goes into a hospital, and role play doctors and nurses with toy stethoscopes. Be as honest as you can about why she's going to the hospital, and emphasize that it's to make her better. Make sure, too, that other family members are positive about it. Reassure her that you will be with her as much as you can, and if she is old enough to understand, tell her when she'll be well enough to come home.

If your child requires an operation she'll probably be curious about what's going to happen to her. Answer her questions as honestly as you can – if she asks you whether the operation will hurt, don't pretend that it won't, but tell her that doctors have medicines to make the pain go away quickly.

WHAT TO TAKE

You can help your child prepare for a stay in the hospital by packing a bag with her. One of the most unsettling things for her will be the unfamiliar surroundings and the change of routine, so let her have some of her own things with her: a personal stereo and tapes or a radio, travel games, cuddly toys, a photograph for her bedside, and any other special item that would make her feel "at home." On a practical level, for a short stay pack the following items:

- A toilet bag containing a hairbrush, comb, soap, washcloth, toothbrush, and toothpaste.
- Three pairs of pajamas or three nightgowns.
- A dressing gown and a pair of slippers.
- Three pairs of socks.
- Three pairs of underpants.

IN THE HOSPITAL

Many hospitals allow parents to stay with their children 24 hours a day. Whether yours does or not, try to spend as much time as possible with your child, especially at first, when her surroundings are unfamiliar. Let her know when you are going to come, and always keep your promises about visiting. Ask the nurses on the unit whether you can bathe, change, and feed your child. If she is well enough, you can read to her and play games with her. If you can't stay at the hospital all the time, encourage your partner, friends, and relatives to visit at different times rather than all at once so that your child has someone she knows well with her almost all the time.

COMING HOME

Depending on how long your child has been in the hospital, you may notice some changes in her habits. She probably woke up and went to sleep much earlier in hospital than she does at home, and these sleeping and waking patterns may continue for a while. She may resent the discipline at home after having been spoiled and indulged a little, and she may be reluctant to go back to school. The best approach to these things is to be tolerant, as your child will soon adapt to life at home again.

IMMUNIZATION

The incidence of potentially fatal childhood diseases such as diphtheria has declined dramatically since the introduction of vaccination programs, which provide immunity. Some vaccines are long-lasting (rubella), others need to be "boosted" at regular intervals (tetanus).

In the first five years, your child will need several immunizations: five DPT injections, one MMR injection, three or four Hib injections, one Varicella injection, and four polio immunizations. A vaccine against hepatitis B is also available. Children whose mothers have tested positive for hepatitis B antibodies should receive the first vaccination within 12 hours of birth, then at one, four, and six months. For other children, vaccination at two, four, and six months is optional. Vaccines do not provide instant protection against disease; in some cases, they take up to four weeks to be effective. Give acetaminophen elixir to ease any discomfort. More serious side effects or complications are very rare, but should be reported to your child's doctor.

IMPORTANCE OF IMMUNIZATION

Because immunization programs have been so successful, it is easy to forget how prevalent diseases like whooping cough and polio once were. Many first-time parents nowadays have never seen a child in leg braces – a common sight in their parents' generation when the possibility of paralysis or even death from polio was a very real one.

Immunization protects both individuals and whole communities from infectious diseases. Every child should therefore be properly immunized. Some parents are alarmed by stories about the side effects of vaccinations, but these are actually quite rare. Your child shouldn't be vaccinated, however, if she has a fever, or if she's had an unusually severe reaction to a previous dose of vaccine. Your child's doctor will advise you.

TETANUS INJECTIONS

There is a danger of tetanus with any deep penetrating wound. Tetanus bacteria thrive only where there is hardly any oxygen, so superficial wounds carry little risk. Tetanus bacteria and spores live in soil and manure, so it's dirty wounds that are dangerous. The bacteria produce a poison that attacks the nerves and brain, causing muscle spasm, particularly of the face – hence the common name lockjaw. Patients always require hospital treatment. Tetanus can be completely prevented by immunization. The first tetanus injection should be given at two months and boosters should be given at ten-yearly intervals up to a total of five doses. If your child has a dog bite or a deep, dirty cut and has not been immunized, she must have a tetanus injection right away.

VACCINE	PROTECTS AGAINST	COMMENTS
DTP.	Diphtheria, tetanus, and pertussis (whooping cough).	Five injections at 2, 4, 6, and 15–18 months, and at 4–6 years; tetanus and diphtheria at 11–12 years, and then every 10 years.
Inactivated polio vaccine (IPV).	Polio.	IPV injected at 2 and 4 months, then given by mouth at 6–18 months and at 4–6 years.
MMR.	Measles, mumps, and rubella.	Given at 15–18 months; a second dose may be given at 4–6 years.
Varicella (Var.).	Chicken pox.	Given at 12–18 months.
Hib.	The bacterium H. influenzae type B (can cause bacterial meningitis, severe croup, blood poisoning, and other infections).	Given at 2, 4, and 6 months.

COMMON COMPLAINTS

Any illness in a child is different from an adult illness. Childhood illnesses may become serious because the immune system is not fully developed until about one year and because complications can occur. On the other hand, children over one year normally have robust immune systems and recover well from common illnesses.

This section describes the most common childhood complaints, and gives advice on when your child should be seen by a doctor and what you can do at home. Try to become familiar with the material in these pages; it will help you avoid worry while taking prompt and appropriate action whenever your child complains of feeling ill.

EARS

Ear infections are common in children because their eustachian tubes are narrow and horizontal; this makes drainage poor and the tubes are easily blocked, leading to middle ear infections.

WAXY EAR

Ear wax is produced by glands in the outer ear canal and protects the ear from dust, foreign bodies, and infection. If wax accumulates and hardens, it can result in hearing loss. Although it's not usually serious, you should consult your child's doctor.

Symptoms Ear wax can become hard and compacted and cause impaired hearing, a ringing sound in the head, or a sensation of fullness in the outer ear. It may be possible to see the buildup of wax.

Treatment Ear drops may be effective. Drops are more likely to be used if the wax has formed a hard plug, as they will soften it, allowing it to come out overnight on soft cotton wool placed at the opening of the canal. You should never try to insert anything into your child's ear to try to clear wax, not even a fingernail or a cotton bud. They will only push the wax further into the canal or damage the lining of the ear.

OUTER EAR INFECTION

The passage leading to the eardrum from the ear flap can sometimes become infected as a result of excessive cleaning or scratching, the presence of a foreign body in the ear, or after swimming. This can be painful, but is not usually serious.

Symptoms Your child will complain of earache and her ear and outer ear passage may be red and tender. You may notice a puslike discharge from the ear, and a dry scaly appearance. A boil within the ear canal can also cause great pain.

Treatment Home treatment includes keeping the ear clean, giving acetaminophen elixir to relieve pain and keep the temperature down, and covering the ear with a cotton pad. Your doctor may prescribe antibiotics or ear drops. Any foreign body or boil in the ear must be dealt with by a doctor.

MIDDLE EAR INFECTION

Otitis media, or infection of the middle ear, is quite common in children. Until about age six, some children develop such infections with every cold or sniffle. Infections are caused by bacteria entering the middle ear from the nose and the throat via the eustachian tube. Untreated infections can result in permanent hearing loss. Recurrent middle ear infections are often linked with glue ear (see p.285).

Symptoms The most prominent symptoms are severe earache and loss of appetite. Your child may also have a fever or a discharge from the ear, and there may be some hearing loss. A baby with a middle ear infection may be distressed and pull and rub her ear. She may also have general symptoms such as loss of appetite, vomiting, and diarrhea.

Treatment The usual treatment is antibiotics and pain-relieving medication. At home, keep your child comfortable and cool and give lots of drinks as well as her medicines. The child should avoid getting water in the ear until the infection has cleared. Unless she feels very unwell, she can go to school; ear infections are not contagious.

GLUE EAR

If your child has repeated infections of the middle ear, the middle ear can gradually fill with jelly-like fluid. As the fluid cannot drain away through the eustachian tube, it becomes sticky and impairs hearing because the sounds are not being effectively transmitted across the middle ear to the inner ear, where they are actually heard. It's important to deal with glue ear promptly, especially when your child is learning to speak.

Symptoms Glue ear generally causes no pain, but partial hearing loss and a feeling of fullness deep in the ear may occur. A child with chronic glue ear may sleep with the mouth open, snore when asleep, and speak with a nasal twang. If glue ear is not treated it can cause permanent deafness, resulting in speech and learning problems.

Treatment The fluid may drain away if left for a few weeks. Your doctor may prescribe decongestants to help drainage. If the fluid does not clear, surgery may be recommended; in this operation, a tiny hole is made in the eardrum and the fluid is sucked out. Then a tympanostomy tube may be inserted; this tiny plastic tube allows air to circulate in the middle ear. Any fluid that forms can drain away through the tympanostomy tube and flow down the eustachian tube.

The tympanostomy tube usually falls out after a few months and the eardrum heals. Occasionally the tube has to be inserted again if the fluid reaccumulates. Doctors usually advise that children avoid getting their ears wet for the first six weeks after the operation, but after that they can usually do anything they like.

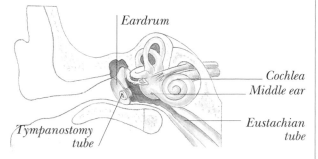

Tympanostomy tube
This is a tiny plastic tube that allows air to circulate in the middle ear. Any fluid that forms can drain away through the tube.

NOSE

A blocked nose, due to a cold, flu, or more rarely from an allergy, is quite common in childhood; so are minor nosebleeds. Neither is usually serious.

BLOCKED OR RUNNY NOSE

Excess mucus in the nose, which results in sniffling or a runny nose, is usually caused by a cold virus (see p.294). The mucous membranes lining the nasal passages become inflamed, swollen, and congested, and consequently block the nose. Other causes include allergic rhinitis (see pp.292–93) or a foreign body, like a bead, lodged in the nose (see p.343).

Symptoms The secretions produced by a cold virus usually start as clear and runny, but may be thick and yellow by the time the body's defenses attack the infection. Mucus from a sinus infection may be thick and yellowish-green.

Treatment Encourage your child to blow her nose frequently. Demonstrate how to do it, clearing one nostril first, and then the other. Be aware that many children do not master nose blowing until they are five or older. Consult your doctor if a runny nose persists for more than three days. Antibiotics may be prescribed for an infection such as sinusitis.

NOSEBLEED

Most nosebleeds can be stopped easily. If a nosebleed is severe, lasts more than 30 minutes, or follows a blow to the head, go to the doctor. Children's nosebleeds are often caused by nosepicking.

Symptoms The bleeding usually comes from tiny blood vessels on the inner side of the nostril. A clot may form in the nose; it shouldn't be removed.

Treatment Sit your child down with her head forward while you firmly squeeze the soft tissue of her nose. Keep applying pressure for about ten minutes or until bleeding has stopped. Your child shouldn't blow her nose for at least three hours after a nosebleed. Never put your child's head back, as she may swallow blood and become nauseated. If a nosebleed is severe, consult your child's doctor, who will probably pack the bleeding nostril with gauze.

THROAT

Throat infections such as tonsillitis and adenoiditis are rare in babies under one year. They are more common in children who have just started school and are being exposed to a new range of bacteria.

SORE THROAT

An uncomfortable or painful throat is usually due to infection by a bacterium such as streptococcus or a virus such as the cold viruses.

Symptoms Your child may tell you that her throat hurts, or you may notice that she finds it hard to swallow. Depress her tongue with a spoon handle and tell her to say "aaahhh" so you can look down her throat for signs of redness (inflammation) or enlarged red tonsils.

Treatment Give lots of drinks, and liquefy your child's food if she finds it difficult to swallow. Your doctor may prescribe an antibiotic if there is a bacterial infection or tonsillitis.

TONSILLITIS AND ADENOIDITIS

The tonsils, situated on both sides of the back of the throat, trap and kill bacteria that invade the throat, preventing them from entering the body. This can result in the tonsils themselves becoming swollen and infected. The adenoids, located at the back of the nose, may be affected at the same time.

Symptoms Your child will complain of a sore throat and may find swallowing difficult. On examination by a doctor, the tonsils appear red and enlarged, possibly with whitish patches. She may have a raised temperature, the glands in her neck may be swollen, and her breath might smell foul. If the adenoids are swollen, too, her speech may sound nasal.

Treatment Consult your doctor, who may take a throat swab and examine your child's ears and neck glands. The treatment for bacterial tonsillitis is a course of the appropriate antibiotic medication. Removal of the tonsils is considered after many severe recurrent attacks.

LARYNGITIS

An infection of the larynx, or voice box, may accompany any cold or sore throat. As long as it does not develop into severe croup (see p.296), laryngitis is rarely a serious condition.

Symptoms The most common symptoms are loss of voice or hoarseness. Your child may find it uncomfortable or painful to swallow, and may also have a dry cough and a mild fever. When it is severe, a child with laryngitis may develop a croupy cough (see p.296).

Treatment Most cases of laryngitis are short-lived. Your child should rest, preferably in a humid environment in which the air can circulate. Give her lots of fluids and encourage her to rest her voice. Make sure she doesn't overheat (see p.281) and should she have difficulty breathing (stridor) (see p.296), seek medical help as soon as possible.

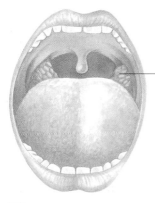

Whitish spots on tonsils

Tonsillitis
Swollen, infected tonsils cause a sore throat and difficulty in swallowing. Whitish spots may also appear on the tonsils.

LYMPH NODES

With a local infection, extra white blood cells are produced at the lymph nodes nearest the site of the infection to kill and mop up the bacteria. The production of white cells causes lymph glands to become inflamed and sore.

Swollen glands
Lymph nodes in front of the ear and below the angle of the jaw swell due to throat infections. To feel them run your fingers down your child's neck from a point just below her ears. Never push or prod.

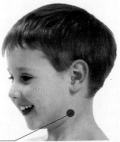

Lymph nodes

EYES

The most common childhood eye problems are infections or inflammations that can be cured with good hygiene, and sometimes antibiotic eye drops.

BLEPHARITIS

This is inflammation of the eyelid margins, found in conjunction with eczema and cradle cap, and usually recurring. It is not serious and can usually be alleviated with simple measures. Consult your doctor if your child's eyes become sticky or if the condition does not clear up within a week.

Symptoms The eyelid margins appear red, scaly, and inflamed, and you may notice tiny crusts of dried pus on your child's eyelashes.

Treatment Using a cotton wad dipped in warm water, wipe each eye from the nose outward. Use a fresh piece of cotton each time you wipe the eye. Bring it up with your pediatrician, who may prescribe eye drops or ointment for an infection.

CONJUNCTIVITIS (PINK EYE)

In this common eye complaint, the membrane covering the eyeball and lining the eyelids (the conjunctiva) becomes inflamed and red. The main causes of conjunctivitis are viral or bacterial infections, damage by a foreign body, and an allergic reaction. Infectious conjunctivitis is very contagious; if one eye is infected, the other may become infected, too.

Symptoms Inflammation causes pain on blinking, and your child may be uncomfortable in well-lighted rooms or bright daylight. When pink eye is caused by an infection, the eye will be sticky and there may be a crust of pus on the lower eyelid. Allergic conjunctivitis causes teary eyes and swollen eyelids.

Treatment Conjunctivitis can be treated by wiping the eye with saline solution or water. Even if only one eye is infected, both need to be treated because the infection is easily transferred from one to the other. When a foreign body is visible, try flushing it out with clear water. If that doesn't work and the particle doesn't wash out with tears, bring your child to the doctor, who may prescribe an antibiotic ointment or drops for an infection or anti-inflammatory drops and antihistamines for allergic conjunctivitis. Always seek medical advice for pink eye.

STYE

When the follicle of an eyelash becomes infected, a stye, or small abscess, develops on the margin of the eyelid. Rubbing the eyes may encourage styes to develop. A stye requires medical treatment because it's painful and may obscure vision.

Symptoms At first the eyelid appears red and a bit swollen, then the swelling fills with pus and the stye may protrude noticeably from the eyelid.

Treatment The swelling can be relieved temporarily with warm compresses; use a clean washcloth or cotton handkerchief and plain warm (not hot) water, holding it over the eye for a few minutes. A stye should be seen by a doctor, who may prescribe antibiotic ointment. Although styes are not as contagious as other eye infections, keep your child's washcloth and towel separate from the rest of the family's.

STRABISMUS (CROSSED EYES)

Your baby's eyes may appear to point in different directions, sometimes convergent (toward each other) and sometimes divergent (away from each other). Until the age of eight weeks, this is normal, but if the baby's eyes have not aligned by two months, your pediatrician may suggest taking your baby to an eye doctor. The usual causes of strabismus are an imbalance in the muscles of the eyes or one eye being farsighted and the other nearsighted.

Symptoms If you suspect that your baby has strabismus, observe how light is reflected in her eyes. It should be reflected from exactly the same place in each pupil; if it does not appear to, ask your baby's doctor to check.

Treatment Usually, the stronger eye is covered with a patch; this forces the muscles in the weaker eye to strengthen. The eyes should become aligned within about five months, though it can take longer. If the strabismus is related to far- or nearsightedness, your child will be prescribed glasses. When patching the eye is ineffective, surgery may be needed to adjust the muscles of the misaligned eye or eyes. It must occur before age six if normal depth perception is to develop. After that age, the surgery will improve the child's appearance only, not her vision.

MOUTH

Childhood mouth problems are generally minor; thrush is the only condition that needs immediate medical attention, since it does not respond to the usual home remedies. Your child may refuse food when his mouth is sore. Give him pureed bland foods that he can suck through a straw.

TEETHING PAIN

A child's teeth usually begin to come through at about six months and are complete by his third birthday (see p.175). During the period when the teeth are erupting, the gums may be red and swollen. Some children suffer terribly with teething while others take it in stride or seem not to notice it at all. The molars usually cause more discomfort than other teeth.

Symptoms If you touch the swollen, red gums you may feel a hard lump beneath them. Your baby will salivate and dribble much more than usual and will chew objects. He may have trouble sleeping and be more irritable and clingy than usual. He may also find eating painful.

The ring can be cooled in the refrigerator

Pain relief
Chewing on a cool teething ring – never frozen – rubbing the gums with your finger, and acetominophen elixir can ease the pain.

Treatment Don't think other symptoms, such as loss of appetite, fever, runny nose, or vomiting, are caused by teething. They never are. Consult your pediatrician if your baby seems very uncomfortable. She may recommend acetominophen elixir for the very bad times. More often, however, something cool but firm to chew on will provide relief.

MOUTH ULCERS

Open sores in the mouth occur inside the lower lip, although they are common on the tongue, gums, and inside the cheeks. They are usually caused by viruses, including herpes and coxsackie. They should go away by themselves in 10–14 days, but if they're recurrent or prevent eating, consult your doctor.

Symptoms All mouth ulcers are painful. Your child may have difficulty eating, especially food that is acidic or salty, and may refuse food.

Treatment Follow your pediatrician's advice. An anti-inflammatory cream may be prescribed or acetominophen elixir be given to relieve discomfort.

While the mouth feels sore, puree and liquefy your child's food, give him a straw to drink through, and avoid salty, acidic, or other strong tastes.

THRUSH

When the mucous membranes become infected by a fungus called *Candida albicans*, it is called thrush. The growth of candida is usually kept in check by the normal presence of bacteria, but when these bacteria are eradicated by antibiotics, candida begins to multiply unrestrictedly. (The antibiotic is used to kill a disease-causing bacterium, but "good bacteria," which help digestion and other body functions, are killed as well.) Alternatively, candida can be passed from a mother at the time of birth. Although thrush is not serious, it can cause a young baby discomfort while he is sucking or feeding.

When it infects the gastrointestinal tract and the anal area it is called candida or monilia (familiar to adult women as "yeast infection"). Candida is sometimes associated with diaper rash (see pp.110–11).

Symptoms Thrush produces white, curdlike patches on the gums, cheeks, tongue, and roof of the mouth. If you attempt to wipe them off, they become raw and may bleed. Around the anus, monilia appears as red spots or a rash. If your child has diaper rash as well, there may red, elevated spots.

Treatment Thrush can be treated quickly and simply with antifungal medications, in liquid form for oral and gastro intestinal infection and cream form for the anal and diaper areas. These are available only on prescription. Liquefied, bland, cold, or lukewarm foods are best if your child has oral thrush.

Fungi flourish in warm, moist conditions, so if your baby has monilia, you should keep him as dry as possible. Leave his bottom exposed to the air as much as you can and avoid plastic pants. Be meticulous about hygiene.

SKIN

Childhood skin complaints may be caused by an infection, an allergy, or a response to very high or very low temperatures. Most of them are minor and can easily be treated. Rashes occur with a variety of complaints, some of which are serious; if you are at all worried about a rash, you should consult your child's doctor.

CHAPPED SKIN

Chaps are little cracks in the skin, sometimes raw and deep. Exposure to the cold makes skin dry and prone to chapping, particularly at the extremities where circulation is poor – hands, fingers, and ears. Damp skin around the lips chaps, too. Failing to dry properly after washing and washing so frequently that the skin's natural oils are removed can both contribute to chapping.

Symptoms Chapped skin has a dry, cracked appearance. If the cracks are deep, there may be some bleeding and pain, and if they become infected, you may notice pus and inflammation.

Treatment Unless chapped skin becomes infected or is very slow to heal, you can probably solve the problem with home remedies. Apply rich emollient creams to your child's skin, use lip balm on his lips, avoid using soap (use baby lotion instead), and dress him warmly in cold weather. Avoid icy winds and sudden changes in temperature. Infected chapped skin should be treated by your child's doctor.

COLD SORES

The virus responsible for cold sores is called herpes simplex and is a relative of chicken pox and shingles. All sufferers from cold sores carry the virus in their skin, where it lies dormant in the nerve endings. Some children have a single attack of the virus; in others, however, cold sores come and go for years. The virus is transmitted through close contact. A rise in skin temperature due to intense sunlight, flu, a cold, stress, or overexertion can reactivate the virus and result in a cold sore. Cold sores are not usually harmful, except near the eye, where they can cause ulceration of the conjunctiva (the transparent covering of the white of the eye and inner eyelids).

Symptoms There is usually warning of an attack in the form of a hot, itchy, tingling sensation for 24 hours before the cold sore appears. The skin becomes red and then tiny blisters appear, usually around the lips or the nostrils. The blisters enlarge, join up, and then burst, revealing the classic cold sore. Fluid from the blisters forms a crust, which gradually shrinks and falls off as the skin underneath heals. This takes 10–14 days. While a cold sore is at the blister and weeping stage, it will be very painful and your child may complain of pain over the whole side of the face, earache, and pain on chewing because the facial nerves are inflamed by the virus.

Cold sores are very contagious, and your child can spread them to other parts of his face by touching them with his fingers.

Treatment Your pharmacist can recommend or your doctor may prescribe an antibiotic cream if the cold sore becomes infected. Discourage your child from touching his face, kissing other children, and sharing his washcloth and towel for the duration of a cold-sore attack. Applying petroleum jelly may prevent a cold sore from cracking and bleeding.

It's helpful to identify the triggers that bring on cold-sore attacks. For instance, if it is sun, your child should wear a high SPF sunblock around his lips during the summer and a brimmed hat.

SUNBURN

Babies and children are extremely vulnerable to sunburn, which can result after what might seem to be a brief exposure to the sun. Sunlight is strongest between 10:00 A.M. and 2:00 P.M., and the danger of overexposure exists even during the winter and on overcast days.

Babies under six months should be kept out of direct sunlight and protected by clothing, brimmed bonnets, and canopies on their strollers or carriages. After six months of age, protect your child with a waterproof and fragrance-free sunscreen rated SPF 15 or greater, clothing, and hats with brims.

In the near term, a sunburn can be painful and excessive sun exposure can lead to heatstroke (see page 340). In the long term, severe sunburns and repeated sun exposure can develop into skin cancer later in life, particularly in fair-skinned people.

Symptoms The affected skin is hot, inflamed, red, and tender. Sometimes the skin looks "bubbly" and blistered. After a few days, the dead skin will flake and peel, at which point your child may complain of itchiness. If sunburn is severe, particularly on the back of the neck, look out for symptoms of heat-stroke: fever, vomiting, and dizziness, and if they are present, seek medical help immediately.

Treatment Immediate relief can come from apply-ing cool, wet sheets or towels to the affected areas. Acetaminophen elixir may also be helpful to keep your child's temperature normal. Treat sunburned skin very gently; let your child go without clothes indoors; if he is going outdoors, dress him in loose-fitting clothes and apply a high SPF (15 or above) sunscreen to all exposed areas. A hat that covers the nape of the neck should be worn. Your child's doctor may prescribe an anti-inflammatory cream for sunburn. Do not apply any creams or lotions unless the doctor advises it.

BOILS

When a hair follicle becomes infected, a red, pus-filled swelling can result. Boils are rarely serious if they are treated appropriately, but they can cause pain, particularly if they are in the armpit or but-tocks. Boils rarely heal by themselves, and can form a carbuncle – a cluster of boils with many heads.

Symptoms Initially the skin is red and swollen. As yellow pus collects beneath the skin, the swelling increases. Boils usually appear singly, but because hair follicles are so close together, it's possible for infection to spread and for a crop of boils to appear.

Treatment Consult your pediatrician if your child has a boil. The doctor may prescribe an antibiotic and/or warm soaks, or may lance the boil to drain the pus away, which provides immediate pain relief. Crops of boils require antibiotics and investigation of the cause. Don't try to squeeze a boil at home; this will spread infection and be very painful.

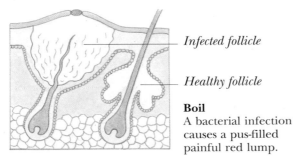

Infected follicle

Healthy follicle

Boil
A bacterial infection causes a pus-filled painful red lump.

IMPETIGO

The bacteria streptococcus and staphylococcus, which are present in the nose and on the skin, can cause a skin infection around the nose, mouth, ears, and elsewhere. Impetigo is characterized by a bright yellow, crusted rash or small pus-filled blisters; it is highly contagious, so you should keep your child away from school until it has been treated.

Symptoms The first sign of impetigo is reddened skin. This is followed by the appearance of blisters full of pus; when they burst they leave patches of oozing skin. The fluid dries into a yellow crust. Impetigo spreads rapidly if left untreated.

Treatment Take your child to see the doctor, who will prescribe an oral or cream antibiotic and dress-ings to keep the skin covered. Be meticulous about hygiene – wash away crusted areas with warm water and pat dry with a paper towel. Use disposable wash-cloths and towels to protect the rest of the family from infection.

DERMATITIS

This is an inflammation of the skin that occurs in response to stress, to contact with something that the child is allergic to (contact dermatitis), or very occasionally to light (photodermatitis). Seborrheic dermatitis affects the face, especially the nostrils, eyebrows and eyelids, ear canal, and scalp – all areas where there are a lot of sebaceous glands.

Symptoms Dermatitis is a red, itchy, and scaly rash, sometimes with blisters. In contact dermatitis, the rash usually appears where the skin has been in con-tact with the allergen. Photodermatitis appears as clusters of spots or blisters on skin that has been exposed to the sun. Seborrheic dermatitis shows up as yellowish as well as red scales.

Treatment If dermatitis is severe, the doctor may prescribe a weak steroid cream and, for seborrheic dermatitis, a special shampoo. Keep the affected areas clean and do not scrub or rub. Gentle cleans-ing with a nondrying soap is best. Discourage scratch-ing and keep your child's fingernails trimmed.

INFANTILE ECZEMA

This inflammatory skin condition is caused by an inherited tendency plus a trigger factor such as an infection or an allergy. Occasionally it is simply a

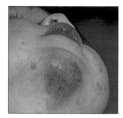

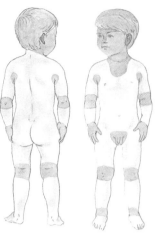

Affected area
Atopic eczema (above) typically occurs on the face, hands, neck, ankles, and knee and elbow creases. The gray areas indicate the usual sites of seborrheic dermatitis.

response to stress. The type of eczema that usually affects children is atopic eczema, and it appears between 2 and 18 months of age. Children who have atopic eczema may tend also to have seborrheic dermatitis (see p.290).

Symptoms Skin affected by atopic eczema is raw, dry, scaly, red, and itchy, and there may be small white blisters, like grains of rice, that burst and weep if scratched. Itchiness is the most irritating symptom of eczema, driving your child to scratch and causing sleeplessness.

Treatment If you suspect your child has eczema, see your pediatrician, who may prescribe an anti-inflammatory cream and antihistamines in order to curb the itching and to combat any allergy. If the skin has become infected, antibiotics may be necessary. The doctor will also try to identify the cause of the eczema: a pet, laundry detergent, or a particular food or group of foods, for example.

Keep contact with water to a minimum. When you do bathe your child, put baby oil in the bath. Stop using soap, and make sure that your child's clothes are thoroughly rinsed and contain no trace of laundry detergent or fabric softener. Minimize your child's contact with potential allergens, use emollient cream on his skin, and keep his fingernails short so that he cannot damage the skin by scratching. Use cotton fabrics, never wool.

HEAT RASH

A hot, poorly ventilated environment in which the skin can't cool encourages heat rash; the body responds by sweating excessively and the sweat glands

become enlarged and red. Heat rash is quite common in babies as their sweat glands are immature and can't switch off as ours can.

Symptoms A faint red rash appears on parts of the body that get hot easily and where sweat glands are most numerous. Typical areas include the neck, the face, and skin folds such as the groin, elbows, and behind the knees.

Treatment Don't overdress or swaddle your baby. Bathe him in tepid water and pat him dry, leaving his skin slightly damp. Be sure the temperature of his room is not too high and keep air circulating by opening a window. Consult your child's doctor only if the rash has not cleared up after 12 hours, to exclude other possible causes.

WARTS (VERRUCAE)

Warts may occur singly or in great numbers. They are caused by viruses; most disappear without treatment after two years. There are more than 30 types of wart virus. Children usually get warts on the hands or areas subject to injury, such as the knees, and on the soles of the feet (plantar warts). Although mildly contagious, warts are not at all serious.

Symptoms Common warts, such as those found on the hands, appear as firm, flesh-colored or brown growths. They are composed of dead skin cells. Although they may look unsightly, common warts

---

RASHES

Infectious diseases like chickenpox, German measles, or measles, as well as allergies and blood disorders may all cause rashes.

A rash may be confined to one area or appear all over the body; it may be, blotchy, flat, or bumpy; it may disappear on pressure or not; and it may contain blisters. If your child has a rash, check to see if he has a fever (this may indicate an infectious disease), and consider whether he has been exposed to any potential allergens (see p.292). An itchy rash between his fingers may indicate scabies.

A rash that doesn't disappear on pressure, such as purpura, is nearly always serious and can result from a fault in the blood clotting mechanism or from bacterial toxins, as in meningitis. Such rashes should be seen by a doctor immediately.

Although they may look unsightly, common warts should not be painful unless cracked and bleeding. The flat plantar warts, however, may be very painful because of the pressure on the foot.

Treatment Unless warts are painful or unsightly, don't worry since they may disappear spontaneously. They are not very contagious, so the risk of their being passed on to other children is minimal. If you do decide to treat a wart at home, use one of several products available over the counter in pharmacies. Never use these on the face or the genitals, as they are too harsh and can scar delicate skin. If you consult your doctor, he may refer your child to a dermatologist to have the warts removed. If you notice warts or bumps on your child's genitals, consult your pediatrician right away.

ALLERGIES

An allergy is an abnormal response of the immune system to a specific chemical or substance. The most common form is hay fever – an allergy to pollen – but children may be allergic to a range of things, from foods and plants to light and drugs.

Allergies can develop at any age, and it is not uncommon to grow out of childhood allergies. The tendency to allergies sometimes runs in families, though one family member might be allergic to one thing – a food, for example – while another is bothered by pollen. Often a child will be allergic to more than one substance. With food, in particular, it is important to distinguish between an intolerance (the inability of the digestive system to process the food) and a true allergy. Your child's doctor can help determine whether and to what your child is allergic. Although various tests for allergies are available, they are rarely done on young children as they are time-consuming and uncomfortable. It is preferable to avoid the suspected substance or substances and, if the allergy persists into adolescence, do testing and give desensitizing injections at that age.

A very severe form of allergic response, called anaphylaxis, is potentially life-threatening. It can be brought on by a reaction to an insect bite, drug, or food. Call 911 or bring your child to an emergency room immediately if he shows signs of severe dizziness, difficulty breathing, profuse sweating, and cloudy consciousness.

URTICARIA (HIVES)

An allergic skin rash that takes the form of itchy, raised red blotches with white centers, urticaria is usually the result of an allergy. Histamine (a chemical found in cells throughout the body) is released in response to contact with an allergen and causes fluid to leak into the skin from the blood vessels, leading to the typical weal.

Named after the nettle plant (*urtica*), urticaria may in fact arise if skin comes in contact with a nettle plant. Once your child is mobile, check your yard for this weed and remove any plants you find.

Symptoms The skin is extremely itchy and there are raised white lumps (weals) surrounded by a flare of inflammation. The weals are small and circular or large irregular patches. The rash usually appears on the limbs and the trunk, although it can appear anywhere on the body. Urticaria lasts a few minutes to a few hours, disappears, and then reappears at a different site. If it is accompanied by facial swelling (angioedema), consult your doctor without delay. Occasionally hives occur on the mouth, tongue, and throat, causing difficulties with breathing (anaphylaxis). This should be treated as an emergency.

Treatment Apply calamine lotion to your child's skin or give her a coolish bath. Your doctor may prescribe antihistamine tablets.

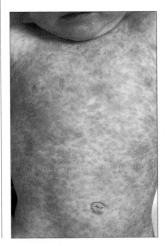

Urticaria rash
Raised white lumps form, surrounded by inflammation. Sometimes these join together forming large patches on the skin.

HAY FEVER
(ACUTE ALLERGIC RHINITIS)

When the mucous membranes are exposed to an allergen they may become swollen and the child suffers the symptoms of allergic rhinitis (see below). It usually occurs in the spring and summer months, when the pollen count is high. Pollens from hay and grasses are potential allergens, but so are trees and certain flowering plants. Hay fever is relatively unusual under the age of five, it tends to run in families, and it may disappear spontaneously.

Symptoms These include sneezing, a runny nose, and red, itchy, watery eyes. Unlike a common cold, hay fever is seasonal and causes no fever.

Treatment Your child will inevitably be exposed to the allergen unless you keep her indoors in the summer. Pollen counts are usually lower in the morning and after rain; it may be practical to schedule outdoor time accordingly. During "allergy" season, the pollen count may be broadcast on the news.

Your child's doctor may prescribe an antihistamine and a steroid nasal spray to relieve symptoms if they are severe. The doctor may also arrange for skin tests to identify the particular pollen causing the symptoms and may prescribe a course of desensitizing injections.

CHRONIC ALLERGIC RHINITIS

Chronic allergic rhinitis is just like hay fever, but happens all year round and the usual culprit is the house-dust mite rather than pollen. Other causes are feathers and cat and dog fur.

Symptoms The symptoms of chronic allergic rhinitis are the same as those of hay fever. Your child's doctor will be able to diagnose it.

Treatment The most effective treatment is avoidance of the allergen or allergens. You may have to get rid of a favorite pet, change bedding, or vacuum the carpets frequently.

Antihistamines and other drugs help prevent symptoms occurring. Steroid sprays, given in very small, safe doses, often bring rapid relief.

PHOTOSENSITIVITY

This condition is an allergy to light, or rather to certain wavelengths of light. A very rare form is in-herited, but more commonly photosensitivity is caused by ingesting a photosensitizing substance or applying it to the skin. Examples of such substances are some medications, dyes, chemicals, and plants. It is not uncommon to have a photosensitive reaction to the perfumes used in soaps and sunscreens. If your child has photosensitive skin, she should use unscented products.

Symptoms Photosensitivity usually shows as a rash that is easily distinguishable because skin areas covered by clothes are free of inflammation, and a clear line demarcates skin that has been exposed to sun.

Treatment The photosensitizer and/or sunlight should be avoided until the rash clears. A susceptible child should cover up well and always wear high SPF sunscreens when outdoors.

FLEA BITES

Children quite often get one flea bite, develop an allergy to it, and then break out in a crop of spots that resemble the first bite. These spots may be mistaken for more bites but are in fact an allergic rash, which is very itchy but will subside in 10–14 days.

Treatment The family cat or dog has to be sprayed for fleas. Also, spray any carpets or soft furnishings, which may harbor flea eggs. The doctor may prescribe an antihistamine to relieve the itching.

DRUGS

The most common drug allergy is to penicillin or any of its derivatives. Once diagnosed, your child should wear a bracelet or medallion stating he is allergic to penicillin so that he won't be given it again. Any drug at any time, however, can cause an allergy, particularly if there's a family history of allergies, eczema, and asthma. A severe drug reaction may result in anaphylaxis, a potentially life-threatening emergency (see p.292).

Symptoms A rash appears up to ten days after exposure to the drug, possibly with swelling of the face and tongue. In severe cases, there may be problems with breathing, vomiting, and diarrhea; seek immediate medical attention.

Treatment Stop using the drug immediately. For mild allergies, antihistamines are usually sufficient. Once a drug is identified as an allergen it should be avoided for life.

COLDS AND INFLUENZA

Infections with cold or flu viruses are common in childhood because children have not yet developed immunity to specific viruses. There are roughly 200 cold viruses producing similar symptoms – your child will never get the same cold twice.

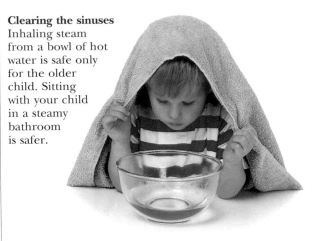

Clearing the sinuses
Inhaling steam from a bowl of hot water is safe only for the older child. Sitting with your child in a steamy bathroom is safer.

COMMON COLD

Colds are not serious unless your baby is very young, or a complication such as bronchitis (see opposite) sets in. Colds are also frequent when your child starts nursery school, because she's suddenly exposed to lots of new viruses.

Symptoms Most cold viruses start with "catarrhal" symptoms (stuffy or runny nose, cough, sore throat), fever, and listlessness. The nasal discharge is first clear and then thick and yellow as the body's defenses take over. The rise in temperature that accompanies a cold can cause cold sores (see p.289), hence their name.

Treatment Only symptoms can be treated, not the virus itself; there's no cure for the common cold. If a secondary infection such as sinusitis or bronchitis develops, your child's doctor will prescribe antibiotics; otherwise, home remedies suffice. Give your child plenty of fluids, and apply petroleum jelly to her nostrils and top lip if they become sore or chapped. When congestion is severe, ensure that she sleeps with her head propped up with pillows and stay with her for brief periods in a bathroom made steamy by running a hot shower. You may carefully use nose drops if a blocked nose interferes with sleeping or feeding. Other symptomatic remedies include acetaminophen elixir to reduce the temperature and to treat aches and pains.

SINUSITIS

The sinuses are cavities in the bones around the nose and cheeks and above the eyes that are lined with mucous membranes. Mucus usually drains from them into the nose. Sinusitis occurs when drainage is impaired, usually during a bout of a cold or flu, and a bacterial infection results, or if an infection spreads to the sinuses from the throat.

Symptoms Nasal secretions are clear and runny at first with a cold. A change to a thick, yellow discharge is normal, but if it is persistent (lasting 10–14 days), sinusitis has probably developed. Other symptoms include a feeling of fullness and discomfort around the top of the nose, headache, diminished sense of smell, stuffy nose, and sometimes fever.

Treatment Sinusitis can be treated with antibiotics. At home, keep the atmosphere humid, including brief periods in a steamy bathroom, and treat facial and forehead pain with acetaminophen elixir.

INFLUENZA

This is a specific viral infection similar to the common cold but with more severe symptoms. Influenza can be very debilitating; it is serious because it can weaken the body, making the ears, sinuses, and chest vulnerable to secondary infections by bacteria.

Symptoms Flu symptoms resemble cold symptoms, but in addition to the usual sore throat, runny nose, and cough, your child will have quite a high temperature, a headache, and muscle aches, and she may complain of feeling hot, cold, and shivery. She will be lethargic and weak, and may feel nauseated.

Treatment The only remedies for flu are symptomatic ones. Let your child rest in a warm and well-ventilated room, and give her acetaminophen elixir and plenty of fluids. Take your child's temperature regularly – if it fails to come down or if other symptoms develop, such as persistant nasal discharge, earache, or chesty cough, call your pediatrician. Sinusitis or an ear infection requires medical treatment, usually an antibiotic.

CHEST INFECTIONS

In very young children the air passages – the sinuses, ear, nose, and throat – are all one system because the tubes are so short. A chest infection can develop from an infection elsewhere in the upper respiratory tract. Chest infections are always serious. The airways may become so narrow that breathing is impaired and pneumonia may develop. If your child's breathing is ever labored, you should seek medical help immediately.

COUGHS

The cough is a reflex action that clears the throat of any irritant such as mucus, food, dust, or smoke. A cough may be due to the irritation of a cold, sore throat, tonsillitis, sinusitis, or chest infection. The cause should always be evaluated since a cough is merely a symptom of an underlying condition.

Symptoms There are two types of cough: a productive cough, in which mucus is produced, and a nonproductive cough, in which there is no mucus. The first has a "wet" sound, whereas the second is dry and hacking. Both will prevent sleep. In a small baby, mucus running down the back of the throat can cause vomiting. A cough may also be a nervous symptom, though rarely in a child younger than four. If a cough is hacking or croaking, your child may have croup (see p.296). Coughing can be so distressing that it causes vomiting.

Treatment If you suspect that your child has croup (see p. 296) or asthma (see pp.260–63), you should seek medical help right away. An underlying acute infection like sinusitis or tonsillitis should be treated separately. As long as they don't stop your child from sleeping or eating, most other coughs can be treated at home. Discourage your child from running around, as breathlessness may bring on a coughing fit, and get her to lie on her stomach or side at night; this keeps mucus from running down the throat. Give your child plenty of warm drinks, and if she is coughing up lots of mucus, lay her over your lap and pat her on the back. Suppress a dry cough, but never suppress a productive cough.

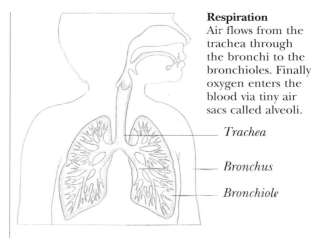

Respiration
Air flows from the trachea through the bronchi to the bronchioles. Finally oxygen enters the blood via tiny air sacs called alveoli.

Trachea

Bronchus

Bronchiole

BRONCHITIS AND BRONCHIOLITIS

The larger airways in the lungs are the bronchi and the smaller are the bronchioles. Bronchitis or bronchiolitis occurs when a viral infection causes the linings of these airways to swell and mucus to build up. The two can appear the same. Bronchiolitis, most common in babies and very young children, is more serious because it can cause severe breathing difficulties and pneumonia. Bronchitis is not usually serious in children over a year old.

Symptoms The symptoms of bronchiolitis are a cough and breathlessess, which may lead to difficulty feeding. Your child may have a raised temperature and may wheeze. He is pale and seems quite ill. There may be indrawing of the chest in the struggle to get air into the lungs; the lips and tongue may appear blue. The symptoms of bronchitis are a dry cough that develops into a cough producing green or yellow phlegm, labored breathing, raised temperature, and possibly loss of appetite. If phlegm is swallowed your child may vomit it up. If his illness worsens, possibly with difficulty breathing, severe infection or pneumonia may be present.

Treatment If you suspect that your child has a lung infection, call the doctor, who will prescribe antibiotics as necessary. Labored breathing and a gray or blue complexion may be treated in the hospital; your child will be put on oxygen to help her breathe.

Keep your child warm and rested, give plenty of fluids, and encourage her to cough up the mucus. If she has a fever, sponge her with tepid water (see p.281) and give her acetaminophen elixir to keep her temperature down. Don't give a child a cough suppressant as it is important to bring up the mucus.

PNEUMONIA

This is an inflammation of the lungs caused by a virus or bacterium. Your child will be ill for two reasons: first because of the bacterial or viral toxins, and second because the affected lung is out of action. The initial cause of pneumonia is often a cold or flu. Conditions like asthma, cystic fibrosis, whooping cough, and measles increase the risk of pneumonia. Pneumonia is always serious, and small children are often treated in the hospital because supplemental oxygen may be needed.

Symptoms Pneumonia usually starts with a fever and cough and your child may be breathless. He may look pale and unwell and seem lethargic. His breathing may be rapid and shallow.

Treatment Labored breathing is always a reason for you to seek medical advice urgently. You should consult your child's doctor right away if you suspect your child has pneumonia. The doctor will prescribe antibiotics and may decide that immediate hospitalization is necessary if your child is in need of oxygen therapy.

CROUP

When a small child's air passages become inflamed and congested as a result of an infection, breathing can be difficult and croup can result. The croup sound is made when air is drawn in through a swollen and narrowed larynx, usually as a result of a viral infection. Croup usually occurs between the ages of one and four. It can appear suddenly: your apparently well child will wake in the night with croup.

Symptoms The predominant symptom is a barking cough, accompanied by hoarseness and by noisy breathing known as stridor. In severe cases your child may be fighting for breath and her face may turn gray or blue. Attacks most often occur at night and usually last for a number of hours.

Treatment Stay calm. If your child is upset, her breathing will become even more labored. Make sure the air around your child is moist – take her to the bathroom and run hot water in the shower to create steam, sit with her near an open window, or take her outdoors, if practical.

If your child's face turns blue, you must get medical help immediately. Even if croup is mild, you should still report it to your child's doctor.

PARASITES

Parasites are very contagious, so if your child has lice or worms the whole family should be treated. Always inform your child's nursery, playgroup, or school of the infestation and keep your child home until it clears. Ticks are not parasites, but they may carry diseases and so are more serious.

LICE

Head lice are common in children of school age. The louse is a small insect that lives on the scalp, lays eggs (nits), and cements them to the base of the hairs. Nits become visible as the hair grows. Contrary to the belief that lice are a sign of uncleanliness, head lice prefer clean hair.

Symptoms Your child will complain of an itchy scalp, which feels worse in hot weather. You may see grayish white eggs firmly attached to the hair near the scalp.

Treatment Wash the hair and saturate it with conditioner while damp. Comb the hair thoroughly for 20 minutes with a nit comb, cleaning the comb after each stroke. Rinse and dry the hair. Repeat this treatment every two or three days until the hair is clear of nits; this will take at least two weeks. Alternatively wash your child's hair in insecticidal shampoo. The whole family should be treated.

Louse and nit
The adult louse lays its eggs (nits) at the root of the hair (right). The eggs become firmly attached and hatch after about two weeks unless they are removed by combing or the hair is treated with insecticidal shampoo.

Adult louse

SCABIES

This is an infestation by a microscopic mite that burrows into the skin and lays eggs. Although not serious, it can be very itchy, especially at night, and it's highly contagious. A child can get scabies by physical contact with someone suffering from scabies or from infested bedding.

Symptoms The backs of the hands, finger clefts, feet, ankles, and toes are affected by an intensely itchy rash. Burrows are usually visible as gray, scaly trails across the skin with a black pinhead spot (the mite) at the end.

Treatment Your child's doctor will probably prescribe a lotion to treat scabies. This should be left on for four hours and the treatment repeated after a day. The whole family should be treated.

Mites can live independently of human skin for up to six days, so you should wash all clothes and bed linen to prevent reinfection.

Scabies mite
The mite burrows into the skin and the opening of the burrow is visible as a gray, scaly swelling. The classic site of the rash is between the fingers. The mite may be visible as a dark spot at the head of the burrow.

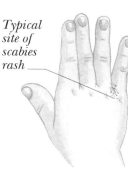

Typical site of scabies rash

PINWORM

Pinworms are extremely common in children, but are not serious. They are passed along due to poor hand washing and hygiene. The child ingests worm eggs, which, when they hatch, cause itchiness around the anus. A child who scratches may transfer eggs to the mouth and begin the cycle again (see below).

Symptoms The most distressing symptom is the itchiness around the anal area, which feels worse at night. Tiny white worms may be visible in the stools.

Cycle of infestation
Pinworms enter the body through the mouth and lay eggs around the anus. A child can become re-infested by scratching the anus, then transferring the eggs to her mouth.

Eggs are passed from the anus to the mouth via the fingers

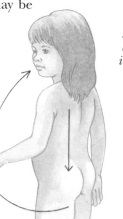

Eggs are swallowed and hatch into larvae inside the intestines

Female worms lay eggs around the anus at night, causing itching

Treatment Your pediatrician will prescribe a medication for the whole family. Pay attention to hygiene: encourage hand washing after using the toilet, keep your child's fingernails short, and get her to wear underpants in bed to discourage scratching.

TICKS

Two kinds of ticks are cause for concern. The deer tick may carry Lyme disease and the wood tick may carry Rocky Mountain spotted fever, which despite its name is more common in the eastern U.S.

You may see a wood tick on your child as it is about ¼ inch in diameter. The deer tick is tiny and often falls off without being seen. If you spot a tick on your child, remove it (see p.341). If symptoms develop, bring your child to the doctor.

Symptoms The symptoms of Rocky Mountain spotted fever are fever, headache, and muscle pain. A raised but nonitchy rash appears on the wrists and ankles, eventually spreading to the, trunk, and face. The first sign of Lyme disease is a characteristic bull's-eye rash that appears 7–14 days after the bite. It begins as a red dot at the site of the bite and spreads outward; usually the center of the circle clears as the rash enlarges. Not everyone gets the rash, however. In addition to, or instead of the rash, flulike symptoms develop. These may go away after a week or so, but fatigue may linger for some time. If untreated, Lyme disease may later lead to nerve and heart problems and a type of severe arthritis.

Treatment Both Rocky Mountain spotted fever and Lyme disease can be treated with antibiotics that your child's doctor will prescribe.

PREVENTING TICK INFECTIONS

Although Lyme disease and Rocky Mountain spotted fever can be treated successfuly, prevention is still the best approach.

When your child is outdoors – especially in the spring, in areas where Lyme disease or Rocky Mountain spotted fever have been reported, and when in woods and grassy areas – dress her in light-colored clothing (this makes it easier to see any ticks) with socks, long pants, and long-sleeved shirts. Check your child's clothes and body carefully at least once a day and remove any ticks you see (see p.341). Use insect repellent cautiously.

STOMACH AND ABDOMEN

Babies are affected by few of the conditions that cause abdominal pain in adults, like gallstones and peptic ulcers. Several causes of abdominal pain in infants are, however, potentially very serious; call the doctor immediately if a child with abdominal pain is distressed or if a temperature, diarrhea, or vomiting accompanies the pain.

Tension at home, between parents, between siblings, or at school can cause a child to feel nauseated, vomit, and suffer abdominal pain. When other causes have been eliminated, stress should be considered. Your child's doctor can advise.

COLIC

This type of crying usually occurs in the first four months of life, then clears spontaneously without treatment. It's thought to be due to spasm of the intestines, though there is no proof of this and the cause is unknown. The condition is very distressing though the baby is in no danger.

Symptoms A baby who is otherwise well will have bouts of crying in which he screams and draws his legs up toward his abdomen.

Treatment No drugs are needed. The baby may be soothed by any rhythmic activity such as rocking, swaying, being taken in the car for a ride, or being laid on his tummy on your lap while you rhythmically pat his back.

Often, nothing will calm a colicky baby. The important thing is to remain relaxed yourself. Since colic often occurs at the same time each day, typically in the evening, it may help to plan your day accordingly to reduce the stress on you.

GASTROENTERITIS

A general term for an inflammation of the stomach and intestine for various known or unknown causes. It may be due to contaminated food (by salmonella, for example), other types of bacterial or viral infection, or the toxins they produce (as with *E. coli*), or food intolerance, spicy foods, and antibiotics.

Gastroenteritis causes diarrhea and vomiting; pain is a lesser symptom. The complaint is extremely common and fairly mild. It rarely lasts for longer than three days, and the child tends to recover without any specific treatment other than replacement of fluid and minerals. A small baby, however, cannot tolerate dehydration, and if he vomits or has diarrhea for longer than 6–12 hours, you should contact your pediatrician without delay.

Symptoms The first symptom is poor appetite; this is followed by vomiting and possibly diarrhea.

Treatment Mild cases can be treated at home with a doctor's advice, though if vomiting or diarrhea continue, the child may have to be treated in a hospital, where fluids will be given intravenously.

INTUSSUSCEPTION

In this rare condition affecting babies, the intestine telescopes on itself, forming a tube within a tube, usually causing a blockage, which is very serious. It's most common at the junction of the small and large intestines. The cause is unknown.

Symptoms Your baby may scream intermittently and draw up his legs. There may be vomiting and diarrhea and he may pass blood and mucus. His abdomen may be swollen and he may become dehydrated. The condition may be complicated by a ruptured bowel and peritonitis (inflammation of the lining of the abdomen) if left untreated.

Treatment Intussusception must be treated by a doctor. Sometimes passing air into the bowel causes the intussusception to unfold. If it doesn't, then in practically all cases surgery is successful. In severe cases, a segment of bowel may have to be cut out.

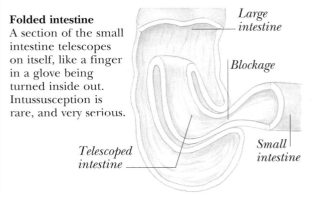

Folded intestine
A section of the small intestine telescopes on itself, like a finger in a glove being turned inside out. Intussusception is rare, and very serious.

Large intestine

Blockage

Telescoped intestine

Small intestine

APPENDICITIS

Inflammation of the appendix, a small, fingerlike sac at the junction of the cecum and the ileum in the small bowel, is a common cause of abdominal pain. The cause is not known, but it may be obstruction by a small piece of feces or very occasionally by pinworms. The appendix becomes inflamed, swollen, and infected. Appendicitis is not a serious condition as long as it is diagnosed early. However, if the symptoms are mistaken for something else, such as constipation, and there is any delay in treatment, the appendix can burst, and an abscess or even peritonitis (inflammation of the abdominal lining) can result.

Symptoms The first symptom is pain around the navel that, after a few hours, shifts to the right lower side of the abdomen, where it becomes intense. The child may have a slight temperature and refuse food. The tongue may become coated and there may be vomiting, diarrhea, or constipation.

Treatment Consult your child's doctor without delay. The appendix must be removed before it ruptures. If this is not done soon enough, it will perforate and cause an internal abscess. The abscess must then be drained and the appendix removed after treatment with large doses of antibiotics.

Site of pain
The first symptom of appendicitis is a slight ache in the navel area. This develops into a sharper, more localized pain, which is usually most intense in the lower right-hand side of the abdomen.

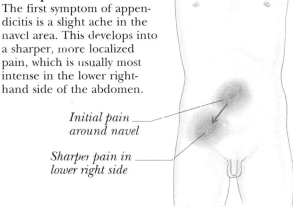

Initial pain around navel

Sharper pain in lower right side

TYPE OF PAIN	OTHER SYMPTOMS	CAUSE
Sudden pain causing your baby to scream and draw his legs up.	*Common in babies under four months.*	*Colic (see opposite).*
Crippling abdominal pain that causes your baby to scream.	*Blood and mucus in the stools and vomiting.*	*Intussusception (see opposite).*
General abdominal pain.	*Vomiting and diarrhea.*	*Gastroenteritis (see opposite).*
Severe pain near the navel that moves toward the lower right of the abdomen.	*Normal to low-grade fever, refusal of food, vomiting.*	*Appendicitis (see above).*
Generalized stomachache.	*Anxiety, clinginess, tearfulness, aggression, and nausea.*	*Stress (see introduction opposite).*
Sudden crippling pain in the lower abdomen.	*Swelling and pain in the scrotum.*	*Torsion of the testis (see p.301).*
Generalized stomachache.	*Sore throat, nasal congestion, and slight fever.*	*Throat infection (see p.286) or common cold (see p.294)*
Dull abdominal ache extending around into the back or down into the groin.	*Pain on urinating, bedwetting when previously dry, and, rarely, blood in the urine.*	*Urinary tract infection (see p.300).*

UROGENITAL COMPLAINTS

Symptoms such as painful urination or blood in the urine may be due to a bladder infection, a kidney disorder, or in rare cases an injury. Correct diagnosis is important in all urinary tract and genital complaints so they don't become chronic.

URINARY TRACT INFECTION

The urinary tract consists of the kidneys, where urine is produced from water and waste products; the ureters, which carry urine from the kidneys to the bladder; the bladder, which stores urine; and the urethra, which carries urine away from the bladder. The female urethra is much shorter than the male urethra, so bacteria entering the female urethra have a much shorter distance to travel to the bladder, increasing the likelihood of infection.

A common cause of urinary tract infections is poor hygiene. It occurs most frequently in girls and uncircumcised boys. A tendency to repeated infections can be caused by an anatomical abnormality of the urinary tract.

Preventing infection

Urinary tract infections are usually spread from the rectum via the urethra to the bladder or kidneys. Girls should wipe from front to back.

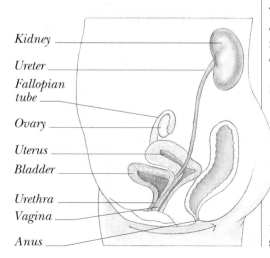

Kidney

Ureter

Fallopian tube

Ovary

Uterus

Bladder

Urethra

Vagina

Anus

Symptoms Urgent, frequent urination is the most prominent symptom of a urinary tract infection. The child may complain of a burning or stinging sensation at the beginning and end of urine flow. This is due to the bladder muscle contracting on the inflamed lining. The child may also pass urine involuntarily, and start to wet the bed again at night. Pain in the lower abdomen and back is common. Severe back pain, fever and chills, refusal to eat, headache, and blood in the urine indicate a kidney infection and the child will be very ill.

Treatment All urinary tract infections require medical treatment. The doctor will take a sample of urine to confirm the presence of a bacterial infection and find the most suitable antibiotic to treat it. A bladder infection can spread upward toward the kidneys, but early treatment can prevent this.

If the doctor suspects that the urinary tract infection is due to an anatomical abnormality, the child will be referred for special studies and checked for kidney damage.

The child should be given plenty of fluids to keep the bladder flushed out. Cranberry juice is often recommended. Encourage your child to urinate as often as possible. Acetaminophen elixir and a wrapped hot-water bottle on the lower abdomen can help to relieve pain.

Show your daughter how to wipe herself from front to back after passing a stool and your son, if he is not circumcised, how to wash beneath the foreskin. For the duration of an attack, washing should be very gentle, as the urethra is sensitive.

BALANITIS

This is an inflammation of the foreskin and head of the penis as a result of bacterial infection. The foreskin is nearly always tight. Products such as laundry detergent can cause irritation and swelling.

Symptoms The glans (tip of the penis) and foreskin are red, swollen, and tender to the touch, and pus may be noticed coming from inside the opening. The child will have pain on passing urine.

Treatment Medical treatment is always necessary to avoid a stricture of the foreskin, making it too tight to retract. A doctor will prescribe an antibiotic cream and may suggest circumcision if the foreskin is tight – either now or if it doesn't stretch by the time the child is six.

Parents should change baby's diapers frequently, keep the penis clean, apply antiseptic cream to any soreness and a barrier cream to the entire genital area. Children's clothes should always be rinsed thoroughly to remove any traces of detergent.

UNDESCENDED TESTES

Before a baby boy is born, his testes develop inside his abdomen; they descend into the scrotum (the pouch that hangs below the penis) shortly before birth. Occasionally, one of the testes fails to descend. The testes need to hang outside the body, where the temperature is lower, for efficient sperm production to take place; a testis at body temperature cannot produce sperm. When both of the testes are undescended, their position must be corrected surgically to prevent infertility. A man is fertile with only one testis.

Retractile testes move up into the abdomen in response to cold or touch. This is normal in young children, and can persist into adulthood. It does not affect fertility.

Symptoms One or both testes are absent from the scrotum. This condition is otherwise symptomless and will not cause your child any discomfort.

Treatment Often the testes descend during the first year of life. If they do not, corrective surgery may be carried out, usually between one and two years.

Development of the testicles
In a fetus, the testicles grow inside the abdomen, near the kidneys. Not long before a boy is born, they move downward into their normal position in the bag of skin called the scrotum.

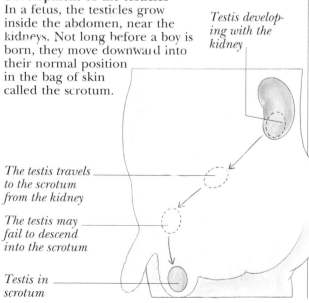

Testis developing with the kidney

The testis travels to the scrotum from the kidney

The testis may fail to descend into the scrotum

Testis in scrotum

TORSION OF THE TESTES

If one of the testes becomes twisted on its stalk, the blood supply will be interrupted and it will become red, swollen, and very painful. If left untreated, the testis will be irreversibly damaged. This is a medical emergency that requires immediate attention.

Symptoms The first symptom is severe pain. Later, the testis becomes swollen and tender. The child could feel sick and may vomit. The scrotum turns red, purple, and then blue.

Treatment The testis must be surgically untwisted as soon as possible to restore blood flow. Occasionally, the testis will untwist spontaneously, but you mustn't wait for this to happen.

BLOOD IN THE URINE

The medical name for blood in the urine is hematuria. It may be only a streak or sufficient to color the urine deep red. The cause may be in any part of the urinary tract from the kidneys to the urethra. Cystitis (inflammation of the bladder) and urethritis (inflammation of the urethra) are two common causes. Nephritis (inflammation of the kidneys) is less common but more serious. A child with hemophilia may pass blood in the urine from internal bleeding.

The slightly red tinge in a newborn baby's urine may be mistaken by a new parent for blood (see p.17). This is perfectly normal, but if you are in doubt, consult your pediatrician.

If you notice any blood in your child's urine, seek medical advice immediately. Although infections such as cystitis are not serious, they cause great discomfort and it's important to stop bacteria spreading from the bladder up to the kidneys.

Symptoms Slight bleeding may not be visible, found only when urine is examined under a microscope or when a special diagnostic dipstick is put into the urine. The symptoms of a urinary tract infection (see opposite) may be present or the child may have a kidney infection or glomerulonephritis.

Treatment Since blood in the urine is only a symptom of an underlying disorder, a doctor must perform special tests to determine the cause and treat it. The urine must be cultured to find an infection and urinary tract X-rays performed to find any anatomical abnormalities.

INFECTIOUS DISEASES

An infectious disease is one that is caused by a microorganism – that is, a bacterium or a virus. The infection is most commonly spread via the air or by direct contact, though it may also be spread

via food, water, or insects. In countries where standards of sanitation are high, appropriate drugs are readily available, and health and nutrition are generally good, infectious diseases pose far

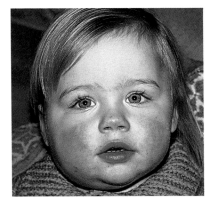

Mumps
In this viral disease (see p.304), the salivary glands swell up, changing the shape of the child's face; the swelling may appear on either or both sides of the face, just below the ears or the chin.

DISEASE	POSSIBLE SYMPTOMS
Chickenpox *A common and usually mild viral disease.* **Incubation** *17 to 21 days*	*Red, itchy spots that become fluid-filled blisters and then scabs. Headache and slight fever.*
Streptoccal infection *A bacterial infection whose effects are similar to those of tonsillitis. Sometimes it is accompanied by a rash (scarlet fever). When treated appropriately, it is rarely serious.*	*Enlarged tonsils, sore throat, high temperature (up to 104°F or 40°C), abdominal pains, vomiting, sometimes a rash resembling a pink-red flush that starts on the chest, then spreads, and a furry tongue with red patches (strawberry tongue).*
Fifth disease *A fairly common viral infection with a characteristic rash but rarely any fever.*	*Starts with "slapped cheek" rash, which appears as rosy cheeks and lasts 1–2 days before disappearing. A lacy rash on the arms and legs and sometimes the torso follows and lasts 2–3 days or comes and goes for 10–14 days.*
Roseola *A relatively rare viral infection caused by a type of herpes virus. It rarely appears after age 3.*	*A temperature of 102.2–104°F (39–40°C) for about three days. Red or pink spots may appear on the trunk, limbs, and neck as the fever wanes. The rash fades after about 48 hours.*
Hepatitis *A viral infection causing inflammation of the liver. There are many viral causes but Type A is the most common in children.*	*Loss of appetite, nausea, and jaundice. In severe cases, the child may pass dark brown urine and pale stools.*

less of a threat than they once did. In addition, many serious and potentially fatal infectious diseases have been virtually eliminated in the West through immunization. Those that still are common are described first, beginning with the most common. The characteristics of many childhood infectious diseases are similar: rash, fever, general malaise, and cold symptoms. If you notice a rash and your child has a fever, consult your pediatrician. The dangers with most illnesses are that your child may become dehydrated from vomiting or refusing food and drink, have difficulty breathing due to constricted airways, or suffer febrile convulsions (see p.281).

PREVENTION/TREATMENT

COMPLICATIONS

Apply calamine to the rash, keep your child at home, and discourage scratching. Your child's doctor may prescribe an antiseptic cream. Never give aspirin.

In very rare cases, chickenpox may lead to encephalitis (inflammation of the brain) and, if aspirin is mistakenly given, Reye's syndrome, a serious illness whose symptoms are vomiting and fever.

Your doctor may prescribe antibiotics. Home treatment includes giving your child plenty of fluids and liquefying food to make it easier to eat. Give acetominophen elixir to lower temperature.

If your child is sensitive to the streptococcus bacterium it may cause complications, including nephritis (inflammation of the kidneys) and rheumatic fever (inflammation of the joints and heart). These are rare.

Child is no longer contagious by the time rash appears so there is no need to keep him home. No treatment necessary as rash causes no discomfort and goes away by itself.

Generally none, though the virus can cause aplastic crises in children with sickle cell disease (see pp. 272–73).

Keep child rested and sponge him down with tepid water to reduce his fever. Give acetominophen elixir to lower his temperature.

If the child's temperature is very high, he may have febrile convulsions (see p.281).

Vaccines are being developed that may eliminate most hepatitis types. Be meticulous about hygiene as hepatitis is highly contagious. A child with hepatitis needs bed rest, plenty of fluids, and as good a diet as he'll take.

Some children suffer posthepatitis symptoms for up to six months. These may include poor appetite and consequent weight loss.

Applying lotion
The rash that accompanies chickenpox is very itchy. Rub in calamine lotion to soothe the itch; the pox may leave scars if they are scratched vigorously.

DISEASE	POSSIBLE SYMPTOMS
Meningitis *An inflammation of the membranes that cover the brain and spinal cord, resulting from a viral or bacterial infection. Epidemics of meningitis are caused by the meningococcus bacterium.*	*Fever, stiff neck, lethargy, headache, drowsiness, and intolerance of bright light; slightly bulging fontanels in children under 18 months. In meningococcal meningitis, there may be a purple-red rash (purpura, see* **Rashes,** *p.291) covering most of the body.*
Tuberculosis *A highly infectious bacterial infection that most commonly affects the lungs, but can also affect the kidneys, meninges, joints, bones, and pelvis if long-term.*	*Persistent coughing (possibly with blood and pus in the sputum if the lungs are affected), chest pain, shortness of breath, fever (especially at night), poor appetite, weight loss, and fatigue.*
Diphtheria *A serious and highly contagious bacterial infection. It is now very rare because of widespread immunization.*	*Enlarged tonsils possibly covered by a gray membrane. The child may have a mild fever, a cough, and a sore throat. Breathing difficulties may develop.*
Rubella (German measles) *A viral infection that is usually mild in children.* **Incubation** *14 to 21 days*	*Small red spots, first on the face and then all over the body, slight fever, and enlarged lymph nodes at the back of the neck and behind the ears.*
Measles *A highly infectious and potentially serious viral illness.* **Incubation** *8 to 14 days*	*Brownish-red spots appear behind the ears and then spread to the rest of the body; white spots appear in the mouth. Fever, runny nose, cough, headache. Possibly sore eyes.*
Mumps *A viral illness that is seldom serious in children.* **Incubation** *14 to 21 days*	*Tender, swollen glands below the ears and chin; fever, headache, and difficulty with chewing and swallowing; possibly earache. Less common: painful testicles (boys) and swollen ovaries (girls).*
Whooping cough *A bacterial infection that causes inflammation of the airways.*	*A cough with a distinctive "whoop" sound as the child tries to breathe, common cold symptoms (see p.294), and vomiting.*

Checking the throat
Use a spoon or spatula to hold your child's tongue down while you check his throat. Enlarged tonsils and a sore throat may be symptoms of streptococcal infection (see p.302) or, more rarely, diphtheria (see right).

TREATMENT

Intravenous antibiotics are used to treat bacterial meningitis. If a purple rash appears, the child must be taken to hospital at once.

Tuberculosis is a serious disease if left untreated, and its incidence is on the rise in some places. A test for tuberculosis antibodies is recommended for young children. Treatment is with antibiotics.

The DTP vaccine has made this a rare disease. Due to breathing difficulties, may require hospitalization. Treated with antibiotics and possibly a tracheostomy (a small tube inserted into the windpipe to ease breathing).

MMR vaccine has made this a rare disease. Acetaminophen elixir may be given for fever. Child should be isolated.

MMR vaccine has made this a rare disease. Bed rest during fever, no school until 7 days after rash appears; acetaminophen elixir; plenty of fluids; antibiotics for secondary infections.

MMR vaccine has made this a rare disease. Keep child away from school, give acetaminophen elixir and plenty of fluids, and liquefy food.

The DTP vaccine has made this a rare disease. A doctor may prescribe antibiotics; severe cases may require hospitalization for oxygen therapy and to treat dehydration.

COMPLICATIONS

Viral miningitis is not usually serious and clears up within a week. Bacterial meningitis is potentially fatal because of the risk of meningococcal septicemia, and so should always be treated as a medical emergency.

The possible complications of tuberculosis are pleural effusion (fluid between lungs and chest wall) and collapse of areas of lung tissue (air between lungs and chest wall); meningitis and miliary (a disease) may result.

Without treatment, diphtheria can cause other serious and potentially fatal complications. Bacteria can release a toxin that damages the heart and nervous system, causing heart failure and paralyzing muscles for breathing.

May cause birth defects if a non-immunized pregnant woman comes into contact with a child with rubella. Slight risk of encephalitis.

Ear and chest infections, which require treatment with antibiotics, may occur; slight risk of pneumonia, encephalitis, and seizures.

Occasionally, a testis is affected, and decreases in size; meningitis, encephalitis, and pancreatitis. Rarely, both testes are affected, which can lead to infertility.

Small babies are most at risk. They may stop breathing for short periods and are also at risk from convulsions, pneumonia, brain damage, and, very rarely, death.

MENINGITIS

Putting myself in the position of the parent of a child, I'd want to know how to be alert to the possibility of meningitis.

The warning signs to look out for are:
- *Headache and sensitivity to bright lights.*
- *Stiff neck – your child won't like pulling her head forward when lying on her back.*
- *A rash that doesn't disappear when you press a glass on it.*

If you spot any of these signs, call your doctor immediately.

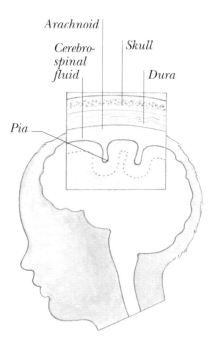

Meningitis
The three membranes that cover the brain and spinal cord – dura, arachnoid, and pia – are called the meninges. Inflammation of the meninges results in meningitis.

305

SAFETY

Many household items are dangerous to children. Every year a large number of children are admitted to hospitals because they have fallen from windows, burned themselves on stoves, choked on small objects, or swallowed household chemicals. Your child is naturally adventurous and inquisitive, and it is all too easy for you to underestimate the dangers presented to him as he explores his environment, especially in the light of his developing mobility and manipulative abilities.

FALLS

The causes of accidents from falling vary according to the age of the child. Babies under the age of one are most likely to fall from a stroller or walker, or from a raised surface, such as a table top; children aged between one and four are more likely to tumble down stairs, fall out of windows, or topple off playground equipment.

You can minimize the risk of your child's falling by careful supervision – make sure you never leave a baby unattended on a raised surface – and by making a few changes in your home, such as installing window guards and safety gates on the stairs. Check that the railings on balconies and banisters are no more than 4 inches (10 centimeters) apart or your child may fall through or get his head stuck between the rails. If you do not have a harness for your baby's high chair or stroller, you should buy one. A built-in harness may not be adequate. Look for one that is easy to fasten and adjust. Make sure you buy one and *use* it.

WINDOWS AND DOORS

The types of accidents associated with windows and doors include falling out of an open window, being cut by broken glass, and getting limbs and fingers trapped in closing doors. Various door slam protectors are available that prevent fingers being trapped in closing doors. The glass that is usually used for doors and windows is particularly dangerous as it breaks into long, sharp shards. Safety glass, on the other hand, is less likely to break and when it does, it doesn't form sharp pieces. Laminated glass stays in one piece when broken, and toughened

SAFETY EQUIPMENT

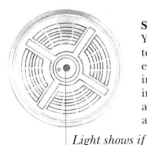

Light shows if battery is working

Smoke alarms
Your home should be protected with smoke alarms on each level. These alarms are inexpensive and easy to install. They must be attached to the ceiling, not a wall, to be totally effective.

A chemical extinguisher is most suitable for kitchens

Fire extinguisher and blanket
The kitchen is the most likely place for a fire to start, so you should keep firefighting equipment there. Extinguishers need to be checked regularly for pressure and may need to be replaced annually.

A dead-bolt can be opened only with a key

Safety locks
Make sure that windows remain firmly closed, or can be opened only a little, especially on upper stories.

An adjustable gate will fit most stair widths

Stair gates
These can be installed at the top or bottom of the stairs. The bars should be vertical so your child can't climb on them, and the gate should have a child-proof lock.

glass shatters into small rounded pieces. Another, cheaper option is to use safety film, but this can only be used on unpatterned glass that is completely smooth and, once applied, cannot be removed.

To prevent your child from falling out of a window, you can install window locks that allow the window to open by only 4 inches (10 centimeters). Tape the key to part of the window frame so you can use the window for emergency escape, if necessary. Window guards are required by many localities for homes with children.

FIRE SAFETY

House fires can be fatal if you or your child inhale smoke and toxic fumes. Fortunately, there are lots of ways to minimize the likelihood of a fire and lessen the damage that it can do.

- Don't smoke indoors.

- Don't leave pans containing hot fat unattended.

- Keep flammable liquids locked away.

- Use fireguards on any open or gas fire.

- Store matches out of your child's reach.

- Buy flame-resistant furniture.

- Replace fire extinguishers every year.

- Keep a fire extinguisher and a fire blanket in the kitchen.

- Install smoke alarms and check the batteries twice a year.

- Never leave your child unattended near lighted candles, stoves, or fireplaces.

BURNS AND SCALDS

Scalds occur when a child is exposed to hot liquids – they usually affect the face, neck, chest, and arms. As a child gets older and his hand-eye coordination improves, he will be able to pull saucepans, mugs, and kettles containing hot liquids off work surfaces. Other causes of scalding are putting a baby in water that is too hot or leaving him unsupervised in a bathroom where there is a bath or sink full of hot water. A child can be scalded by less water, at a lower temperature, than an adult.

A good way to avoid scalds is to turn your hot water thermostat down to 130°F (54°C). At this temperature, scalding will start to occur only after 30 seconds of exposure. When running a bath for your child, put the cold water in first, then add the hot water afterward; don't leave a young child unsupervised in the bathroom.

In the kitchen, prevent your child from pulling things off work surfaces by making sure that there are no trailing cords. Try to buy coiled cords for electrical appliances or shorten the existing cord and use hooks to prevent trailing cords. After you have finished with a mug, kettle, or pan full of hot liquid, empty it immediately, and, when cooking on the stove, use the back burners rather than the front ones and always keep saucepan handles turned in.

ELECTRICAL SAFETY

Make your child aware of the dangers of electricity and block unused sockets with heavy furniture or with socket covers. These are dummy plugs made of plastic that prevent your child from sticking his fingers or objects into the socket. Avoid brightly colored socket covers, as these will only serve to attract your child's attention.

POISONOUS SUBSTANCES

Children aged between one and three years are most prone to accidental poisoning because they learn how to climb and open cupboards. Before the age of 18 months, children cannot tell by taste whether something is bad for them. Common household poisons include bleach, floor and furniture waxes, disinfectants, detergents, medications, including pain-killers such as aspirin and acetaminophen. Fortunately, however, only one in 500 incidents of accidental poisoning has very serious consequences.

Poisoning is largely preventable. You should keep all drugs and household chemicals in a high place out of reach of your child or, preferably, in a locked cabinet. When using them, watch your child the whole time – this is when most accidents happen. Both prescribed and over-the-counter drugs should be kept in bottles with child-resistant tops – avoid taking medicines out of their original containers; out-of-date or unused drugs should be thrown away.

Household chemicals, such as bleach, should also be stored in an inaccessible place and should never be transferred into containers that are familiar or attractive to children, such as soda or juice bottles. Keep pet food bowls away from children as they can harbor bacteria and don't keep toxic plants or flowers in the house. Post the phone number of your local poison control center on or near every telephone in the house.

SAFETY AT HOME

There are some general rules that apply to all rooms of the house. These include avoiding having trailing electrical cords, loose carpets, and flammable items of furniture. Choose furniture that is child friendly; for example – avoid tables with sharp corners. Keep all electric outlets covered and all windows fitted with window locks and/or guards. Teach your child from an early age that hot things such as fireplaces, open flames, and ovens are dangerous and that she should never go near them, but maintain safety precautions until your child is at least three years old.

When your child visits other people's homes, scan the room for potential dangers. If you are in a house where there are no children, carry out a quick check for breakable items, heavy ornaments that can be pulled off surfaces, open, low-level windows, and sharp objects.

KITCHEN

- Install a guard on the stove and always point saucepan handles toward the back of the stove.
- Keep matches out of your child's reach and install a smoke alarm.
- Remove stove knobs if they are on the stove front.
- Set the hot water thermostat to a maximum of 130°F (54°C) – at this temperature, it will take half a minute for serious scalding to occur.
- Keep plastic bags out of reach.

- Store sharp knives in a locked drawer.
- Don't use tablecloths . Your toddler can pull them and everything on the table on to her head.
- Don't leave hot pans or mugs containing hot drinks around.
- If you spill fat or liquid on the floor, mop it up immediately.
- Turn your washing machine and dishwasher off at the circuit breaker or fuse box.
- Store glasses and breakable dishes out of reach.
- If you are not using the iron, put both the iron and the ironing board away.
- Keep bowls of pet food out of reach to avoid bacterial infection.
- Never leave your child unattended while he is eating – he could choke.

HALL AND STAIRS

- Install safety gates at top and bottom of the stairs.
- Don't leave objects lying on the stairs.
- The stairway should be protected on both sides by walls or banisters.
- The gaps between the banisters should not be more than 4 inches (10 centimeters) wide so your child can't get an arm or a leg caught in them.
- Stair carpets should fit the stairs exactly so that your child can't trip on them.
- Mend any loose carpet on the stairs without delay.
- Make sure that it is impossible for your child to get out of the front door and run into the street.

DANGERS IN THE HOME

Your child could pull a tablecloth on top of herself

Remove all harmful plants

Never leave objects on the stairs

BATHROOM

- Store medicines in a locked cabinet or on a high shelf and throw away unused or old medicines.

- Keep disinfectants and bleach locked away and in their original containers, preferably with child-resistant tops, and make sure they are always out of reach while you are using them.

- Never leave a child alone with a filled bath.

- When preparing your child's bath, always add hot water to cold, never the other way round.

- Use nonslip mats in the bathtub.

- Keep the toilet lid closed.

- Keep razors (electric and blade) well out of reach.

BEDROOM

- Crib toys should not have strings that are longer than 1 foot (30 centimeters).

- Never leave your baby with the crib side down.

- Never leave your baby alone on the changing table, even for a second.

- Put window locks and/or guards on windows.

- Avoid lights with trailing cords.

- Crib bars should not be spaced more than 2 1/2 inches (6 centimeters) apart, as your child could get part of her body stuck between them.

- Don't use a pillow in your baby's crib until she's one year old.

- Choose furniture with rounded corners.

- Don't leave gas or electric heaters or fans on when your child is by herself.

LIVING ROOM

- When you replace the glass in patio doors, choose laminated glass or tempered glass.

- Install a firescreen in front of all fireplaces and make sure it's securely fitted to the wall. Don't put cups, mugs, or ashtrays near the fireplace.

- Use outlet covers on all unused sockets so your child can't poke objects into them.

- Avoid trailing cords from lights, TV, stereo, and video equipment.

- Avoid poisonous houseplants (see p.311).

- Don't leave any alcohol, cigarettes, matches, or lighters lying around.

- Keep fragile, breakable items out of reach.

- Don't place hot or heavy objects on low tables.

- Attach all shelving securely to the wall.

PLAY AREAS

- Keep older children's toys separate from younger children's toys. Toys with small parts, modeling kits, and chemistry sets can be especially dangerous to babies and toddlers.

- Store toys safely in a box and don't leave them lying around on the floor.

- Throw broken toys away.

- A playpen is a good way of keeping a young child out of potential danger. Make sure that it is at least 2 feet (60 centimeters) deep.

- Store toys and games at floor level or somewhere within your child's reach so he doesn't have to stretch or climb to get them.

SAFETY MEASURES

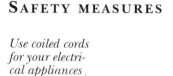

Keep electric outlets covered

Use coiled cords for your electrical appliances

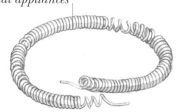

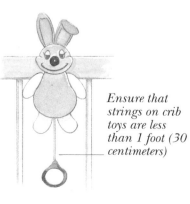

Ensure that strings on crib toys are less than 1 foot (30 centimeters)

SAFETY AT PLAY

The most common accidents that result from playing are cuts and bruises from falling over or off toys, or injuries from swallowing part of a toy or inserting it into a nostril. Sometimes an accident occurs because the child is not properly supervised, sometimes because the toy is broken or of a poor quality, and sometimes because the toy is simply too sophisticated for the child.

Many toys can injure a child in some way, but construction kits, toy cars and trains, and rocking and wheeled toys cause the most injuries. Even soft toys can cause choking and suffocation.

TOY SAFETY CHECKLIST

- Check packaging and labels to ensure that the toy is appropriate to your child's age. In general, toys with small components are not suitable for children under the age of 36 months.

- Check warning labels for flammability or for any toxic ingredients.

- Don't stick pictures on the inside of your baby's crib as he may put them in his mouth.

- Crib toys should not be suspended on strings longer than 1 foot (30 centimeters).

- If your baby can stand up in his crib, remove toys from the side, as he can use them as a stepping stone to climb out.

- For a child under three, avoid toys with small detachable components, as these can be swallowed by very young children.

- If you have children of different ages, store each child's toys separately.

- Show your child how to use a toy.

- One- and two-year-olds can easily fall off rocking toys and rideable vehicles, so keep an eye on your child, especially if he is playing on hard ground.

- Regularly check the batteries in battery-operated toys. Replace them if there's leakage.

- Make sure toys have no sharp or abrasive edges.

- Throw broken toys away rather than giving them to charity or to a rummage sale.

- Store toys safely in a box with a lid that doesn't slam shut.

- If a toy comes wrapped in a plastic bag, unwrap it for your child and dispose of the plastic bag.

CHOKE HAZARD TESTER

Once your baby acquires the pincer grasp, he is in danger of picking up and swallowing small objects.

A choke hazard tester checks if an object is small enough to lodge in a child's windpipe. If the object slips into the tester, it's potentially dangerous.

Toys
It's tempting to buy toys on impulse, but check for potential hazards first.

Ears should be firmly stitched on

The eyes should be firmly attached

The paint should be nontoxic

The fabric should be flame resistant

Check for splits or tears; loose stuffing might be eaten or inhaled

The edges should be curved or flexible, not sharp or rigid

The wheels should not be detachable

OUTDOOR SAFETY

Your child will like playing outdoors – he'll be able to run around freely, get dirty, and explore a different environment. The main danger associated with playing outside is that he may run out of the yard or playground and into the street. Drowning is also possible if there is water or a pool in the garden. You can prevent this by making sure that your child always plays in an enclosed environment and that yard gates are locked at all times with child-resistant locks. Fence swimming pools and empty wading pools after use. The other main dangers include ingesting poisonous plants, animal feces, and chemicals used in gardening.

YARD SAFETY CHECKLIST

• Ensure that any poisonous plants (see opposite) are removed and pull up all types of mushrooms as soon as they appear.

• Store garden tools and chemicals, such as weed-killer, in a locked garden shed.

• Make sure that garden chairs are always put up properly – injuries can be caused by unstable deck chairs and loungers.

• Check the safety of play equipment regularly.

• Don't allow animals to defecate in the yard.

• Put climbing toys on grass or rubber matting, not on paved areas.

• Make sure that your child cannot run out of the yard into the street – install child-resistant locks.

• If you have a pond or a swimming pool you should drain it, cover it, or fence it off.

• Don't use power tools or mow the lawn if your child is running around. Always put power tools away after use.

• Cover sandboxes to prevent fouling by animals.

• Cover up drains.

POISONOUS PLANTS

Although eating garden plants is rarely fatal, they can cause unpleasant symptoms, which range from irritation of the skin, mouth, throat, and stomach, to nausea and vomiting. Make sure that you tell your child never to eat any plants or berries from the garden and remove any of the plants that you know to be poisonous. Daffodils, hyacinths, irises, buttercups, snowdrops, sweetpeas, and privet cause irritation of the gastrointestinal tract, and rhubarb, many fungi, tomato leaves, willow, laurel, rhododendron, mistletoe, and lily of the valley all cause general poisoning.

Playgrounds
Young children need challenging equipment to test their skills and use up energy, but make sure they're safe.

Young children should sit in box swings, not open ones

The play area should be surrounded by a fence so animals cannot get in

Climbing equipment should be situated on grass, sand, or rubber matting

The sandbox should be too shallow for your child to bury himself

Equipment at ground level, like tubes and tires, is safest for toddlers

Swings should be surrounded by a fence

Your child should not put his feet under a merry-go-round or jump off one when it's moving

The slide surface should have no joints in it

Slides constructed on an earth mound will break a fall

311

CAR AND ROAD SAFETY

The most basic rule of car safety is to make sure that your child is always strapped in. Rear-facing seats are best for infants and should be used only in the back of the car. A child should never sit in a front seat equipped with a passenger-side airbag.

Until your child is six, use child locks on the rear doors of your car, and don't let your child lean out of the window or stick her hands and arms out. Never take your eyes off the road to turn around and talk to your child when you are driving. If she is crying or needs your attention, stop the car first.

Accidents can happen when a car is stationary as well as when it is moving. A child can get her fingers stuck in car doors or windows as they are being closed or get out of a car on the traffic side.

BABY CAR SEATS

The safest way for your baby to travel by car is in an approved baby car seat. A seat belt alone is not sufficient because her pelvic bones are not strong enough to protect the pelvic organs from the pressure of the belt in a crash. Baby seats are designed for babies from birth to nine months, and they can be used in the front or backseats of cars, although they are safer in the back. The best design is a rear-facing seat which can be buckled into a seat belt. This means that in a crash the impact is against the

---

TAKE CARE

Baby seats should never be used in the front of a car with a safety airbag fitted on the passenger side. In the event of a crash, the airbag can inflate with such force that the impact could seriously injure your baby's head, possibly even causing brain damage.

---

baby's back, not the delicate pelvic organs. Some models can be converted to a forward-facing child seat when your baby is old enough.

BABY CARRIERS

Although a proper baby seat is better, it is safe for your baby to travel in a carrycot in the back seat as long as it is attached with seat belts. The restraining straps should be secured to the back seat and bolted to the car frame. Keep the carrier cover in place so that it is impossible for your baby to be thrown out.

CHILD SEATS

By the age of one year, your baby will need a child seat. Some of these are fitted with a four-point anchorage kit, although these are not practical for all types of car. Other types are secured with the adult seat belt, and some have integrated harnesses. Make sure you install your child seat according to the manufacturer's instructions, since a badly installed seat will not offer any protection in a crash.

When your child has grown out of a car seat – some types will last until she is six – she can use a booster cushion with an adult seat belt.

Child safety
Infants over the age of one year need a child seat. This is forward facing and should be used in the backseat.

Baby safety
The best seats for babies from birth to one year are rear-facing.

ROAD SAFETY

Road accidents are usually more serious and require longer hospitalization than any other childhood accidents, so safety is of paramount importance. The responsibility for your child's safety when out in traffic lies with you, of course, not just when she is in her stroller but when she reaches school age. Children do not develop the ability to judge the speed of traffic until they are about 10 or 11 years old and they are not good pedestrians until the age of 12. You can, however, instill the basics of street safety from an early age, by teaching her and, more importantly, by setting a good example.

TEACHING YOUR CHILD

The first thing your child must learn is that streets are dangerous places. It doesn't matter what the circumstances are – whether she has lost her ball or pet, or wants to greet someone – she must never run out into a street. Unless your street has no traffic, don't let your child play on the sidewalk – encourage her to play in parks, playgrounds, or in the backyard instead, and make sure that these areas are secured with a fence or a locked gate. Tell your child she must never play on a bike or scooter near the road, that she shouldn't stand between parked cars, and that if she loses a ball in the street, she should ask an adult to retrieve it. And teach your child about traffic lights and don't walk signs.

SETTING AN EXAMPLE

The best way to teach your child road safety is to show her how you behave as a pedestrian. Most of us develop bad habits as adults, such as weaving through traffic or crossing a street without allowing ourselves sufficient time. When you are with your child, you should practice the following, even if it takes you longer to reach your destination. This way your child will learn by example.

When you cross the street with your child, hold her hand and explain what you are doing and why. Go to the curb and tell your child that it is the safety line that must not be crossed without an adult. Look left and right and wait for a green light or, if there is no traffic light, a clear break in the traffic before you cross over. If pushing a stroller, keep it on the sidewalk until you are ready to cross. Show your child how to press the buttons at controlled crossings, and how to wait for the traffic to stop before you cross a zebra crossing. Never run across the road in front of traffic when with your child.

Your child's awareness of street safety is in part determined by the area she grows up in. A child who grows up in a rural area and only has to cross quiet country roads may need extra supervision when she goes to a town or city because she has not made a strong association between streets, traffic, and danger. If this is the case with your child, you can still teach her about road safety when you are driving in the car. When you stop at a pedestrian crossing, point out what they are for and how pedestrians use them. Show your child sensible places to cross, such as straight stretches of road, and point out the dangers of crossing at places such as sharp bends or between parked cars, where you cannot see traffic coming. Point out pedestrians who are crossing well or badly, and explain why.

ENVIRONMENT

Make a careful assessment of the traffic and road conditions on your street. Although traffic speed is an important factor, recent research has shown that main roads pose six times as great a risk to pedestrians as residential or local streets. In other words, if you live on a main road you should never allow your child to go out of the house on her own.

If you live in a residential area, you could try to increase the safety of roads by asking your local government to install speed bumps or to narrow the road at specific points. If possible, get together with other parents and discuss a campaign for safe neighborhood play. Local authorities can play an important role in helping you achieve this.

THE SAFETY CODE

This simple road safety routine is really intended for children of eight years and older, but start to teach it as soon as your child is old enough to follow your example.

- *Repeat these steps to your child every time you cross the street together.*

- *Find a safe place to cross the street, such as a pedestrian crossing or traffic-lighted intersection.*

- *Stop, look, and listen for traffic. Watch the traffic lights.*

- *If there is any traffic, let it pass.*

- *Look in both directions, and when the light is green and the street is clear, walk across. Keep looking and listening as you cross the street.*

PERSONAL RECORDS

Your baby's early milestones – her first smile, her first word – will seem unforgettable to you, but as time passes you'll find that your memory becomes hazy, not just about small details, like when she first held her head up, but crucial ones, like vaccination dates.

BIRTH RECORD: FIRST BABY

Name _Mykenzie Noël Francis_
Date and time _2-14-01_   _2:15 p.m._
Place _Anne Arundel Medical Center_
Estimated date of delivery _2-27-01_
Length _20"_
Weight _7 lbs. 1.8 oz._
Blood group _____
Duration of labor _~~Caesarean~~_
Type of delivery _Caesarean_
Doctor/midwife _Dr. Wells_
People present _Daddy (delivery room)_ _Grandma Salley & DeFelice Aunt Beth (waiting area)_

DEVELOPMENT RECORD: FIRST BABY

First smile _4/01_
Achieves head control _4/01_
First tooth _____
Starts solids _4/29/01_
Sits unsupported _____
Feeds self _____
Responds to own name _____
Uses mature "pincer" grip _____
Learns to "ungrasp" _____
First word _____
Understands "No" _____
Crawls _____
Fully weaned _____
Jargons _____

Stands _____
Bowel control _____
Bladder control _____
Walks _____
Makes simple statements _____
Dresses self _____
Obeys simple requests _____
Climbs stairs unsupported _____
Runs _____
Jumps _____
Counts to ten _____
Draws a circle _____
Starts nursery school _____
Starts school _____

The following pages will help you keep track of these important events. The medical records on pp.334–35 are particularly important. You can use them to refresh your memory each time you take your child to the doctor; they may remind you of some forgotten but relevant detail. Fill in your own medical history, too, and that of your partner; these can often provide important clues to your child's state of health.

NOTES

BIRTH RECORD: SECOND BABY

Name _____

Date and time _____

Place _____

Estimated date of delivery _____

Length _____

Weight _____

Blood group _____

Duration of labor _____

Type of delivery _____

Doctor/midwife _____

People present _____

DEVELOPMENT RECORD: SECOND BABY

First smile _____

Achieves head control _____

First tooth _____

Starts solids _____

Sits unsupported _____

Feeds self _____

Responds to own name _____

Uses mature "pincer" grip _____

Learns to "ungrasp" _____

First word _____

Understands "No" _____

Crawls _____

Fully weaned _____

Jargons _____

Stands _____

Bowel control _____

Bladder control _____

Walks _____

Makes simple statements _____

Dresses self _____

Obeys simple requests _____

Climbs stairs unsupported _____

Runs _____

Jumps _____

Counts to ten _____

Draws a circle _____

Starts nursery school _____

Starts school _____

Medical Records: First Baby

Name _____

Illness	Date	Comments

Injuries

Allergies

Mother's Medical History

Illnesses

_____
_____
_____
_____
_____
_____
_____
_____
_____

Allergies

_____
_____
_____

Chronic conditions

_____
_____

Immunizations: First Baby

Type	Date	Reaction
DTP: Diphtheria, tetanus, whooping cough (5 vaccinations)	4-16-01 / 6-2-01	Cried & fever / " "
Polio (4 immunizations)	4-16-01 / 6-2-01	Cried & fever / "
MMR: Measles, mumps, rubella (1 plus optional 2nd)		
Varicella: Chickenpox (1 vaccination)		
Hib: see p.283 (3 or 4 vaccinations)	4-16-01 6-02-01	Cried & fever
Hepatitis B	2-16-01	

MEDICAL RECORDS: SECOND BABY

Name _____

Illness	Date	Comments
_____	_____	_____
_____	_____	_____
_____	_____	_____
_____	_____	_____
_____	_____	_____

Injuries
_____	_____	_____
_____	_____	_____
_____	_____	_____
_____	_____	_____

Allergies
_____	_____	_____
_____	_____	_____
_____	_____	_____

FATHER'S MEDICAL HISTORY

Illnesses
_____
_____
_____
_____
_____
_____
_____
_____
_____

Allergies
_____
_____
_____

IMMUNIZATIONS: SECOND BABY

Type	Date	Reaction
DTP: Diphtheria, tetanus, whooping cough (5 vaccinations)	_____	_____
	_____	_____
	_____	_____
	_____	_____
	_____	_____
Polio (4 immunizations)	_____	_____
	_____	_____
	_____	_____
	_____	_____
MMR: Measles, mumps, rubella (1 plus optional 2nd)	_____	_____
	_____	_____
Varicella: Chickenpox (1 vaccination)	_____	_____
	_____	_____
Hib: see p.283 (3 or 4 vaccinations)	_____	_____
	_____	_____
Hepatitis B	_____	_____

Chronic conditions
_____
_____
_____

LENGTH, HEIGHT, AND WEIGHT

The most important criteria in assessing your baby's progress are happiness and general well-being. If these are apparent, there's no need for you to worry about his measurements.

You may find it interesting to plot your baby's increasing height and weight on the following charts, but you should become anxious about it only if his growth pattern veers away from that of the average. Don't compare your child to others of his age.

The range of "normal" heights or weights at a given age is very wide. A newborn boy may weigh anything from 5 lbs. 8oz. to 10 lbs. (2.5 to 4.5 kg) without giving cause for concern; a five-year-old boy from 30 lbs. to 58 lbs. (13.5 to 26.5 kg).

Each chart shows the range of heights or weights into which the vast majority of children will fall. The black line in the middle of each colored band represents the "average child"; that is, about half the children will fall below the line, and about half above it. The outer lines represent extremes beyond which very few children will fall. If your child does, you should consult your pediatrician.

A child's measurements, plotted regularly, should form a line roughly parallel to the central line. If not, the measurements may not have been correctly plotted or the correct chart may not have been used. If in doubt, consult your child's doctor.

GIRL'S LENGTH 0–6 MONTHS

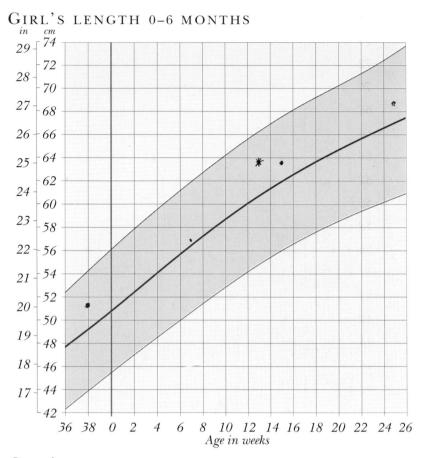

Age in weeks

GIRL'S WEIGHT 0–6 MONTHS

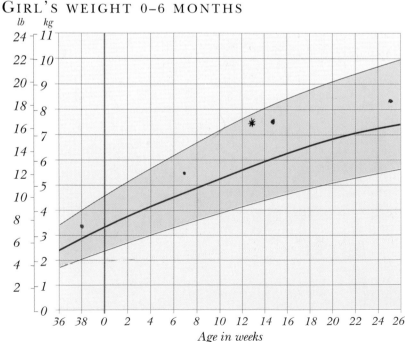

Age in weeks

BOY'S LENGTH 0–6 MONTHS

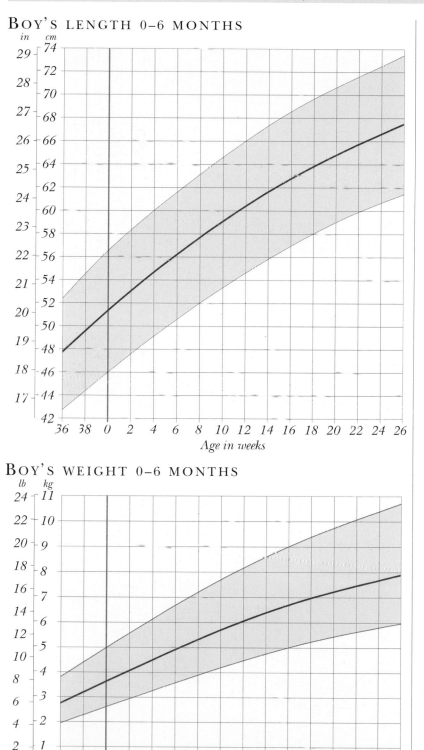

Age in weeks

BOY'S WEIGHT 0–6 MONTHS

Age in weeks

USING THE CHARTS

I believe that parents need not weigh and measure their baby, but we've included charts for parents who are eager to follow their child's progress.

• *You'll probably need to ask your obstetrician or midwife for your baby's birth weight and length*

• *For a baby, you could fill in the charts using the measurements taken by your pediatrician at well-baby check ups*

• *For a preterm baby, you will have to adjust her age accordingly, at least until she is a year old. If, for example, your baby was born at 36 weeks, start recording her measurements at the appropriate point to the left of zero on the chart, and continue to subtract four weeks from her age each time you fill in the chart*

• *To measure your child's height once she's three or four, get her to stand against a wall with her feet together and her heels and shoulderblades touching the wall. Make sure she holds her head up straight by gently tilting her chin upward. If you like, measure her again at six-monthly intervals so she can see how she's growing*

• *To enter your child's measurements on the chart, find her age along the bottom axis and trace a straight line up from it. Now find her weight or height along the vertical axis, and trace a line across. Mark a solid dot where the two lines meet. The row of dots is your child's growth curve*

Notes

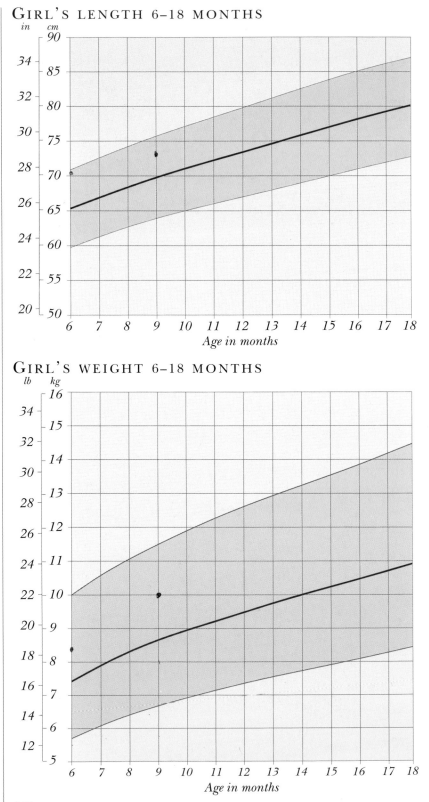

Girl's length 6-18 months

in / *cm*

Age in months

Girl's weight 6-18 months

lb / *kg*

Age in months

BOY'S LENGTH 6–18 MONTHS

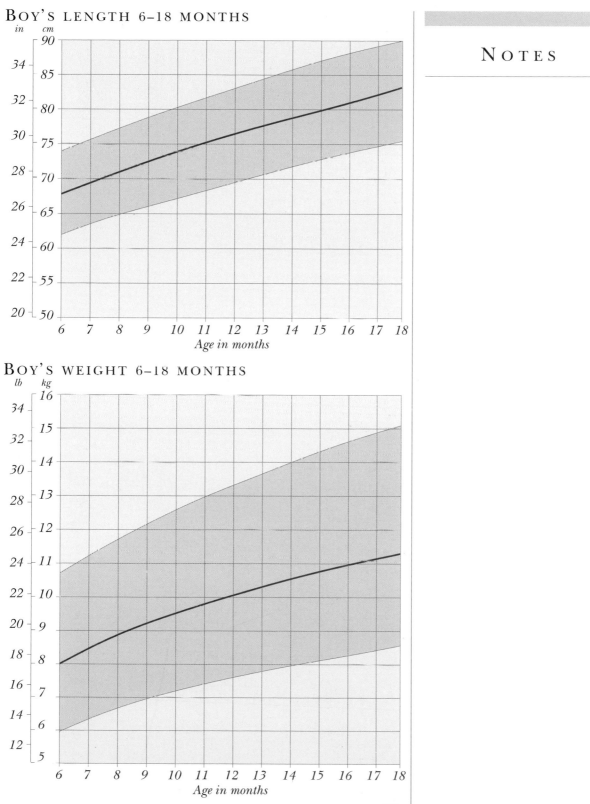

in / *cm*

Age in months

BOY'S WEIGHT 6–18 MONTHS

lb / *kg*

Age in months

NOTES

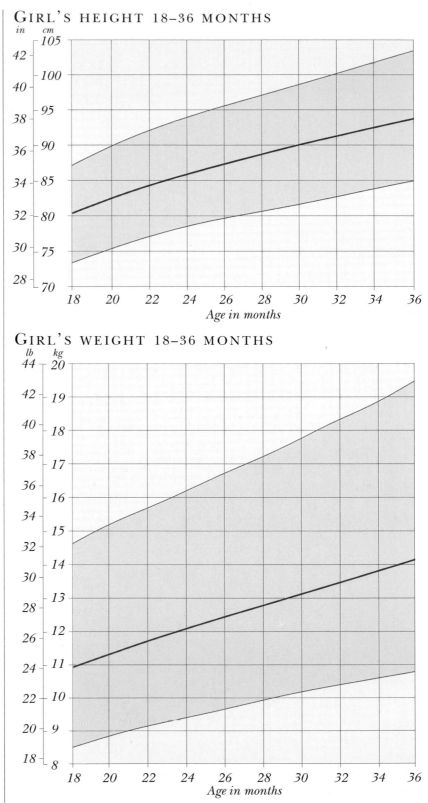

GIRL'S HEIGHT 18–36 MONTHS

Age in months

GIRL'S WEIGHT 18–36 MONTHS

Age in months

BOY'S HEIGHT 18–36 MONTHS

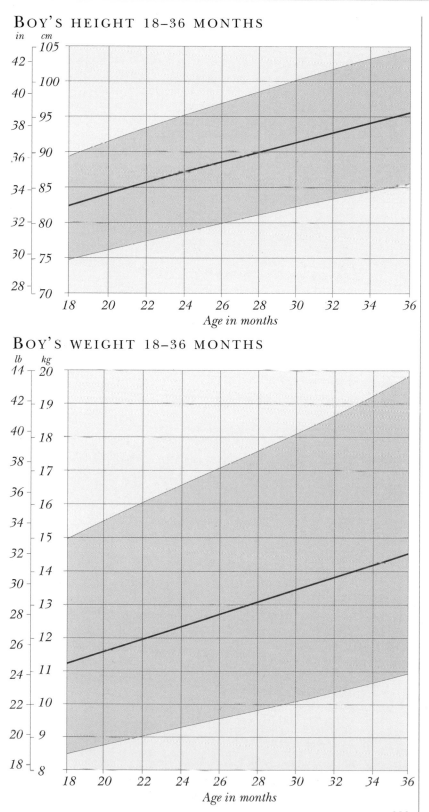

in   *cm*

Age in months

BOY'S WEIGHT 18–36 MONTHS

lb   *kg*

Age in months

NOTES

GIRL'S HEIGHT 3–5 YEARS

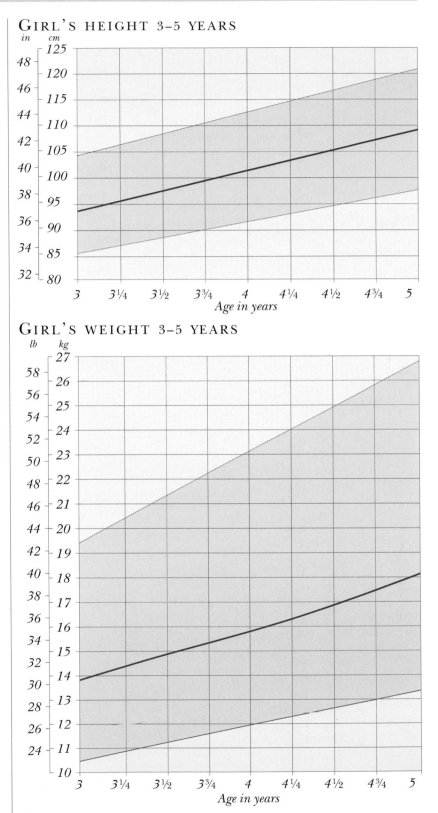

GIRL'S WEIGHT 3–5 YEARS

BOY'S HEIGHT 3–5 YEARS

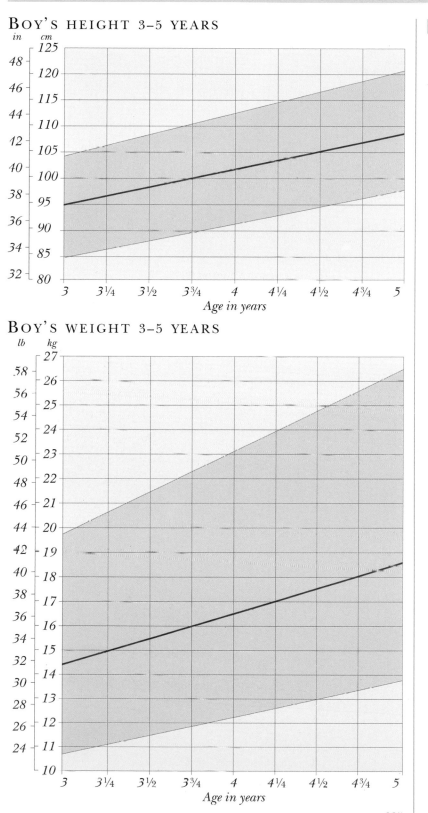

Age in years

BOY'S WEIGHT 3–5 YEARS

Age in years

FIRST AID

As a parent, you will inevitably have to cope with minor accidents as your child grows up. Most of the time, these will be minor cuts and bruises, but you should be equipped to cope with major accidents or emergencies, should they occur. All parents should know the basic first-aid techniques to deal

with accidents quickly, effectively, and calmly. To give first aid effectively, you need to understand and practice the techniques detailed on the following pages, and you should also keep a first-aid kit in your home. This should be accessible in an emergency but stored out of reach of your child.

EMERGENCY FIRST AID

A severe accident with the loss of much blood or other body fluids may precipitate shock (see p.333), which is always serious. Other emergencies include choking (see pp.332–33), a very severe respiratory tract infection that blocks the airways, drowning, and unconsciousness. Prompt action on your part can be lifesaving.

PRIORITIES

When your child has an accident, you must get your priorities straight. Tell any adult present to call 911 while you go through the checklist of priorities, right. Detailed instructions for the procedures involved are shown on pp.328–333. If there isn't an adult there to help you, you should go through the checklist before calling 911.

Is your child in danger? If appropriate, remove your child from the danger or the danger from your child. Do not put yourself at risk, and do not move your child if you suspect a fracture.

Is he conscious? Shake your child gently by his shoulders and keep calling his name.

Is his airway blocked? Open your child's airway by supporting the chin and tilting the head back. Then clear any obstruction (see pp.328-29).

Is he breathing? Lean close to your child's mouth to listen for breathing and feel it against your cheek. Look at his chest to see if it is rising and falling. If there are no signs of breathing after five seconds, give five breaths of artificial respiration (see p.330).

HOME FIRST AID KIT

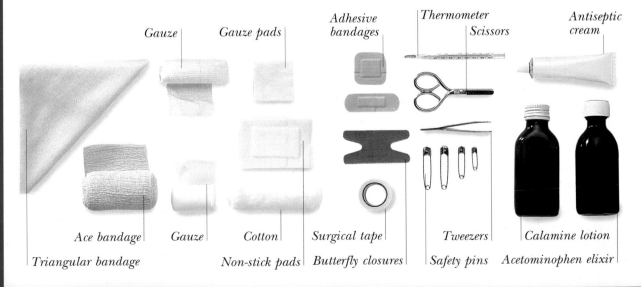

Gauze | Gauze pads | Adhesive bandages | Thermometer | Scissors | Antiseptic cream

Triangular bandage | Ace bandage | Gauze | Cotton | Non-stick pads | Surgical tape | Butterfly closures | Tweezers | Safety pins | Calamine lotion | Acetaminophen elixir

FIRST-AID TRAINING

You must learn the procedures on these pages by heart in order to make use of them. If you have to waste time referring to this book to refresh your memory, your delay could be the difference between life and death.

This book cannot make you a "First Aider." To learn first aid properly you should complete a course of instruction and pass a professionally supervised examination. First-aid and CPR courses are available in many localities through Ys, hospitals, and private organizations (see **Useful addresses,** pp.344–45). Many focus on first aid for children.

Does he have a pulse? Check for a pulse in the arm or neck (see p.328–30), or place your hand on your child's chest and count the beats. A normal pulse rate is about 120 beats per minute for a baby; less for an older child. If no pulse is present, or if the pulse is less than 60 beats per minute in a baby, give CPR (see pp.330–31) for one minute, call 911, taking your child with you if you can, then continue to carry out CPR.

Call 911 If your child is having breathing difficulties or is unconscious, call 911, or get another adult to do this. Try not to leave your child unattended and be prepared to carry out resuscitation on him until help arrives.

RESUSCITATION

In order for the vital organs, such as the brain, to function, they need a continuous supply of oxygen. If any part of the process by which oxygen is carried to body cells and tissues is interfered with, unconsciousness might result. Air must be inhaled to supply oxygen to the blood, and the oxygenated blood must be pumped around the body by the heart. If the brain is deprived of oxygen for more than three minutes, it will begin to fail. If the heart fails, death will occur unless emergency action is taken.

Resuscitation is necessary if, for whatever reason, your baby or child has stopped breathing or if his pulse has stopped (see pp.328–29).

HOW RESUSCITATION WORKS

Oxygen supply

Three factors are involved in the transport of oxygen to the brain. The air passage, or airway, must be open so that oxygen can enter the body; breathing must occur so that oxygen can enter the bloodstream in the lungs, and the heart must be pumping so the blood travels around the body (circulation), taking the oxygen to all the tissues, including those of the brain.

Air must be inhaled to provide oxygen

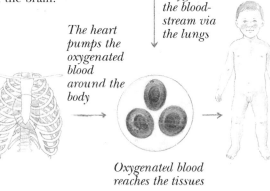

The heart pumps the oxygenated blood around the body

Oxygen enters the blood-stream via the lungs

Oxygenated blood reaches the tissues

THE ABC OF RESUSCITATION

In an emergency, when your child stops breathing or loses consciousness, these are the three steps you must remember:

A is for Airway *Open the airway, look in the mouth, and check for obstructions. Clear the airway if you can by tilting your child's head back (see pp.328–29). Never sweep the back of the throat if your child is choking (see pp.332–33).*

B is for Breathing *If your child shows no signs of breathing, you will have to breathe for him with artificial respiration (see p.330, steps 1–3).*

C is for Circulation *Check that your child has a pulse. If not, or if it is very faint, you will have to give CPR, chest compressions along with artificial respiration (see pp.330–31).*

RESUSCITATION

If your child is unconscious and isn't breathing, she's at risk of brain damage and heart failure. You need to make a fast assessment of her condition in order to know what first-aid treatment to give. If she is unconscious but still breathing and has a pulse, call for help and place her in the recovery position (see p.329). If she's not breathing but has a pulse, give artificial respiration. If she is not breathing and has no pulse, *start cardiopulmonary resuscitation (CPR) immediately. The procedures differ slightly for babies and children (see pp.329–31).*

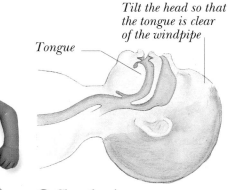

Tilt the head so that the tongue is clear of the windpipe

Tongue

ASSESSING A BABY

1 Check for consciousness
See if your baby is conscious by calling her name, gently shaking her, and tapping or scratching the sole of her foot. If she doesn't respond after about ten seconds, shout for help.

Run a finger along the sole of your child's foot

2 Clear the airway
Look in your baby's mouth. If you can see an obstruction, remove it with your finger, but be careful not to poke it farther in. Open the airway by lifting the chin with one finger (for a baby) and tilting the head back very slightly.

Place the thumb on the outside of the arm and two fingers on the inside

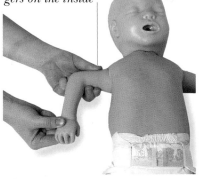

Support the chin with one finger

Look along your baby's chest and abdomen to see if they are moving up and down

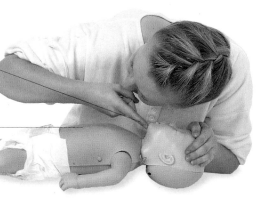

3 Check for breathing
Look, listen, and feel for signs of breathing. Look along your baby's chest and abdomen to see if they're moving up and down. Listen closely for sounds of breathing and feel for her breath on your cheek. If there are no signs of breathing after five seconds, you will need to give five breaths of artificial respiration (see p.330, steps 1–3), then check her pulse.

4 Check the pulse
Place two fingers on the inner side of the arm above the elbow and press gently. If you can't feel any pulse after five seconds, give CPR (see p.331, steps 4–6) for one minute, then call 911 and continue.

ASSESSING A CHILD

1 Check for consciousness
See if your child is conscious by shaking her gently and pinching her skin. Keep calling her name. If she doesn't respond, call for help.

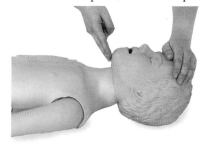

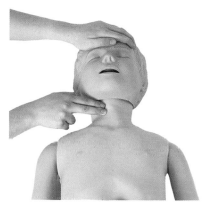

2 Clear the airway
Look in the mouth to see if it is obstructed. If it is, clear it with your fingers, but take care that you don't push any obstruction farther in. Open the airway by putting two fingers under your child's chin and lifting the jaw. Tilt the head back by placing your other hand on her forehead.

3 Check for breathing
Look, listen, and feel for signs of breathing. Look along your child's chest and abdomen for movements; listen for sounds of breathing; and feel for her breath on your cheek. If she is not breathing, give five breaths of artificial respiration (see p.330, steps 1–3), then check her pulse.

4 Check the pulse
See if your child's heart is still beating by checking her carotid pulse. You can find the pulse by placing your fingers just in front of the large muscle at the side of the neck under the angle of the jaw. If there's no pulse, you must give one minute of CPR (see p.331, steps 4–6), call 911, then continue.

THE RECOVERY POSITION

An unconscious child who is breathing and has a regular pulse should be placed in this position, provided there are no suspected fractures, to prevent his tongue blocking the airway and allow liquids to drain from the mouth.

The uppermost leg should be bent at a right angle so that the hip and knee act as a "prop"

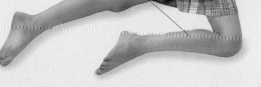

Place the arm at right angles to the body with the elbow bent

For a baby
Cradle a small baby in your arms, with her head tilted slightly back in order to keep the airway open.

1 If the child is lying on his back or side, kneel beside him. Straighten his legs and place the arm nearest you at right angles to his body with the elbow bent.

2 Bring the other arm across the chest and place the back of the hand against the cheek.

3 Still pressing your child's hand to his cheek, grasp the thigh farthest away from you and pull the knee up. Keep the foot flat on the ground and place it next to the nearer knee.

4 Roll your child over into a resting position with his knee bent and his head resting on his hand.

RESUSCITATION FOR BABIES

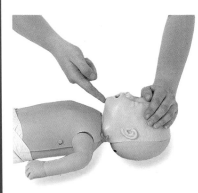

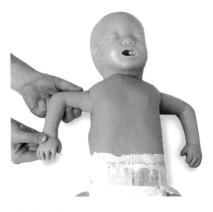

1 Open the airway
Lay baby down on a firm surface, gently lift the chin with one finger, and tilt the head back very slightly.

2 Give artificial respiration
Inhale, put your lips over the baby's nostrils and mouth to make a complete seal, and breathe out gently for about one and a half seconds into her mouth and nose so that her chest rises. Remove your lips and let the chest fall. Repeat, then check pulse.

3 Check pulse
Check for a pulse in the arm (see p.328). If there is none, or if it is less than 60 beats per minute, give CPR: five chest compressions (steps 4–5) for every breath of artificial respiration. If there is a pulse, do not proceed with steps 4–6 but continue to give breaths, checking the pulse every minute.

RESUSCITATION FOR CHILDREN

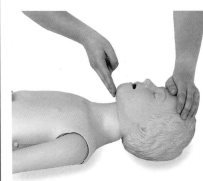

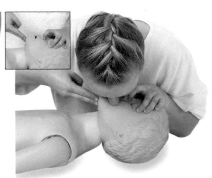

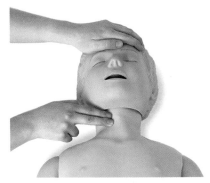

1 Open the airway
Lay the child on a firm surface. Place two fingers under his chin and tilt his head back.

2 Give artificial respiration
Using your finger and thumb, pinch the child's nostrils closed. Inhale, put your mouth over his mouth, making a complete seal, and breathe out for one and a half seconds so that his chest rises. Remove your mouth and watch the chest fall. Repeat, then check pulse.

3 Check pulse
Check the pulse in the child's neck (see p.329). If there is no pulse, give CPR: five chest compressions (steps 4–5) for every breath of artificial respiration. If there is a pulse, do not proceed with steps 4–6 but continue breaths, checking the pulse every minute.

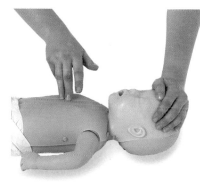

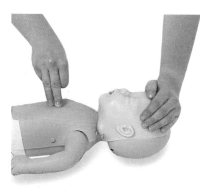

4 Position the fingers
With the baby on a firm surface position your index finger just below an imaginary line between the nipples and put the tips of the next two fingers on the breastbone. Then raise the index finger, leaving the other two in position.

5 Give chest compressions
Press down sharply with the tips of your two fingers to a depth of ½ to 1 inch. You should give five compressions during a three-second period. Be careful not to thrust too vigorously or too deeply, or you could cause harm to your baby.

6 Give artificial respiration
After five compressions, give one breath of artificial respiration (step 2). Alternate chest compressions with artificial respiration: for every five compressions over a three-second period, give one breath.

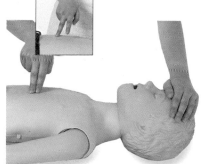

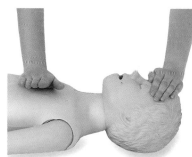

4 Positioning the hand
With the child on his back on a firm surface, slide your middle finger along the edge of the rib cage until you find the point where the ribs meet in the middle. Place your middle finger here and and your index finger above it.

5 Give chest compressions
Look at the position of your index finger. Now lift your hand up and place the heel of your hand on the breastbone just above where your index finger was. Keeping your fingers off the child's chest, press down sharply to a depth of 1–1½ inches. Give five compressions in three seconds.

6 Give artificial respiration
After five compressions, give one breath of artificial respiration (step 2). Don't stop to take your child's pulse unless he shows signs of reviving.

CHOKING

If your child's airway becomes completely blocked, she may lose consciousness. At that point, she may begin to breathe again as her muscles relax. If she is not breathing, you must begin artificial respiration immediately (see pp.330).

If something is blocking the airway, encourage your child to cough it out by patting her back. If that doesn't work, immediately begin the steps below. (For a baby under one year, or for any small child, follow the sequence for a baby). If it doesn't work at first, call 911 and keep trying until help arrives. Use the Heimlich Maneuver only for a conscious child, never for a baby or anyone who is unconscious.

FOR A BABY

1 Back blows
Lay baby face down along your forearm, with her head low and shoulders supported on your hand. Give five sharp slaps between the shoulder blades.

2 Chest thrusts
Turn the baby face up and lay her along your other arm. Place two fingers in the center of her chest just below the nipples, and give five sharp downward thrusts about ¾ inch (2 centimeters) deep.

3 Check the mouth
Place your finger on her tongue. If you can see an object, hook it out with a finger, but do not put your finger down her throat. If the blockage hasn't cleared, call 911 and repeat the steps until help arrives.

FOR A CONCIOUS CHILD (HEIMLICH MANEUVER)

1 Position
Position yourself behind the child with one fist clenched, the thumb on the child's navel.

2 Position
Cup the other hand over your fist, keeping your elbows out and away from the child.

3 Thrust
Press in and up in one firm but smooth motion. If this does not clear the obstruction, call 911 and repeat steps until help arrives.

FOR AN UNCONCIOUS CHILD

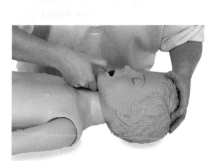

1 Check the mouth
Lay the child on her back on a firm surface. Tilt her head back using two fingers under her chin. Check her mouth for an obstruction, placing a finger on her tongue, and if it is visible, try to hook it out with your finger.

2 Artificial respiration
Pinch the child's nostrils closed, inhale, and put your mouth over hers, making a complete seal. Try to give two slow breaths. If the chest does not rise, retip the head and try again for two breaths only.

3 Chest thrusts
Stand next to or straddle child, put hands palms down and on top of each other, heel of bottom hand on child's navel, fingers pointing to the chin. Thrust in and up 6–10 times. Return to mouth and alternate 2 breaths with 6–10 thrusts.

SHOCK

In a medical context, "shock" refers to a perilous drop in the flow of oxygen to organs and tissues. If shock is not dealt with quickly, the vital organs can stop functioning and the child can die. Shock is made worse by fear and pain.

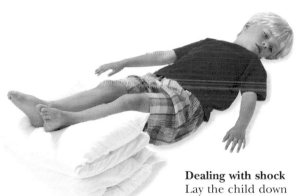

Dealing with shock
Lay the child down with his legs higher than his chest.

Symptoms Initially, the body responds with a flow of adrenalin. This gives rise to a rapid pulse, pale, grayish-looking skin, especially around the lips, sweating, and clamminess. As shock progresses, the child may be thirsty, she may feel sick, and she may vomit. She is likely to be weak and dizzy, her breathing will be shallow and fast, and her pulse (see p.328) will be fast and irregular. In very severe cases, when the oxygen supply to the brain is insufficient, the child may become restless and anxious, and she may be yawning and gasping for air ("air hunger"). Eventually, she will lose consciousness and the heart will stop.

WHAT TO DO

If you suspect that your child is suffering from shock, call 911 as soon as possible. If she's lost a lot of blood, try to stop the bleeding (see p.335), and deal with any burns (see p.336). Move her as little as possible but get her to lie down with her legs raised on some pillows so her legs are higher than her chest. Undo fastenings around the neck, chest, and waist, and turn her head to one side in case she vomits.

A child in shock will be very anxious so it is important to stay with and keep reassuring her. Keep her as calm and comfortable as possible. Make sure she is warm, but not too hot. A blanket on top of her and around her head will keep her insulated. (In a very young child, the blanket should be wrapped around the body.) If she is injured, she may need surgery, so don't give her anything to eat or drink. If she is thirsty, wet her lips with some water. Keep checking her breathing and pulse rates, and be prepared to give CPR (see pp. 330–31) if necessary.

ELECTRIC SHOCK

A child may receive an electric shock from frayed electrical cords or wires, light switches, defective electrical appliances, or from touching an appliance with wet hands. It is important to warn your child about the hazards of electricity from an early age and stress that water and electricity are a dangerous combination. Replace frayed wires and put dummy plugs in any electrical outlets not in use.

Symptoms In severe cases, the child may lose consciousness and his heartbeat may stop. In mild cases, he may have slight burns.

WHAT TO DO

Before you go to help a child, you must break the contact between him and the source of electricity. Either switch the current off at its source or pull out the plug. If you have to break the contact manually, make sure you do it safely: push your child away using an object made of a nonconducting material such as wood or plastic and stand on an insulating material while you do it. If there is no alternative, drag your child away by his clothes. This can be very dangerous, however, because if you touch his skin or if his clothes are damp, you will receive a shock, too.

Once the contact has been broken, examine your child for burns. If burns are severe or your child is unconscious, call 911. In the meantime, treat the burns by pouring on cold water and then placing a sterile dressing on them (see p.336). Monitor your child's condition closely; if he starts to show signs of shock (see p.333), you may have to resuscitate him. If he is unconscious but breathing, place him in the recovery position (see p.329).

POISONING

Common poisons include bleach, weed-killer, and certain plants and fungi. You should leave medicines and chemicals in their original containers, which should be tamperproof where possible, and lock them away. Always call a poison control center or 911 if you suspect poisoning.

Symptoms A corrosive chemical often burns around the mouth and it is usual for the child to feel nauseated and vomit or to have diarrhea. With very poisonous chemicals, your child may lose consciousness or he may have convulsions. There may be a poisonous substance such as berries, pills, or a bottle containing household chemicals lying near by – keep this to show to the doctor.

Use a wooden broom-handle to break contact with the source

A telephone directory makes a good insulator

Breaking contact
Stand on a dry insulating material while you push your child's limbs away from the source with a nonconductive object of wood or plastic. Do not touch your child's skin with your hands.

WHAT TO DO

Try to identify the poison. Call your local poison control center or 911. If you can, tell whomever you speak to how much your child took and when. Keep a sample of the poison to show to the doctor.

If you suspect or know that your child has swallowed a poison, don't try to induce vomiting. If the chemical is regurgitated, it may cause as much damage on the way back up as it did when it was first swallowed. Instead, give your child sips of milk or water. Traces of poison on hands or face should be washed away with water.

If your child has lost consciousness, check her pulse and breathing and, if necessary, resuscitate her (see pp.330–31). When she is breathing, lie her in the recovery position (see p.329).

DROWNING

A child can drown in as little as 2 inches (5 centimeters) of water, so it's very important that you do not leave your child alone near a wading or swimming pool, a bathtub, or even a bucket of water. If a drowning child is not rescued quickly, he will be asphyxiated.

RESCUE

Drowning in a large body of water is a hazard to you as well as your child, so first, you should attempt to rescue him without entering the water. Try to reach him with your hand or a pole, or throw him a life-preserver. Get into the water only if there is no alternative. In shallow water, carry your child to land by wading through the water. While you are carrying him, make sure his head is lower than his chest – if he vomits, there will be less risk of his inhaling vomit.

WHAT TO DO

Take your child to the nearest warm, dry place and, without undressing him, lay him down on blankets or a coat. Check his airway, breathing, and pulse (see pp. 328–29), and give CPR if necessary (see pp. 330–31). If he is unconscious but still breathing, put him in the recovery position (see p.329) and monitor his breathing all the time. Replace his wet clothing and insulate him from the cold.

Your child should receive medical attention as soon as possible; either call 911 or take him to the hospital yourself; even if he appears to recover there is a chance that he may suffer from a condition known as "secondary drowning" in which the air passages swell up. Your child may also need treatment for hypothermia.

BLEEDING

Cuts and bruises (see pp.342–43) are rarely serious and, unless infected, can be dealt with at home. Severe external or internal bleeding, however, can lead to shock and eventually loss of consciousness. These should be treated as emergencies.

WHAT TO DO

Profuse bleeding is both serious and distressing. It should be dealt with quickly before your child goes into a severe state of shock.

Severe external bleeding Expose the wound if it is covered – cut away clothing if necessary – and apply pressure to the wound with a clean dressing or cloth. If there is glass sticking out of the wound, don't remove it. Instead, apply pressure on either side; this will compress the ends of the damaged blood vessels. Lay your child down, keeping the injured part of the body in a position above the heart to slow down the flow of blood to the wound.

Do not use a tourniquet to stem bleeding, but do apply a dressing to the wound and secure it with bandages after applying pressure to the wound. If blood appears through the bandage, put another one on top. If there is glass sticking out of the wound, build up the bandages on either side until you can bandage over the top without pushing the glass deeper into the wound. Call 911 or take your child to the hospital.

Internal bleeding If your child shows signs of shock (see p.333), if there is pattern bruising (bruises that follow the pattern of the object that crushed against the body), or if there is bleeding from the ears, nose, mouth, or vagina, you should suspect internal bleeding. You should treat your child for shock and call 911.

BURNS AND SCALDS

Burns are usually described in terms of the amount of damage to the skin. Superficial burns (first degree) are the least serious and can result from a minor spillage or touching a very hot surface. Partial-thickness burns (second degree) are more serious, and fluid-filled blisters form on the skin. Full-thickness burns (third degree) are very serious since all layers of the skin are damaged, fluid loss is high due to weeping of the skin, and the nerves and muscles may be damaged. Unless a burn is very minor, you should always seek medical help.

WHAT TO DO

If the burn is minor, run cold water over the affected part of the body for about ten minutes. This will cool the skin and halt further tissue damage. Cover it with a sterile dressing to protect it from bacteria. A clean plastic bag will make a good temporary dressing if you have nothing else suitable.

If the burn is major, call 911 first, then lay your child down and pour cold water over the affected area for ten minutes or until the ambulance arrives. Check that your child is breathing and take his pulse. You may need to treat him for shock (see p.333). If he loses consciousness, be prepared to resuscitate him (see pp.330–31). Unless your child's clothes are sticking to the burned area, you should gently take or cut them off him.

Do not

- Touch the affected area or burst any blisters.

- Apply lotion or fat to the area.

- Stick a bandage or adhesive dressing to the burn.

- Cover the burn with a "fluffy" dressing or any cloth that sheds lint.

- Remove anything that is sticking to the burn: you may cause further damage or introduce infection.

- Overcool your child if he has severe burns; this could lead to hypothermia (see p.340).

CLOTHES ON FIRE

Douse with water
Make your child lie down as quickly as possible with the burning side of his body facing upward. Put out the flames with water. Do not pour water on your child if he has been burned by an electrical object that is nearby. Throw water downward along the body to stop flames from reaching the face.

Smother flames
If there is no water nearby, wrap your child in blankets or a thick coat or rug to deprive the flames of oxygen. Do not use a flammable fabric to smother flames.

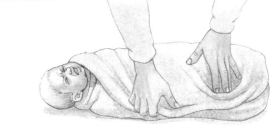

TAKE CARE

Severe burns are dangerous: a child can rapidly go into shock (see p.333) because of loss of body fluids. Untreated shock leads quickly to unconsciousness. The larger the area of the burn, the greater the likelihood of shock. Burns affecting more than one-tenth of a child's body need immediate treatment for shock. Call 911.

HEAD INJURIES

If your child bangs or knocks his head, he will normally have recovered within minutes. If he bangs his head quite hard, he may have some temporary swelling. Head injuries that should give cause for concern are those that produce severe bleeding or those that give rise to the symptoms of concussion, even several hours after the injury. Look out for drowsiness, headaches, and nausea.

Symptoms Mild symptoms resulting from a slight knock include a headache and a bump or swelling where the impact occurred. If the injury is more severe, the child may lose consciousness and the symptoms of concussion may follow (see below right). He may be drowsy, stunned, or dazed, and he may suffer nausea and vomiting. Disturbances in vision and headaches are common. If the skin of the scalp is cut, bleeding may be profuse.

Straw-colored fluid or watery blood leaking from the ears or the nose may indicate a skull fracture. Other symptoms include a depression of the scalp and unconsciousness. A suspected skull fracture should be treated and followed up carefully by a doctor.

WHAT TO DO

If your child is unconscious, you should call 911 and place him in the recovery position (see p.329). Keep checking his pulse and level of response (see pp.328–29). If he recovers consciousness after a short time, keep checking his level of consciousness by getting him to answer simple questions or just to respond to his name. Do not leave him alone.

If there is bleeding, press a clean pad firmly to the area to stop the flow but do not touch the wound with your fingers. If the bleeding stops, clean and dress the wound, though not if this causes the bleeding to start again. If the wound if long or jagged, take your child to the hospital to have it stitched. Smaller wounds should be cleaned with soap and water and then covered with a sterile dressing. Any discharge from the ear should be allowed to drain away. Any child who has lost consciousness or in whom concussion is suspected should be seen by a doctor as soon as possible, even if he seems perfectly all right afterwards.

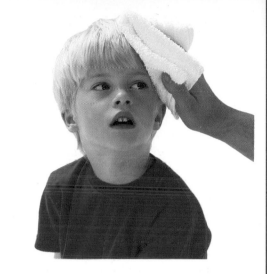

Scalp wounds
Apply firm, steady pressure to the injury with a sterile dressing or clean pad for ten minutes or until the bleeding stops.

CONCUSSION

A child who has suffered a blow to the head may show symptoms of concussion, which is a temporary disturbance of the brain.

The child may lose consciousness for a short time and then recover completely. He may feel dizzy or nauseated and have a slight headache, and may even be unable to remember what led up to his injury. Concussion can occur several hours after a blow to the head, so you should monitor your child closely for 24 hours for these symptoms. If the symptoms occur, consult your child's doctor.

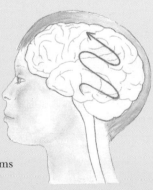

Cause of concussion
Because the brain is not fixed rigidly inside the skull, it is free to move around a little. This means that a blow to the head can shake or knock the brain against the skull, giving rise to the symptoms of concussion.

SEIZURES AND CONVULSIONS

The most common causes of convulsions are fever (see p.281), epilepsy (see pp.270–71), head injuries, diseases that damage the brain, and poisoning. Convulsions may also occur for no apparent reason. During a convulsion, there is a disturbance in the normal electrical impulses in the brain, causing muscles to jerk involuntarily. It is important that the child not be restrained except to prevent injury. Convulsions usually occur on isolated occasions, but children with epilepsy suffer repeated attacks.

Symptoms Children with epilepsy may suffer from minor fits (known as "petit mal"), which appear as a lapse of concentration or daydreaming, or from major fits ("grand mal"), which are seizures. In a mild seizure, the child may experience a tingling or twitching in some part of his body, such as his arm or leg. In a grand mal convulsion, the child may cry out and then lose consciousness and fall to the floor. His body will become stiff and he will hold his breath. This "stiff" phase is followed by rhythmic jerking movements of the arms and legs and arching of the back. The child has no control over his bodily functions, and he may become incontinent. He may clench his teeth and bite his tongue, or froth at the mouth.

After the convulsion, the child's muscles will relax and he will begin to breathe normally again. When he regains consciousness, he is likely to be dazed or confused and he will want to sleep.

WHAT TO DO

It's very important not to try to intervene while a child is having a convulsion. Even if you think he is at risk of biting his tongue, you should not try to open his mouth or put anything in it. Clear a space around the child so that he cannot hurt himself, call a doctor, and stay with the child all the time. If the child remains unconscious, put him in the recovery position (see p.329). You should tell the doctor the duration and the symptoms of the child's convulsion as it will help diagnosis of the cause.

EYE INJURIES

Any injury to the eye should be taken seriously. Common injuries include a foreign body or chemical in the eye, a blow to the eye causing bruising or a black eye, and a cut in or near the eye.

Symptoms These vary according to the type of injury, but may include some bruising around the eye socket, pain, inability to open the eye fully, or spasms of the eyelid. There may be impaired vision, a bloodshot appearance, and if the eyeball has been punctured, blood or fluid leaking from the eyeball.

WHAT TO DO

Treatment will depend on the type of injury, but in all cases it should be prompt. The child will probably need to be taken to an emergency room.

- If your child has a foreign body in his eye, try to remove it by flushing out his eye (see below). If it is embedded in the eye or is on the iris, tape a pad or handkerchief over his eye and take him to an emergency room.

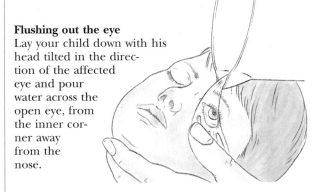

Flushing out the eye
Lay your child down with his head tilted in the direction of the affected eye and pour water across the open eye, from the inner corner away from the nose.

- For a blow to the eye, place a pad soaked in cold water over the eye to minimize bruising.

- If your child has a chemical in his eye, take him to an emergency room, but first try to flush out the eye with water from a pitcher (see picture) or by getting him to lean under a running tap, the affected eye lowermost for about 15 minutes.

- If your child cuts his eye, hold a sterile pad against the wound and take him to an emergency room.

FRACTURES AND DISLOCATIONS

The most common type of childhood fracture is a greenstick fracture, in which the bone bends and only partially breaks. Other types of fracture include simple fractures (a clean break) and compound fractures (the bone breaks through the skin). A dislocation is a bone that is displaced from its joint, usually after a wrenching force.

TYING A SLING

Symptoms Typically, there is difficulty moving and a limb may look oddly shaped. There will be pain, swelling, bruising, and possibly a wound at the site of the injury. With a dislocation, your child may experience a "sickening" pain.

WHAT TO DO

All fractures and dislocations should be treated promptly in a hospital. You should keep your child as still as possible until an ambulance arrives and don't let him have anything to eat or drink. You can prevent the worsening of an injury by immobilizing the joints above and below a fracture.

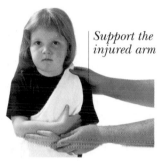

Support the injured arm

1 Positioning the bandage
Bend the injured arm across the chest. Place the bandage (use a triangular bandage or a scarf or cloth folded diagonally) between the arm and the chest. Pull one corner around the neck to reach the shoulder of the injured arm.

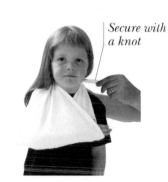

Secure with a knot

2 Tying the bandage
Bring the bottom of the bandage up over the child's forearm and tie the bottom corner of the triangle with a knot to the corner resting at the injured shoulder. Tuck in the ends of the knot.

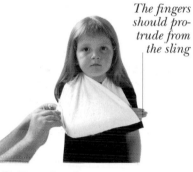

The fingers should protrude from the sling

3 Fastening the corner
Using a safety pin, secure the loose point of the bandage at the front of the elbow. If you don't have a safety pin, tuck the point into the sling. The hand should be left exposed.

LEG BANDAGE

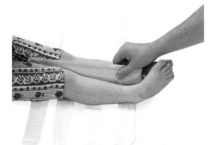

1 Improvising a splint
Lay the child down and place padding between his legs. Use newspaper, rolled blankets, or a pillow.

A rolled newspaper makes a good splint

2 Tying the bandages
Using the broadest bandages you can find, tie the broken leg to the uninjured leg at the knee, calf, and ankle. Make a figure-eight at the ankles. All the knots should be on the side of the uninjured leg.

TAKE CARE

If you suspect that your child has fractured his spine or his neck, there may also be damage to the delicate spinal cord carried by the vertebrae, so it is essential that you not move the child until an ambulance arrives. Don't let him move his head. If there is spinal cord injury, the child will experience burning, tingling, or even a loss of sensation in his limbs.

HEATSTROKE

When the body overheats as a result of exposure to extreme heat, the temperature-control mechanism in the brain fails and the sweat glands stop working. The child cannot lower his temperature in the normal way. This is a relatively common occurrence among children who go out in strong sun before they have the chance to acclimatize. The child's temperature may rise above 104°F (40°C) and in extreme cases he may lose consciousness and stop breathing. Most cases, however, are mild.

Symptoms Although the skin looks and feels hot, it remains dry. The child will seem drowsy and lethargic, and he may have a rapid pulse rate. In severe cases, the child may become confused, start to lose consciousness, and stop breathing.

WHAT TO DO

Take the child's clothes off and lay him down in a cool place. Call a doctor if the child's temperature is as high as 104°F (40°C) and, while you are

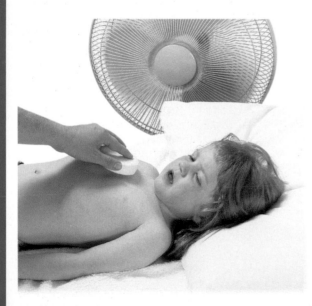

Lowering body temperature
Take your child out of the sun, and sponge her with tepid water or aim a fan at her skin.

waiting, sponge him with tepid water or wrap him in a cool wet sheet. Place a covered icepack on his forehead, give him lots of cool drinks, and aim a fan at his body. Monitor his pulse rate and temperature closely. Check his temperature every minute until it lowers to 99°F (37.2°C), then stop cooling but continue to monitor his temperature.

If he begins to lose consciousness, place him in the recovery position (see p.329) and check his breathing. If he has stopped breathing, give artificial respiration (see p.330) and call 911.

HYPOTHERMIA

If your child gets cold as a result of being exposed to cold, wet, and windy weather, a near-drowning, or simply being in a room that is too cold, he may suffer from hypothermia. Clinically, hypothermia is defined as a body temperature below 95°F (35°C). Deep hypothermia occurs when the body temperature drops to below 79°F (26°C), and this can be fatal since the heart, liver, lungs, and intestines may slow down and cease functioning.

Symptoms The child may be shivering and his skin will feel cold and dry. He may look pale and blue (although babies may look pink) and his breathing may be slow and shallow. He will be lethargic and might show behavioral signs like apathy, confusion, and quietness. In severe cases of hypothermia, the child may start to lose consciousness.

WHAT TO DO

Take off any wet clothing, wrap the child in warm, dry clothes and blankets, and hold him close to your body. Call 911.

Older children can be warmed up by giving them a warm bath and warm (not hot) sweet drinks. Monitor the child's temperature constantly with a thermometer or by feeling his skin. If your attempts to warm him up are not working or if he has lost consciousness, call 911. If your child seems to be warming up, put him in a warm bed and stay with him until the ambulance arrives or you are sure his temperature is back to normal. Never place a direct source of heat, such as a hot water bottle, on a child's skin.

EVERYDAY FIRST AID

As your child grows up, he will inevitably experience some commonplace accidents such as cuts, bruises, blisters, bites, and stings. Most of the time, they are not serious and can be treated at home with comfort and some simple first-aid techniques.

ANIMAL BITES

Animal bites can happen if your child is teasing or playing boisterously with a pet, usually a dog or a cat. Although being bitten can be traumatic for a child, bites are not usually very serious. The main danger is that if the bite is deep, bacteria will be lodged in the wound. If your child is bitten by a wild animal – a bat, badger, raccoon, or skunk – bring him to a doctor. Although rabies is rare, there is a risk from wild animal bites, as well as occasionally from cats.

The first thing you should do is reassure your child, as he will probably be quite frightened. If he was bitten because he was teasing the animal, you should explain this to him and emphasise that it is an isolated incident.

What to do

Wash the wound thoroughly with warm water. Apply an antiseptic cream and cover the bite over with a dressing. If the bite is very severe, try to control the bleeding with direct pressure, raising the wounded part of the body and wrapping it tightly with a bandage. Cover the wound with a dressing and take your child to the hospital. He may need a tetanus injection if he hasn't received his routine immunizations, as well as antibiotics to prevent infection.

SNAKE BITES

Most snakes in the U.S are not poisonous and the venom of those that are is often not fatal. If your child is bitten by a snake, make a note of the snake's appearance so that the appropriate antidote can be given. Depending on the snake, the symptoms of a snake bite can include puncture marks in the skin, pain, redness, and swelling around the bite, and in very severe cases, impaired breathing, sweating, vomiting, and impaired vision.

What to do

It is important to keep your child calm, since if he panics this can speed the spread of venom around the body. Wash the area of the bite with water, immobilize the affected part of the body with bandages, and take your child straight to a hospital.

INSECT BITES AND STINGS

Stings and insect bites are not usually serious unless there is an allergic reaction. Stings in the mouth or throat, however, are serious, as the swelling they cause can obstruct the airway. Stinging insects include bees, wasps, and hornets. Biting insects include fleas, mosquitoes, and ticks (see p.297). A sting is felt as a sudden, sharp pain and appears as a raised, white area on an inflamed patch of skin. A bite is much less painful and normally causes only mild discomfort and inflammation.

What to do

A dab of ammonia or a paste made with baking soda and water will neutralize the irritating substances many insects inject in the skin. Apply a cold compress and, later, calamine lotion to a sting to relieve discomfort. If you can see the stinger sticking out of your child's flesh, scrape it off with a blunt knife.

If you see a wood tick on your child, remove it with a tweezer, holding firmly to the tick's body and pulling it out gently. Deer ticks usually fall off by themselves, but can be removed by scraping with a blunt knife. If your child is bitten by fleas, have family pets treated and your house disinfected. Mosquito bites can be avoided with insect repellent, and the itching relieved with calamine lotion. Tick bites are painless but can cause infection and disease, so you should seek medical treatment.

Removing a stinger
If the stinger is still in the skin, remove it with tweezers. Grasp the stinger as close to the skin as possible and carefully pull it out. Don't pull the stinger at the top. You may squeeze the poison sac and the poison may enter the wound.

If your child is stung in the mouth, give him an ice cube to suck (unless he is under one year old) and seek medical help at once since swelling can restrict breathing. If your child has an allergic reaction to a sting, you should treat it as an emergency. Symptoms of an allergic reaction include swelling of the face and neck, puffy eyes, impaired breathing, red blotchy skin, wheezing, and gasping.

In certain parts of the United States, poisonous spiders, tarantulas, and scorpions may be found. If you live or are traveling in an area where these are common and your child is bitten, seek immediate medical attention, as their bites may be very serious, especially in a small child.

JELLYFISH STINGS

If your child comes in contact with a jellyfish, he may experience a severe local reaction – jellyfish have stinging cells that discharge venom when touched. The severity depends on the type of jellyfish. Most are not very toxic and are unlikely to produce severe symptoms – just a rash that may itch or be slightly painful. In certain parts of the world, however, rare jellyfish exist that are much more poisonous. These can produce a very severe reaction that may be life-threatening.

What to do

The stinging cells that stick to your child's skin release their poison gradually as they burst. You can help by inactivating the cells or preventing them from bursting. Alcohol or vinegar will do this, and any fine powder, such as sand or talcum powder, will make the cells stick together. You should wash the area with sea water. Apply a paste of baking soda or meat tenderizer. Rinse off after 10 minutes and apply ice, then calamine lotion or hydrocortisone cream to relieve the pain and irritation. If your child experiences a severe allergic reaction or develops any symptoms of shock (see p.333) as a result of any sting or wound caused by a marine creature, take him to a hospital immediately.

BLISTERS

When the skin is burned or subjected to pressure or friction, a blister may form as a protective cushion. Blisters are bubbles of skin with tissue fluid underneath. They are common on the heels of the feet if your child's shoes don't fit correctly or if he wears shoes without socks. Blisters are not usually serious, but if they result from bad sunburn, burst and become infected, or are very large and painful, you should consult your child's doctor.

What to do

Do not burst a blister. In a day or two, new skin will form underneath the blister, the tissue fluid will be reabsorbed, and the blistered skin will dry and peel off. To aid this healing process, you should cover the blister with a clean dressing (not an adhesive bandage, since this can burst the blister when you peel it off), and keep it dry. If your child's blister is very large, your pediatrician may burst it.

SPLINTERS

Small shards of wood, glass, metal, or a thorn from a plant can easily become embedded in your child's skin, particularly if he is playing out of doors. Unless splinters are deeply embedded or very painful to remove, they can be dealt with easily at home.

What to do

First try to find out from your child what kind of splinter it is. If it is glass, you should not try to remove it yourself as you could cut your child. Seek help from your child's doctor. Look for the end of the splinter. Take a pair of sterilized tweezers (you can sterilize them by holding them over a flame; then let them cool) and gently pull the protruding end of the splinter out. Squeeze the area to make it bleed a little, since this will help clean it. When you have removed the splinter, clean the skin with soap and water, then apply a little antiseptic cream. If the splinter is completely embedded in your child's skin, it may need to be removed by a doctor under local anesthetic – don't poke or probe the area with a needle. If you think that there is dirt in the wound, your child may need a tetanus injection (see p.283).

Pull the splinter out in the same direction it went in

Removing a splinter
If the end of the splinter is visible, use sterilized tweezers to pull it out gently. Don't try to remove a glass splinter yourself.

CUTS AND SCRAPES

As long as a cut is superficial and is not infected (this is a risk with cuts by fingernails, plants, or animals), it should not require treatment other than a smear of antiseptic cream. A scrape is simply an abrasion of the skin that leaves the surface raw and tender. A deep cut that bleeds profusely can lead to shock (see p.333), so treat it as an emergency. A very jagged cut may require stitches, and with a deep or dirty cut there is a risk of tetanus unless your child's immunizations are up to date (see p.283).

What to do

Run cold water over the wounded area and wash thoroughly with soap. Dry by patting with a clean cloth, apply an antiseptic cream, and cover with a sterile dressing or adhesive bandage. If your child has an incision wound with two straight edges, you can hold them together using a butterfly closure. If the wound is dirty or deep, there is a risk of infection and you should take your child to a hospital to see if he needs a tetanus injection.

If a cut is very deep or bleeds profusely, you should take your child to a hospital right away, as he may need stitches. Before he gets to the hospital, apply pressure to the wound using a clean pad or handkerchief (or your hand if nothing else is available) and make sure that the wounded part of the body is raised to slow the flow of blood.

BRUISES

Active children often get bruises from falls and knocks, and they are rarely serious; they usually take 10–14 days to disappear completely.

What to do

If the bruise is large, apply a cold compress for half an hour or so to contain the bruising. You should consult your child's doctor immediately if pain on the site of a bruise gets worse after 24 hours (this could indicate a fracture) or if your child repeatedly has bruises with no apparent cause (this could indicate a serious underlying condition).

CRUSHED FINGERS

This is a fairly common accident in very young children who don't understand how doors, windows, and drawers operate. A crush injury can be serious so it is vital to release the trapped hand as quickly as possible and to comfort your child.

What to do

If the skin is not broken, hold your child's hand under a cold running tap or hold a bag of crushed ice or frozen food against it. When the pain has subsided, wrap the hand in a bandage. If the crush is severe and there is internal bleeding or swelling, bring him to a hospital emergency room.

FOREIGN BODY IN THE EAR

The commonest objects for children to push into their ears are small beads, bits of crayon, and small components from construction toys. Occasionally, an insect can fly into the ear or cotton can be left behind after cleaning. A foreign body in the ear may cause temporary deafness, it may result in an ear infection, and it may damage the eardrum.

What to do

If your child has an insect in his ear canal, lay him on his side with the affected ear uppermost and pour tepid water from a pitcher into the ear. The insect should float out. Any other type of foreign body needs to be treated by a doctor. If you attempt to remove it yourself, you may cause more damage. Your child's doctor can remove it and treat any resulting infection or damage to the skin. You can reduce the risk of foreign bodies in the ear by making sure your child isn't given toys with small parts, particularly if he is under three years old.

FOREIGN BODY IN THE NOSE

If your child has pushed something into his nose, you may not notice, though he will probably complain of pain. Occasionally it takes several days for symptoms to become apparent. Your child may develop a blood-stained discharge from the nose, he may find it difficult to breathe, and there may be swelling, inflammation, and bruising around the bridge of the nose. A foreign body in the nose is rarely serious, but there is a risk that your child will inhale the object, so it requires hospital treatment.

What to do

Do not try to remove the object, as you could cause your child an injury or push the object in farther. Keep him calm, get him to breathe through his mouth, and take him to the hospital.

At the hospital, a doctor will remove the foreign body using forceps; if your child is very young, he may need a general anesthetic beforehand.

USEFUL ADDRESSES

HEALTH AND SAFETY INFORMATION

The American Academy of Pediatrics
141 Northwest Point Blvd.
PO Box 927
Elk Grove Village, IL 60007
Tel: 847-434-4000
Online: www.aap.org

American Red Cross
431 18th St. NW
Washington, DC 20006
Tel: 202-639-3520
Online: www.redcross.org

US Consumer Product Safety Commission
Publication Request
Washington, DC 20207
Hotline tel: 1-800-638-CPSC
Online: www.cpsc.gov

National Health Information Center
PO Box 1133
Washington, DC 20013
Tel: 1-800-336-4797
Online: www.nhic.org

National Lead Information Center
Hotline tel: 1-800-LEADFYI

CHILDREN WITH BIRTH DEFECTS

National Down Syndrome Society
666 Broadway, 8th Floor
New York, NY 10012
Tel: 1-800-221-4602;
in NYC: 212-460-9330
Online: www.ndss.org

March of Dimes/Birth Defects Foundation
1275 Mamaroneck Avenue
White Plains, NY 10605
Tel: 888-663-4637
Online: www.modimes.org

Office of Rare Diseases
National Institutes of Health
31 Center Drive
Bethesda, MD 20892
Tel: 301-402-4336
Online:
rarediseases.info.nih.gov/ord

Spina Bifida Association of America
4590 MacArthur Blvd. NW
Suite 250
Washington, DC 20007
Tel: 1-800-621-3141
Online: www.sbaa.org

BEREAVEMENT

The Compassionate Friends
PO Box 3696
Oak Brook, IL 60522
Tel: 708-990-0010
E-mail: tcf_national@prodigy.com

Pregnancy and Infant Loss Center
1421 E. Wayzata Blvd., #30
Wayzata, MN 55391
Tel: 612-473-9372

American SIDS Institute
2480 Windy Hill Rd.
Suite 380
Marietta, GA 30067
Tel: 1-800-232-SIDS
Online: www.sids.org

SIDS Alliance
1314 Bedford Avenue, Suite 210
Baltimore, MD 21208
Tel: 1-800-221-SIDS
Online: www.sidsalliance.org

CHILDREN WITH SPECIAL NEEDS

National Information Center for Children and Youth with Handicaps
PO Box 1492
Washington, DC 20013
Tel: 1-800-695-0285
Online: www.nichcy.org

Federation for Children with Special Needs
1135 Tremont St., Suite 420
Boston, MA 02120
Tel: 617-236-7210
Online: www.fcsn.org

The Arc of the US
1010 Wayne Avenue, Suite 650
Silver Spring, MD 20910
Tel: 301-565-3842
Online: www.thearc.org
(mental retardation)

ERIC Clearinghouse on Disabilities and Gifted Education
1110 N. Glebe Rd.
Arlington, VA 22201
Tel: 1-800-328-0272
Online: ericec.org
(special education)

Children and Adults with Attention Deficit Disorders (CH.A.D.D.)
8181 Professional Place, Suite 201
Landover, MD 20785
Tel: 1-800-233-4050
Online: www.chadd.org

National Autism Hotline
PO Box 507
Huntington, WV 25710
Tel: 304-525-8014

American Council of the Blind
1155 15th St. NW,
Suite 1004
Washington, DC 20005
Tel: 1-800-424-8666
Online: www.acb.org

American Foundation for the Blind
11 Penn Plaza
Suite 300
New York, NY 10001
Tel: 1-800-232-5463
Online: www.afb.org

United Cerebral Palsy
1660 L St. NW
Suite 700
Washington, DC 20036
Tel: 1-800-USA-5-UCP
Online: www.ucp.org

Alexander Graham Bell Association for the Deaf and Hard of Hearing
3417 Volta Place NW
Washington, DC 20007
Tel: 202-337-5220
Online: www.agbell.org

Internation Dyslexia Association
8600 LaSalle Rd.
382 Chester Building
Baltimore, MD 21286
Tel: 1-800-ABCD123;
in MD 410-296-0232
Online: www.interdys.org

National Down Syndrome Society
(*see* CHILDREN WITH BIRTH DEFECTS)

The Gifted Child Society
190 Rock Rd.
Glen Rock, NJ 07452
Tel: 201-444-6530
Online: www.gifted.org

National Association for Gifted Children
1707 L St. NW
Suite 550
Washington, DC 20036
Tel: 202-785-4268
Online: www.nagc.org

Stuttering Foundation of America
PO Box 11749
Memphis, TN 38111
Tel: 1-800-992-9392
Online: wwww.stutteringhelp.org

CHILDREN WITH CHRONIC CONDITIONS

Asthma and Allergy Foundation
1233 20th St., NW
Suite 402
Washington, DC 20036
Tel: 1-800-7-ASTHMA
Online: www.aafa.org

Cystic Fibrosis Foundation
6931 Arlington Rd., #200
Bethesda, MD 20814
Tel: 1-800-FIGHTCF
Online: www.cff.org

American Diabetes Association
1701 N. Beauregard St.
Alexandria, VA 22311
Tel: 1-800-DIABETES
Online: www.diabetes.org

Juvenile Diabetes Association
120 Wall St.
New York, NY 10005
Tel: 1-800-JDF-CURE;
in NYC 212-785-9500
Online: www.juvenilediabetes.org

Epilepsy Foundation
4351 Garden City Dr.
Landover, MD 20785
Tel: 1-800-332-1000;
in MD 301-459-3700
Online: www.efa.org

Hydrocephalus Association
870 Market St.
Suite 705
San Francisco, CA 94102
Tel: 415-732-7040
Online: www.hydroassoc.org

National PKU News
6869 Woodlawn Ave. NE, #116
Seattle, WA 98115
Tel: 206-525-8140
Online: www.pkunews.org

Sickle Cell Disease Association of America
200 Corporate Point
Suite 495
Culver City, CA 90230
Tel: 1-800-421-8453
Online: www.sicklecelldisease.org

National Tay–Sachs and Allied Diseases Association, Inc.
2001 Beacon St.
Brighton, MA 02135
Tel: 1-800-906-8723
Online: www.ntsad.org

PARENT SUPPORT

Parent Care, Inc.
9041 Colgate St.
Indianapolis, IN 46268
Tel: 317-872-9913
(*premature and high-risk infants*)

Depression After Delivery, Inc.
PO Box 278
Belle Mead, NJ 08502
Hotline tel: 1-800-944-4773

La Leche League International
PO Box 4079
Schaumburg, IL 60168
Tel: 847-519-7730
(*breastfeeding*)

Parents Helping Parents
140 Clarendon St.
Boston, MA 02116
Tel: 1-800-882-8077
Online:
www.parentshelpingparents.org

Adoptee-Birthparent Support Network
3421 M Street NW, #328
Washington, DC 20007
Tel: 202-686-4611

National Organization of Mothers of Twins Clubs
PO Box 438
Thompson Station, TN 37179
Tel: 877-540-2200
Online: www.nomotc.org

Mothers at Home
8310A Old Courthouse Rd.
Vienna, VA 22182
Tel: 703-827-5903
Online: www.mah.org

Single Parent Resource Center
31 East 28 St
Second Floor
New York, NY 10016
Tel: 212-951-7030

Single Mothers By Choice
PO Box 1642
Gracie Sq. Station
New York, NY 10028
Tel: 212-988-0993

Parents Sharing Custody
420 S. Beverly Dr.
Suite 100
Beverly Hills, CA 90212
Tel: 310-286-9171

Mothers Without Custody
PO Box 27418
Houston, TX 77227
Tel: 713-840-1622
Online:
www.motherswithoutcustody.org

Parents Without Partners
1650 S. Dixie Hwy.
Suite 510
Boca Raton, FL 33432
Tel: 1-800-637-7974
Online:
www.parentswithoutpartners.org

Stepfamily Foundation
333 West End Ave.
New York, NY 10023
Tel: 212-877-3244
Online: www.stepfamily.org

Stepfamily Association of America
650 J St.
Suite 205
Lincoln, NE 68508
Tel: 1-800-735-0329
Online: www.stepfam.org

INDEX

A

Abdominal pain 298, 299
Access, after separation 243
Accidents 306–7, 310–13
   see also **First aid**
Addresses 344–5
Adenoids 286
ADHD 255
Affection, showing 80–1, 233
Air travel 146–7
Allergy 292–3
   food 71
Amblyopia 177
Ammonia dermatitis 111
Anemia, sickle cell 272
Animal bites 341
Anti-inflammatory medication 262
Anus, imperforate 29
Anxiety 134–5
Apgar score 24
Apnea 27
Appendicitis 299
Appetite, loss of 70–1, 277
Assertiveness 208
Asthma 260–3
Attention, dividing 81
Attention deficit hyperactivity disorder (ADHD) 255
Autism 250, 258–9

B

Baby blues 19, 236
Baby listener 35
Backpack 36, 37, 78, 142
Balance 161, 167
Balanitis 300–1
Bathing
   boys 91
   equipment 32
   fear of 95, 96–7
   girls 90
   older baby 96–7
   play 97, 98
   preschool child 100
   safety 96, 97, 98
   sponge bath 92
   technique 94–5
   toddler 98–9
   toiletries 92
   topping and tailing 90
   young baby 90–5
Bed 35
   move from cot to bed 126, 128–9
Bedding 32, 33, 34–5,
   and temperature 123

Bedtime 80, 125, 127
   crying at 135
Bedwetting 116, 220, 221
Behavior
   at nursery school 225
   newborn baby 20–3
   social *see* **Social behavior**
Behavioral disorders 220, 222–3
Birthmarks 16, 17
Bites 341
Bladder 104
Bladder control 115–16
   gender differences 112, 113
   regression 116–19
Bleeding, first aid 335
Blepharitis 287
Blisters 342
Blood glucose self–monitoring 267
Body care 91–2
Boils 290
Bonding 12, 13, 206
   breastfeeding and 42
   father 13
   massage 76
   premature baby 26, 49
Books 185, 186, 187, 188–9, 193, 203
Boredom 134
Bottlefeeding 39
   equipment 52
   fathers and 50
   milk flow 52
   position 53
   routines 54–5
   supplementary 43, 45
   technique 53–4
   see also **Milk formulas**
Bottles 50
Bouncing chair 37, 156
Bowel control 114, 116
   gender differences 112, 113
   regression 116–17
Bowel function 105
Bowel movements 17, 104–5, 112–13
   celiac disease 112
   changes in 104–5, 112
   diarrhea 105
Bragging 218, 219
Brain, gender differences 180, 181
Bras, nursing 41
Breast milk 38, 39, 40
   expressing 39, 44–5
   low-milk syndrome 43
   storage of expressed milk 44
   supply 40, 41
Breast pads 46
Breast shells 46
Breastfeeding 40–7
   advantages 38–9
   bras 41
   breast problems 47

Breastfeeding (cont.)
   drugs and 46–7
   effects on mother 39
   feeding problems 43
   frequency 41
   illness of mother 46
   management 46–7
   positions 41
   preterm baby 48, 49
   supplements 43, 45
   technique 42
Breasts
   abscess 47
   care in breastfeeding 46
   effects of breastfeeding 39
   newborn baby 15
   problems in breastfeeding 47
Breathing
   difficulty in 277
   newborn baby 13
   premature baby 27
Bronchiolitis 295
Bronchitis 295
Bronchodilator 262
Bruises 343
Building blocks 171, 173
Bullying 220
Burns 307
   first aid 336

C

Candy 72, 102
Cardiopulmonary resuscitation (CPR) 330-31
Car journeys 144–5, 312
Car sickness 145
Carriage 34, 36
Carrier 36, 37
Carrying baby
   shopping trips 142
   young baby 36–7, 75
Celiac disease 112, 113
Cereals 57
Cerebral palsy 268–70
Chairs
   booster seat 68
   bouncing 37, 156
   clip-on 68
   high chair 60
   restaurants 73
Chest compression 331
Chest infections 295–6
Chickenpox 302–3
Child care 241–2
Choking
   first aid 332-3
   food 60
   toy hazards 310

ACKNOWLEDGMENTS

Carroll & Brown Limited would like to thank:

Photography
Jules Selmes

Illustration
Aziz Khan: 33, 40, 50, 87, 104, 105, 109, 175, 262, 265, 266 (right), 267, 271, 273, 278 (bottom), 279, 285, 291, 295, 298, 299, 300, 301, 306, 308, 309, 310, 311, 312, 327, 337, 338; Coral Mula: 29, 290, 296, 297, 305, 336; Howard Pemberton: 103, 179, 266, 269; Ian Thompson: 25, 278, 286

Medical consultants
Dr. Margaret Lawson; Dr. Frances Williams; Dr. Penny Preston; Kate Mactier

Advice and assistance
Association for Spina Bifida and Hydrocephalus; Child Accident Prevention Trust; Child Growth Foundation (height and weight charts); Cleft Lip and Palate Association; National Childbirth Trust; The Vegetarian Society. The first aid information on pp.326–343 has been validated by Joe Mulligan, Training Officer, British Red Cross.

Typesetting
Debbie Lelliott; Rowena Feeny; Axis Design

Film output
Disc To Print (UK) Ltd; revised edition, Brightside Partnership

Equipment
Boots the Chemist; Children's World; Debenhams; Freeman's Mail Order

Models
Julia Alcock; Milo Baraclough; Cassie-Ella Bernard; Gertrud Blomberg; Lena Larsson Blomberg and Fredrik; Zoë Bothamley; Georgina and Elliot Bourke; Alison Briegel, Alice, and Charlie; Jayde Caines; Niyazi Caykara; Oliver Clarke; Ricardo Cohen; George Cooper; Hannah and Charlotte Coster; Ella Crawley; Cora Eugene and Kairone; Emily Fogarty; Keitel and Stone Frankle; Joseph Gavshon; Julia Gibbon; Candy Gummer; Hannah Heyes; Katie Hogben; Natalie Joseph; Elliott Kenton; Sami Khan; William King; Beverley Lagna; Malcolm Langton; Lee Lawer; Angela Loveday and Jack; Georgina McCooke; Ursula Macfarlane and Josiah Ackerman; Kelly MacNabb; Joan Marcello and Marco; Antonio Marcello; Joseph Milner Sweeney; Cordelia Nelson; Reiss Ng; Stephanie Parker and Daniel; Jordan Raymond; Temuera Reefman; Millie Satow; Caroline Sims and Michael; Alice Smith; Jayde, Mairéad, and Michael Snell; Aisling Walsh; Tess Watson; Mark Weegmann; Beresford Williams; Jessica Williams; Albert Wood

Additional editorial assistance
Kesta Desmond; Richard Emerson; Steve McGrath; Cathy Meeus; Jennifer Rylaarsdam

Index
Anne McCarthy

Additional design assistance
Juanita Grout, Richard Horsford

Picture credits
Collections/Anthea Sieveking, 26; Mother and Baby Picture Library, emap/1; Mike Good/ Zartec Studios, 114; Taeke Henstra, Petit Format/ Science Photo Library, 12; John Radcliffe Hospital/ Science Photo Library, 292; Dr. H.C. Robinson/Science Photo Library, 291; Science Photo Library, 302; Ron Sutherland/ Science Photo Library, 15; Katrina Thomas/ Science Photo Library, 13; Stock Market Photo Agency/2-3; Stock Market Photo Agency/30-31; Stock Market Photo Agency/ Michael Keller,148-149; Stock Market Photo Agency/ Steve Prezant, 228-229; Stock Market Photo Agency/248-249; Stock Market Photo Agency/274-275; Telegraph Colour Library/Mel Yates, 10-11